SAP FINANCE

CONFIGURATIONS & TRANSACTIONS

YOGI KALRA

ACKNOWLEDGMENTS

I am very thankful foremost to my clients and their employees who have given me the opportunity to work on their SAP systems, always learning from them and their Businesses; notable among them being, Stericycle, Shred-it, Kemira, Johnson & Johnson, BELL Industries, Chevron Phillips, Freightliner and many more. Without their support and my learning their Business Processes, this manual would not have been possible.

I am grateful to my family for tolerating my absence while I composed this manual ignoring them most of the time. I will have to make up to them one day! I am thankful to my wife Michelle for helping me edit the proof of this manual and finding it's numerous errors.

Finally, and not the least, I am grateful to you, the reader for selecting this book among the thousands available, never an easy choice and I hope it met or exceeded your expectations. . I am happy to answer any questions you may have on the topic or if, for better learning, you would like access to the demo system on which this book was written – ykalra@shefaria.com. The author will be grateful for your review and feedback on the public fora if the book helped you increase your understanding of the subject.

CONTENTS

FOREWORD

This manual, written with the objective of providing detailed training to both, consultants and users goes deep into the subject from initial configurations to setting up the Income Statement and Balance Sheet of the company. The integration points of Finance with Purchasing/Inventory and Shipping/Billing are explained in detail and the chapters marked clearly if it is a Configuration (C) or Transaction (U) or both. Since most of the book has been written in standard SAP, once a company code is set up along with some other basic configurations defined in the first few pages, a SAP user, if so desires, can stay only with the areas marked 'U', by passing the 'C' since not everything in standard SAP depends on specific company code configurations. Consultants or to-be consultants, of course, need to understand both sides of SAP. The effects of changes done in configuration are immediately followed by their effect on the transactions, thereby making the learning relational in real time for better understanding. From the user's perspective, not much from the subject has been left out in writing this manual and every effort has been taken to keep it relevant to the Corporate Finance functions of day-to-day working on SAP in an orderly flow.

This manual has been written keeping standard Business processes proposed by SAP. In writing this book, I have stayed away from all frills and concentrated on providing only useful subject matter with tips and tricks based on over my many years of experience in SAP implementations and consulting. This book is not a result of overnight arrangement but a composition of several years of training and understanding of Business processes across multiple industries in various disciplines. I believe it is as comprehensive as any book can be for users and consultants, new and old, to conducting any Corporate Finance and Banking functions in SAP.

For New users: One of the primary learning curves in SAP is navigation. The data in SAP is so well organized that first time users are often astonished to see the integrative nature of this

ERP system. It is no exaggeration to say that everything you need to know in SAP is at one, two or maximum three clicks away. Mastering navigation in SAP is half the battle won. This becomes even more vital in Finance, being at the tail end of all the processes. Good navigation skills will guide you in finding sources of the data in the documents. It would be very worth the while to spend time on navigation on the different screens and get familiar with them as for the most part, there is a commonality in the way SAP is structured across different areas in terms of screen layouts. To get a better understanding of Navigation in a structured form, read the author's book *SAP Navigation & General Components*. Use the F1 key for help liberally – it will help you wade through the screens understanding everything thoroughly. As is the case with all seemingly multifaceted structures, the base is very simple. In spite of SAP's complexity as an ERP system, it's edifice is built on very elementary processes as you will notice while going through this book. Processes that are uniform, scalable and easily comprehensible. One of SAP's masterstrokes is the Transaction code and the philosophy that drives it. Usually a 4 alpha-numeric or alpha code (but can be often longer, especially in Finance reporting), it is used to invoke a program which will guide you through the entire process. Thus, a user need only to remember this transaction code for the function to be performed and entering it in the transaction window to begin your activity. This manual endeavors to cover over 400 such transactions; bear in mind, each of them will perform a related and unique business function. Further, to simplify learning, a transaction code is usually ended as 01, 02 or 03 signifying create, change or display respectively. Thus, FB01, FB02 and FB03 become Post (Create) Accounting document, Change Accounting document and Display Accounting document, respectively. Also, for the most part, transaction codes and configurable objects are case insensitive i.e. FB01 is same as fb01.

For SAP Users and Process Owners: This book covers over 110 standard processes and transactions in Corporate Finance and daily banking in depth in easily understandable language and with only relevant screen shots. It is unlikely that any organization will be required to call upon any other substantial transactions other than these in its normal functioning. Towards the end, the book also touches on some cross application components, which if you have access to, will simplify your work in SAP tremendously. Anyone new to the SAP world is advised to read the chapter on 'Variants' after getting a good feel of the first couple of transactions while leaving the rest to the end. Again, for users new to SAP, the best and perhaps fastest way to learn from this book is to think of what you do or did in your legacy system and look up this manual on how to perform the same process in SAP. The transaction code to perform that function is provided right in the beginning of the chapter.

For Consultants: This book covers all configurations relating to Finance and some Controlling in depth. The effect of the changes in configurations in real time is explained as you go along, making your learning easier. Also detailed are the relationship between Finance and MM/SD wherever applicable to enable you to become more robust consultants. The ability to understand how FI gets it's data from Logistics and Purchasing/Inventory is critical to setting up the FI module. Most importantly, you will learn a lot by diving into the details of the transactions also as explained in this book and that will help you face the users more confidently. I can't recount the number of times I was embarrassed in my early days at client's sites when the experienced users explained to me navigation on the screens I did not know myself!

Your inputs and criticism are very welcome. If there is anything the author can do to help you understand the subject better or guide you in any way, please feel free to drop an email to shefariaentinc@gmail.com noting the name of the book and topic in the subject of the email. Since nothing is perfect, there may be some errors and omissions in the book. I will be very grateful for your comments and responses if you find them or even otherwise give your suggestions since they will work to make the next edition better.

FINANCIAL ACCOUNTING MENU (C)

T Code SPRO

SAP Implementation begins from the IMG (Implementation Guide) screen.

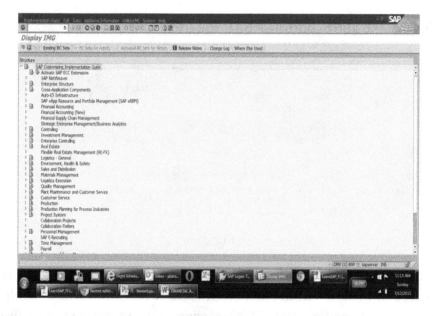

Fig 1

To go to the above screen, log in to SAP and in the transaction window, type SPRO and Hit Enter:

Fig 2

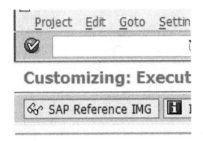

Fig 3

Click on the above button – SAP Reference IMG:

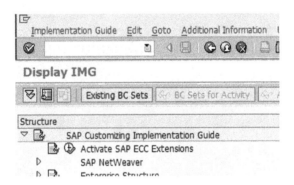

Fig 4

The IMG is divided into different modules arranged in no particular order. Within each module there are more sub-modules relating to specific areas. Within each sub-module one can find configuration areas at each node for each particular activity, some of which we will explore in this course.

SETTING UP A COMPANY (C)

T Code SPRO

The first step in SAP is to set up a company, much in the same way as we would in the real world. The path to set up a company is:

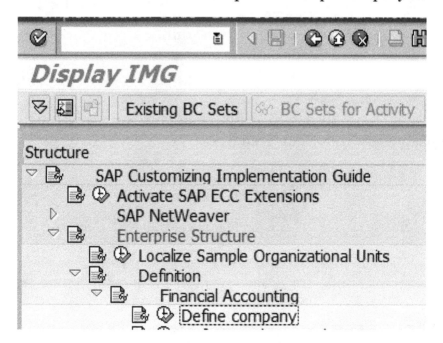

Fig 1

The company is the highest level of organizational structure that is created in SAP in FI. A company is used to consolidate the financial statements of the legal entities of any Business group. Usually a company will comprise of many CCs (discussed next). On the FI side, the use of a company is to consolidate this data and pass it on to the Controlling module, which is set up separately based on how the group company needs to do their filings or otherwise use this data.

Clicking on the Execute - ▷ ⊕ button will lead us into a table in which the company will be set up:

Company	Company name	Name of company 2
	Ledger Co. G00000	
0	Michael Company	Mick's Company Training
4	amcercian company	benny
8	Saran	
12	twelve company	
109	PINEAPPLE	APPLE
111	VB Company	PLEASE DO NOT CHANGE. THANKS
123	Logistic sap	Logistic sap
139	Test Hungary	Test
300	zenith logistics	

Fig 1

Click on New Entries to define your own company (up to 6 alphanumeric code) and its address.

Fig 2

At many places in SAP, based on countries and their formats, there are inbuilt error checks like the Postal Code check for country Canada as below:

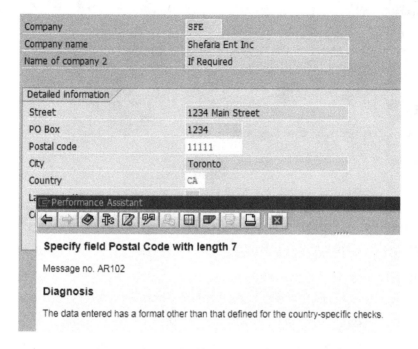

Fig 3

Thereby forcing the user to enter the correct data:

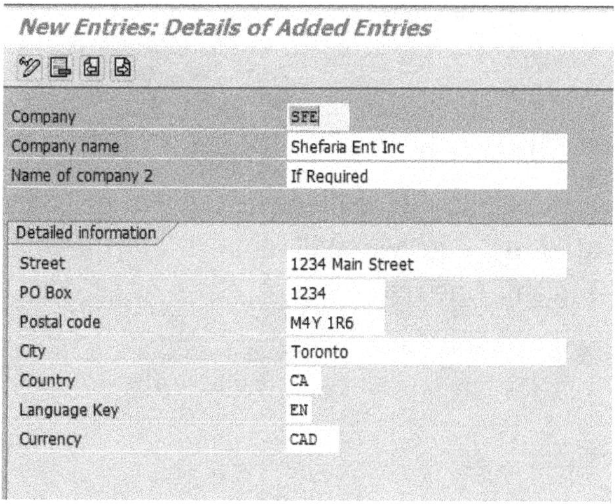

Fig 4

Save the data. A window pops up asking the user to create a transport:

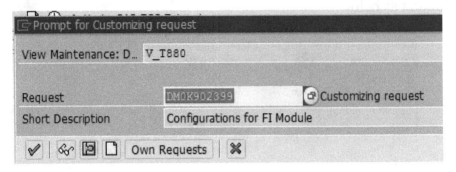

Fig 5

You must create a new transport if it proposes any transport number which is not your own. This transport number will be moved from one system to another carrying with it all the changes done. To create a new transport, click on ▢ . If you want to add this change to your own pre-existing transport, you have the ability to choose that from Own Requests also.

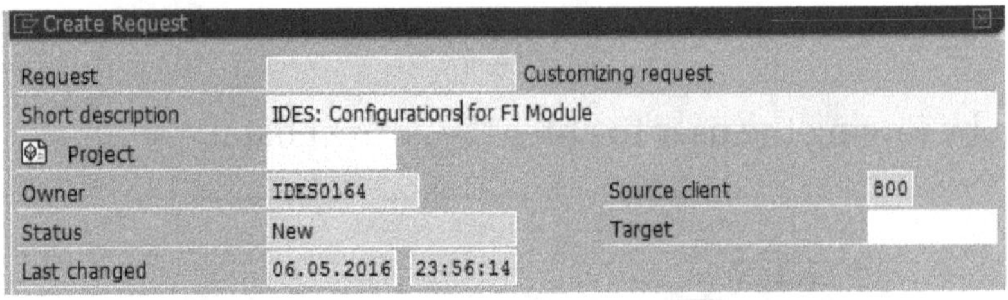

Create Request			
Request		Customizing request	
Short description	IDES: Configurations for FI Module		
Project			
Owner	IDES0164	Source client	800
Status	New	Target	
Last changed	06.05.2016 23:56:14		

Fig 6

Give a description that will make sense to you or is specific to the change being done e.g. we will collect all the configurations relating to FI in this one transport.

Clicking on Save will give you a different (new) number as below:

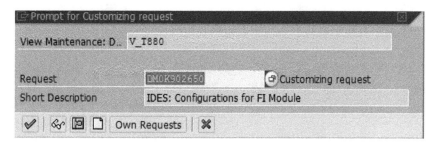

Fig 7

Hit Enter and the system will have saved your changes under the transport Number as above. As we go along, we will add more changes onto this same number so that we do not have to have multiple unnecessary numbers to remember and look for.

SETTING UP THE COMPANY CODE

(C)

T Code SPRO

A Company Code (CC) is a legal entity in whose name the Income statements and Balance Sheet will be filed. It is different from the Company. One company may have multiple CCs, which may require to be set up depending on the prevailing legal requirements. The path to it is after the option to set up the CC in the same tree.

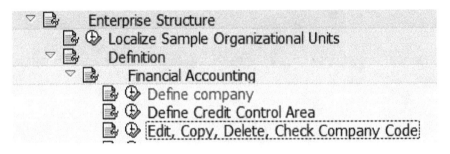

Fig 1

The company code we will set up is SFE1 on which this entire manual is based.

Double click the second option (Edit CC Data) in the below window:

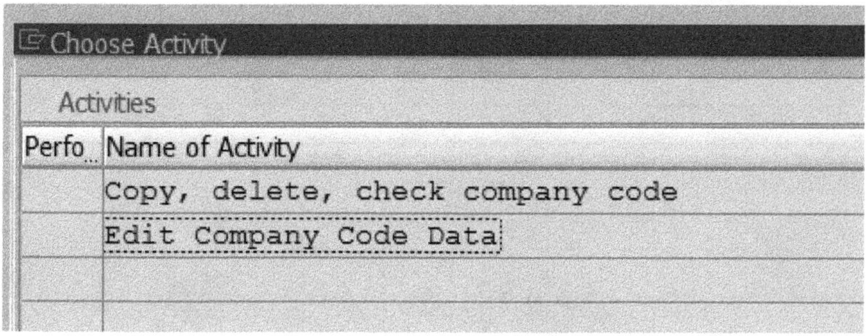

Fig 2

Alternatively, simply place the cursor in the 2nd line and Hit Enter.

Click on New Entries as previously and add your CC (4 characters maximum):

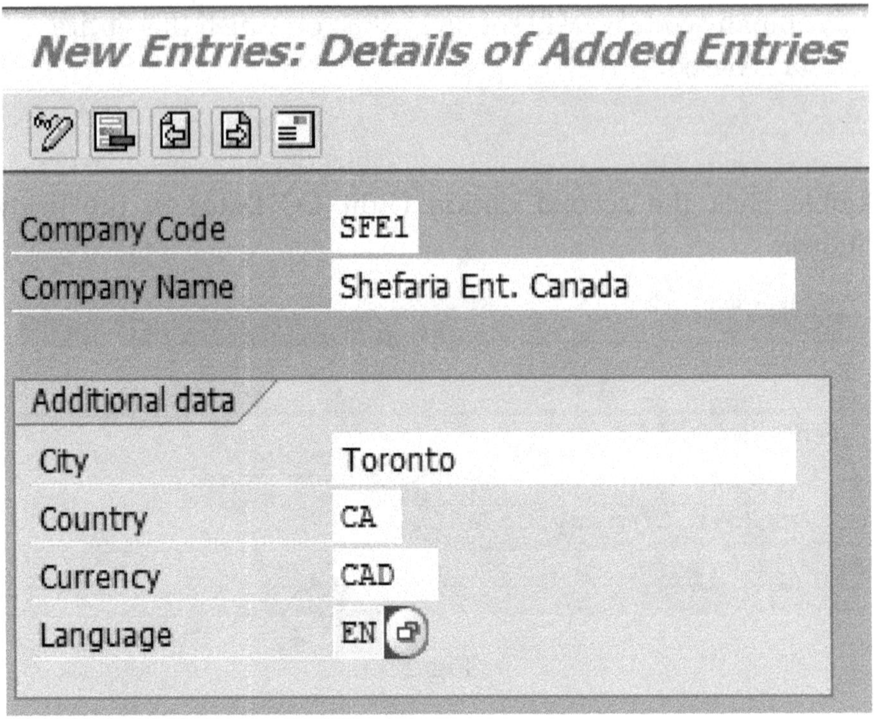

New Entries: Details of Added Entries

Company Code	SFE1
Company Name	Shefaria Ent. Canada

Additional data

City	Toronto
Country	CA
Currency	CAD
Language	EN

Fig 3

On Hitting Save, a window comes up asking for the address:

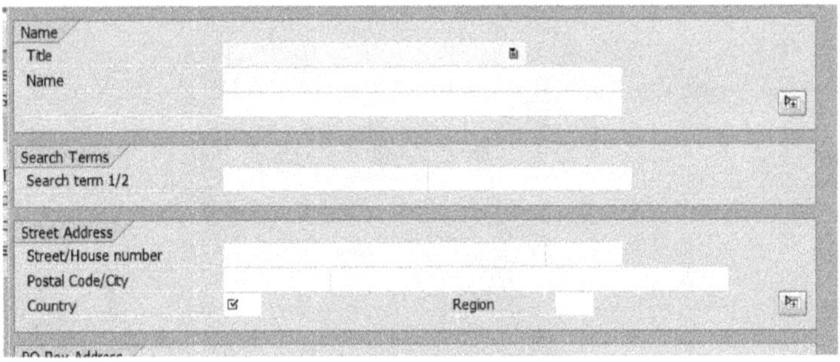

Name
Title
Name

Search Terms
Search term 1/2

Street Address
Street/House number
Postal Code/City
Country   Region

Fig 4

While only the country is mandatory (shown by the Check Mark inside the field), it is advisable to enter the complete address as it may be used for printing on documents later.

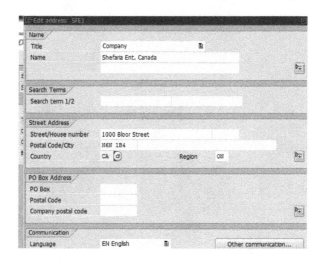

Fig 5

Hit Enter and Save. If a window asking for a transport comes up, use the same number as above. At the bottom, a message will come up saying your data was saved:

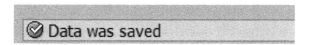

Fig 6

ASSIGNMENTS (C)

T Code SPRO

All objects in SAP are mere placeholders and have no real use unless they are connected with each other in a meaningful way. In our case, since a company is representing multiple CCs, which are legal entities on their own, it is necessary to form a link between them. This link is called 'assignment' and these assignments are done across all modules for their respective organizational objects. This assignment is done in the Menu tree right after Definition in the respective module:

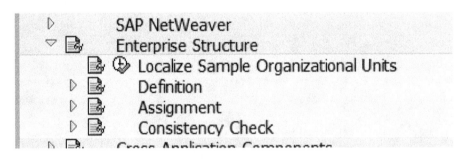

Fig 1

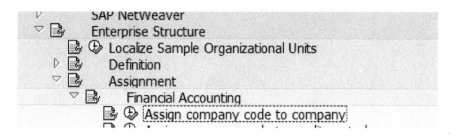

Fig 2

Click on the Position window at the bottom and search for the CC SFE1 by typing it in and hitting Enter:

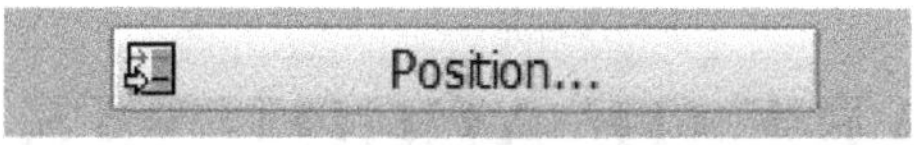

Position...

Fig 3

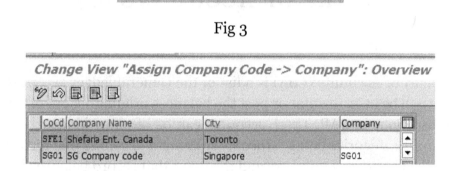

Fig 4

Add the company SFE in the field on the right most column and save:

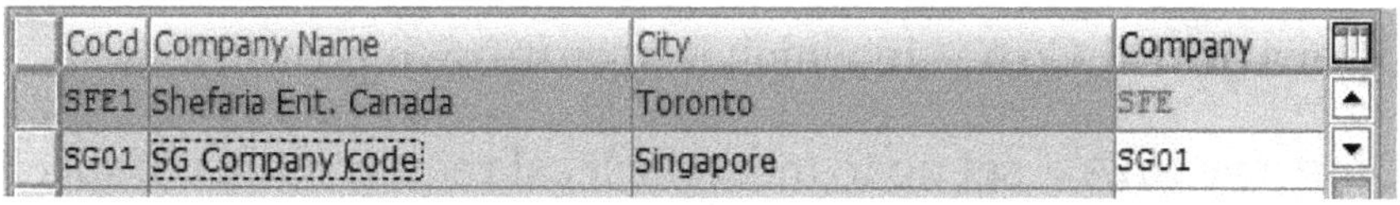

CoCd	Company Name	City	Company	
SFE1	Shefaria Ent. Canada	Toronto	SFE	▲
SG01	SG Company code	Singapore	SG01	▼

Fig 5

Add it to the same transport #.

CHART OF ACCOUNTS (C)

T Code SPRO

A Chart of Accounts (CoA) is a list of the General ledger accounts that will be used to enter or post the balances originating out of the transactions in SAP. These accounts can be of many kinds- the 2 primary categories being – *Income statement accounts* that record the Profit and loss numbers and the other that record balances i.e. *balance sheet accounts*. Often, large corporations retain the same CoA across all CCs for ease of reporting, however that is not mandatory and each CC can have its own CoA. In SAP, the same CC can have, depending on requirements, up to 3 CoAs:

1 **Operational CoA** – in which it does its own postings

2 **Country CoA** – set up to meet the legal requirements of specific countries

3 **Group CoA** – for multi-national corporations, this is used to amalgamate the postings from different CoAs of different CCs in multiple countries to report 'as a group'

For our purpose here, we will set up only the Operational CoA. It is set up in transaction OB13 or by following the path in IMG as below:

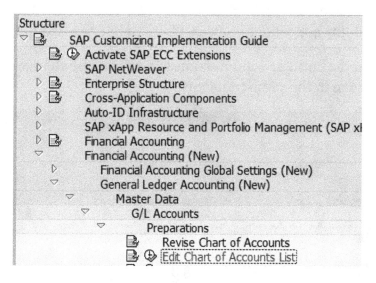

Fig 1

Click on New Entries and define the CoA as below. Since a COA can be used by many CCs concurrently for ease of operations and accounting, it is best to give them a generic or group name instead of one based on the CC:

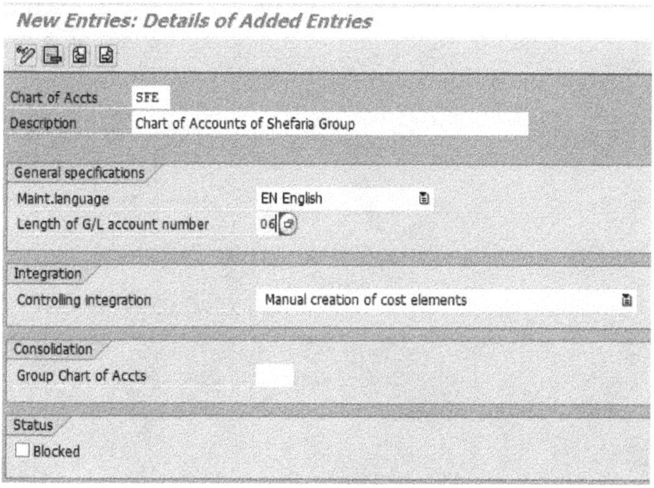

Fig 2

The G/L accounts can range from 4 to 10 digits and depending on a nomenclature that a company may choose, they can be defined as such. Normally, 6 digit good enough for the # of G/L accounts a CoA will have so we will choose 6 too. For the moment, since we are not doing consolidation, we will not define the Group CoA.

Save and the familiar window comes up to save the changes, which can be done in the same transport:

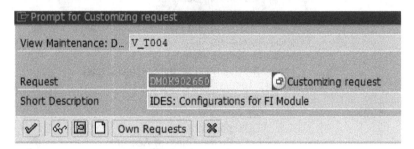

Fig 3

ASSIGNING CO CODE TO COA (C)

T Code SPRO

Now we need to make our CC recognize the CoA to enable postings from its transactions into this CoA. To do that, we assign the CoA to the CC in the path:

Financial Accounting
Financial Accounting Global Settings
General Ledger Accounting
G/L Accounts
Master Data
Preparations
Revise Chart of Accounts
Edit Chart of Accounts List
Assign Company Code to Chart of Accounts

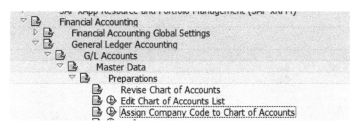

Fig 1

Alternatively, simply use transaction code OB62:

Search for the CC as previously, assign the CoA to it, and save:

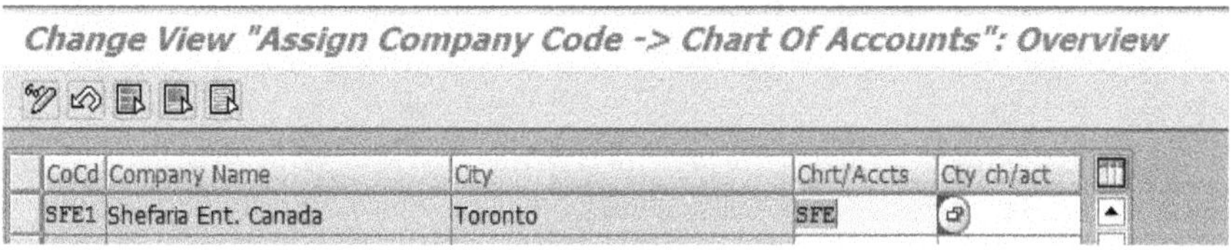

Change View "Assign Company Code -> Chart Of Accounts": Overview
CoCd
Company Name
City
Chrt/Accts
Cty ch/act
SFE1
Shefaria Ent. Canada
Toronto
SFE

Fig 2

This now makes the CC hold its numbers in the G/L accounts of the CoA of the group. Later, we will set up some G/L accounts and see how all this aligns together.

CREATING G/L ACCOUNT GROUPS

(C)

T Code SPRO

To meet the statutory requirements of most countries, 2 account groups are mandatory – the Income statement group and the Balance sheet group. Some others could be like Fixed assets accounts, Data Conversion Acts (to hold temporary balances esp. at times of mergers/acquisitions) etc. The different account groups will drive how postings will be done, and what fields will be mandatory to fill in while setting up different G/L accounts. This configuration will also define the number ranges we give to the different account groups, which will also differentiate them from each other.

Menu path:

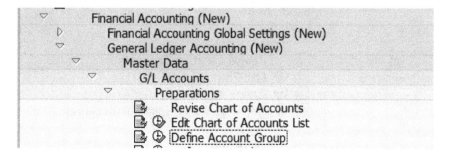

Fig 1

Alternatively, use transaction OBD4.

For our purpose we will set up 2 account groups for PL and BS and give them appropriate number ranges:

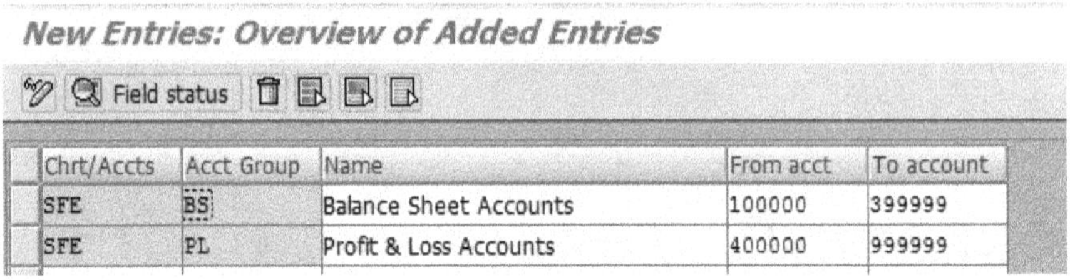

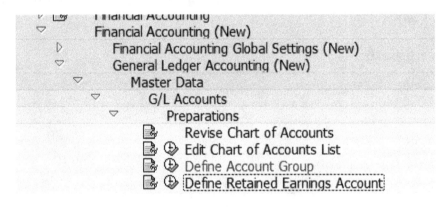

Chrt/Accts	Acct Group	Name	From acct	To account
SFE	BS	Balance Sheet Accounts	100000	399999
SFE	PL	Profit & Loss Accounts	400000	999999

Fig 2

These ranges mean that when we set up a Balance sheet G/L Account, SAP will require us to give a number between 100000 and 399999 and for an Income statement account, between 400000 and 999999. The numbers cannot overlap between the 2 groups thus keeping them independent of each other.

This is also a good time to set up the Retained Earnings account. Without a RE account, the other P&L accounts can't be set up. This account is a configuration also unlike others, which are master data only and can be set up directly in all systems.

The RE account is set up in transaction OB53 or in the path:

Fig 3

Enter the CoA when the window prompts you to and Set the account you wish the retained earnings to be posted to, keeping in mind it is a BS account:

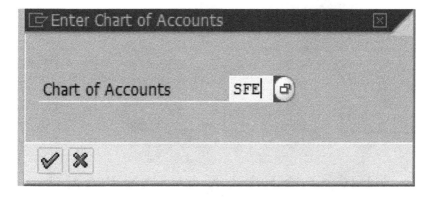

Fig 4

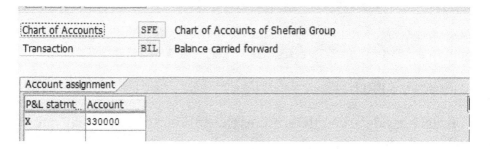

Fig 5

You may get a message at the bottom:

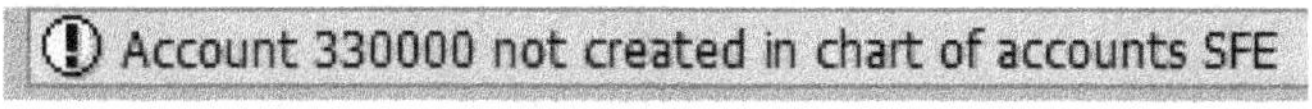

Account 330000 not created in chart of accounts SFE

Fig 6

This message is because we have not actually set up any GL account with this number, for the moment, Hit Enter and ignore the message. Save as usual.

FISCAL YEAR VARIANT AND

POSTING PERIODS (C)

I.   FISCAL YEAR VARIANT

T Code SPRO

A fiscal period variant determines the period a company will adopt to keep its accounts. It may be the calendar year or one in which a company can make it's own periods – e.g. begin the year in July with period 1, August period 2 etc. or follow a different methodology which could even include half periods. Most companies prefer to set up 16 periods - 12 of them could be used as normal posting periods and the rest 4 for special postings. Normally, it is helpful to keep one such 'extra' period per quarter for tax adjustments and companies often do that. To mirror the actual posting periods in the real world to open and close the books, SAP provides the ability to set up fiscal year variants, which can be replicated to multiple CCs thereby making the process of setting up fiscal year variants, a lot simpler. The path to assigning a fiscal year variant is in Fig 1.

Fig 1

Choose your company using the Position Key if it is not visible on the screen:

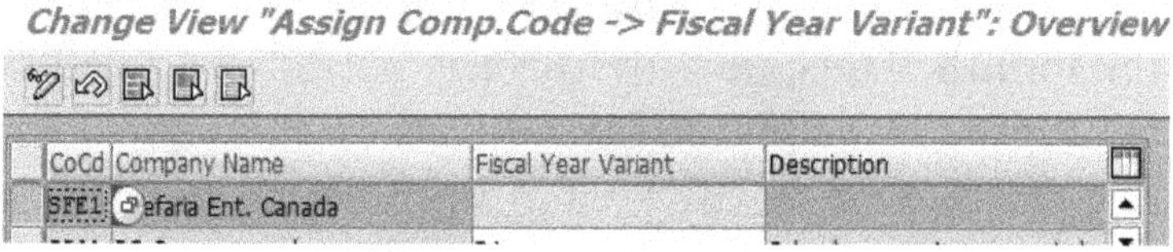

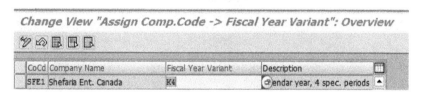

Fig 2

Press F4 in the field Fiscal Year Variant or click on the icon to bring up the possible entries:

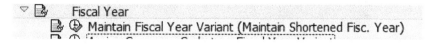

Fig 3

Normally the K4 period which divides an year into 4 quarters is most commonly used and there should be no need to set up any new ones as an available one will suffice.

We choose K4 and Save.

If a new one is required for any reason, it can be set up in the previous step:

Fig 4

II. POSTING PERIOD

T Code SPRO

Posting Period is the actual time during which documents can be posted to the accounting database. They usually mirror the actual dates for which the fiscal year variants are valid e.g. if we have a variant that is set up to divide the entire year into 12 calendar months, then the Finance dept. will maintain the posting period from the 1st to the end of the month. Thus, on July 18th the period open will be July, on August 1, the period open August and so on. Documents have to be necessarily posted in the open periods only. If, for any reason, documents are created later, then, quite likely, they will have to be posted in a later period as one normally does not go back and open closed periods.

Posting periods are also set up as posting period variants to reduce redundancy of set up.

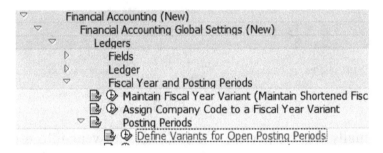

Fig 5

Again, make your entry as earlier:

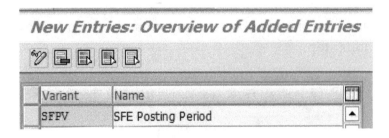

24

Fig 6

Normally, different CCs under the same company can share the same posting period variant unless dictated differently for legal reasons. It is not necessary though it helps in keeping the books in sync with each other and the business users then have to open/close only the variant and automatically it affects all the CCs that are using that variant.

In the next step, we will assign this variant to the CCs, in our case, just one for the moment

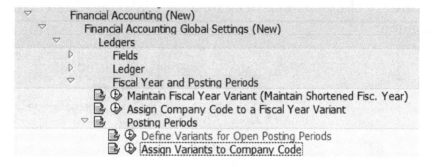

Fig 7

Search for your CC using the Position tab or otherwise by scrolling and assign the posting period variant to it:

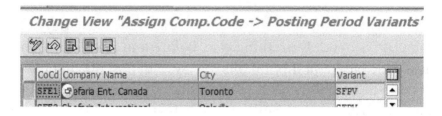

Fig 8

Save.

Now we look at how posting periods are opened and closed. T Code to Open and close posting periods is OB52 or S_ALR_87003642.

New Entries

Var.	A	From acct	To account	From per.1	Year	To period	Year
SFPV	+			2	2017	2	2017
SFPV	A		ZZZZZZZZZZ	2	2017	2	2017
SFPV	D		ZZZZZZZZZZ	2	2017	2	2017
SFPV	K		ZZZZZZZZZZ	2	2017	2	2017
SFPV	M		ZZZZZZZZZZ	2	2017	2	2017
SFPV	S		ZZZZZZZZZZ	2	2017	2	2017

Fig 9

There are different kinds of accounts in SAP represented in the 2nd column:

Var.	A	From acct	To account	From		
SFPV	+			2	**A**	**Short text**
SFPV	A		ZZZZZZZZZZ	2	+	Valid for all account types
SFPV	D		ZZZZZZZZZZ	2	A	Assets
SFPV	K		ZZZZZZZZZZ	2	D	Customers
SFPV	M		ZZZZZZZZZZ	2	K	Vendors
SFPV	S		ZZZZZZZZZZ	2	M	Materials
SMI	+			8	S	G/L accounts
					V	Contract accounts

Fig 10

The entry in Fig 9 simply tells us that for SFE1 only 02/2017 i.e. Feb 2017 is open. Everything else, before and after this month, is closed. So based on this, on this day, we can post documents in the co code SFE1 only with a posting date of Feb, 2017 because it's posting period variant SFPV has only this one month as open.

We would normally define the posting periods for all kinds of accounts separately but not differently from each other though it is technically possible to close vendors, keep customers open etc. This overview simply states that only Feb 2017 is open to post accounting documents to, no other. Therefore, we can't pre-date or post-date documents other than of 02/2017 and post them. We can, in reality allow only vendor postings to be posted while preventing the AR (customers) or vice versa etc., though most companies would follow the right business practice of closing all of them as the period ends.

Now, all the CCs that get the posting period variant SFPV attached to them will have their posting periods open and close together based on SFPV. Create these entries for all these kinds of G/L accounts for your posting period variant in the above table.

FIELD STATUS GROUPS & VARIANTS

(C)

T Code SPRO or OBC4

Every document has bits of data, which is necessary for some functional area of the organization to understand its impact on their particular domain. That data is often carried from the beginning to the end of the transaction's life cycle. It would be very cumbersome as well as prone to errors if that data were to be entered manually at every stage. Field status groups are one of the many such objects in SAP that enable us to keep fields as necessary – as mandatory, optional, suppressed or only to display (i.e. no change possible). Thus, configuration is done to mark them as such so that this data like plant, profit centers, cost centers, once determined, are allowed to flow from one preceding document to the next, with some of it unchangeable.

The transaction code is OBC4 or the path to set these field statuses and field status variants is:

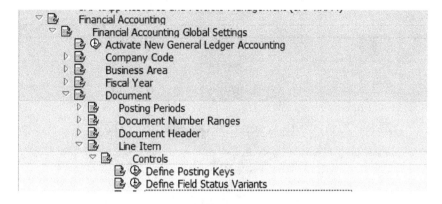

Fig 1

Change View "Field status variants": Overview

FStV	Field status name
0001	Field status for 0001
1000	IDES Group
1100	ABC LTD FIELD STATUS
1234	Field status for 0001
1983	OKIR
2200	IDES Group
2700	IDES Group
3000	Field status for 0001
5535	IDES Group
7000	IDES Brazil
8500	IDES Australia Group
9876	9876_AP
F100	IDES Banking
F220	IDES France Bank Group
LFV	Lenin Field Status Varian
ZUSA	ZUSA Incorporation

Dialog Structure
▽ ⊟ Field status variants
    ☐ Field status groups

Fig 2

We will use the SAP standard defined 0001 but for our purpose, we will copy it into our own. As their names suggest, SAP has created them with the view of utilizing them for specific kinds of G/L accounts, e.g. G004 for Cost accounts, G025 for Inventory adjustment accounts etc. (see Fig 7).

Then, we have the ability to modify it as needed without disturbing the existing one. Select 0001 as above and click on the Copy button:

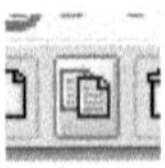

Fig 3

In the window that comes, replace 0001 with SFE1.

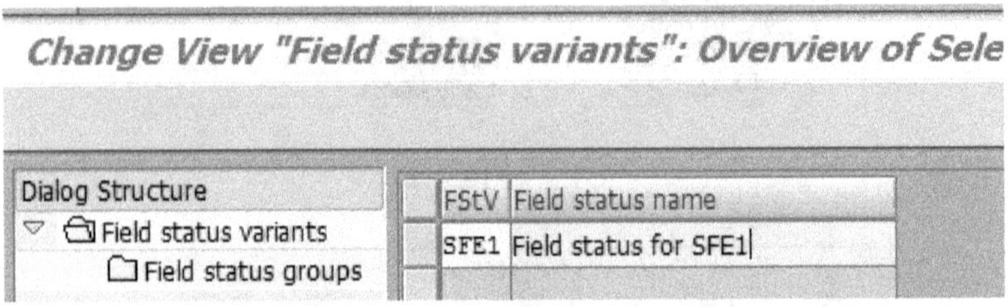

Change View "Field status variants": Overview of Sele

Dialog Structure	FStV	Field status name
▽ 🗁 Field status variants	SFE1	Field status for SFE1|
🗀 Field status groups		

Fig 4

Hit Enter

In the window, say Copy All:

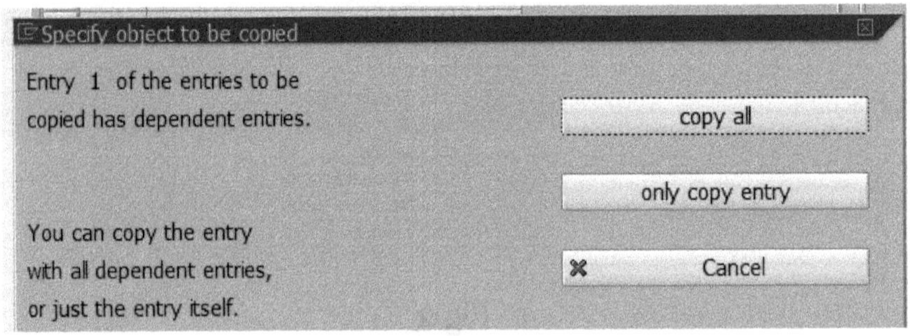

Specify object to be copied

Entry 1 of the entries to be copied has dependent entries.

[copy all]

[only copy entry]

You can copy the entry with all dependent entries, or just the entry itself.

[✖ Cancel]

Fig 5

A window informs you the copying was done.

Hit Enter again and we can see our field status variant:

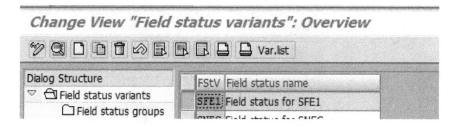

Fig 6

The 41 entries it referred to in the screen shot above are the underlying field status groups. These can be seen by checking the line SFE1 and double clicking on the line Field Status groups:

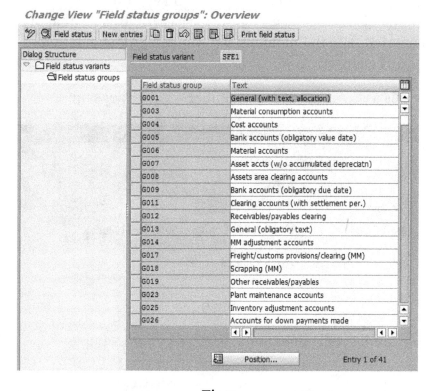

Fig 7

Note the same number 41 at the bottom. This is what was copied.

These G001 to ICCF are SAP defined field status groups:

Dialog Structure	Field status variant	SFE1	
▽ ☐ Field status variants			
☐ Field status groups			

	Field status group	Text	
	G068	Reconcilatn accts (payables - Austria)	
	G069	Cost accounts (travel expenses)	
	G070	Clearing accounts (travel expenses)	
	G071	Reconcil.accts (KIDNO/foreign payment)	
	ICCF	CO <-> FI reconciliation posting	

Fig 8

They should never be changed and if required to, a copy should be made and that changed. Copies of standard SAP objects must begin with a Z or Y, usually the former as to keep differentiation, SAP recommends that 'Y' be used only for local objects i.e. that are not transported. For the moment, we will use SAP standard and not make any changes.

Save this assignment and the familiar window pops up:

☞ Prompt for Customizing request	
View Cluster Mainten...	V_T004V
Request	IMDK902650 ☞ Customizing requ
Short Description	IDES: Configurations for FI Module
✓ ⏐ ⬚ 🗎 🗎 Own Requests ⏐ ✖	

Fig 9

To see more detail about them, let's look at an example:

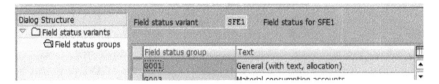

Dialog Structure	Field status variant	SFE1	Field status for SFE1
▽ ☐ Field status variants			
☐ Field status groups			

	Field status group	Text	
	G001	General (with text, allocation)	
	G003	Material consumption accounts	

Fig 10

Check the first one and click on the field 'Field Status'

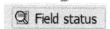

Fig 11

Underlying each variant (here G001) is a list of the field group:

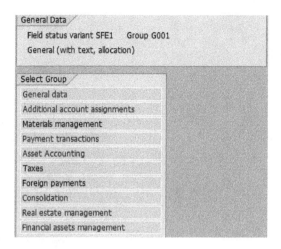

Fig 12

These field status groups relate to different data on the document and each signifies a kind of data. Double clicking each one of them gives more details about the fields and how they have been set up (ROS – Required/Optional/Suppress):

Maintain Field Status Group: General data

Field check

General Data   Page 1 / 1
Field status variant SFE1   Group G001
General (with text, allocation)

General data

	Suppress	Req. Entry	Opt. entry
Assignment number	○	○	●
Text	○	○	●
Invoice Reference	●	○	○
Hedging	●	○	○
Collective Invoice	●	○	○
Reference specification 1/2	●	○	○
Reference specification 3	●	○	○
Inflation Index	●	○	○

Fig 13

33

The next step is to assign our field status variant to the CC so it can be used. The T code for that is OBC5 or we can follow the path:

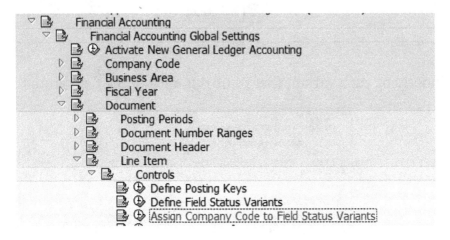

Fig 14

Find your CC using the Position key or by scrolling and then add the FSV SFE1 to it:

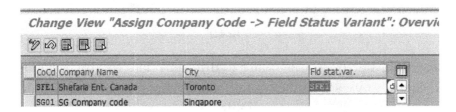

Fig 15

Hint: If there will be multiple CCs i.e. more to be set up down the road and normally, since in larger organizations, the CoA is common to all the CCs, it may be advisable to give a more 'generic' FSV code name like 1000, like we did for the Posting Period Variant.

NUMBER RANGES (C)

T Code SPRO or FBN1

The entire SAP is a litany of numbers and dates. With the combination of the two plus some other relevant data the entire data flow can be constructed. Every document that posts in FI must have some sort of a number, system either generated or external. The users have the ability to decide on any number range they wish. The number range can be repeated over different CCs though it is advisable that for clear accounting and audit trails, it is not done. It can also be repeated over different document types (we will discuss this later) i.e. different types of documents can share one number range. Number ranges are set up in different systems separately, a concept we will visit when we discuss testing of the system at the end of the course. The ranges on the FI side are set up in transaction FBN1. Alternatively, the path:

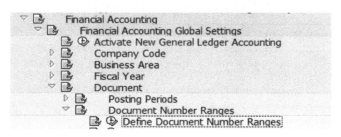

Fig 1

Since SAP has already pre-defined ranges for the template in this system, co code 0001, we will merely copy it, later, if we need to re-visit it, we can.

Enter 0001 as below and then click on the Copy button -

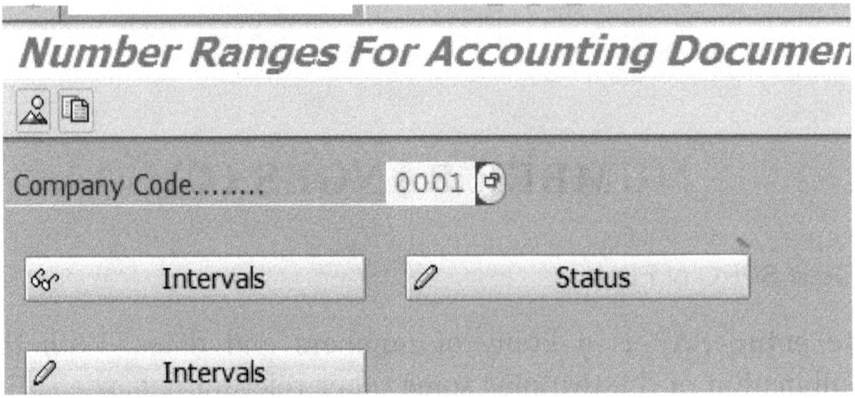

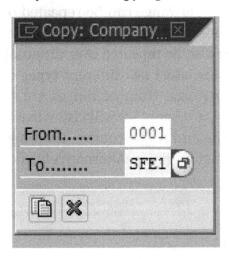

Fig 2

In the window, enter your CC – copying from '0001' to 'your CC':

Fig 3

Click on the Copy button again and a window comes up advising you to transport them separately. Normally, they can also be set up separately in the systems as noted above.

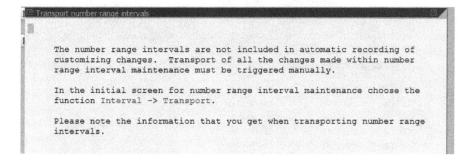

Fig 4

Hit Enter and you get a message at the bottom:

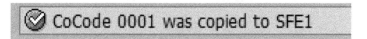

Fig 5

To verify, enter your CC on the screen and click on Display or Change mode of the intervals:

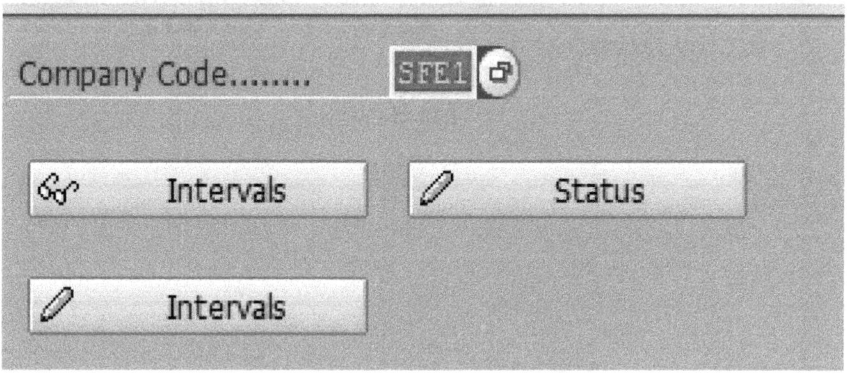

Fig 6

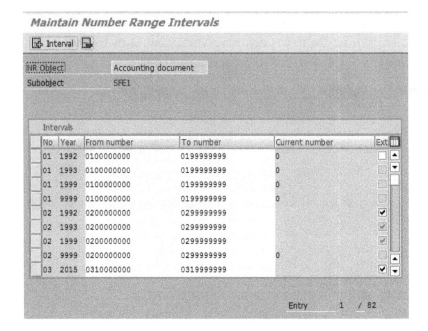

Fig 7

By clicking on Interval>Maintain you do have the ability to add/delete/modify the numbering per your choice:

Fig 8

GENERAL LEDGER IN SAP (U)

T Code FS00 (Area Menu)

The General ledger, henceforth, G/L Accounts in SAP is simply 'buckets' in which amounts pertaining to different activities or balances are held. We saw previously there are different types of account groups under which G/L accounts are set up. Further, the G/L accounts usually belong to a Chart of Accounts and a CoA may be repeated over multiple CCs, thereby indirectly assigning the G/L account to a CC. However, the G/L accounts then need to be created/extended to the CC itself also.

There are 3 different types of G/L accounts in SAP:

1. Accounts to which we must post via transactions i.e. no direct JEs are possible to these accounts. Typically, these entries are posted from a different module like SD posts revenues/receivables and MM posts purchases/payables. No direct entry to these accounts is possible. Instead, the entries emanate from a sub ledger – there are also reconciliation accounts, which fall in this definition.
2. Direct entry accounts like direct purchases e.g. consumption accounts, balance sheet accounts etc.
3. Indirect accounts where postings take place as a part of a different posting – typically a tax account will be like that where the taxes are a certain % of the revenue or expense and get posted accordingly

Alternatively, we can set up G/L accounts in a CoA and later extend them to the CCs we wish to. The G/L account must exist in the CC to enable postings to take place to the account.

G/L accounts are best explained by creating one to represent different business activities or balances. For the sake of brevity, we will set them up in 2 major groups that represent the P & L and a Balance sheet:

1. Balance Sheet
2. P & L

Re-visiting our numbering sequence will tell us what numbers we can give them:

New Entries: Overview of Added Entries

Field status

Chrt/Accts	Acct Group	Name	From acct	To account
SFE	BS	Balance Sheet Accounts	100000	399999
SFE	PL	Profit & Loss Accounts	400000	999999

Fig 1

The people running the accounting and finance areas in the organization generally set up G/L accounts. Let us set up a G/L account and understand the significance of each field in this set up. The transaction to set up a G/L account is in a menu called FS00 or we can follow the below path on the transactional SAP menu (not IMG/SPRO). This is on the Menu at log in time:

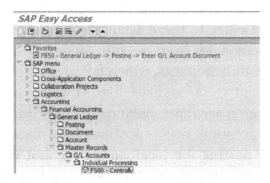

SAP Easy Access

- ▽ 🗀 Favorites
  - 🗎 FB50 - General Ledger -> Posting -> Enter G/L Account Document
- ▽ 🗀 SAP menu
  - ▷ 🗀 Office
  - ▷ 🗀 Cross-Application Components
  - ▷ 🗀 Collaboration Projects
  - ▷ 🗀 Logistics
  - ▽ 🗀 Accounting
    - ▽ 🗀 Financial Accounting
      - ▽ 🗀 General Ledger
        - ▷ 🗀 Posting
        - ▷ 🗀 Document
        - ▷ 🗀 Account
        - ▽ 🗀 Master Records
          - ▽ 🗀 G/L Accounts
            - ▽ 🗀 Individual Processing
              - 🗎 FS00 - Centrally

Fig 2

Enter the G/L account and company code in the window. Let us create a revenue account 451010:

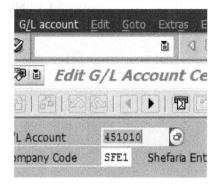

Fig 3

Enter the Account # and CC as in Fig 3, and Go to G/L Account> Create:

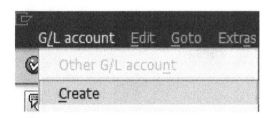

Fig 4

Select PL as we know this is a P&L Account:

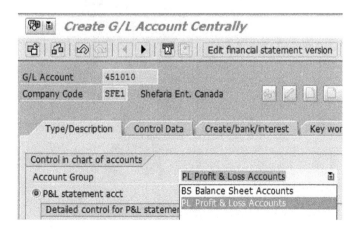

Fig 5

To enable reporting for functional areas (if configured), we can assign the G/L account to a relevant functional area e.g. this is a Revenue account we defined for Business Division 1, so we can link it to Functional Area 4000:

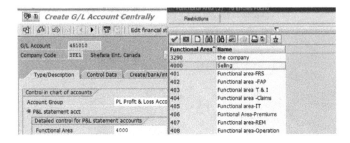

Fig 6

Give it the appropriate description i.e. it's purpose:

Description	
Short Text	Revenue Stream 1
G/L Acct Long Text	Revenue from Furniture Division

| Consolidation data in chart of accounts | |

Fig 7

On the next tab, the main field is currency, which should auto, populate from the CC currency e.g. CAD in our case:

G/L Account	451010	
Company Code	SFE1 Shefara Ent. Canada	With Template

Type/Description | Control Data | Create/bank/interest | Key word/translation | 1.

Account control in company code

Account currency	CAD Canadian Dollar
☐ Only balances in local crcy	
Exchange rate difference key	
Valuation group	
Tax category	+ Only output tax allowed
☑ Posting without tax allowed	
Recon. account for acct type	
Alternative account no.	
☐ Acct managed in ext. system	
Inflation key	
Tolerance group	

Account management in company code

☐ Open item management	
☑ Line item display	
Sort key	000 Assignment number

Fig 8

- **Tax category** – in SAP the output taxes (on sales) and input taxes (on purchases) are different categories. Since this is a revenue account, it makes sense to mark it as such
- **Posting without tax allowed** – generally, keep this checked for nontaxable customers.
- **Line item display** – keep this checked generally. This will provide reporting on line item of the transaction instead of clubbing them together
- **Sort Key** – this enables the reporting sequence. Usually 000 is the preferred one as it gives the listing in sequence of the transaction # (assignment #)

Click on the Create/Bank/Interest tab:

Fig 9

- **Field Status group** – this is the same that we saw in the step of Field Status variants. Use the SAP standard for revenue accounts – G029
- **Post automatically** – this button ensures no manual postings can be done to this G/L account. Since it is an account that will collect the revenue and since revenue is a result of sales orders from customers, the postings into this account should originate from Sales side. Thus, we ensure nobody can post revenue directly in the system.

The other tabs are not important for anything specific that can affect the postings.

Save the account and a message appears at the bottom:

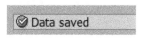

RECONCILIATION ACCOUNTS (C/U)

T Code SPRO, FS00

Reconciliation accounts are provided by SAP as secondary accounts into which the main accounts pour their numbers. These accounts merely act as a 'one point' storage to see amounts relating to total receivables, payables, assets etc and are very useful at the time of generating the P&L and Balance Sheet. When we set up customers and vendors, this account is a mandatory field that needs to be filled up so the system can recognize the account that needs to be updated with the sale or purchase transaction with that customer or vendor.

A typical transaction will occur like this:

A purchase of $1000 of a product has occurred and the vendor has submitted an invoice for it, which is posted to AP.

This transaction will perform the Vendor and expense direct entries:

```
            Vendor                                    Expense
    Dr            Cr                          Dr            Cr
              |  1000  1                   1      1000|
              |                                        |
                                                       |


              A/P Reconciliation
                   Dr          Cr
                           |  1000  1
                           |
                           |
```

Fig 1

Based on the reconciliation account defined in the customer master, SAP will post another entry in the background to it to the A/P Reconciliation account. Thus, with hundreds of such vendor invoice receipts taking place, the A/P Reco account will hold all those balances and one can look up the payables amount at one spot. The Recon acct is the general ledger account, which is updated via the sub-ledger accounts.

Once the vendor is paid, the following will happen in the system:

```
            Vendor                              Bank Balance A/c
       Dr          Cr                          Dr          Cr
  2    1000|    1000  1                               |  1000 2
           |                                          |


              A/P Reconciliation
                   Dr          Cr
               2   1000|    1000  1
                       |
```

Fig 2

Let us create a reconciliation account 211000 for Trade Payables – Domestic for the vendors that will provide goods or services to the SFE1. Again, the T Code is the same, FS00:

Since, this account will hold the total amount of payables at any point of time; it must be a Balance sheet account:

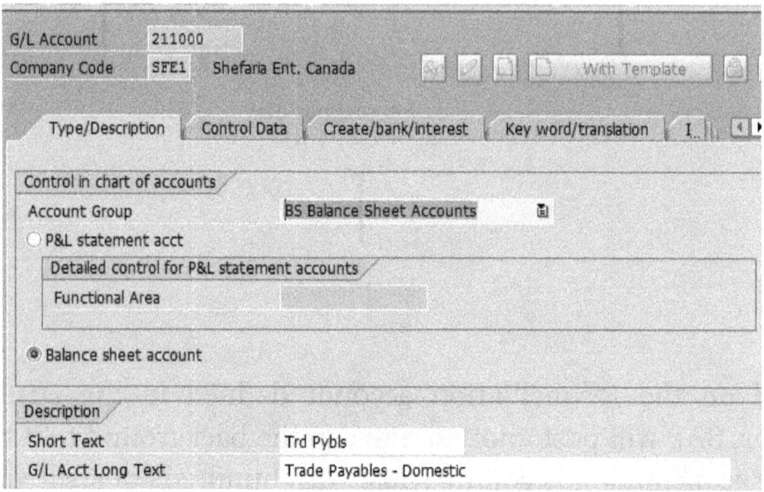

Fig 3

Control Data tab:

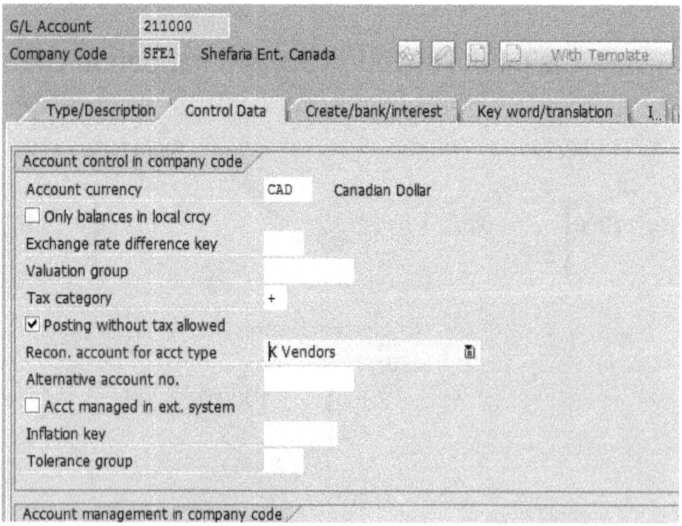

Fig 4

The notation 'K' is the same 'K' we saw in the posting period open/close screen. It is K here because this account 211000 (a part of the BS sheet series of accounts) is for trade payables (to vendors). Had it been for trade receivables, we would have used D (from customers). We have to open or close posting periods for the account type K to enable the postings to flow in the same way as they would for the normal revenue G/L accounts thus, to maintain balance between the two, it is generally recommended to open and close all kinds of accounts synchronously.

Again, the currency will pre-populate based on the CC of the CoA. It is recommended to allow all kinds of tax categories by using a '*'.

It is not recommended to check the boxes Open line item management or line item display as the former is unnecessary since postings take place only indirectly to the recon accounts and the latter will cause a lot of time to be taken to run the reports relating to the recon accounts due to the high volume of transactions with each transaction also posting to the recon account. However, it is possible to select line item display if one really feels the need to.

Create/Bank/Interest Key tab:

Use G067 – provided by SAP for recon accounts.

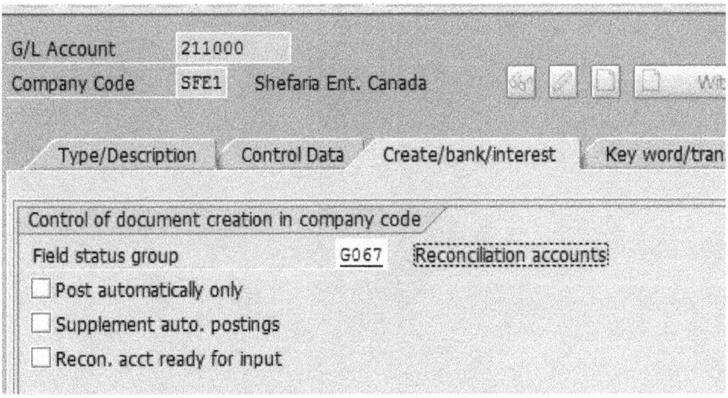

Fig 5

Do not check any other boxes are they are not relevant to a recon account. A recon account by default can only be posted to automatically via a transaction from the sales or purchasing side.

The other tabs are not significant and mainly relate to descriptions in different languages, relationships to cost elements etc.

Save the G/L account, the message should come at the bottom:

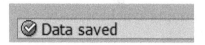

Fig 6

Along with the others, also set up the retained Earnings G/L account we configured earlier – 330000. It is a BS sheet account.

DEFINING EMPLOYEE TOLERENCE

(C)

T Code SPRO

Before we can make any real postings to a G/L account, we must define Employee tolerance limits. These limits set up the following information:

1. Maximum amount that can be posted in a single accounting document
2. Maximum amount that can be posted to a vendor or customer account. This field restricts the amount that can be paid to a vendor or cleared from receivables for a customer.
3. Maximum percentage for a cash discount that can be applied to a line item in this field.
4. Maximum acceptable tolerance for payment differences

These tolerance limits are defined in employee groups which in turn are attached to the user's profiles in the area of SAP roles/authorizations and security. The path to set this up is:

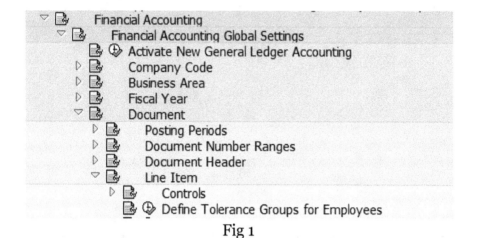

Fig 1

For the purpose of keeping this simple, we will define for only one employee, not as any group of employees. We make the entry for the CC in the table below by clicking on New Entries tab:

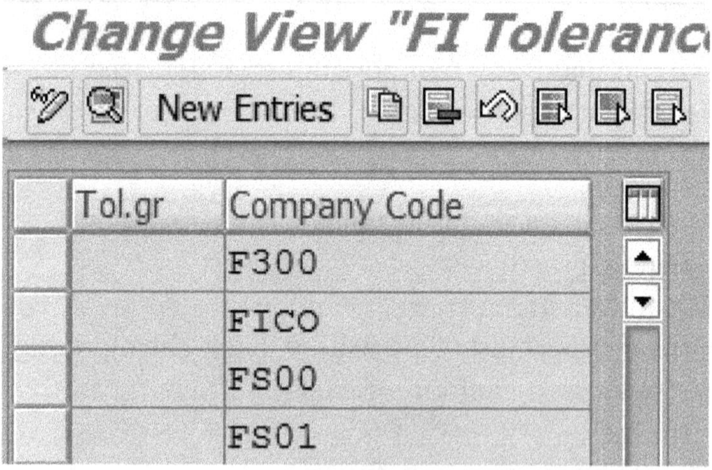

Change View "FI Toleranc

Tol.gr	Company Code
	F300
	FICO
	FS00
	FS01

Fig 2

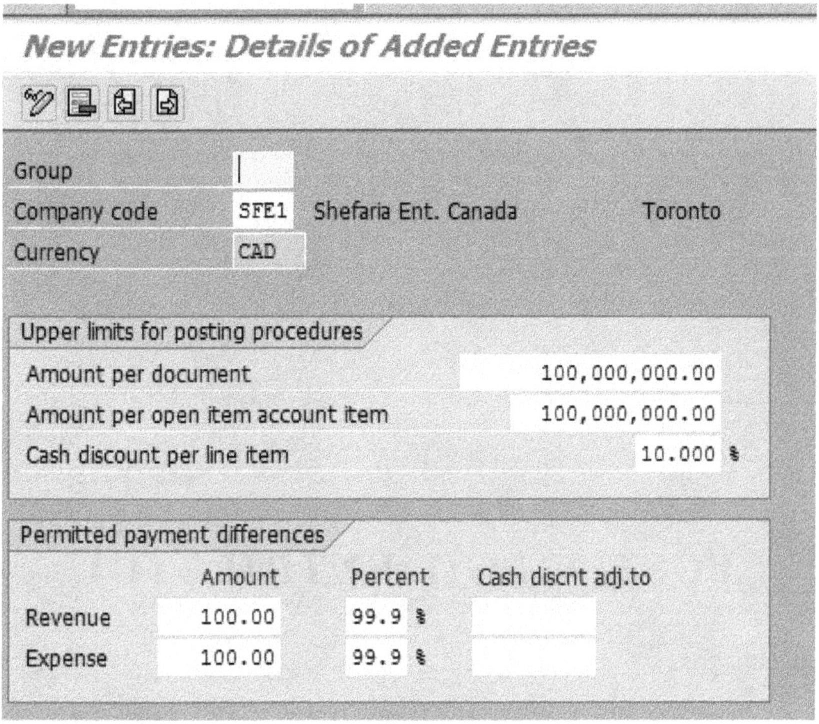

New Entries: Details of Added Entries

Group			
Company code	SFE1	Shefaria Ent. Canada	Toronto
Currency	CAD		

Upper limits for posting procedures

Amount per document	100,000,000.00
Amount per open item account item	100,000,000.00
Cash discount per line item	10.000 %

Permitted payment differences

	Amount	Percent	Cash discnt adj.to
Revenue	100.00	99.9 %	
Expense	100.00	99.9 %	

Fig 3

This means:

- The employee can post a total document till 100 mn CAD and each line of a max 100 mn
- The differences the employee is allowed to apply against the receivable or payable compared to the actual transaction value is 100 dollars or up till 99.9%. The % is valid only for a gain, not loss. SAP chooses the lower of the two, hence if we want to define the limits in absolute terms, the percentage must always be kept to 99.9.

Save this configuration.

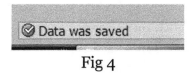

Fig 4

POSTING G/L ENTRIES (U)

T Code FB50

At this point, we have defined the following:

1. Our company code and it's CoA
2. A few G/L accounts, of type P&L, Balance sheet and reconciliation; some allow direct postings, some not
3. Employee tolerances which determine how much an employee can post, both in absolute terms of a manual JE and in relative terms as a % or $ difference from the actual transaction document.

While there are some more configurations like tax codes for accounts that mandatorily require taxes in the amounts to be posted, we will for the moment, proceed with minimal and simplest posting to see how it is done.

When G/L entries are done, every entry must have a debit and credit side to it and both must balance else SAP will not allow the posting to take place. Thus, 2 or more different accounts are needed to make one posting in the system. SAP allows until 999 line items for every document.

The books in SAP are posted to from the point of view of the corporation. The accounting rules that drive them are:

1. To increase the value of an expense or asset account, we post a debit entry to it
2. To decrease the value of the expense or asset account, we post a credit entry to it
3. To increase the value of a revenue or liability account, we post a credit entry to it
4. To decrease the value of a revenue or liability account, we post a debit entry to it

Before we actually create any recurring entries, we need to look at the concept of posting keys in SAP. Posting keys control the line item posting in a document screen. They also control the data underlying them:

A/c Type (A-assets, D-customer, K-vendor and S-GL),
Transaction Type and
Nature of the Transaction (debit/credit)

A unique combination of these 3 elements is a different posting key. Just by knowing the # of the posting key, one can identify what kind of transaction it is. Though not a major utility, it facilitates daily work when posting manual JEs. There should not be any reason to set up any new ones, SAP provided standard ones will always suffice. The different posting keys can be seen in the configuration:

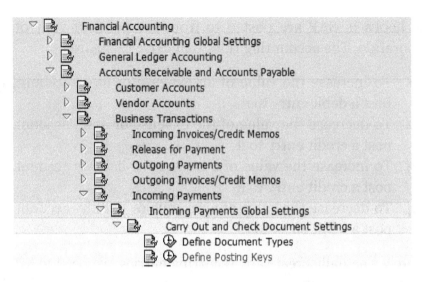

Financial Accounting
    Financial Accounting Global Settings
    General Ledger Accounting
    Accounts Receivable and Accounts Payable
        Customer Accounts
        Vendor Accounts
        Business Transactions
            Incoming Invoices/Credit Memos
            Release for Payment
            Outgoing Payments
            Outgoing Invoices/Credit Memos
            Incoming Payments
                Incoming Payments Global Settings
                    Carry Out and Check Document Settings
                      Define Document Types
                      Define Posting Keys

Fig 1

Maintain Accounting Configuration : Posting Keys - List

Posting key	Name	Debit/Credit	Account type
00	Act assignment model		
01	Invoice	Debit	Customer
02	Reverse credit memo	Debit	Customer
03	Bank charges	Debit	Customer
04	Other receivables	Debit	Customer
05	Outgoing payment	Debit	Customer
06	Payment difference	Debit	Customer
07	Other clearing	Debit	Customer
08	Payment clearing	Debit	Customer
09	Special G/L debit	Debit	Customer
11	Credit memo	Credit	Customer
12	Reverse invoice	Credit	Customer
13	Reverse charges	Credit	Customer
14	Other payables	Credit	Customer
15	Incoming payment	Credit	Customer
16	Payment difference	Credit	Customer
17	Other clearing	Credit	Customer
18	Payment clearing	Credit	Customer
19	Special G/L credit	Credit	Customer

Fig 2

They are categorized into 4 groups:

- ➢ Customer (01 to 20)
- ➢ Vendor (21-39)
- ➢ GL (40&50)
- ➢ Asset (70&75)

A detail screen of 01 reveals more:

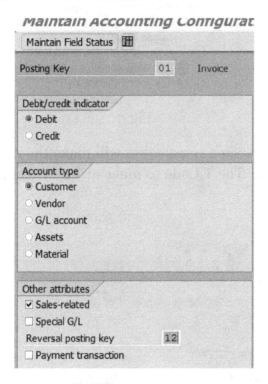

Fig 3

Therefore, now we know, when we have to post a sales related debit entry on a customer, we should use the key 01. One of the most commonly used ones are 40 and 50 (for G/L postings) with both of them also being each other's reversal posting keys.

40	Debit entry	Debit	G/L account
50	Credit entry	Credit	G/L account

Fig 4

As noted, there should not be any reason to create a new posting key, the configuration though lies in the below path to view the details of the keys:

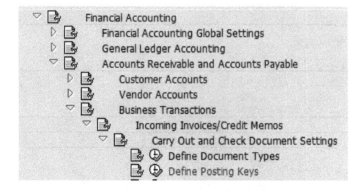

Fig 5

Making an entry via a transaction will make the usage of posting keys more clear. The T Code to make an entry directly is FB50 or follow the path:

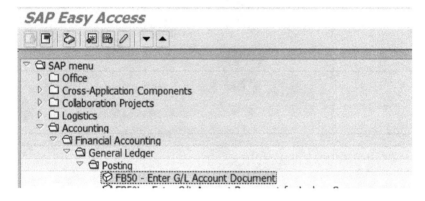

Fig 6

The transaction took us directly to post into SFE1 because we have been working in it, SAP holds that data in it's memory.

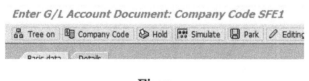

Fig 7

If, however, the correct CC does not show up as 'default', it must be made so by clicking on the option

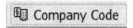

Fig 8

Then choose your co code from the drop down list or enter it directly:

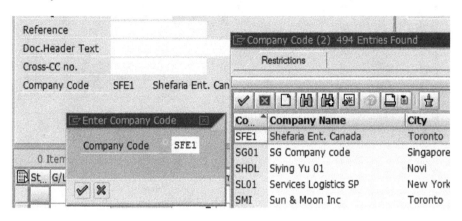

Fig 9

Let us try to purchase goods and increase the inventory. A typical JE will require this information:

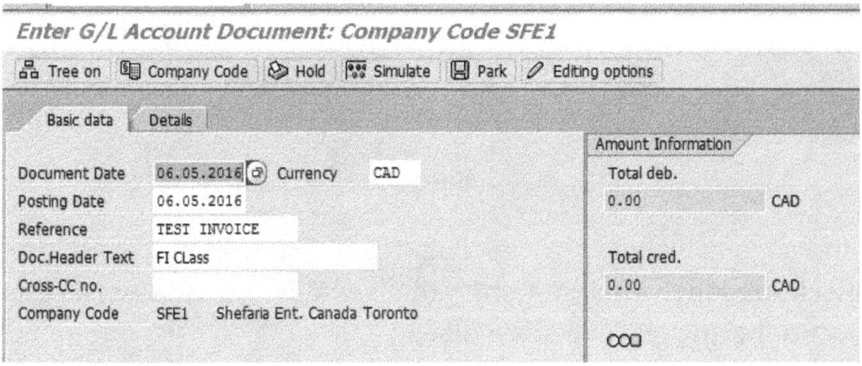

Fig 10

Enter the dates and texts to give the JE a meaning.

In the lower part of the screen, let us try the first line item, debiting the purchase account:

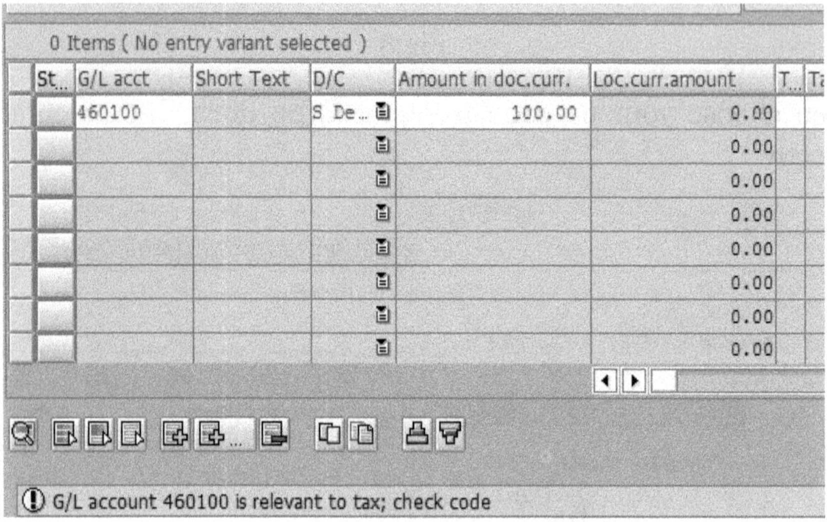

St..	G/L acct	Short Text	D/C	Amount in doc.curr.	Loc.curr.amount	T..	Ta
	460100		S De...	100.00	0.00		
					0.00		
					0.00		
					0.00		
					0.00		
					0.00		
					0.00		
					0.00		

0 Items (No entry variant selected)

⚠ G/L account 460100 is relevant to tax; check code

Fig 11

On the 2nd line, enter the corresponding inventory account to credit it – an asterisk in the amount column will 'copy' the amount from the 1st line, thereby preventing the need to manually enter and make any mistake:

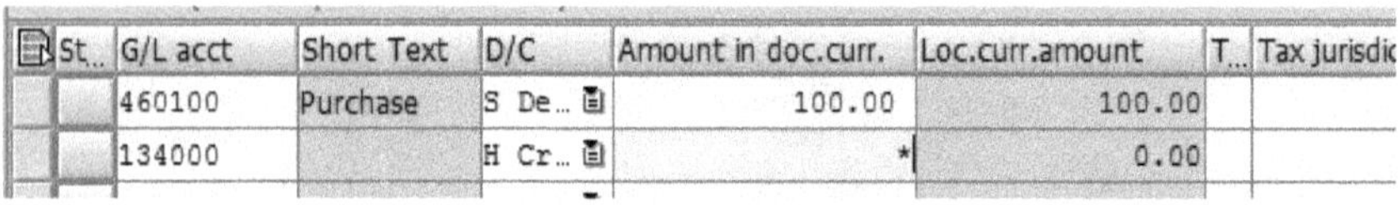

St..	G/L acct	Short Text	D/C	Amount in doc.curr.	Loc.curr.amount	T..	Tax jurisdic
	460100	Purchase	S De...	100.00	100.00		
	134000		H Cr...	*	0.00		

Fig 12

A message in yellow may appear if the G/L account is set up to reflect taxes in it. However entry of taxes is not mandatory as there may not be any taxes to pay/collect.

⚠ G/L account 460100 is relevant to tax; check code

Fig 13

Hit Enter and the data screen changes to a balancing sign at the top right in Green (right most position on the 3 circles)

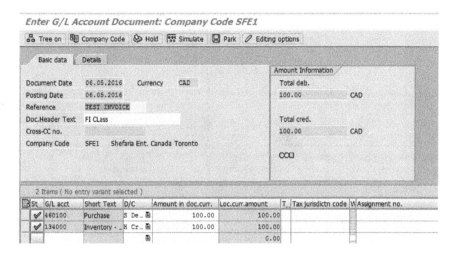

Fig 14

As we know, SAP will allow to make an entry only if the credit and debit balance match as they do in this case. If the amounts do not match, the screen would display the red light (left most position on the 3 circles)

Enter G/L Account Document: Company Code SFE1

▥ Tree on   ▣ Company Code   ◈ Hold   ▦ Simulate   🖫 Park   ✎ Editing options

| Basic data | Details |

		Amount Information
Document Date	06.05.2016 Currency CAD	Total deb.
Posting Date	06.05.2016	100.00 CAD
Reference	TEST INVOICE	
Doc.Header Text	FI CLass	
Cross-CC no.		Total cred.
Company Code	SFE1 Shefaria Ent. Canada Toronto	105.00 CAD
		⬤○○

2 Items (No entry variant selected)

St	G/L acct	Short Text	D/C	Amount in doc.curr.	Loc.curr.amount	T	Tax jurisdictn code	W Assignment
✔	460100	Purchase	S De…	100.00	100.00			
✔	134000	Inventory - …	H Cr…	105.00	105.00			
					0.00			

Fig 15

59

It is also possible to 'simulate' to ensure everything is in sync and correct before posting. Click on the tab:

Fig 16

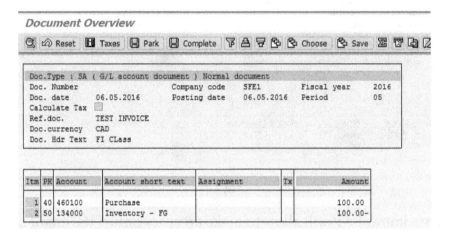

Fig 17

The above posting keys 40 and 50 were self-determined by SAP based on the G/L transaction that is being posted.

At this point, we have the option to Park or Post the document or to go back and make changes. Let us post this document by clicking on the Save button:

Fig 18

A message appears at the bottom informing the document was posted:

Fig 19

60

Note the numbering sequence, it posted this document and took
the number from the sequence we set up earlier for the CC:

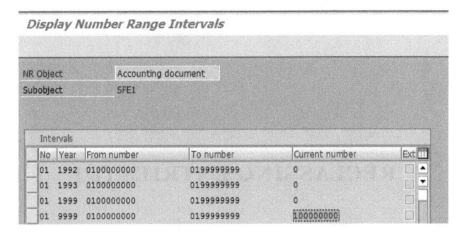

	No	Year	From number	To number	Current number	Ext
	01	1992	0100000000	0199999999	0	
	01	1993	0100000000	0199999999	0	
	01	1999	0100000000	0199999999	0	
	01	9999	0100000000	0199999999	100000000	

Fig 20

RECLASSING ENTRIES (U)

T Code F-02

Occasionally mistakes occur in which a posting to be made manually or automatically in a certain G/L account is inadvertently made to another G/L. Balances can be moved around from one G/L to another using transaction F-02:

Enter the data as necessary relating to the G/L you made the incorrect entry to. E.g. we need to move some amount from G/L 460100 to 460300:

Enter data in F-02 crediting 460100 with the amount:

Fig 1

Hit Enter and on the next screen enter the amount and the account to be debited:

Enter G/L account document: Add G/L account item

More data | Acct model | Fast Data Entry | Taxes

G/L Account	460100	Purchase
Company Code	SFE1	Shefaria Ent. Canada

Item 1 / Credit entry / 50

Amount	1735.50	CAD
Tax Code		☐ Calculate tax

Real Estate Obj ⇨

Asset	⇨ More
Value date	
Assignment	Asst retirement ☐
Text	✐ Long Texts

Next Line Item

PstKy 40 Account 460300   SGL Ind   TType   New co.code

Fig 2

Hit Enter again and on the following screen copy the amount to be debited using * or entering it:

Enter G/L account document: Add G/L account item

More data | Acct model | Fast Data Entry | Taxes

G/L Account	460300	Purchases of MRO materials
Company Code	SFE1	Shefaria Ent. Canada

Item 2 / Debit entry / 40

Amount	*|	CAD
Tax Code		

Fig 3

Now you can simulate the document to see the effects of your changes:

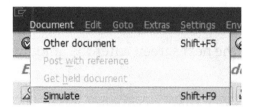

Fig 4

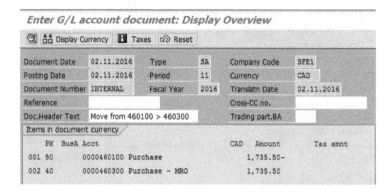

Fig 5

In addition, post:

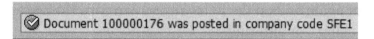

Fig 6

Run FBL3N transaction for the date you did the postings and you will find the 2 corresponding entries:

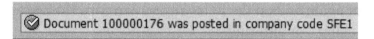

Fig 7

AUTOMATIC CLEARING OF OPEN

ACCOUNT ITEMS (C/U)

T Code SPRO, F.13

Overview : In SAP the Concept of Automatic clearing simply means an automated process of clearing open items in book of accounts using certain criteria. When doing daily transactions there are many line items in GL/ Vendor / Customer section which remain open due to many reasons.

Following items can be considered as open items :

- GR/IR clearing acounts within a G/L
- Items with witholding tax posting
- Down payments can only be cleared if down payment clearing for the same amount has been posted

The remaining open items are grouped together according to fxed system criteria :

- By company code
- Account type

- Account number
- Reconcilliation Account Number
- Assignment Number
- Currency Key
- Spl. GL Indicators

Clearing takes place when, for the group of line items selected according to the above criteria, the balance in document currency (for customers and vendors) or in update currency (for G/L accounts) is zero. The date for clearing is the clearing date according to your selection specifications. In an update run, if the clearing transaction is successful, the clearing document number is generated by SAP.

During the program run, all accounts in which clearing can be performed are blocked automatically. They get unblocked again after the clearing transaction is over. Accounts that are blocked by other transactions intended for the automatic payment run are not considered in automatic clearing.

Pre-requisites : Addressing above criteria we see that F.13 – Automatic Clearing process works on some pre-defined conditions for example if we have raised one invoice for 100 CAD$ and received payment for 100 CAD$; in this case, we will have two open line items in the customer account.

Based on three identical information in both open line items.. customer code, amount and invoice number, F.13 turns these open items into cleared items.

We need to define those conditions or basis on which Automatic Clearing will work :

I. CONFIGURING AUTOMATIC CLEARING (C)

T Code OB74

In this activity, we enter the criteria for grouping the open items of an account for automatic clearing. The program clears open items of a group if the balance in local and foreign currency is zero.

We enter the following standard criteria:

- The account type
- The account number or number range

We can also enter five additional criteria. We choose the five other criteria from the fields in the main accounting tables BSEG and BKPF. If possible we should choose those fields which are also included in table BSIS (G/L accounts), BSID (customers), or BSIK (vendor). More on tables in the concluding sections of this manual.

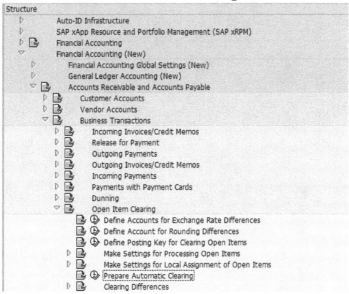

Fig1

In the following screen we put 4 conditions on which Autoclearing process will work on each account type (Customer , Vendor and GL Account) :

- Assignment Number [ZUONR]
- Reference Number [XBLNR]
- Trading Partner   [VBUND]
- Purchase Doc No.   [EBELN]

ChtA...	AccTy	From acct	To account	Criterion 1	Criterion 2	Criterion 3	Criterion 4
SFE	D	A	Z	ZUONR	XBLNR	VBUND	EBELN
SFE	K	A	Z	ZUONR	XBLNR	VBUND	EBELN
SFE	S	0	999999	ZUONR	XBLNR	VBUND	EBELN

Fig 2

II.   How Automatic Clearing Works

Automatic clearing process only works on Accounts which are mananged as Open Item Management (recall this to be one of the settings in a G/L Account).

During the setup and the execution of Automatic Clearing in the output control we select only those documents that can be cleared; then we obtain a detailed list.

The detail list is a list of the line items and gives information about the open or cleared (or clearable) line items selected. Group of items that comply with the system criteria and the user criteria are summarized. If the clearing conditions have been fulfilled, , in an update run, the clearing document number are displayed if the clearing transaction was successful. If an error occurred during clearing, the message No clearing appears.

Now let's take a scenario : Clearing the Vendor with Customer

Scenario Overview: In practice, a specific customer can also be a vendor for the same company code. In this case, open items from the A/P side can be offset with the open items from the A/R side for this specific account. The offset is made using the clearing transaction. Clearing vendor with customer open items can be executed only after the following setup is made:

Settings Required : T Code : FK02 (Vendor Master Change) , FD02 (Customer Master Change)

In tab Account Control enter the vendor account number, company code and hit ENTER

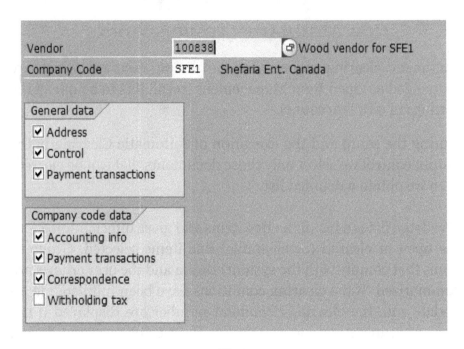

Fig 3

In tab "Account Control", enter the customer number of that vendor as shown below.

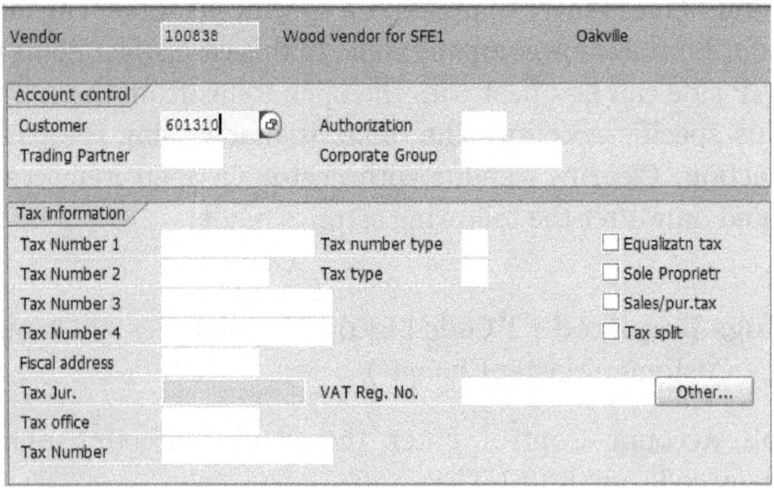

Fig 4

In the tab "Payment transactions", select the "Clrg with Cust." checkbox.

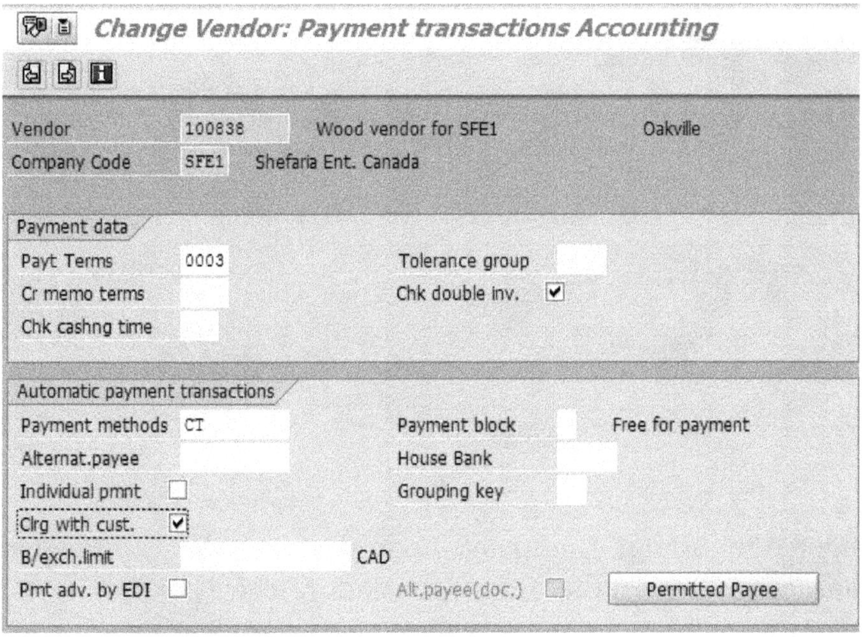

Change Vendor: Payment transactions Accounting

| Vendor | 100838 | Wood vendor for SFE1 | Oakville |
| Company Code | SFE1 | Shefaria Ent. Canada | |

Payment data

Payt Terms	0003	Tolerance group	
Cr memo terms		Chk double inv.	✔
Chk cashng time			

Automatic payment transactions

Payment methods	CT	Payment block	Free for payment
Alternat.payee		House Bank	
Individual pmnt	☐	Grouping key	
Clrg with cust.	✔		
B/exch.limit		CAD	
Pmt adv. by EDI	☐	Alt.payee(doc.) ☐	Permitted Payee

Fig 5

In the same way we will now set up Vendor within Customer Master record for the Account 601310

Under FD02 : Input the customer account number and the company code.

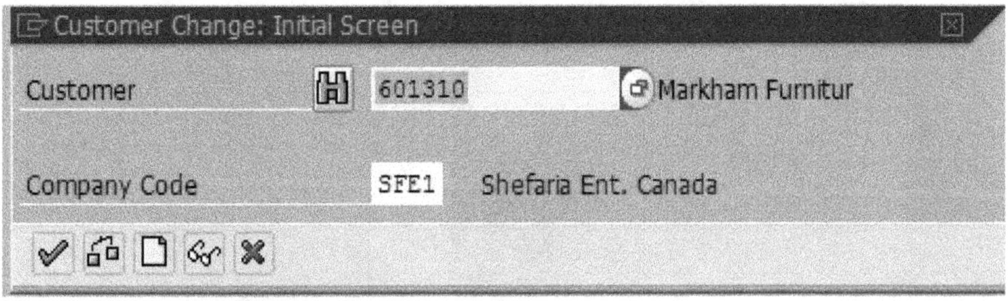

Customer Change: Initial Screen

| Customer | | 601310 | Markham Furnitur |
| Company Code | | SFE1 | Shefaria Ent. Canada |

Fig 6

In the tab "Control Data", enter the corresponding vendor number.

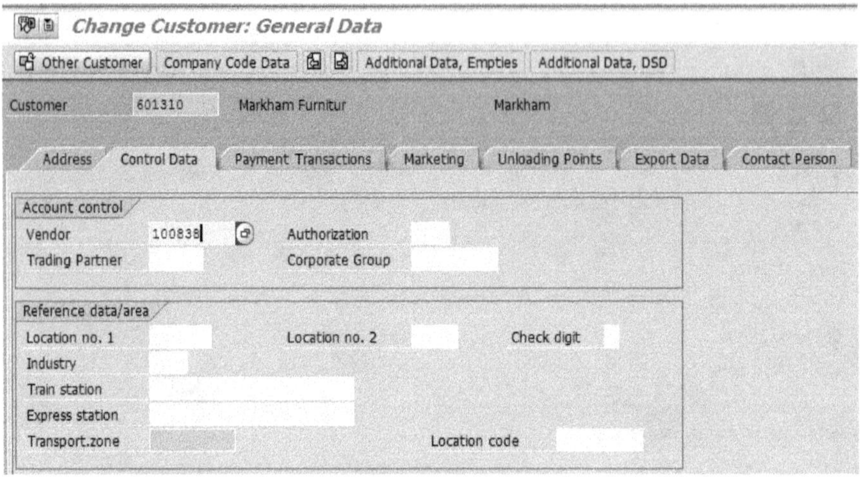

Fig 7

Under the option Company Code Data tab - "Payment transactions", select the "Clrg with vendor." checkbox.

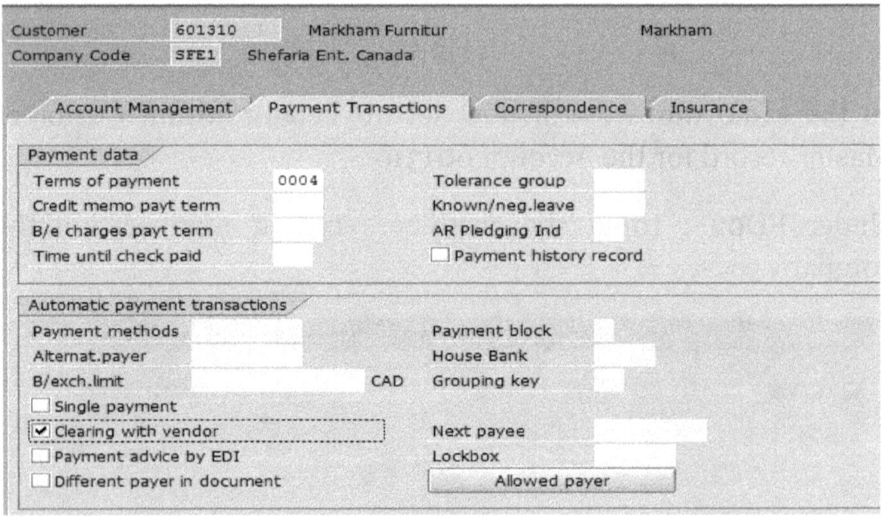

Fig 8

III.   AP, AR, GL Automatic Clearing

T Code F.13

We need to specify Company Code, Fiscal Year, tick Select vendors, customer, GL   checkbox, enter vendor & customer account numbers be cleared, and Clearing date. Next, select Test run checkbox in order to have a preview of the proposed items to be cleared.

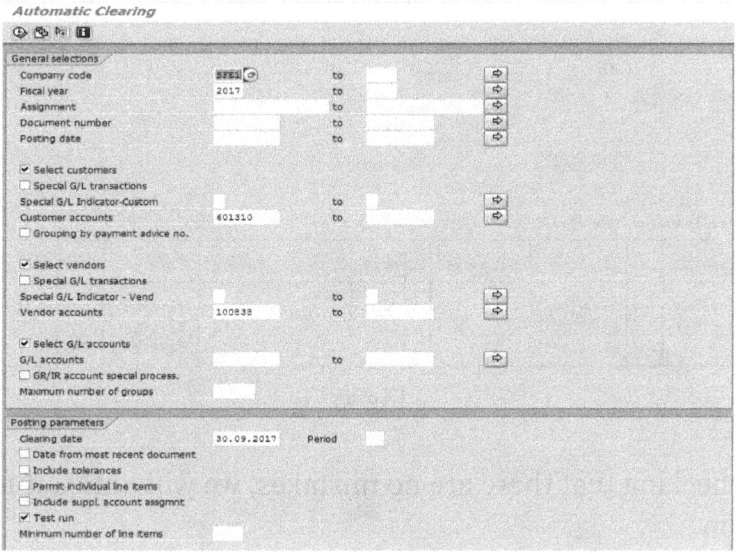

Fig 9

Automatic Clearing Process executed in Test Run to have a preview on list of items to be cleared based on condition grouping.

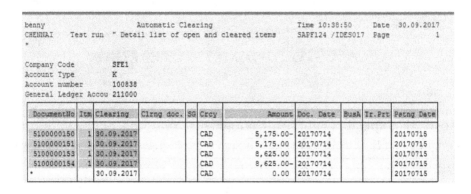

```
benny                      Automatic Clearing              Time 10:38:50    Date  30.09.2017
CHENNAI    Test run  " Detail list of open and cleared items    SAPF124 /IDES017   Page            1
*

Company Code        SFE1
Account Type        K
Account number          100838
General Ledger Accou 211000
```

DocumentNo	Itm	Clearing	Clrng doc.	SG	Crcy	Amount	Doc. Date	BusA	Tr.Prt	Pstng Date
5100000150	1	30.09.2017			CAD	5,175.00-	20170714			20170715
5100000151	1	30.09.2017			CAD	5,175.00	20170714			20170715
5100000153	1	30.09.2017			CAD	8,625.00	20170714			20170715
5100000154	1	30.09.2017			CAD	8,625.00-	20170714			20170715
*		30.09.2017			CAD	0.00	20170714			20170715

Fig 10

```
benny                      Automatic Clearing              Time 11:39:12    Date  30.09.2017
CHENNAI Test run  " Detail list of open and cleared    SAPF124 /IDES017   Page            1
*

Company Code        SFE1
Account Type        S
Account number          200000
General Ledger Accou 200000
```

DocumentNo	Itm	Clearing	Clrng doc.	SG	Crcy	Amount	Doc. Date	BusA	Tr.Prt
100000138	1	30.09.2017			CAD	5.00-	20160913	0001	
100000144	1	30.09.2017			CAD	5.00	20160913	0001	
*		30.09.2017			CAD	0.00	20160913	0001	

Fig 11

After checking that there are no mistakes, we will untick it for the
final run.

```
benny                         Automatic Clearing              Time 06:29:58   Date  30.09.2017
CHENNAI                       Test run  " Error Log           SAPF124 /IDES017   Page            5

CoCd AccTy Account number   G/L        Crcy
Program    Scre MT Msg. MsgNo Message Text


                   No errors were logged during clearing in test run
```

Fig 12

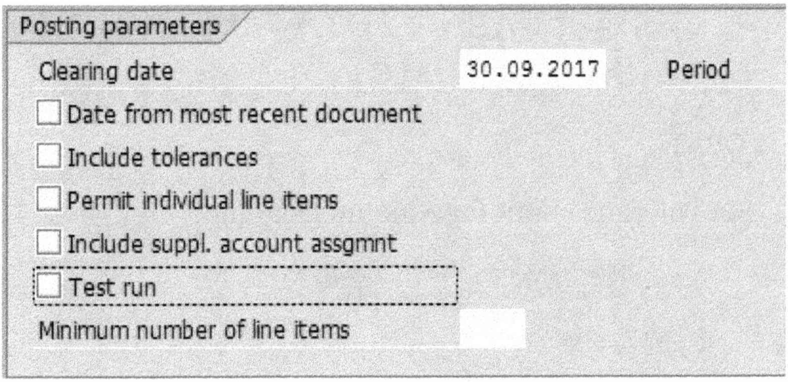

Posting parameters

Clearing date	30.09.2017 Period
☐ Date from most recent document	
☐ Include tolerances	
☐ Permit individual line items	
☐ Include suppl. account assgmnt	
☐ Test run	
Minimum number of line items	

Fig 13

To run the transaction in final run click Execute button for
automatic clearing and posting

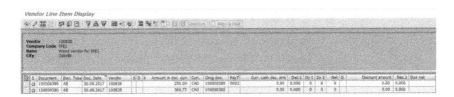

Fig 14

IV. AUTOCLEAR IN THE FOREGROUND/ BACKGROUND (C)

T Code OBA3

Set Tolerance limit for Amount clearence:

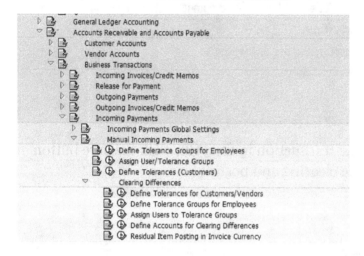

Fig 15

Company Code	Tolerance group	Name
R100		
R100	00	
R300		
R300	R300	
RG		
RG	1000	
S000		
S000	1000	
S300		
S300	3000	
SAUR		
SAUR	3000	
SFC1		Tolerance group of SFC1
SFC1	SFC1	Tolerance group of SFC1
SFC2		Tolerance group of SFC1
SFC2	SFC1	Tolerance group of SFC1

Fig 16

Select **New Entries** to define new tolerance group for Customers / Vendors

Here we will maintain tolerance limit upto 2000 CAD$ as amount difference for autoclearing Customer / Vendor open items.

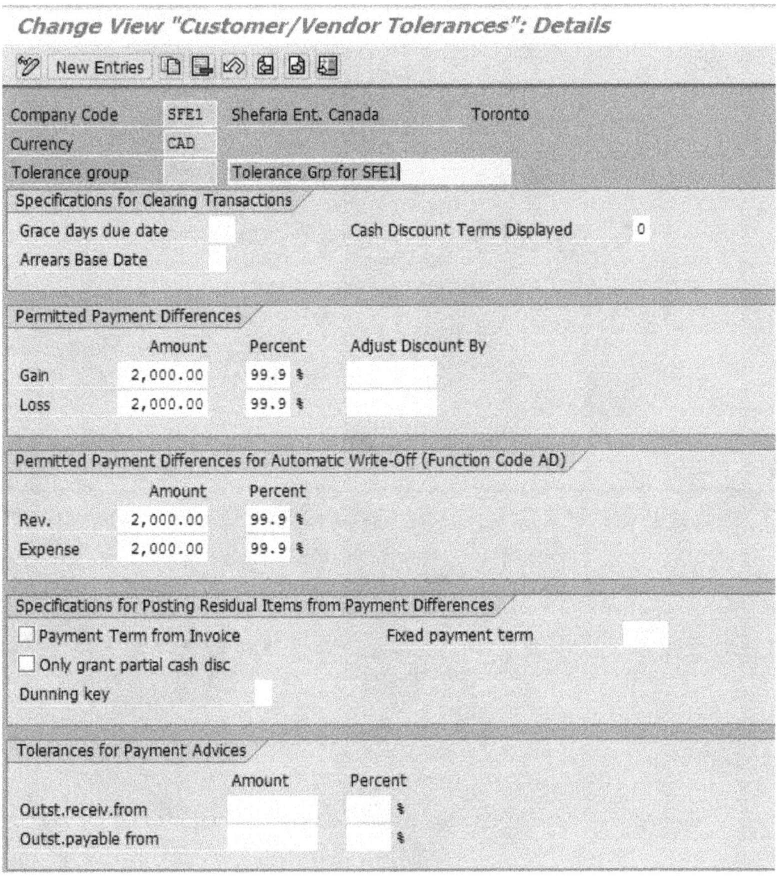

Change View "Customer/Vendor Tolerances": Details

New Entries

Company Code	SFE1	Shefaria Ent. Canada	Toronto
Currency	CAD		
Tolerance group		Tolerance Grp for SFE1	

Specifications for Clearing Transactions

| Grace days due date | | Cash Discount Terms Displayed | 0 |
| Arrears Base Date | | | |

Permitted Payment Differences

	Amount	Percent	Adjust Discount By
Gain	2,000.00	99.9 %	
Loss	2,000.00	99.9 %	

Permitted Payment Differences for Automatic Write-Off (Function Code AD)

	Amount	Percent
Rev.	2,000.00	99.9 %
Expense	2,000.00	99.9 %

Specifications for Posting Residual Items from Payment Differences

☐ Payment Term from Invoice   Fixed payment term
☐ Only grant partial cash disc
Dunning key

Tolerances for Payment Advices

	Amount	Percent
Outst.receiv.from		%
Outst.payable from		%

Fig 17

Assign Tolerance limit for User / Employees (C)

T Code SPRO

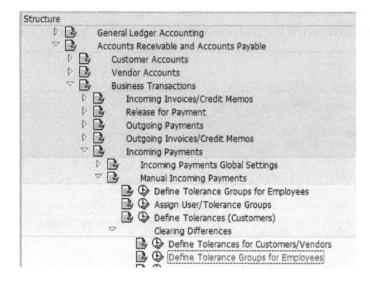

Fig 18

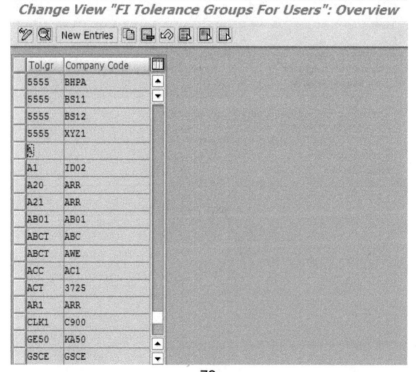

Fig 19

Choose New Entries to define the tolerance group for allowing diferences upto 2000 CAD

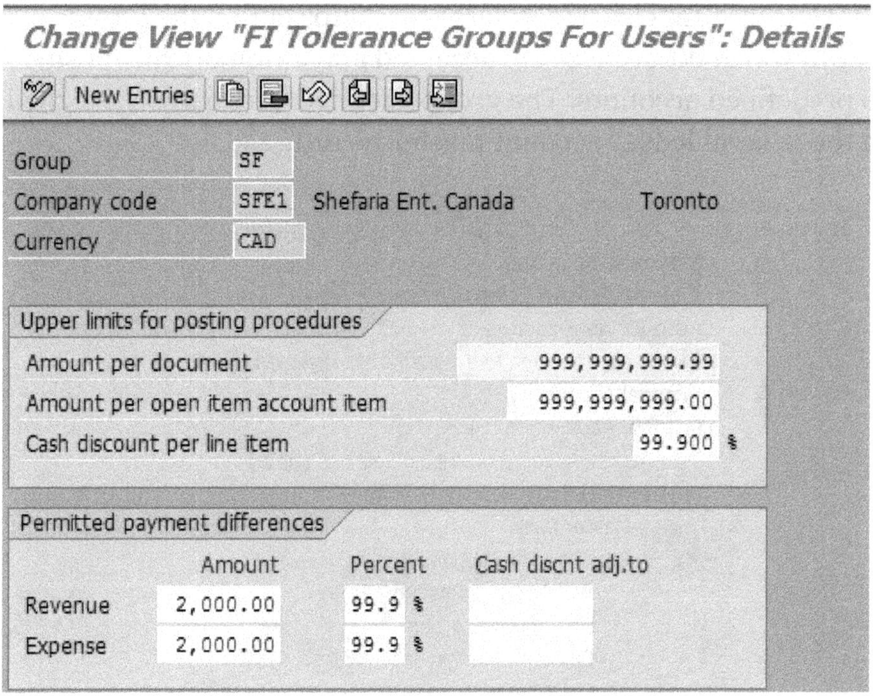

Change View "FI Tolerance Groups For Users": Details

New Entries

Group	SF
Company code	SFE1 Shefaria Ent. Canada Toronto
Currency	CAD

Upper limits for posting procedures

Amount per document	999,999,999.99
Amount per open item account item	999,999,999.00
Cash discount per line item	99.900 %

Permitted payment differences

	Amount	Percent	Cash discnt adj.to
Revenue	2,000.00	99.9 %	
Expense	2,000.00	99.9 %	

Fig 20

V. DEFINE TOLERANCE GROUP FOR G/L ACCOUNTS (C)

T Code SPRO

For G/L account clearing, tolerance groups define the limits within which differences are accepted and automatically posted to predefined accounts. The groups defined here can be assigned in the general ledger account master record.

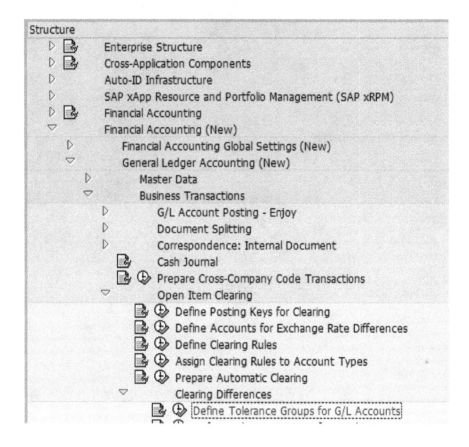

Fig 21

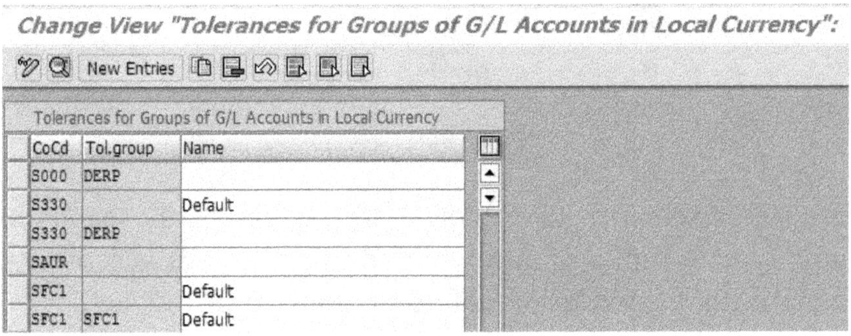
Change View "Tolerances for Groups of G/L Accounts in Local Currency":
New Entries
Tolerances for Groups of G/L Accounts in Local Currency
CoCd
Tol.group
Name
S000 DERP
S330 Default
S330 DERP
SAUR
SFC1 Default
SFC1 SFC1 Default

Fig 22

Choose New Entries to define the tolerance group.

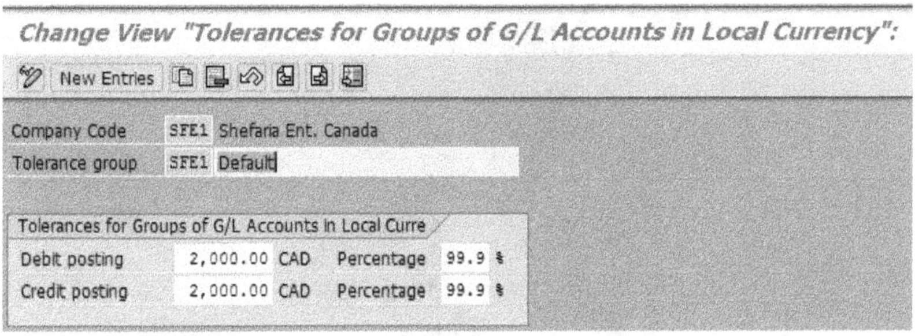
Change View "Tolerances for Groups of G/L Accounts in Local Currency":
New Entries
Company Code SFE1 Shefaria Ent. Canada
Tolerance group SFE1 Default
Tolerances for Groups of G/L Accounts in Local Curre
Debit posting 2,000.00 CAD Percentage 99.9 %
Credit posting 2,000.00 CAD Percentage 99.9 %

Fig 23

Click 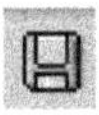 to save the entries.

VI.   DEFINE ACCOUNTS FOR AUTOPOSTING CLEARING DIFFERENCES (C)

T Code OBXL

When you are clearing customer/vendor accounts, these tolerance groups specify limits within which differences are accepted and automatically posted to predefined accounts. In this activity you define the accounts to which these differences should be automatically posted.

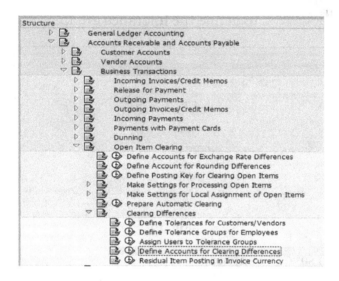

Fig 24

Choose your Chart of Accounts :

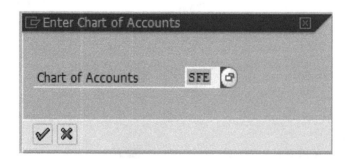

Fig 25

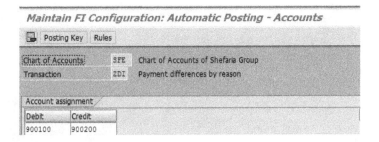

Fig 26

Click to save the entries.

VIII. ACCOUNT DETERMINATION FOR EXCHANGE RATE DIFFERENCE (C)

T Code OB09

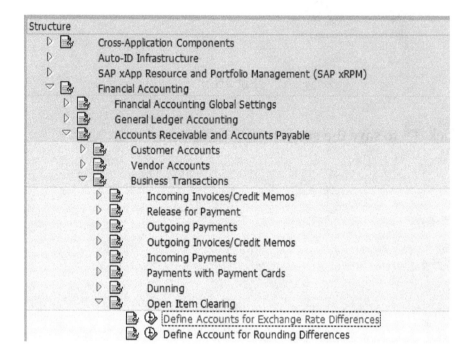

Fig 27

In this activity we define the accounts for valuating open items here. However, we can only make the necessary settings for these accounts when defining the settings for the closing procedures. This step is important incase the clearing is happening in local currency while the company code has Group Currency different from the local currency, which means the system may identify the Exchange rate Differences. As in this case Company code: SFE1 has group currency [30] active in EUR.

Since F.13 is treated as one of the closing procedures, currency valuation comes into effect during autoclearing for local with additional local currency which is set up as group currency.

T Code : OB22

To view the Additional currency set up by Company Code

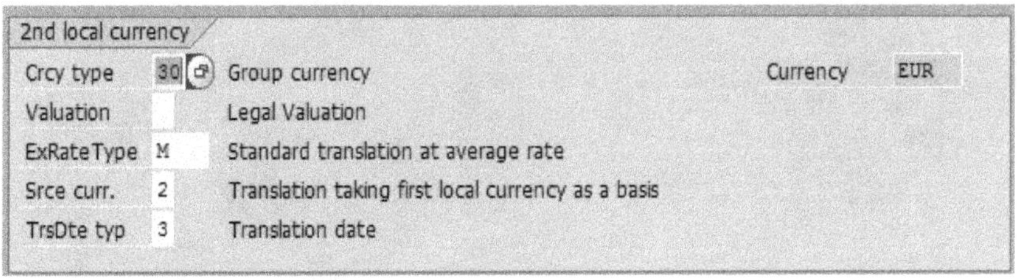

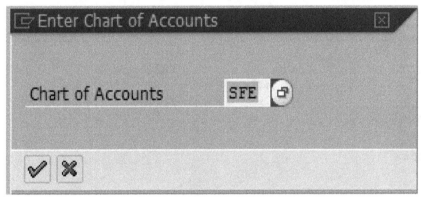

Fig 28

Now let us define the accounts for Exchange rate differences.
Choose your Chart of Accounts :

Fig 29

Since we are proceeding with Autoclearing for customer open
items we might consider the Customer reconcilliation (GL)
account where we will define the account for the realized
Exchange rate difference.

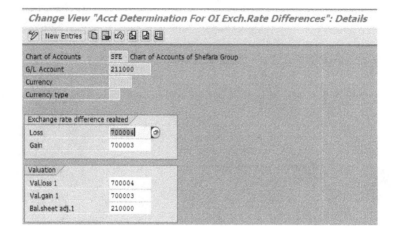

Change View "Acct Determination For OI Exch.Rate Differences": Details

New Entries

Chart of Accounts	SFE Chart of Accounts of Shefaria Group
G/L Account	211000
Currency	
Currency type	

Exchange rate difference realized

| Loss | 700004 |
| Gain | 700003 |

Valuation

Val.loss 1	700004
Val.gain 1	700003
Bal.sheet adj.1	210000

Fig 30

Change View "Acct Determination For OI Exch.Rate Differences": Overvie

New Entries

Chart of Accts   SFE   Chart of Accounts of Shefaria Group

G/L	Currency	Crcy type
121000		
121210		
211000		
211001		
211020		
211050		
212000		
300203		

Fig 31

Click 🖫 to save the entries.

IX.   EXECUTE AUTOCLEARING (U)

T Code F.13

We choose customer Account no. 601321 which has a balance of 500 CAD (Fig 32 of FBL5N) and will autoclear that using the tolerance rules set up earlier.

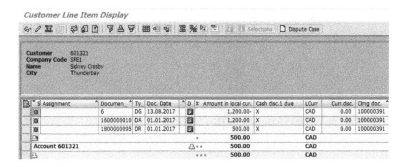

Fig 32

Fig 33

Choose the option

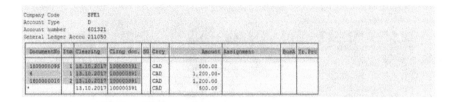

as it will take care of the tolerance rules set up earlier for auto clearing.

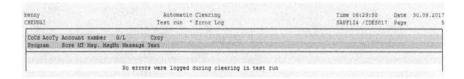

Fig 34

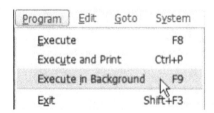

Fig 35

We can also run in test mode first to check for any possible errors. If no errors are found then we can run in foreground / background to process autoclearing as hown below:

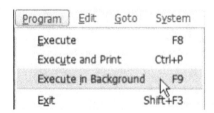

Fig 36

After Succesful clearing the FI Document will be posted as shown at the bottom in Fig 37:

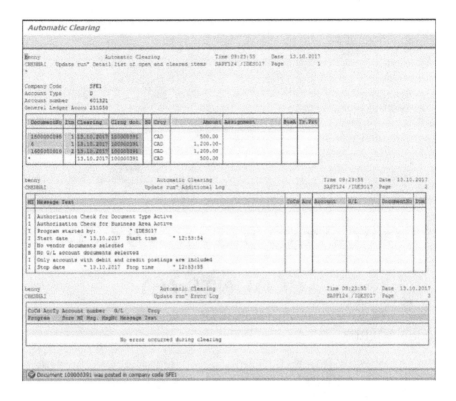

Fig 37

Post processing F.13 - Auto clear : Go to FBL5N again to check the clearence of the customer 601321

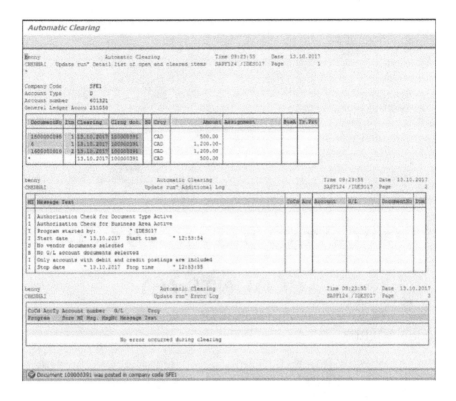

Fig 38

DISPLAYING BALANCES IN G/L

ACCOUNTS (U)

T Code FAGLB03

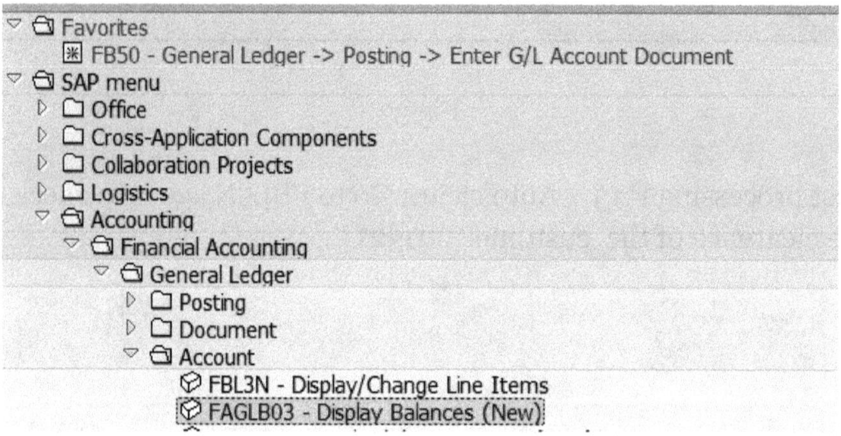

```
▽ 🗁 Favorites
    ⊞ FB50 - General Ledger -> Posting -> Enter G/L Account Document
▽ 🗁 SAP menu
   ▷ 🗀 Office
   ▷ 🗀 Cross-Application Components
   ▷ 🗀 Collaboration Projects
   ▷ 🗀 Logistics
   ▽ 🗁 Accounting
      ▽ 🗁 Financial Accounting
         ▽ 🗁 General Ledger
            ▷ 🗀 Posting
            ▷ 🗀 Document
            ▽ 🗁 Account
               ⊘ FBL3N - Display/Change Line Items
               ⊘ FAGLB03 - Display Balances (New)
```

Fig 1

FAGLB03 will be a transaction every SAP FI user will use fairly often. On the main screen, enter the G/L account, CC (since in a common CoA, a G/L account can be across several CCs) and the year you wish to look up in:

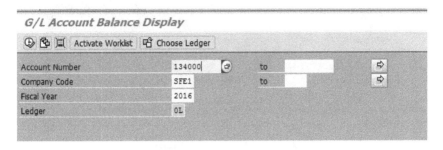

Fig 2

Multiple G/L accounts can be entered at the same time by clicking on the button [⇨] and in the screen that comes up:

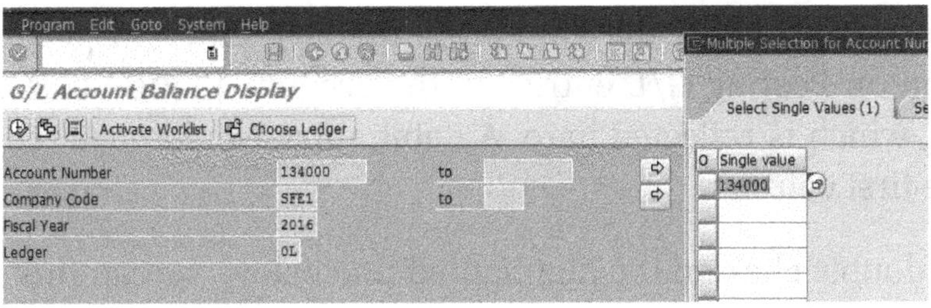

Fig 3

G/L accounts can also be included or excluded as needed in the above tabs. For the moment, we will run this transaction for the G/L 134000.

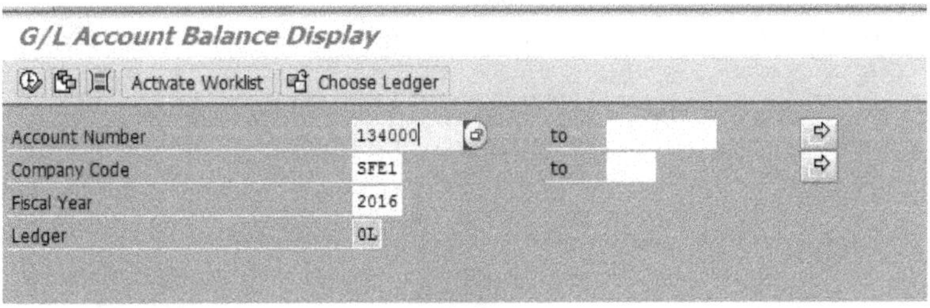

Fig 4

Click on the Execute button ⊕ or hit F8. A new screen comes up giving the balances as in the different months:

Balance Display: G/L Accounts For the Ledger 0L

Document Currency	Document Currency	Document Currency	Individual Account

Account Number	134000	Inventory - FG
Company Code	SFE1	Shefaria Ent. Canada
Fiscal Year	2016	

Display More Chars

All Documents in Currency   *   Display Currency   CAD   Company code currenc

Period	Debit	Credit	Balance	Cumulative balance
Bal.Carryfor...				
1				
2				
3				
4				
5		100.00	100.00-	100.00-
6				100.00-
7				100.00-

Fig 5

As we notice above, the amount is the G/L entry we did in the section on Posting G/L entries in the account 134000 as a credit entry, which is reflected here. A debit entry would have reflected in the first column.

If we double click on the highlighted line below, we can find more details about the balances. Depending on which cell/column you click (Debit or credit or balance), you can see either only the debit, or only the credit or all the postings in that G/L.

Account Number	134000	Inventory - FG
Company Code	SFE1	Shefaria Ent. Canada
Fiscal Year	2016	

Display More Chars

All Documents in Currency   *   Display Currency   CAD   Company code currenc

Period	Debit	Credit	Balance	Cumulative balance
Bal.Carryfor...				
1				
2				
3				
4				
5		100.00	100.00-	100.00-

Fig 6

We will find the actual documents relating to those postings, all the cleared and open items all together when we click on the balance column:

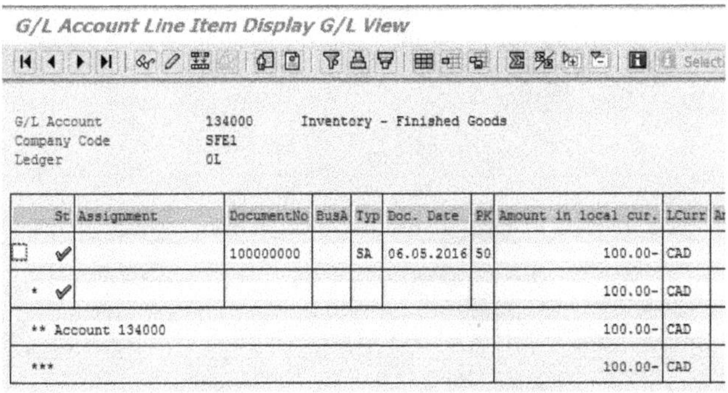

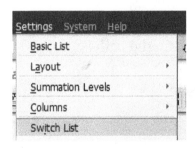

Fig 7

A very neat way of looking at this table to sort the data is by switching the layout mode in Settings>Switch List:

Fig 8

A more pleasing layout emerges:

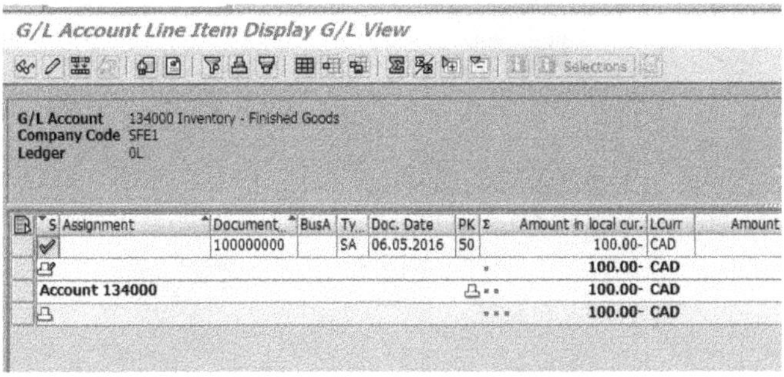

Fig 9

DISPLAYING LINE ITEMS (U)

T Code FBL3N

Line items in SAP are the individual entries that were posted in a document. To view them the path is:

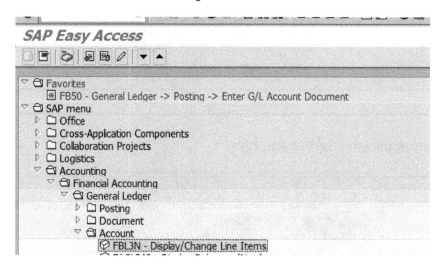

Fig 1

Alternatively, use transaction FBL3N.

Line item display is only possible for the accounts, which are set up, so in G/L account setup under the Control tab:

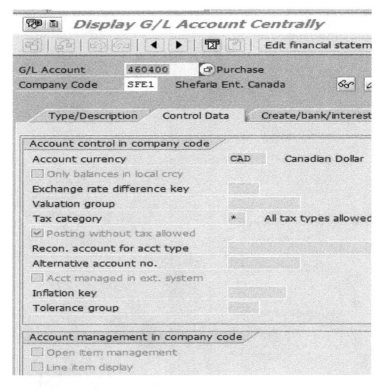

Fig 2

As we note, this account 460400 is not set up for line item display, so if we try to look up it's balances in FBL3N, we get an error (Fig 3)

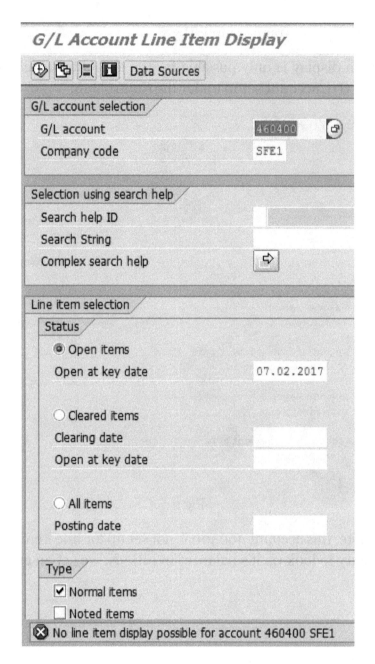

G/L Account Line Item Display

⊕ ⊡)≡(**H** Data Sources

G/L account selection

G/L account · · · · · · · · · · · · · · · · 460400 ⟨⬦⟩

Company code · · · · · · · · · · · · · · · · SFE1

Selection using search help

Search help ID

Search String

Complex search help · · · · · · · · · · ⇨

Line item selection

Status

⦿ Open items

Open at key date · · · · · · · · · · 07.02.2017

○ Cleared items

Clearing date

Open at key date

○ All items

Posting date

Type

☑ Normal items

☐ Noted items

⊗ No line item display possible for account 460400 SFE1

Fig 3

Let us now post in FB50 a G/L entry for accounts that support line item reporting. Let us credit Labor inventory (external labor bought) and debit Purchases account.

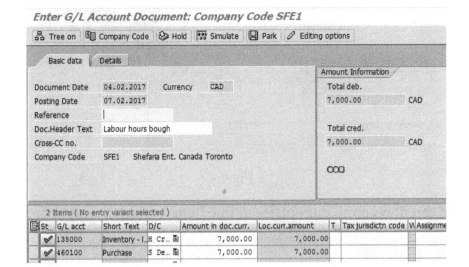

Fig 4

Post the document:

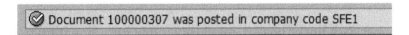

Fig 5

Now, if we want to see the balances in these 2 G/Ls, we can:

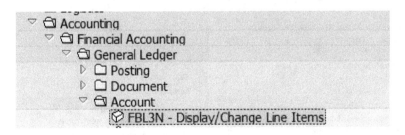

Fig 6

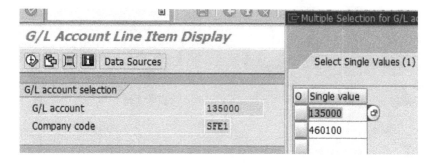

Fig 7

We can now see all our entries at line item level in this report:

G/L Balances
G/L Account
Company Code SFE1

S	Doc. Date	DocumentNo	Doc. Type	Cost Center	LCurr	Σ	Amount in local cur.	Texts	Text	Account	User Name
✔	04.02.2017	100000307	SA		CAD		7,000.00-			135000	IDES0164
✔		100000307	SA		CAD		7,000.00			460100	IDES0164
					CAD	•	0.00				

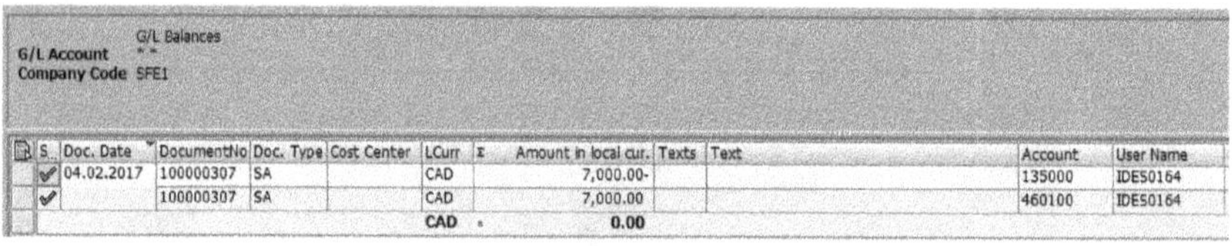

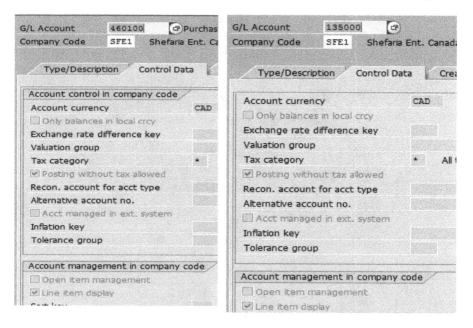

Fig 8

This is because both the G/L accounts allow for a line item display:

Fig 9

Again, the list can be seen a different form also, in settings:

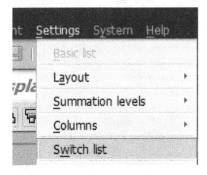

Fig 10

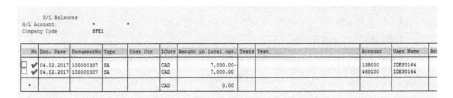

Fig 11

We can also export it on our desktop to work with it; this is especially useful when there are many entries to be analyzed.

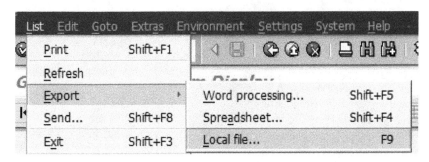

Fig 12

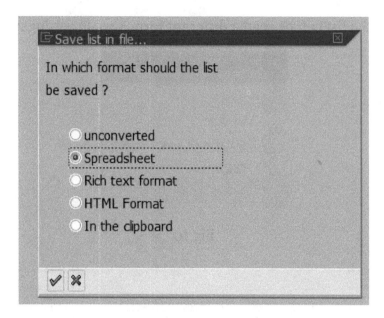

Fig 13

Select the spot where you want the file to be stored like Desktop in Fig 14:

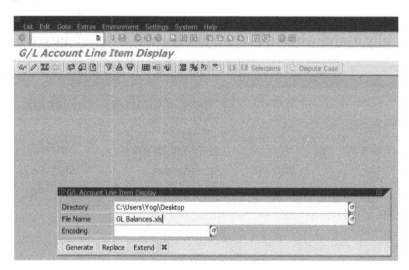

Fig 14

This downloading of data from reports will be a common recurring process throughout and users often use it all the time. For the most part, it is standard across entire SAP.

REVERSING ACCOUNTING ENTRIES

(U)

T Code FB08

A number once used up cannot be cancelled or deleted in accounting. This is to ensure a complete audit trail. However, it can be reversed. The path to do that is:

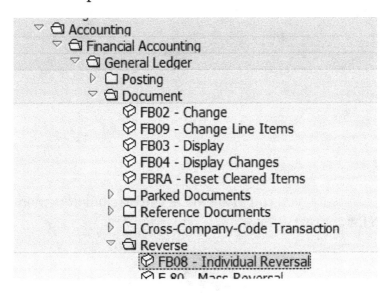

Fig 1

Enter the document # you need to reverse and give the reason thereof which is mandatory:

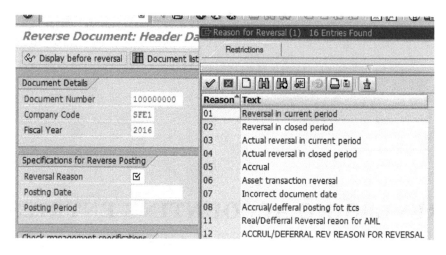

Fig 2

We can define our own reasons also via configuration though it is unnecessary and one of standard SAP ones will work fine, like 01 above.

You can also give a different date if the original posting date belonged to a period, which is now closed:

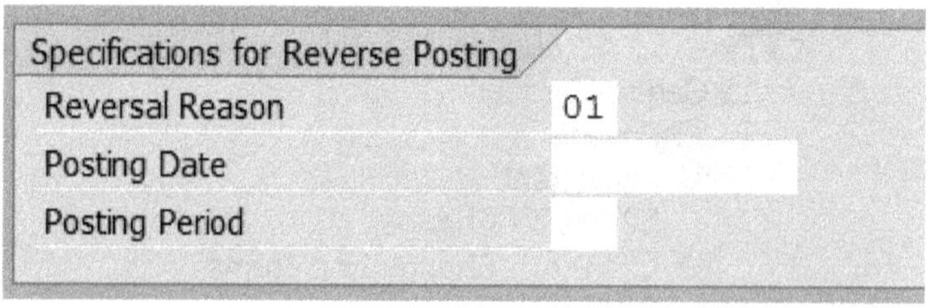

Specifications for Reverse Posting		
Reversal Reason	01	
Posting Date		
Posting Period		

Fig 3

Before reversing, you can also look at the original document if you need to for confirmation:

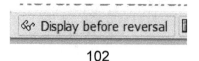

Fig 4

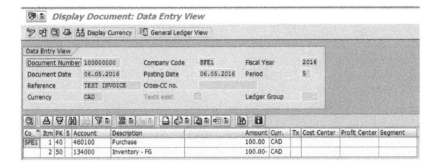

Fig 5

Save and a message is displayed at the bottom:

Document 100000002 was posted in company code SFE1

Fig 6

Note that it took the next available number from the same series. It is possible to have different numbering for reversal documents and often companies do that to ensure better separation and visibility.

When we run the report again, we find the reversal entries have appeared together under the documents that posted them:

G/L Account		G/L Balances						
Company Code SFE1		* *						
S	Doc. Date	Document	Doc. Type	Cost Center	LCurr	Σ	Amount in local cur.	Texts	Text
---	---	---	---	---	---	---	---	---	---
✓	06.05.2016	100000001	SA		CAD		5,000.00-		
					CAD	▪	5,000.00-		
Account 135000							5,000.00-		
✓	06.05.2016	100000000	SA		CAD		100.00		
	06.05.2016	100000002	AB		CAD		100.00-		
					CAD	▪	0.00		
Account 460100							0.00		
✓	06.05.2016	100000001	SA		CAD		5,000.00		
					CAD	▪	5,000.00		
Account 460200							5,000.00		
					CAD	▪ ▪ ▪	0.00		

Fig 7

PARKING A DOCUMENT (U)

T Code FV50

Occasionally, we have situations where we may be expecting more information or changes to the postings in which case we can park the document until we are ready to post it. Documents may also be required to park if there is an informal process of getting authorizations to make postings directly to the G/L. Parking the document has the same effect as posting in terms of obtaining a document number except that it does not update the balances. To park a document, we can either go via the same route of FB50:

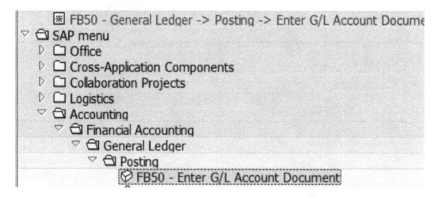

Fig 1

However, choose the option to park instead of post (or save).

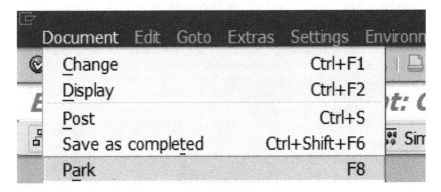

Fig 2

Alternatively, go directly to T Code FV50:

Fig 3

The screens look similar but are not same. FB50, because it is the transaction to post when saved, it will by default, post the document but gives the option to park also:

Fig 4

FV50, because it is the transaction to park, will by default, park the document when saved, but gives the option to post also:

Fig 5

Saving as completed and parking are practically the same things. A list of parked documents for verification and action can be obtained through transaction FBV3.

Let us try to park a document using the same process as earlier.

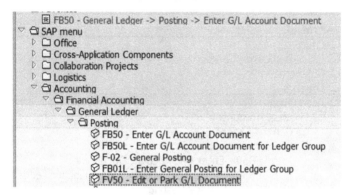

Fig 6

Fig 7

Save the document and SAP will give a number at the bottom:

Fig 8

The difference between this and the posted document is that this number will not show up in G/L line balances when we run the report for these 2 G/L accounts

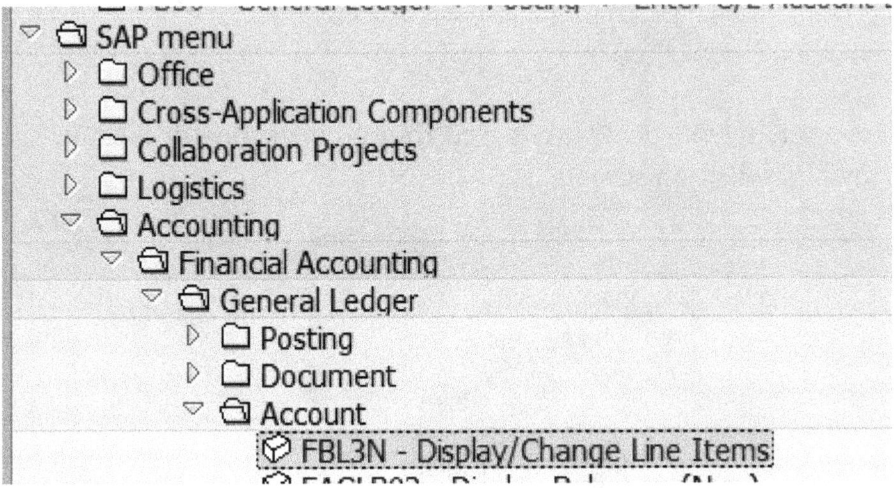

```
▽ 🗁 SAP menu
   ▷ 🗀 Office
   ▷ 🗀 Cross-Application Components
   ▷ 🗀 Collaboration Projects
   ▷ 🗀 Logistics
   ▽ 🗁 Accounting
      ▽ 🗁 Financial Accounting
         ▽ 🗁 General Ledger
            ▷ 🗀 Posting
            ▷ 🗀 Document
            ▽ 🗁 Account
                  ♡ FBL3N - Display/Change Line Items
```

Fig 9

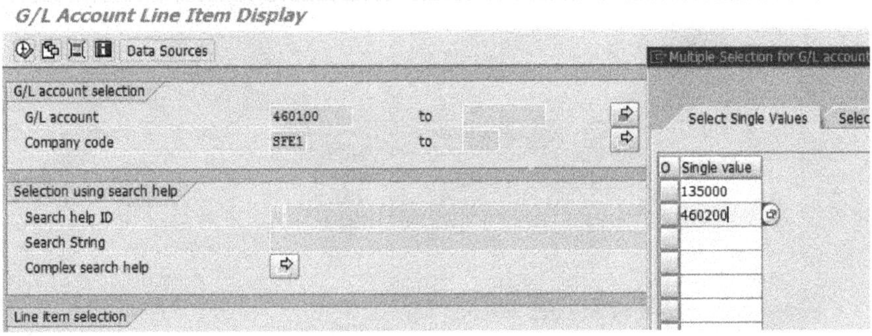

G/L Account Line Item Display

⊕ 🔊 ⊒ ⏃ Data Sources

🖹 Multiple Selection for G/L account

G/L account selection					
G/L account	460100	to		⇨	Select Single Values Selec
Company code	SFE1	to		⇨	

O	Single value
	135000
	460200 ⇨

Selection using search help		
Search help ID		
Search String		
Complex search help	⇨	

Line item selection

Fig 10

On executing the report for these 2 G/Ls, we see other numbers but not the parked one:

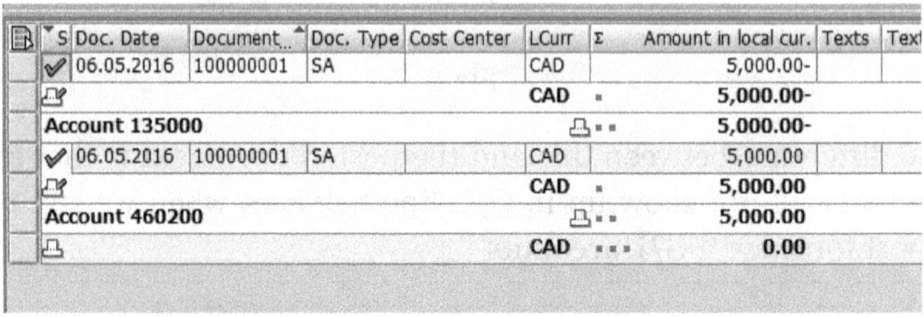

S	Doc. Date	Document	Doc. Type	Cost Center	LCurr	Σ	Amount in local cur.	Texts	Text
✓	06.05.2016	100000001	SA		CAD		5,000.00-		
					CAD	▪	5,000.00-		
Account 135000						▪▪	5,000.00-		
✓	06.05.2016	100000001	SA		CAD		5,000.00		
					CAD	▪	5,000.00		
Account 460200						▪▪	5,000.00		
					CAD	▪▪▪	0.00		

Fig 11

However, if you do want to see them, check on the box in the previous selection screen:

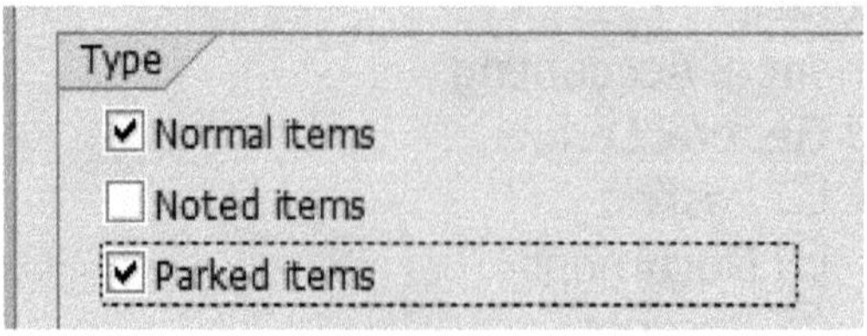

Type
☑ Normal items
☐ Noted items
☑ Parked items

Fig 12

It now appears along with the other actual postings too:

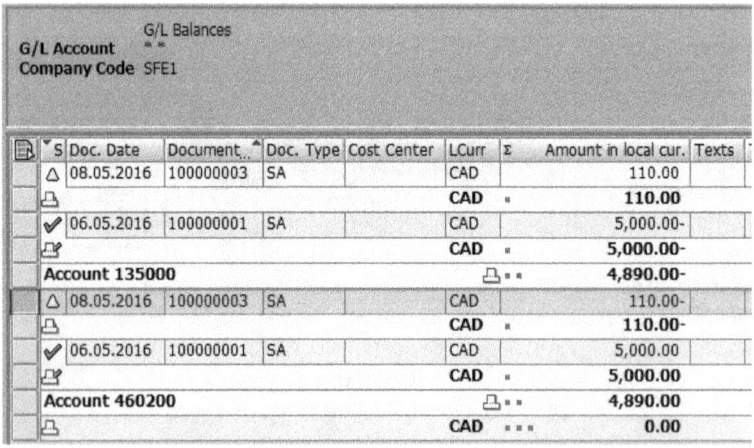

G/L Balances
G/L Account   ★ ★
Company Code SFE1

S	Doc. Date	Document	Doc. Type	Cost Center	LCurr	Σ	Amount in local cur.	Texts
△	08.05.2016	100000003	SA		CAD		110.00	
					CAD	▪	110.00	
✓	06.05.2016	100000001	SA		CAD		5,000.00-	
					CAD	▪	5,000.00-	
Account 135000						▪▪	4,890.00-	
△	08.05.2016	100000003	SA		CAD		110.00-	
					CAD	▪	110.00-	
✓	06.05.2016	100000001	SA		CAD		5,000.00	
					CAD	▪	5,000.00	
Account 460200						▪▪	4,890.00	
					CAD	▪▪▪	0.00	

Fig 13

108

The Yellow upward triangle symbol in the first column tells you it is a parked document:

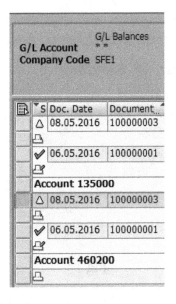

Fig 14

While Green check means it is posted:

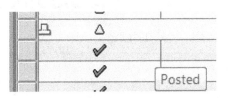

Fig 15

To see just the list of parked postings by G/L for taking action on them, un-select the Posted button and re-run the report:

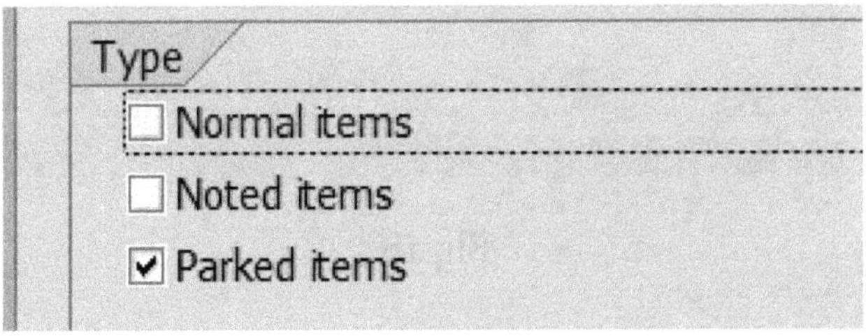

Type
- [ ] Normal items
- [ ] Noted items
- [✔] Parked items

Fig 16

Alternatively, to just get a list of the parked documents, run the transaction FBV3:

Display Parked Document: Initial Screen
Document list
Editing Options
Key for Parking
Company Code
SFE1
Doc. Number
Fiscal Year

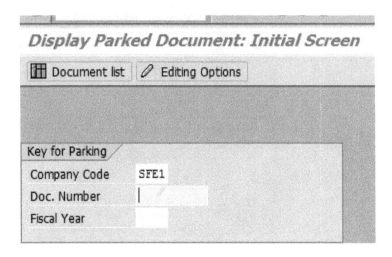

Fig 17

Enter the document # if you know and are specifically looking for it:

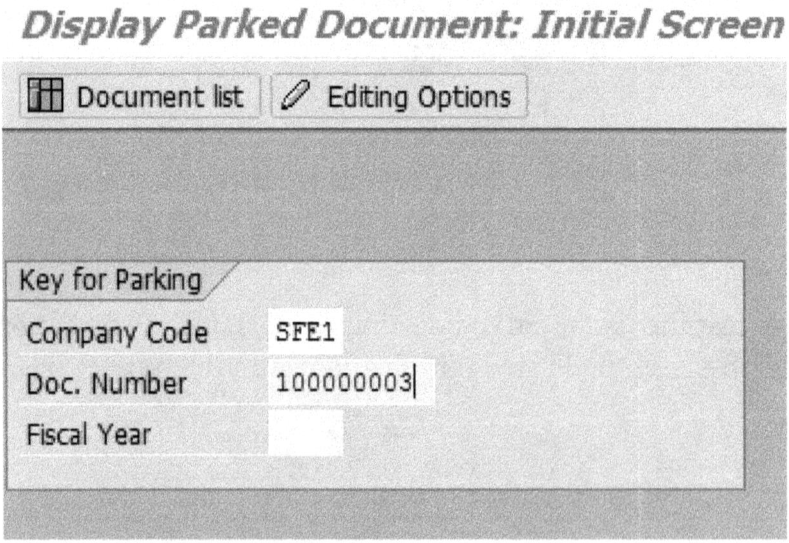

Display Parked Document: Initial Screen
Document list
Editing Options
Key for Parking
Company Code
SFE1
Doc. Number
100000003
Fiscal Year

Fig 18

The fiscal year will also be needed to be entered in case the same document number exists in multiple fiscal years. In our case since it is only in current year, that is not necessary.

If you do not know the document # and just want a list to work on, click on:

Fig 19

Now you have many options – you can run it open i.e. for the report to display all the parked documents in any or all CC/s.

Alternatively, restrict the selection to specific times, people (Entered by), dates etc:

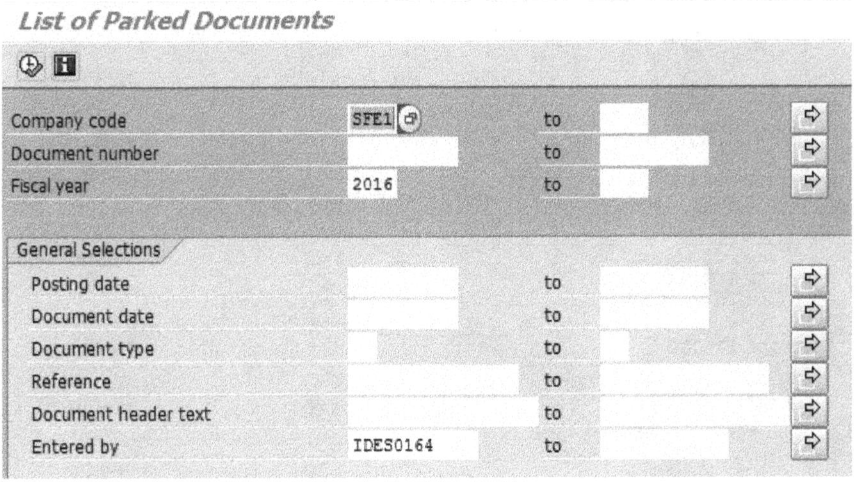

List of Parked Documents

Company code	SFE1	to	
Document number		to	
Fiscal year	2016	to	

General Selections

Posting date		to	
Document date		to	
Document type		to	
Reference		to	
Document header text		to	
Entered by	IDES0164	to	

Fig 20

Executing it will display the parked documents that were entered by IDES0164 in CC SFE1:

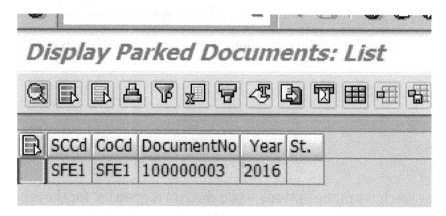

Display Parked Documents: List

SCCd	CoCd	DocumentNo	Year	St.
SFE1	SFE1	100000003	2016	

Fig 21

We saw this same document also appear in the G/L line item display earlier:

G/L Balances
G/L Account   * *
Company Code SFE1

S	Doc. Date	Document	Doc. Type	Cost Center	LCurr	Σ	Amount in local cur.	Texts
△	08.05.2016	100000003	SA		CAD		110.00	
					CAD	▪	110.00	
✓	06.05.2016	100000001	SA		CAD		5,000.00-	
					CAD	▪	5,000.00-	
Account 135000						▫▪▪	4,890.00-	
△	08.05.2016	100000003	SA		CAD		110.00-	
					CAD	▪	110.00-	
✓	06.05.2016	100000001	SA		CAD		5,000.00	
					CAD	▪	5,000.00	
Account 460200						▫▪▪	4,890.00	
					CAD	▪▪▪	0.00	

Fig 22

112

POSTING PARKED DOCUMENTS (U)

T Code FBV0

Once you have obtained all the information and/or authorizations needed, the parked documents can be posted in the system. This will change their status from parked to posted and update the database accordingly. To post a parked document, go to the menu:

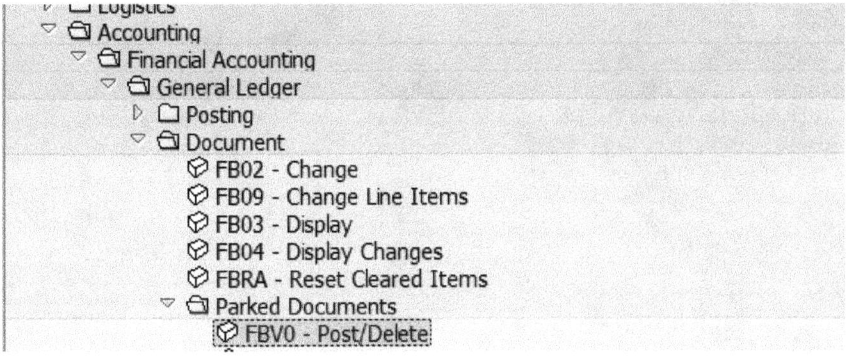

```
  ▷ ☐ Logistics
  ▽ ⬒ Accounting
      ▽ ⬒ Financial Accounting
          ▽ ⬒ General Ledger
              ▷ ☐ Posting
              ▽ ⬒ Document
                    ⊗ FB02 - Change
                    ⊗ FB09 - Change Line Items
                    ⊗ FB03 - Display
                    ⊗ FB04 - Display Changes
                    ⊗ FBRA - Reset Cleared Items
                  ▽ ⬒ Parked Documents
                        ⊗ FBV0 - Post/Delete
```

Fig 1

Enter the document #:

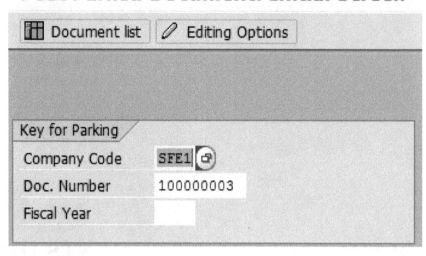

Fig 2

Hit Enter:

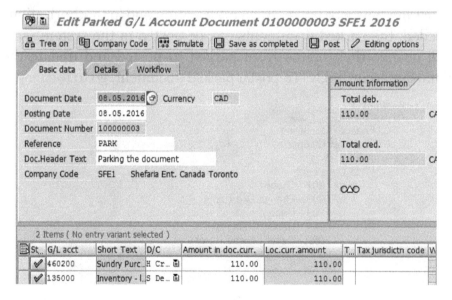

Fig 3

Note that in a parked document, we can practically change anything we need to, except the document # itself, as it has not yet his the database.

Post the document:

Fig 4

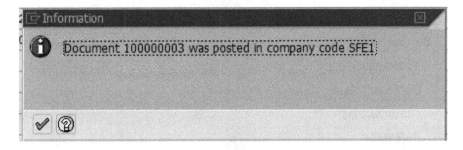

Fig 5

When we re-run the line items or G/L account balances reports, FBL3N, this document will change it's status from Yellow to Green:

G/L Balances
G/L Account   * *
Company Code SFE1

S	Doc. Date	Document	Doc. Type	Cost Center	LCurr	Σ	Amount in local cur.	Texts	T
✓	06.05.2016	100000001	SA		CAD		5,000.00-		
	08.05.2016	100000003	SA		CAD		110.00		
					CAD	▪	4,890.00-		
Account 135000							4,890.00-		
✓	06.05.2016	100000001	SA		CAD		5,000.00		
	08.05.2016	100000003	SA		CAD		110.00-		
					CAD	▪	4,890.00		
Account 460200							4,890.00		
					CAD	▪▪▪	0.00		

Fig 6

115

Also, that document will no longer show up in the parked documents report FBV3:

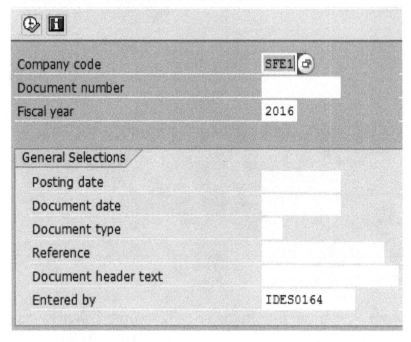

Fig 7

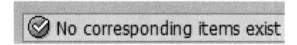

Fig 8

RECURRING OR REPEATED

TRANSACTIONS (U)

I.   SETTING UP FOR REPEATED TRANSACTIONS

T Code FBD1

We often have bills like of rents, telephone; insurance which are recurring amounts i.e. repeat themselves over at certain defined periods. SAP has provided the option of setting them up as recurring to avoid making repeated entries at every payment cycle. When the appropriate times come, the G/L entries are posted either automatically or by the user with the minimal intervention.

Let us now try posting a recurring entry in the system. The path is below or T Code FBD1:

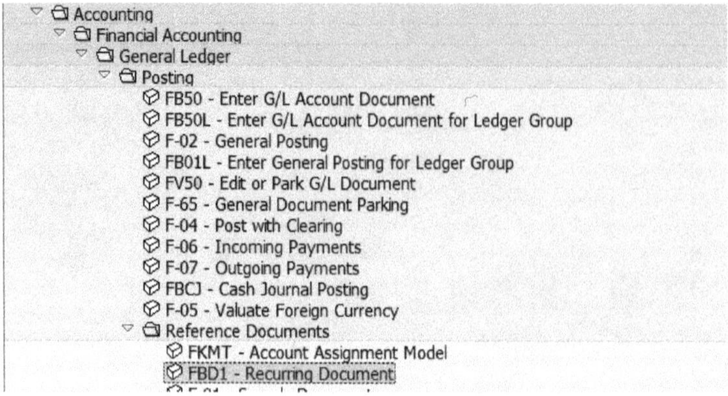

Fig 1

Enter the following information to enable the recurring entries to take place:

1. Company Code
2. When you want the first and the last runs of this fixed amount to occur
3. How often should they occur i.e. the time gap in months between each run
4. Run date – you can have this in lieu of the first run date
5. Reference – usually this would be provided by the vendor as it's invoice# on us
6. Document header text – to give some meaning to the entry
7. Document type – choose SA (G/L entry)

Company Code	SFE1

Recurring entry run

First run on	090516
Last run on	09.12.2016
Interval in months	1
Run date	
Run schedule	
☐ Transfer amounts in local currency	☐ Copy texts
☐ Transfer tax amounts in local currency	

Document header information

Document Type	SA	Currency/Rate	CAD
Reference	123456	Translatn Date	08.05.2016
Document Header Text	Insurance for Buildings		
Trading part.BA			

Fig 2

Hit Enter and the system takes you to the bottom of the screen to make the actual JEs:

Fig 3

Let us debit the Insurance account by the insurance amount:

Fig 4

Hitting Enter takes us to the next screen to make more entries. Enter the amount and tax code if applicable (more on tax codes later, for now leave it blank) and with posting key 50 (to offset 40), enter the bank account that will be credited for this transaction:

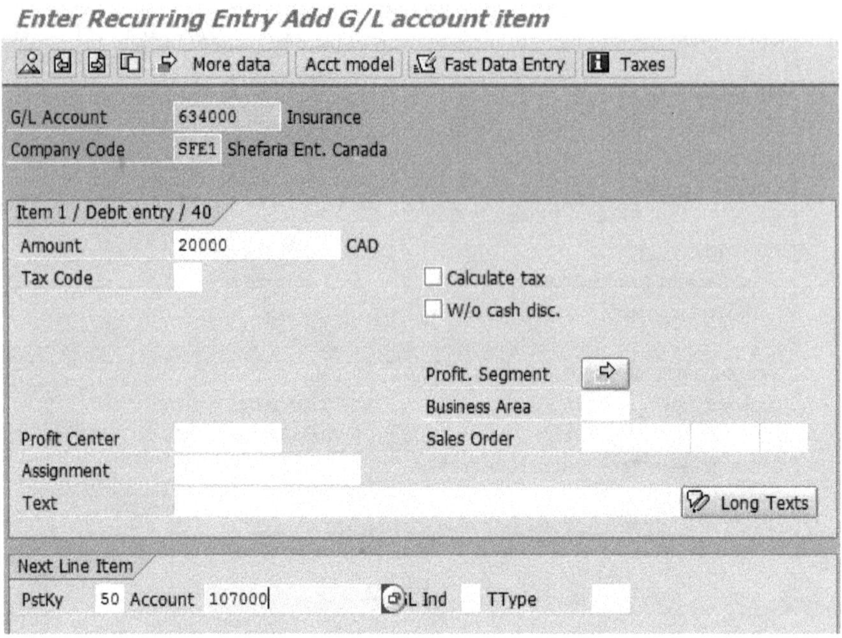

Enter Recurring Entry Add G/L account item

| ♟ 🗐 🗐 🗗 ➯ More data | Acct model | 🔄 Fast Data Entry | 🔢 Taxes |

| G/L Account | 634000 | Insurance |
| Company Code | SFE1 | Shefaria Ent. Canada |

Item 1 / Debit entry / 40

Amount	20000	CAD
Tax Code		☐ Calculate tax
		☐ W/o cash disc.

		Profit. Segment	➯
		Business Area	
Profit Center		Sales Order	
Assignment		
Text		🗐 Long Texts

Next Line Item

| PstKy | 50 | Account | 107000 | 🗗 iL Ind | TType | |

Fig 5

120

Hit Enter and a new screen will come up:

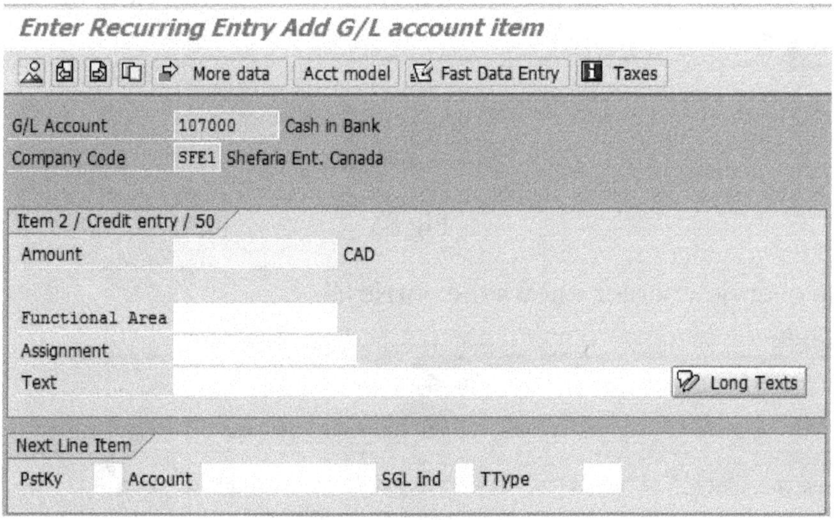

Enter Recurring Entry Add G/L account item

G/L Account	107000 Cash in Bank
Company Code	SFE1 Shefaria Ent. Canada

Item 2 / Credit entry / 50

Amount	CAD
Functional Area	
Assignment	
Text	🖉 Long Texts

Next Line Item

PstKy	Account	SGL Ind	TType

Fig 6

Amount: Enter the amount for your second line item. We can use '*' as before to copy this amount from the 1st line

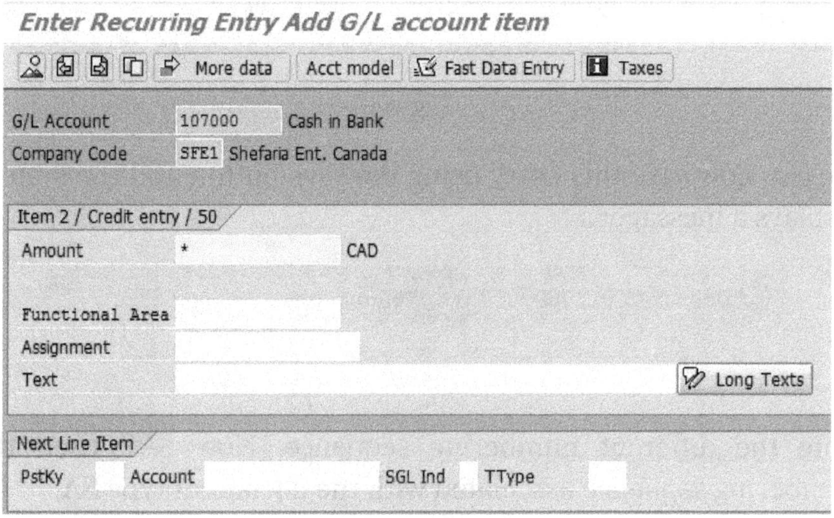

Enter Recurring Entry Add G/L account item

G/L Account	107000 Cash in Bank
Company Code	SFE1 Shefaria Ent. Canada

Item 2 / Credit entry / 50

Amount	* CAD
Functional Area	
Assignment	
Text	🖉 Long Texts

Next Line Item

PstKy	Account	SGL Ind	TType

Fig 7

121

This is the complete data to be entered one time only for recurring transactions. We can use the icons to view an overview or scroll between the line items:

Fig 8

The overview screen shows the entries:

Fig 9

We can now save this entry using the save button and the system displays a message:

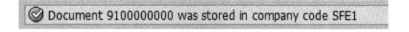

Fig 10

Note the different numbering sequence. Now SAP used the numbering sequence associated with the document type SA.

II.   PROCESSING RECURRING ENTRIES (U)

T Code F.14

Recurring entries can be processed manually or by sessions that can span across different periods. Use transaction code F.14 or follow the path:

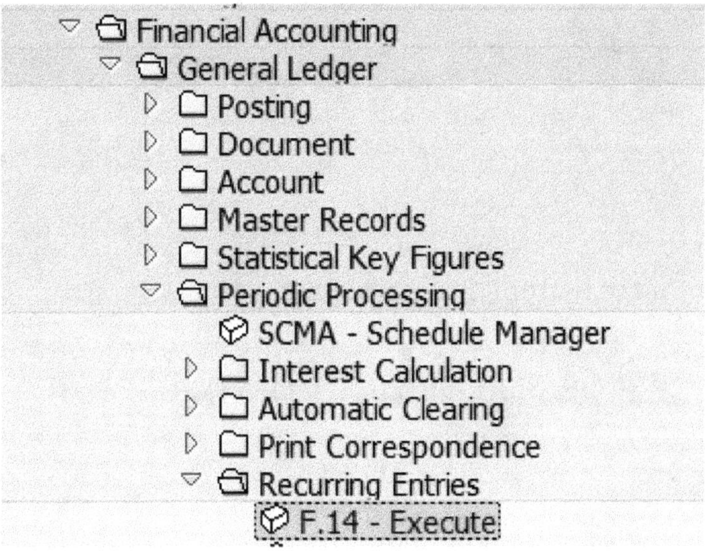

Fig 1

Enter as much data as you need for the runs – the more the restrictions, the lesser the runs will be created, as they will be restricted to only where the data matches up in the required transaction.

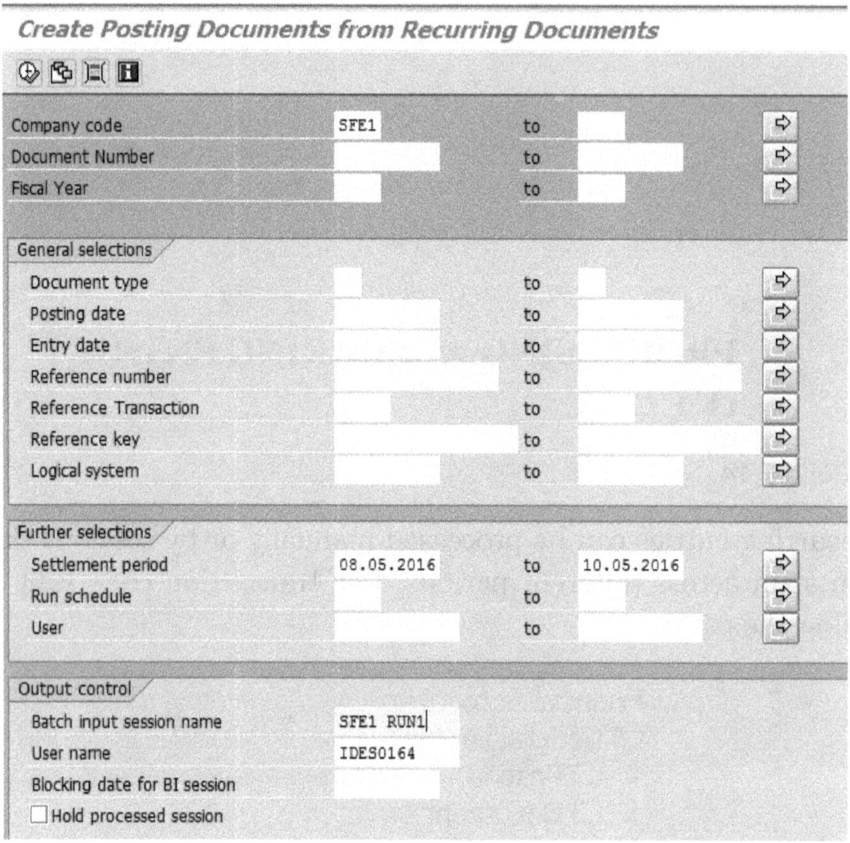

Create Posting Documents from Recurring Documents

Company code	SFE1	to	
Document Number		to	
Fiscal Year		to	

General selections

Document type		to	
Posting date		to	
Entry date		to	
Reference number		to	
Reference Transaction		to	
Reference key		to	
Logical system		to	

Further selections

Settlement period	08.05.2016	to	10.05.2016
Run schedule		to	
User		to	

Output control

Batch input session name	SFE1 RUN1
User name	IDES0164
Blocking date for BI session	
☐ Hold processed session	

Fig 2

Execute. At the bottom, it gives a message:

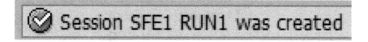

Fig 3

124

III.   RUNNING THE SESSION

T Code SM35

The creation of a run simply means that SAP has collected all the data it needs to post the actual JEs in the system. To actually post them, we have to run this session, which we do by following the path:

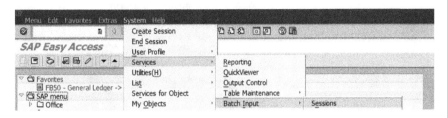

Fig 4

This brings us to a screen where we choose the run it shows under our respective IDs. Depending upon authorizations provided, we can run the sessions of other users also.

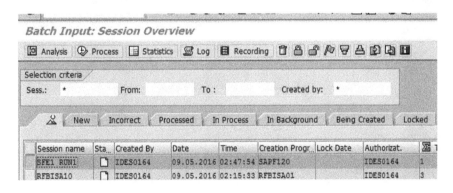

Fig 5

This screen can also be reached directly via transaction code SM35.

Check the line and click on the button to Process it:

Fig 6

In the window, ask it to be processed in 'Display Errors only' mode:

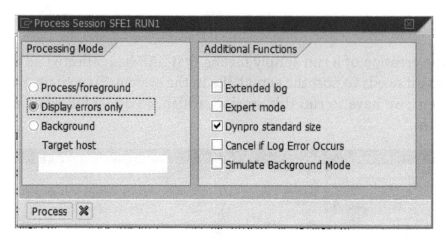

Fig 7

Click on Process and in the windows that appear as below, keep hitting Enter a few times:

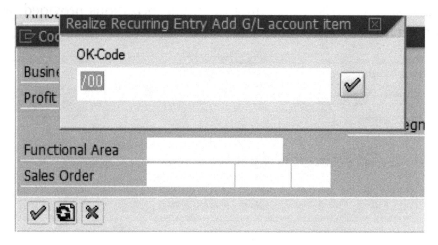

Fig 8

Until you get the below message:

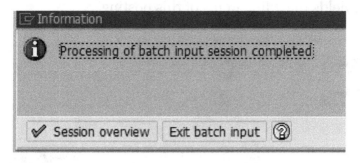

Fig 9

Now if we go to run the G/L balance report FAGLB03 for these 2 accounts:

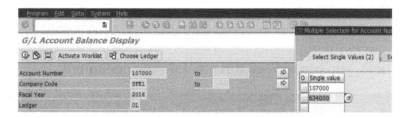

Fig 10

We find the amount appearing and double clicking it, it gives us the details or it's origin:

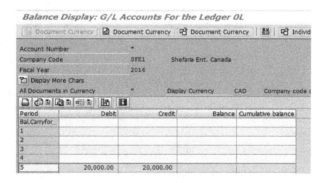

Fig 11

Double clicking the cell under Cumulative Balance & the period of posting yields the 2 line items of this posting

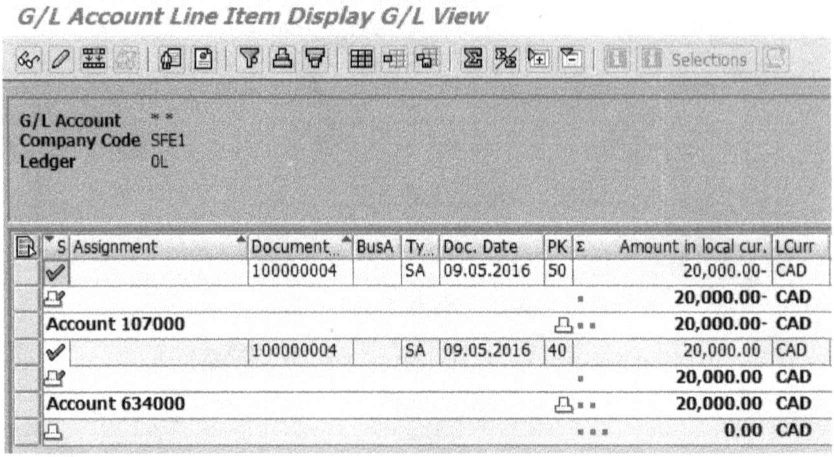

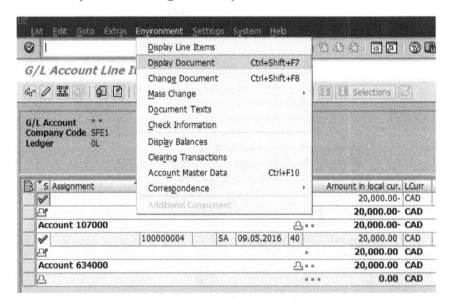

Fig 12

From here, you can also go directly into the document:

Fig 13

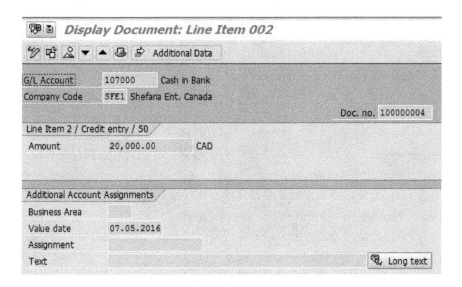

Fig 14

And then click on overview button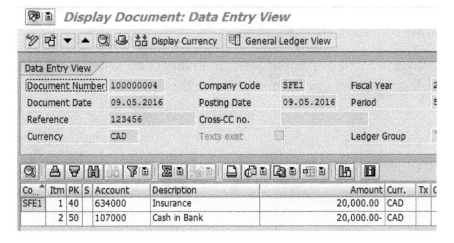

Fig 15

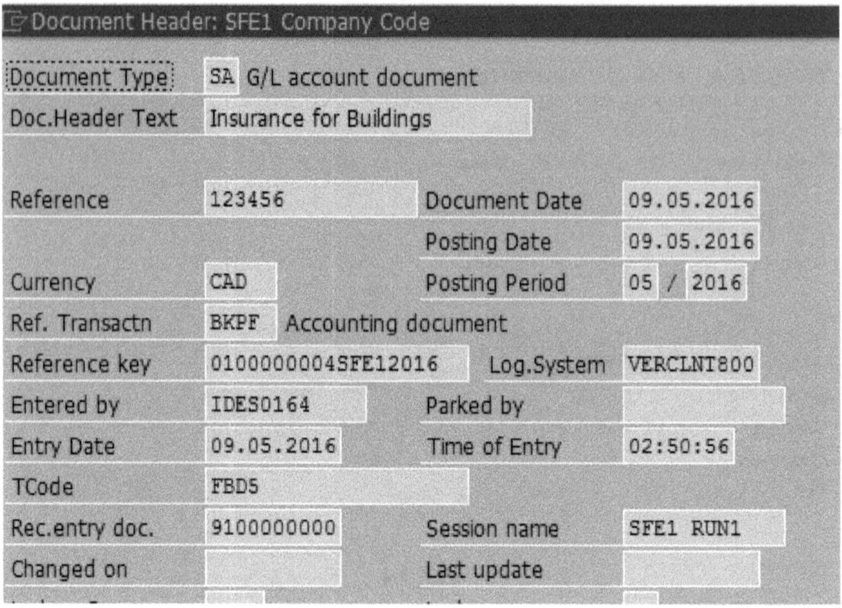
Document Header: SFE1 Company Code

Document Type: SA G/L account document
Doc.Header Text: Insurance for Buildings
Reference: 123456
Document Date: 09.05.2016
Posting Date: 09.05.2016
Currency: CAD
Posting Period: 05 / 2016
Ref. Transactn: BKPF Accounting document
Reference key: 0100000004SFE12016
Log.System: VERCLNT800
Entered by: IDES0164
Parked by:
Entry Date: 09.05.2016
Time of Entry: 02:50:56
TCode: FBD5
Rec.entry doc.: 9100000000
Session name: SFE1 RUN1
Changed on:
Last update:

Fig 16

The Rec. Entry doc. in the above print was the # we got when we set this recurring entry up.

It converted that particular posting to an actual accounting entry, which is what we saw in the G/L report.

CUSTOMER & VENDOR TOLERANCE

(C)

T Code SPRO

Customer and vendor tolerances are required to be set up before we can make any posting of payment from or payment to them as the case may be. This is because it is not necessary that the amounts we post would be the same as the invoices we will raise or receive. SAP does not allow any postings to customer or vendor accounts if these limits are not defined in the configuration.

The path to do this configuration is:

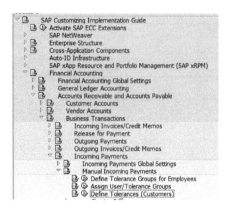

SAP Customizing Implementation Guide
  Activate SAP ECC Extensions
  SAP NetWeaver
  Enterprise Structure
  Cross-Application Components
  Auto-ID Infrastructure
  SAP xApp Resource and Portfolio Management (SAP xRPM)
  Financial Accounting
    Financial Accounting Global Settings
    General Ledger Accounting
    Accounts Receivable and Accounts Payable
      Customer Accounts
      Vendor Accounts
      Business Transactions
        Incoming Invoices/Credit Memos
        Release for Payment
        Outgoing Payments
        Outgoing Invoices/Credit Memos
        Incoming Payments
          Incoming Payments Global Settings
          Manual Incoming Payments
            Define Tolerance Groups for Employees
            Assign User/Tolerance Groups
            Define Tolerances (Customers)

Fig 1

Click on **New Entries** to define one for your company, let us use the values below; the other fields are not important for this purpose:

New Entries: Details of Added Entries

Company Code	SFE1	hefaria Ent. Canada	Toronto
Currency	CAD		
Tolerance group	SFE1	Tolerance Grp for SFE1	

Specifications for Clearing Transactions

Grace days due date   Cash Discount Terms Displayed

Arrears Base Date

Permitted Payment Differences

	Amount	Percent	Adjust Discount By
Gain	100.00	99.9 %	
Loss	100.00	99.9 %	

Fig 2

Save the configuration. This configuration linking the CC with the tolerance group will work for both, customer and vendors.

VENDOR GROUPS (C)

T Code SPRO

All master data in SAP is ordered by way of grouping them for specific purposes. These groups are fundamental to the way the master data will be required to be entered and be visible to the user. A master data record is for the most part, a 'proposal' of the most often repeated or expected scenario to be used in the transaction. Its primary purpose is to save time for the users from entering data repeatedly. Because SAP is such an integrated system, it requires a great amount of data to link different business process documents and modules with each other. It does that by making data relevant at different points in the business cycle of a document. For the most part, substantial elements of this data can be changed in the first document that is created from it.

Vendor group is the highest level of data organization of a vendor master. This is also the first step in setting up the vendor master in any SAP system. In most situations, standard vendor groups provided by SAP should suffice, though if custom ones need to be created, that is also an easy activity.

Vendor groups can be seen in the path:

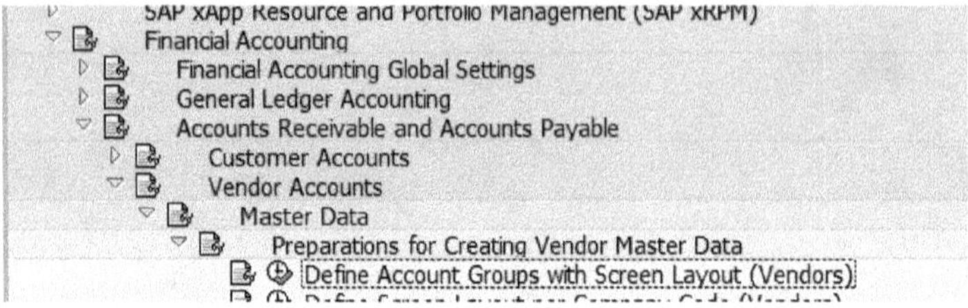

Fig 1

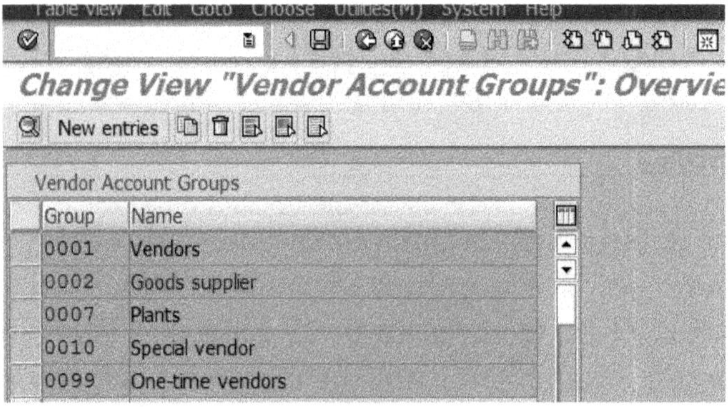

Fig 2

Double clicking on any one of them gives the detail of how the data will be organized, here, in account group 0001, it is split into 3 areas – General data, CC data and Purchasing data:

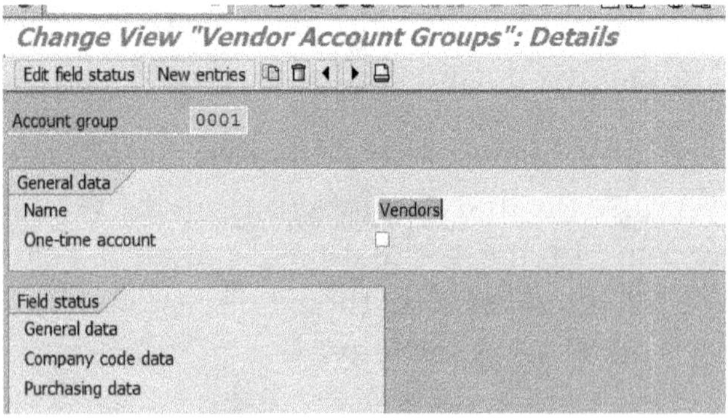

Fig 3

Double clicking on any one of them further reveals the sub-groupings/screens in that section:

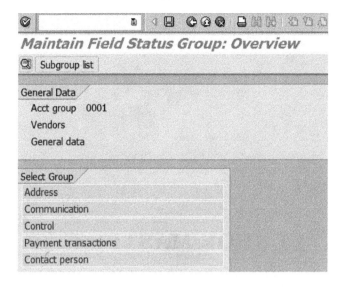

Fig 4

For most business requirements, the existing vendor account groups will work though some companies may prefer to create their own. For our purpose, we will use the existing standard one – 0001.

VENDOR MASTER (U)

T Code FK01 or XK01

We are now ready to create our first vendor. The T Code to create a vendor is XK01 centrally or, from a Finance perspective only, FK01. We can also follow the path on the SAP main menu:

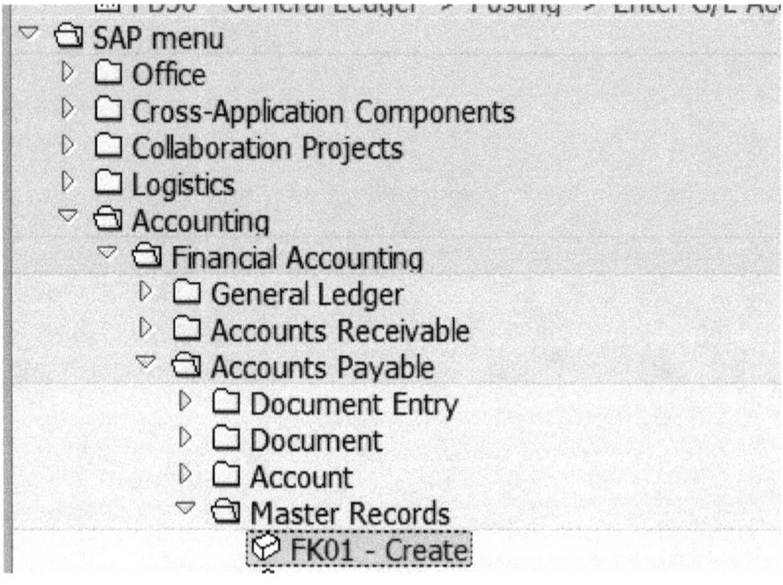

Fig 1

136

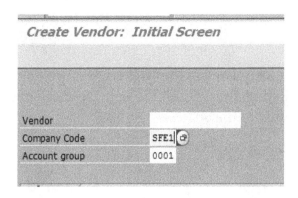

Vendor	
Company Code	SFE1
Account group	0001

Fig 2

Hit Enter and the system takes you to the main address screen where you can enter the data as required. Toggle through the screens using the buttons to fill up all the necessary data. Most fields are self-explanatory; a few important ones are defined below. There is a lot more to the vendor master than we will cover here; however, all that other data is relevant to purchasing departments and thus, is a part of the Material Management module. We will touch upon it later when we create a Purchase Order.

The field Search term is used as an abbreviated form of the name to 'search' for vendors in the huge database.

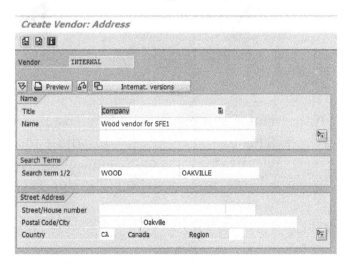

Fig 3

The Plus icon denotes that there are more fields that can be viewed and filled up by clicking this icon. On the above screen, they will relate mainly to the address.

Create Vendor: Control

| | | | Tax categories |

| Vendor | INTERNAL | Vendor for FI Class 2 |

Account control

| Customer | | Authorization |
| Trading Partner | | Corporate Group |

Tax information

Tax Number 1		Tax number type		☐ Equalizatn tax
Tax Number 2		Tax type		☐ Sole Proprietr
Tax Number 3				☐ Sales/pur.tax
Tax Number 4				☐ Tax split
Fiscal address			
Tax Jur.		VAT Reg. No.		Other...
Tax office			
Tax Number			

Reference data

Location no. 1		Location no. 2		Check digit
Industry			
SCAC		Car.freight grp		ServAgntProcGrp
POD-relevant			
Actual QM sys.		QM system to	

Fig 4

Customer: If the vendor also happens to be a customer, enter its customer # here. This can also be used to adjust the payables against the receivables or vice versa once, some other data settings are done as we will see in transaction F.13 for auto clearing accounts.

The field-trading partner is used to denote if it is an inter-company vendor and then populated with it's Inter company customer number.

On the next screen, define the vendor's banking information where payments can be made:

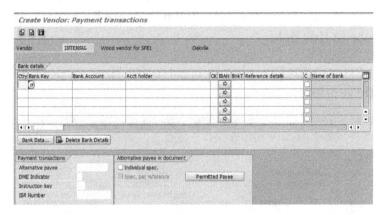

Fig 5

Alternative payee: If the vendor to be paid for the purchases is different from the current vendor #, enter that payee # here

On the next screen, 2 fields are mandatory and marked as such:

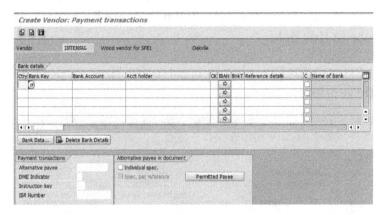

Fig 6

You will recall from the previous chapters that the reconciliation account is the account to which the account payables are posted via the sub-ledger. Enter the account we created or choose from the drop down or press F4 - the reconciliation account is a mandatory field as this is the account to which the account payables are posted via the sub-ledger. Enter the account we created or choose from the drop down or press F4 after positioning the cursor in this field:

Choose 211000 that is what is created for this purpose as it is a domestic vendor:

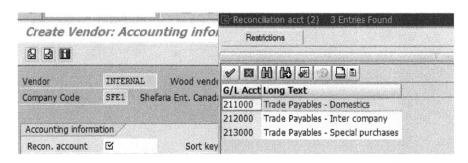

Fig 7

The other mandatory field is Cash management group:

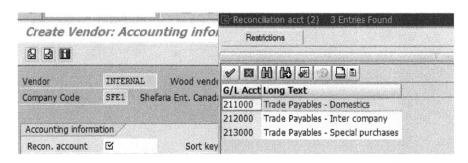

Fig 8

Let us say this will be handled by the domestic payments group and select A1.

The next screen has payment related data:

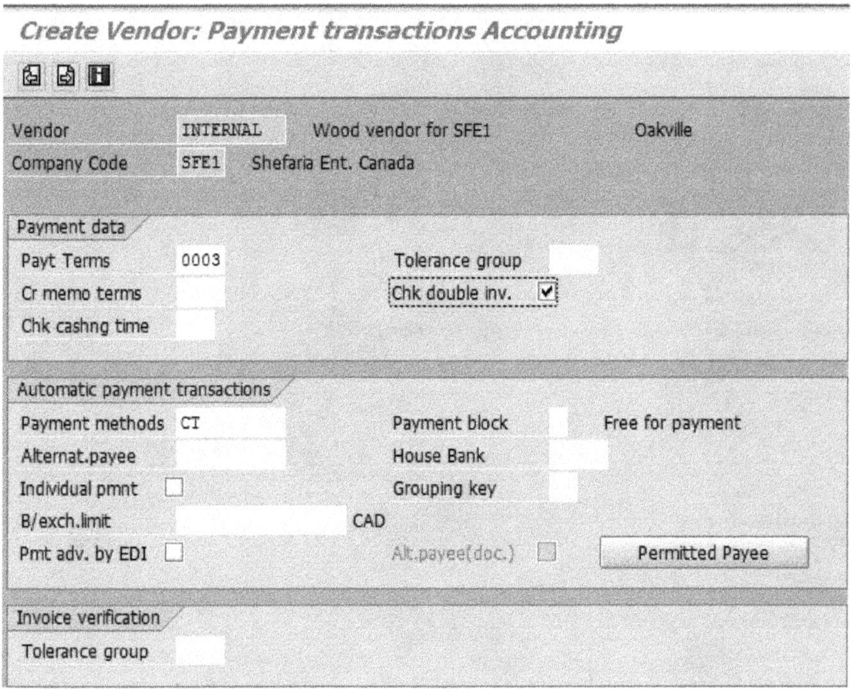

Create Vendor: Payment transactions Accounting

| Vendor | INTERNAL | Wood vendor for SFE1 | Oakville |
| Company Code | SFE1 | Shefaria Ent. Canada | |

Payment data
Payt Terms	0003	Tolerance group	
Cr memo terms		Chk double inv.	✔
Chk cashng time			

Automatic payment transactions
Payment methods	CT	Payment block	Free for payment
Alternat.payee		House Bank	
Individual pmnt	☐	Grouping key	
B/exch.limit		CAD	
Pmt adv. by EDI	☐	Alt.payee(doc.) ☐	Permitted Payee

Invoice verification
| Tolerance group | |

Fig 9

Enter the data as appropriate and always check the indicator – Chk double invoice. This drives that SAP will, at the time of doing invoice verification, ensure we do not book the same invoice from the same vendor for payment again. We will find it's use in a subsequent chapter on 'Duplicate Invoice Check'.

The next screen has data relating to how to correspond with this vendor:

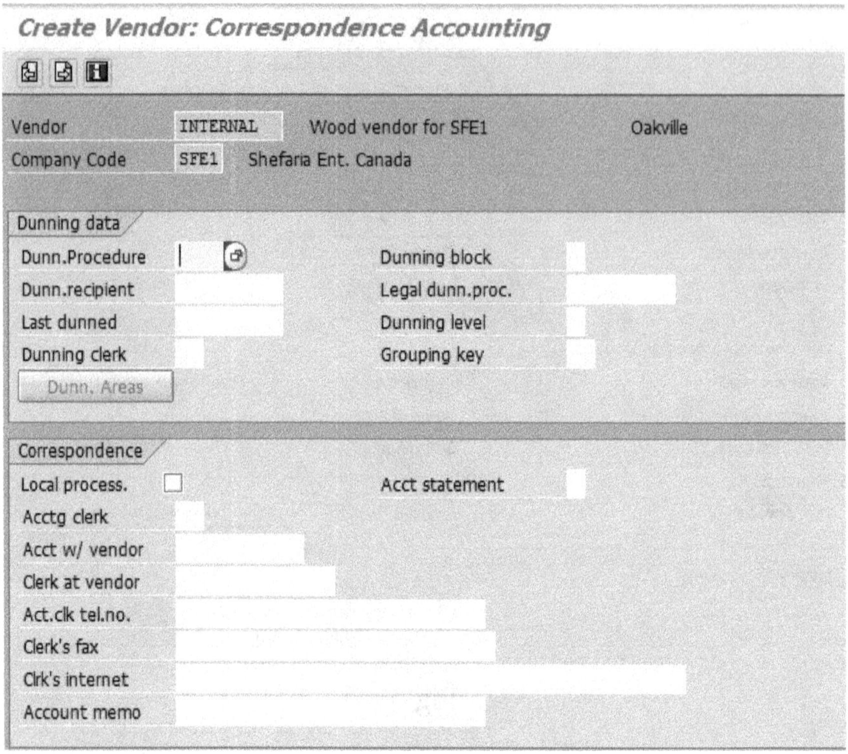

Fig 10

Data like Acct clerk is used to provide visibility to the vendor. The acct clerk is a person or group responsible to make payments to this vendor and if we run reports for accounting clerks, we get the lists of vendors that clerk is responsible for and whose payments are due.

Now when we click on  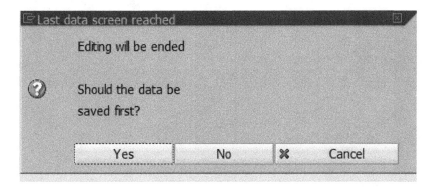, we get the message that the last screen has been reached:

Fig 11

At this point, we have entered in all the data that the system needed on the screens we chose to set up. We now save this vendor by clicking on Yes and the message follows:

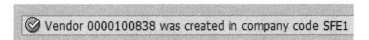

Fig 12

At various times in this manual, we will come back to the vendor master to populate certain more data and see it's effect on our transactions.

CUSTOMER GROUPS (C)

T Code SPRO

Conceptually, the customer master follows the same principles as the vendor master i.e. it proposes the customer related information in the transaction. Information such as which sales office of the company is responsible for the customer, who is responsible for the receivables from this customer, what is their credit terms, whom to contact, their banking information, method or preference of shipping and what locations they can be shipped to, and a lot more, can be made to 'default' from the customer master instead of entering into every transaction. This information though, is not cast in stone and is only a 'proposal' based on the most often repeated scenarios. The user can override most of this information in the transaction if it happens to be different for that particular situation.

Generally, the same rules apply in creation of customer account groups as they do for vendor account groups. SAP has provided some excellent customer account groups based on the way businesses are structured and it is always advisable to use the existing ones or create a custom one by copying and modifying an existing one as needed. However, we will use the standard SAP provided one for our purpose.

The path to do so is:

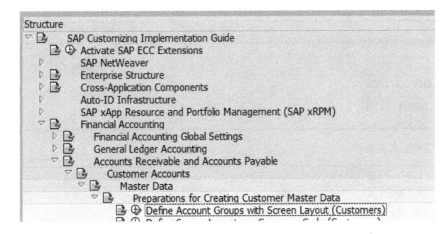

Fig 1

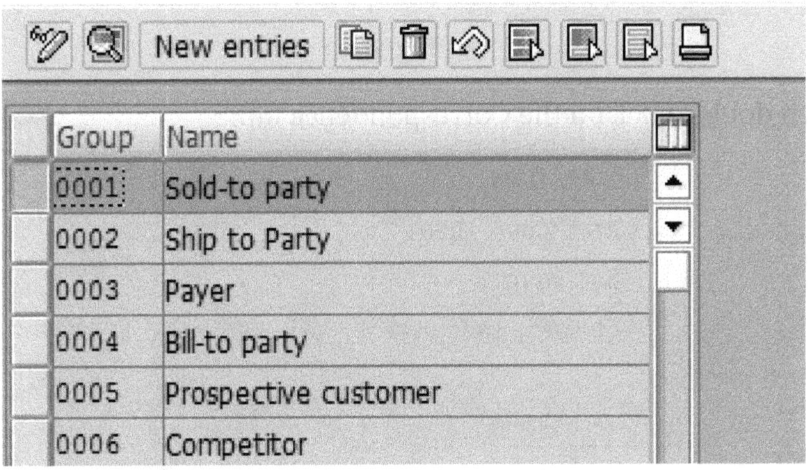

Fig 2

Again, we will use the standard account group 0001 – sold to party.

By default, all the fields on the various screens of the customer master are optional to fill in (Fig 5). However if we need to, we can make some mandatory e.g. if it is a company policy to always have an AR representative (called accounting clerk in SAP) assigned to every customer, then we can make this field mandatory in the CC data. This can be done by first going to the CC data under this account group by double clicking on it:

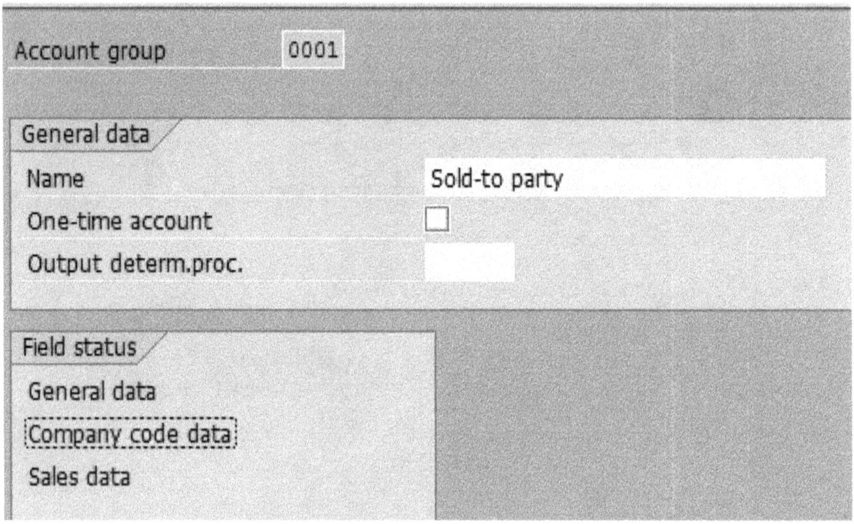

Account group	0001

General data
Name   Sold-to party
One-time account   ☐
Output determ.proc.

Field status
General data
Company code data
Sales data

Fig 3

Then double click on the Correspondence tab:

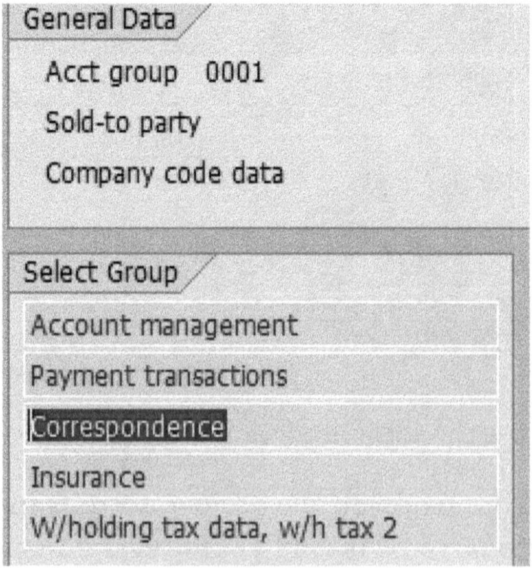

General Data
Acct group   0001
Sold-to party
Company code data

Select Group
Account management
Payment transactions
Correspondence
Insurance
W/holding tax data, w/h tax 2

Fig 4

For the accounting clerk field, check on the radio button Req. Entry instead of Optional:

Maintain Field Status Group: Correspondence

Field check

General Data					Page 1 / 1
Acct group 0001					
Sold-to party					
Company code data					

Correspondence

	Suppress	Req. Entry	Opt. entry	Display
Payment notices	○	○	◉	○
Acctng clerk's communication	○	○	◉	○
Dunning data	○	○	◉	○
Account statement	○	○	◉	○
Local processing	○	○	◉	○
Collective invoice variant	○	○	◉	○
Account at customer	○	○	◉	○
Accounting clerks	○	◉	○	○
Users at customer	○	○	◉	○
Account memo	○	○	◉	○

Fig 5

Save. Now, whenever we try to create a customer's financial accounting data, SAP will insist we fill in this field.

For this field to be filled, we must also have at least one accounting clerk set up in the particular CC. Account clerks are set up in the path below in the vendor tree or in a path under the customer node. Both lead to the same configuration and can be used interchangeably.

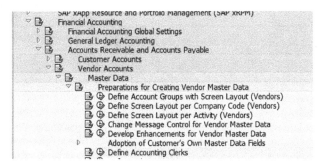

Fig 6

Click on New entries, define yours for your CC, and give it a description – a two-digit charter field:

New Entries

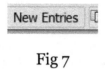

Fig 7

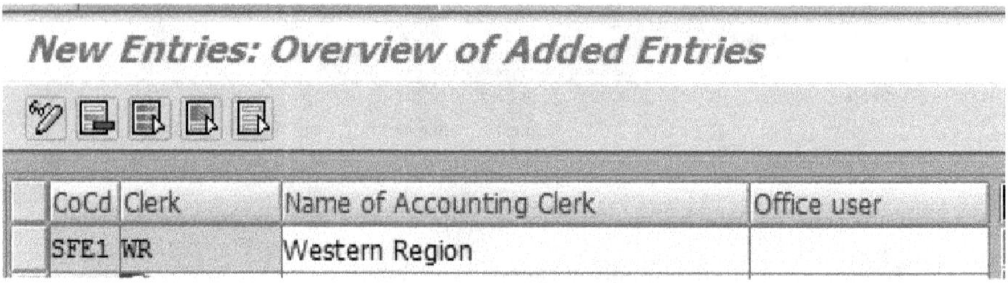
New Entries: Overview of Added Entries
CoCd
Clerk
Name of Accounting Clerk
Office user
SFE1
WR
Western Region

Fig 8

Save the data in the transport.

CUSTOMER MASTER (U)

FD01 or XD01 (mirrors the vendor creation with D replacing K)

The path to create a customer from the Accounting/Finance perspective is

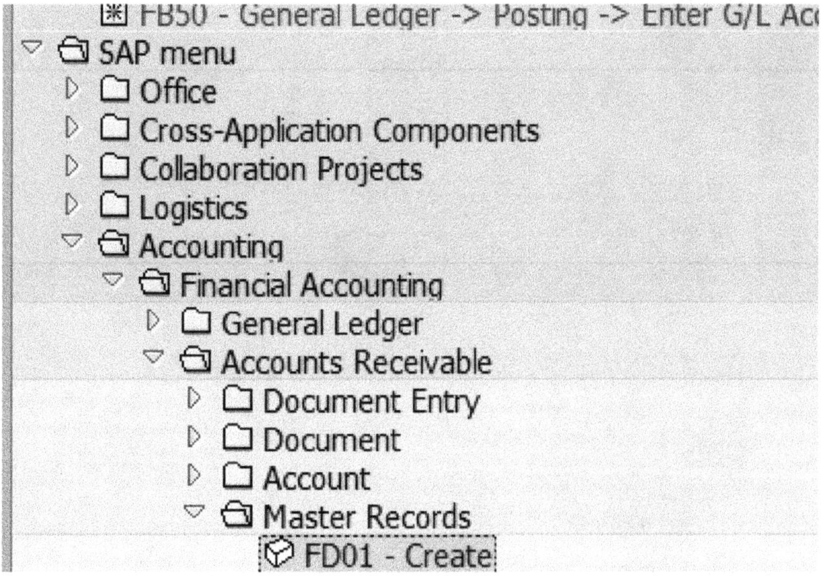

Fig 1

Or use T Code FD01.

Choose the account group 0001, Sold to party:

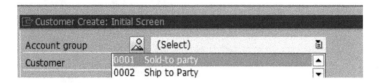

Fig 2

Leave the field Customer blank, as SAP will generate the number. Enter your CC

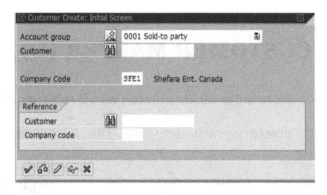

Fig 3

Hit Enter:

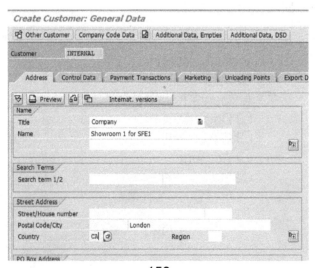

Fig 4

The field Country is mandatory so we enter that – populate the data related to accounting – click on the tab

Fig 5

This view has a few screens:

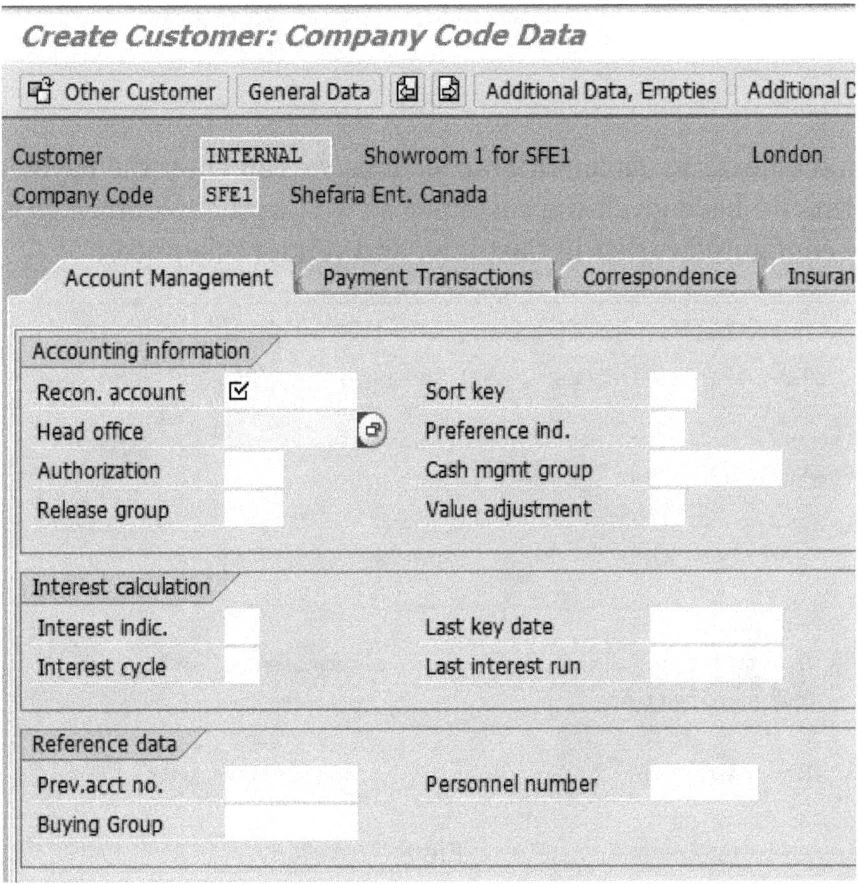

Create Customer: Company Code Data

| 🖳 Other Customer | General Data | 🖫 🖫 | Additional Data, Empties | Additional D |

Customer   `INTERNAL`   Showroom 1 for SFE1   London
Company Code   `SFE1`   Shefaria Ent. Canada

| Account Management | Payment Transactions | Correspondence | Insuran |

Accounting information

Recon. account	☑	Sort key	
Head office	⟳	Preference ind.	
Authorization		Cash mgmt group	
Release group		Value adjustment	

Interest calculation

| Interest indic. | | Last key date | |
| Interest cycle | | Last interest run | |

Reference data

| Prev.acct no. | | Personnel number | |
| Buying Group | | | |

Fig 6

We see that the reconciliation account is mandatory, as was in the vendor master.

So let us enter the appropriate recon account as below:

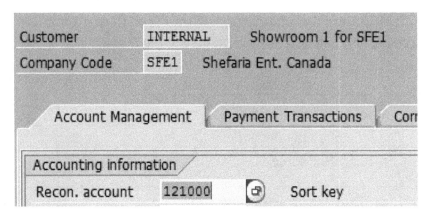

Fig 7

On the next tab, payment Transactions we can enter the payment terms we have given the customer as well as the tolerance group we configured earlier in Customer and vendor tolerances.

Create Customer: Company Code Data

| 📑 Other Customer | General Data 🔲 🔲 | Additional Data, Empties | Additional Data, |

| Customer | INTERNAL | Showroom 1 for SFE1 | | London |
| Company Code | SFE1 | Shefaria Ent. Canada | | |

| Account Management | Payment Transactions | Correspondence | Insurance |

Payment data

Terms of payment	0004	Tolerance group	SFE1
Credit memo payt term		Known/neg.leave	
B/e charges payt term		AR Pledging Ind	
Time until check paid		☐ Payment history record	

Fig 8

152

On the next tab, Correspondence, we find the field Accounting Clerk is mandatory:

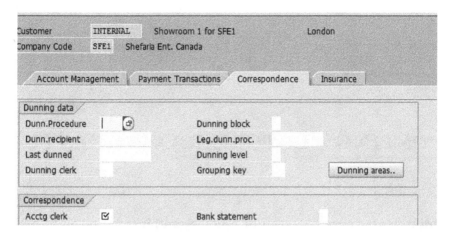

Fig 9

This is because we made it so in the configuration. Populate it with the accounting clerk we had set up and save:

Fig 10

At various times in this manual, we will come back to the customer master to populate certain data and see it's effect on our transactions.

POSTING CUSTOMER INVOICES (U)

T Code FB70

Under normal times, customer invoices will be created as a part of a transaction in which services and/or goods were provided. In SAP, invoicing is a function performed under Sales & Distribution module, as they are a result of goods and/or services provided, however, in reality; the Finance department may do it as most non-SAP legacy systems have billing as a part of the accounting function. Billing in SAP is a very generic term and encompasses invoices, credit notes, cancellation documents, even pro-forma invoices. Every invoice in SAP except the pro-forma invoice, generally leads up to an accounting document.

There are rare times when customers are invoiced or credited directly in accounting and those transactions create accounting documents that show up in the AR reports of the customer. To create one such manual invoice, let us follow the path below:

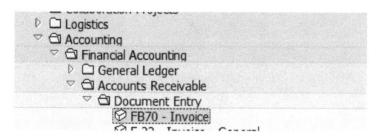

Fig 1

Enter your CC if/when prompted to do so:

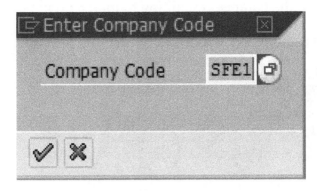

Fig 2

Enter your data, at the minimum, the customer #, date and amount and Hit Enter:

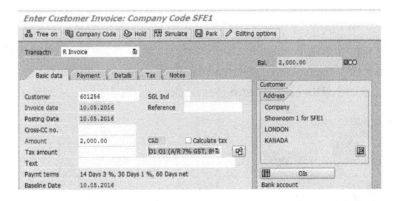

Fig 3

If tax is applicable, check *Calculate tax*, else leave it unchecked.

Enter the revenue account you want to post this amount against:

	St..	G/L acct	Short Text	D/C	Amount in doc.curr.	Loc.curr.amount
		450000		H Cr...	*	
				H Cr...		

0 Items (No entry variant selected)

Fig 4

The * will copy the amount from the main line or, if multiple lines, will calculate the balance remaining to match debits with credits.

It is always a good idea, while one is learning, to simulate the entry using the [Simulate] button before posting it:

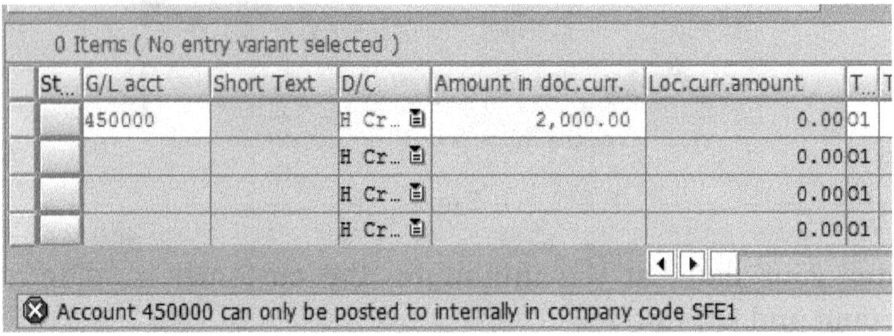

St	G/L acct	Short Text	D/C	Amount in doc.curr.	Loc.curr.amount	T	T
	450000		H Cr…	2,000.00	0.00	01	
			H Cr…		0.00	01	
			H Cr…		0.00	01	
			H Cr…		0.00	01	

0 Items (No entry variant selected)

⊗ Account 450000 can only be posted to internally in company code SFE1

Fig 5

We get an error because the way the GL 450000 was defined prevents us from posting directly to it, only automatic postings (from Sales or Purchase) can be made:

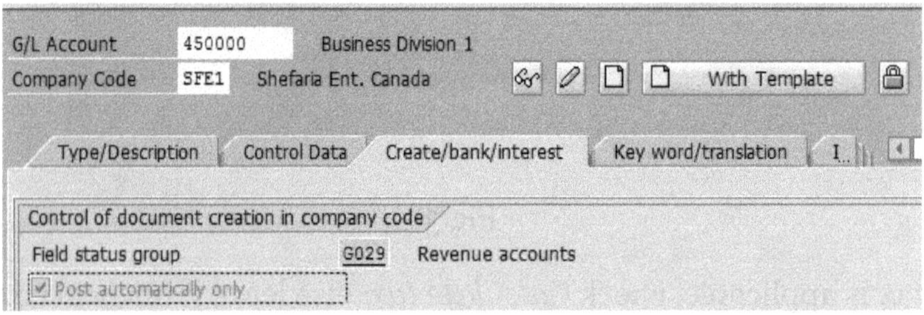

| G/L Account | 450000 | Business Division 1 |
| Company Code | SFE1 | Shefaria Ent. Canada | | | | | With Template |

Type/Description | Control Data | Create/bank/interest | Key word/translation | I

Control of document creation in company code

Field status group   G029   Revenue accounts

☑ Post automatically only

Fig 6

This setting determines that postings to this account can come only from the sales side. Therefore, this would not work obviously. We should change the account to a revenue account that allows direct postings. Normally, companies keep an account or two only for these purposes i.e. to make direct JEs.

We have account 450300 for this purpose. Let us substitute 450000 with 450300 and try the posting again and w/o any taxes to keep it simple:

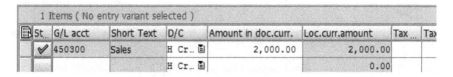

Fig 7

The simulation button gives no errors – only a message in yellow that can be by passed by hitting Enter:

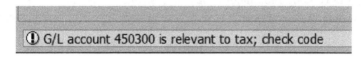

Fig 8

Simulation screen tells us the customer is being debited and G/L account is being credit for the same amount:

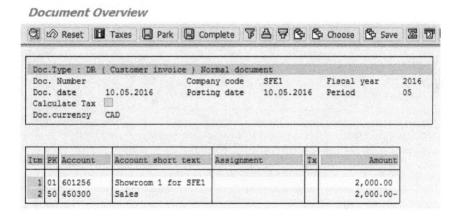

Fig 9

Since no errors were observed, we save this posting:

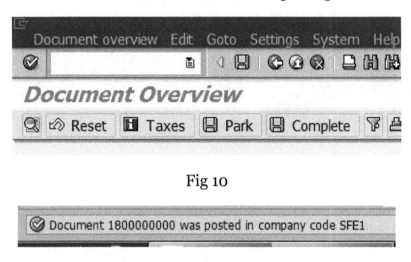

Fig 10

Document 1800000000 was posted in company code SFE1

Fig 11

Note the numbering is yet another sequence. These numbers also tell us what kind of posting was made as they are linked to different document types.

POSTING A VENDOR INVOICE (U)

T Code FB60

The process is the same as posting a customer's invoice except for the G/L accounts and the debit and credit side. FB60 can again be used to post this entry or the path:

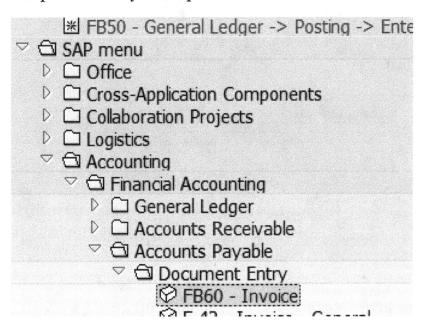

Fig 1

Enter appropriate data for vendor #, amount, G/L being debited and the dates ans/or Reference # of the vendor:

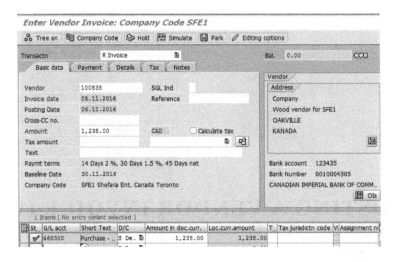

Fig 2

The interesting thing to note is that SAP recognizes what we are doing and defaults the appropriate Dr or Cr indicator for the line item. In FB70, it was Cr and in FB60, it is Dr for the appropriate G/L line item.

Simulate:

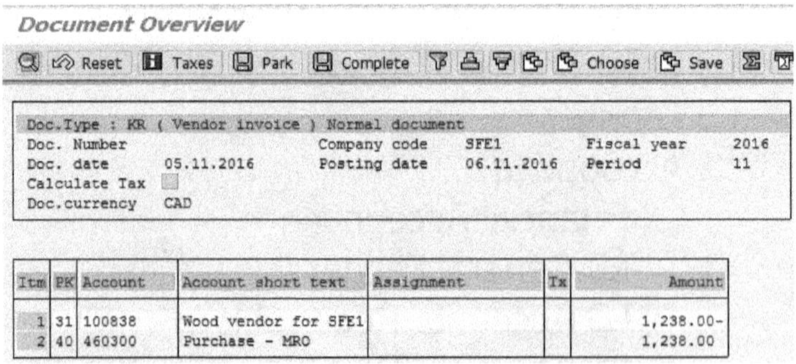

Fig 3

Post and the system gives us yet another numbering sequence:

DUPLICATE INVOICE CHECK (U)

T Code FB60

This functionality has been provided by SAP to ensure multiple bookings of the same vendor invoice do not take place. To activate this, some configurations have been done already; from the vendor master data point of view, the indicator *Chk double inv.* needs to be checked under the Payment Transaction tab in the vendor in FK01:

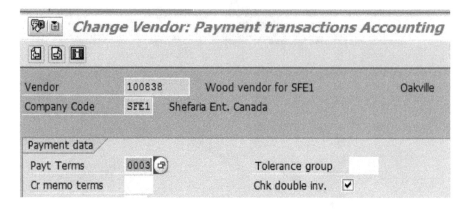

Fig 1

In the screen for posting a vendor invoice, there is a field called Reference:

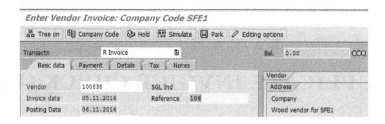

Fig 2

Though a free field that can be used for anything, most companies prefer to insert the vendor's invoice # in this field. At the time of checking for duplicates, SAP looks at the following fields for complete match in data:

CC
Vendor
Currency
Invoice Date
Reference document number

If the reference field is not filled up, it looks for an exact match using these fields:

CC
Vendor
Currency
Invoice Date
Amount in document currency

i.e. replaces the Reference Number with the amount for validation.

Let us post a vendor invoice with the following data in FB60:

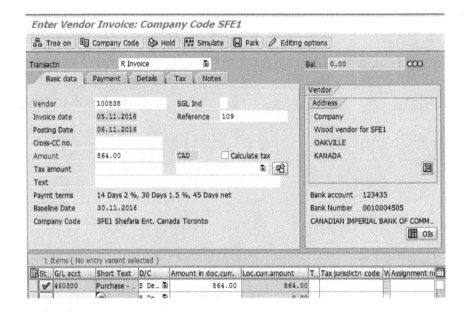

Fig 3

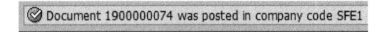

Fig 4

Now if we attempt another posting with the reference even if with a different amount we get the same message:

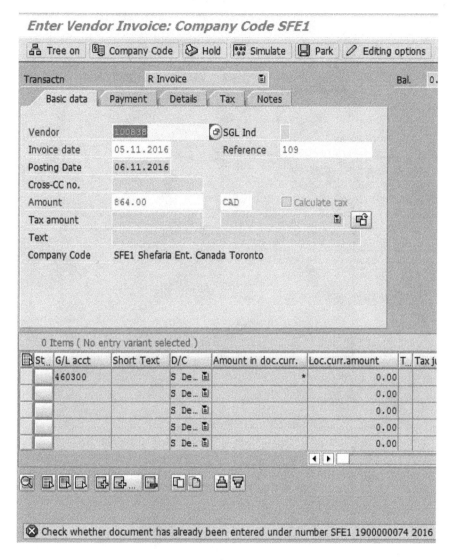

Fig 5

We can post this 2nd invoice only if we remove the reference # from the field or change it to any other as below:

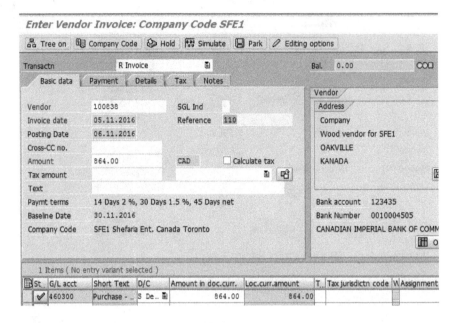

Fig 6

LOOKING UP PAYABLES AND

RECEIVABLES (U)

T Code FBL1N and FBL5N

I.   PAYABLES

T Code FBL1N

The items not yet paid are called vendor open items or payables. These payables can be looked up with the transaction code FBL1N or follow the path below:

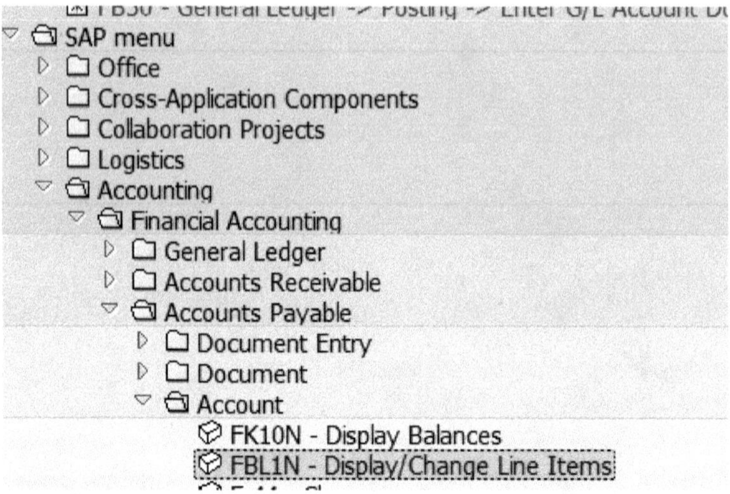

▽ 🗁 SAP menu
   ▷ 🗀 Office
   ▷ 🗀 Cross-Application Components
   ▷ 🗀 Collaboration Projects
   ▷ 🗀 Logistics
   ▽ 🗁 Accounting
      ▽ 🗁 Financial Accounting
         ▷ 🗀 General Ledger
         ▷ 🗀 Accounts Receivable
         ▽ 🗁 Accounts Payable
            ▷ 🗀 Document Entry
            ▷ 🗀 Document
            ▽ 🗁 Account
                ⊘ FK10N - Display Balances
                ⊘ FBL1N - Display/Change Line Items

Fig 1

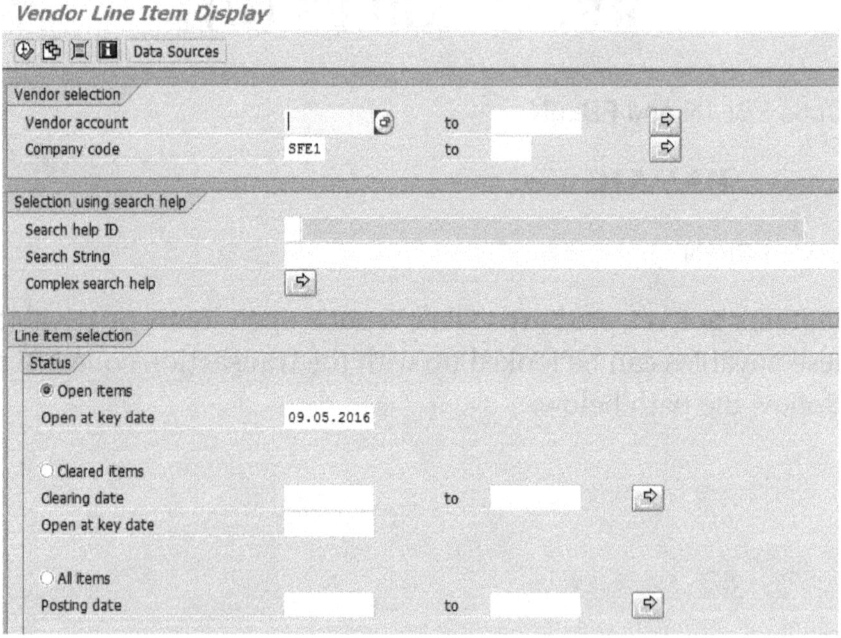

Vendor Line Item Display

⊕ 🕭 ☲ 🗏 Data Sources

Vendor selection
| Vendor account | | 🕀 | to | | ⇨ |
| Company code | SFE1 | | to | | ⇨ |

Selection using search help
Search help ID		
Search String		
Complex search help	⇨	

Line item selection

Status
  ◉ Open items
  Open at key date   09.05.2016

  ◯ Cleared items
  Clearing date   to   ⇨
  Open at key date

  ◯ All items
  Posting date   to   ⇨

Fig 2

This screen is almost identical to what you will see for receivables so let us understand the usage of some of the input fields here:

Vendor account:

Fig 3

This is the actual vendor #. We can look up the payables by including or excluding a range of vendors, or individual multiple vendors using the key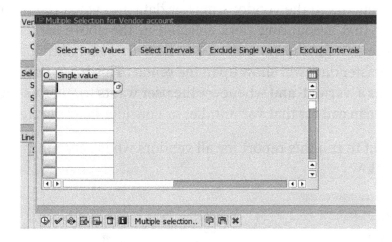

Fig 4

Using the same choices, the vendors' payables can be looked across multiple CCs at the same time:

Fig 5

The more data we give to restrict the inputs on this screen, the faster will be the results. For most people, when running day-to-day transactions, the selection key ▣ will be very useful. It further restricts the inputs to many more fields that are not available on the main screen:

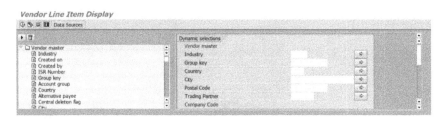

Fig 6

Normally, one will be responsible for certain groups of vendors or certain vendors. That person can be made the accounting clerk for those vendors in the vendor's master data and when the report is run for that accounting clerk selected in the above screen, then only the A/P for those vendors that have this accounting clerk in their master data will show up in the report. This input data can be saved as a 'variant' and whenever the user wants to run this report, he/she can call for that variant. Let us consider an example:

We want to run this report for all vendors whose accounting clerk is as below:

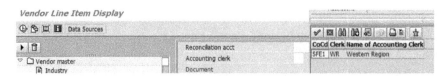

Fig 7

170

We select it and run the report.

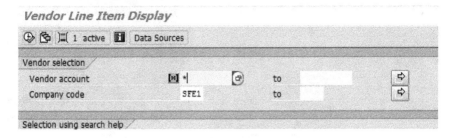

Fig 8

It displays all balances payable to all vendors that have this as their accounting clerk:

Vendor   *
Company Code SFE1
Name   *
City   *

S.	DocumentNo	Doc. Type	PK	Doc. Date	Curr. cash disc. amt	Vendor	S	DD	Amount in doc. curr.	Curr.	Clrng doc.	PayT	Dis
☀	1900000027	KR	31	05.03.2016	0.00	100845	🔲		890.00-	CAD		0001	0.00
☀	1900000026	KR	31	23.02.2016	0.00	100845	🔲		3,350.00-	CAD		0001	0.00
☀	1900000025	KR	31	10.02.2016	0.00	100845	🔲		5,600.00-	CAD		0001	0.00
☀	1900000024	KR	31	05.02.2016	0.00	100845	🔲		7,500.00-	CAD		0001	0.00
☀	1900000023	KR	31	02.02.2016	0.00	100845	🔲		4,300.00-	CAD		0001	0.00
☀	1900000021	KR	31	25.01.2016	0.00	100845	🔲		3,500.00-	CAD		0001	0.00
☀	1900000022	KR	31	25.01.2016	0.00	100845	🔲		6,000.00-	CAD		0001	0.00
☀	1900000012	KR	31	02.01.2016	0.00	100845	🔲		550.00-	CAD		0001	0.00
☀	1900000003	KR	31	01.01.2016	0.00	100844	🔲		750,000.00-	CAD		0001	0.00
☀	1900000000	KR	31	10.05.2016	30.00-	100838	🔲		1,500.00-	CAD	1500000001	0003	2.00
☀	1900000001	KR	31	10.05.2016	60.00-	100838	🔲		1,200.00-	CAD	1500000004	0003	5.00

Fig 9

This link between the vendor and the accounting clerk is formed from the vendor master data.

II. RECEIVABLES

T Code FBL5N

The items for which we have not been paid yet are called customer open items or receivables. These receivables can be looked up with the transaction code FBL5N or follow the path below:

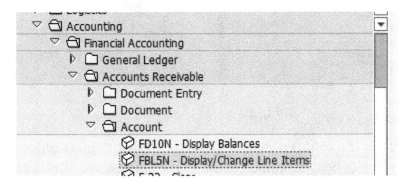

Fig 10

Conceptually, it is exactly the same as FBL1N so we will not go into details of the screen. The way we executed FBL1N, we can execute FBL5N to see the results of one, multiple or all customer open items in one or multiple company codes as on a date of our choosing. We can also look for all or only the cleared postings made during a date range:

Customer Line Item Display				
Customer selection				
Customer account	*		to	
Company code	SFE1		to	
Selection using search help				
Search help ID				
Search String				
Complex search help				
Line item selection				
Status				
⊙ Open items				
Open at key date	05.11.2017			

Fig 11

173

Customer									
Company Code SFE1									
Name									
City									

S.	Assignment	DocumentNo	Account	Ty.	Doc. Date	S	DD	Amount in local cur.	LCurr	Clmg doc.	Text
		90036890	800017	RV	19.07.2017			5,040.00	CAD		
		90036886	800016	RV	30.07.2017			150.00	CAD		
	0080015487	90036882	800016	RV	07.07.2017			2,086.50	CAD		
		90036885	800015	RV	30.07.2017			350.00	CAD		
		1400000009	800010	DZ	04.06.2016			203.00	CAD		
		1800000275	601399	DR	01.11.2017			5,000.00	CAD		shoe rack
		1800000276	601399	DR	01.11.2017			10,000.00	CAD		
		1800000277	601399	DR	01.11.2017			15,000.00	CAD		
		1800000278	601399	DR	01.11.2017			20,000.00	CAD		
		1800000279	601399	DR	01.11.2017			25,000.00	CAD		
		1400000177	601398	DZ	03.11.2017			5,880.00	CAD		
		1800000270	601398	DR	15.09.2017			25,000.00	CAD		Dining sets
		1800000272	601398	DR	01.10.2017			15,000.00	CAD		Ottomans
		1800000273	601398	DR	01.09.2017			17,000.00	CAD		

Fig 12

As we notice in the report above, it is similar to the vendor report and the layout can be customized to our choice to display whatever fields we desire.

TRANSFER AR BETWEEN

CUSTOMERS (U)

T Code F-30

AR can be transferred from one customer to another. Situations like these can arise at time of initial upload of data, re-alignment of customers, customer buyouts/takeover etc. The same can be achieved in the transaction code F-30. Choose the appropriate posting key for debiting/crediting the 2 customer numbers.

S	Assignment	Document	Ty	Doc. Date	DD	Σ	Amount in local cur.	LCurr	Clrng doc.	Text
	0080015387	90036764	RV	10.09.2016			6,420.00	CAD		
		90036749	RV	23.09.2016			1.12	CAD	1400000080	
		1400000076	DZ	05.11.2016			99.00	CAD	1400000088	
		1400000077	DZ	05.11.2016			50.00	CAD	1400000089	
		90036720	RV	15.06.2016			10.50-	CAD	1400000111	
	0080015373	90036716	RV	11.06.2016			267.50	CAD	1400000111	
	0080015375	90036718	RV	11.06.2016			1,337.50	CAD	1400000111	
	0080015375	90036747	RV	19.09.2016			87.50-	CAD	1400000111	
		1400000070	DZ	05.11.2016			4.96	CAD	1400000118	
							8,082.33	CAD		
	Account 601256						8,082.33	CAD		
		1800000034	DR	12.06.2016			80,000.00	CAD		
		1800000036	DR	13.06.2016			2,300.00	CAD	1400000116	
	0080015377	90036723	RV	18.06.2016			267.50	CAD	1400000116	
		1800000035	DR	13.06.2016			40,000.00	CAD	1400000120	
							122,567.50	CAD		
	Account 601263						122,567.50	CAD		
							130,649.83	CAD		

Fig 1

If we want any AR from 601263 to 601256, debit the customer 601256 and credit the customer 601263 with this amount using the appropriate posting keys from the defined series.

In F-30:

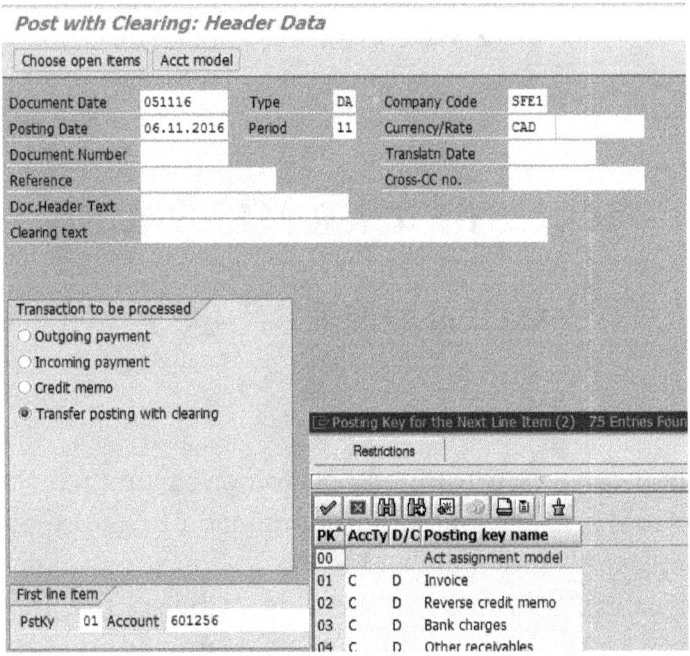

Fig 2

On the next screen, enter the offsetting data:

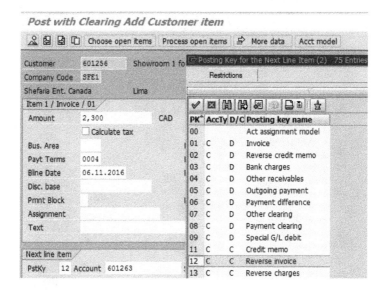

Fig 3

Hit Enter and on the next screen copy the amount using the '*':

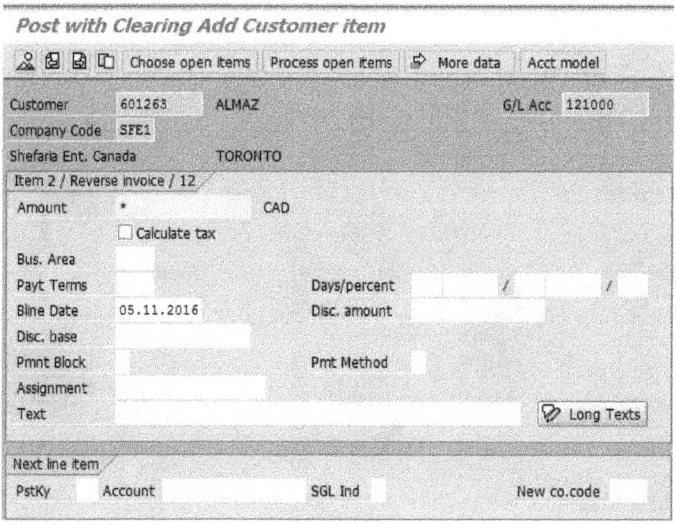

Fig 4

Simulate and/or save:

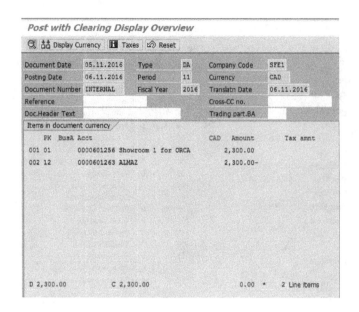

Fig 5

Document 1600000005 was posted in company code SFE1

When you run FBL5N for the customers, the 2 offsetting entries will be available in the line items of the 2 customers:

S	Assignment	Document	Ty	Doc. Date	DD	Σ Amount in local cur.	LCurr	Clrng doc.	Text
☼		100000147	AB	21.09.2016		0.23-	CAD		
☼		1400000066	DZ	21.09.2016		2.50	CAD		
☼		1400000075	DZ	05.11.2016		2.02-	CAD		
☼	0080015387	90036764	RV	10.09.2016		6,420.00	CAD		
☼		90036749	RV	23.09.2016		1.12	CAD	1400000080	
☼		1400000076	DZ	05.11.2016		99.00	CAD	1400000088	
☼		1400000077	DZ	05.11.2016		50.00	CAD	1400000089	
☼		90036720	RV	15.06.2016		10.50-	CAD	1400000111	
☼	0080015373	90036716	RV	11.06.2016		267.50	CAD	1400000111	
☼	0080015375	90036718	RV	11.06.2016		1,337.50	CAD	1400000111	
☼	0080015375	90036747	RV	19.09.2016		87.50-	CAD	1400000111	
☼		1600000005	DA	05.11.2016		2,300.00	CAD	1400000115	
☼		1400000070	DZ	05.11.2016		4.96	CAD	1400000118	
					*	10,382.33	CAD		
	Account 601256					10,382.33	CAD		
☼		1600000005	DA	05.11.2016		2,300.00-	CAD		
☼		1800000034	DR	12.06.2016		80,000.00	CAD		
☼		1800000036	DR	13.06.2016		2,300.00	CAD	1400000116	
☼	0080015377	90036723	RV	18.06.2016		267.50	CAD	1400000116	

Fig 6

CLEARING RECEIVABLES & PARTIAL

PAYMENTS (U)

T Code F-28

A customer invoice remains outstanding or open until it is paid or cancelled or adjusted in some other way. To clear a receivable we must first have an invoice. For this purpose, we will use one of the invoices we posted earlier.

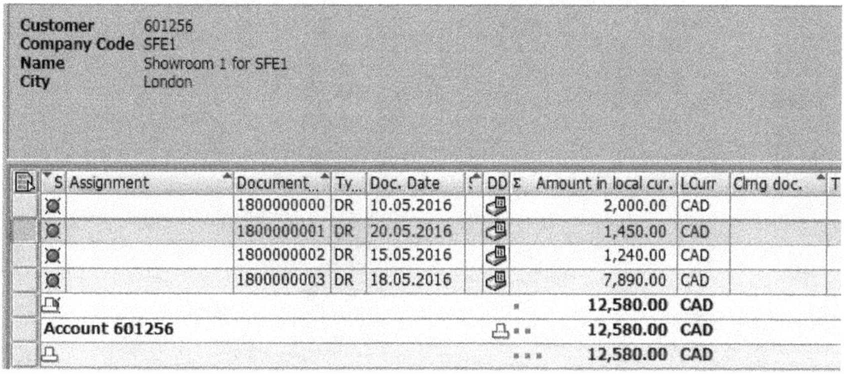

	S	Assignment	Document	Ty	Doc. Date	DD	Σ	Amount in local cur.	LCurr	Clrng doc.	T
			1800000000	DR	10.05.2016			2,000.00	CAD		
			1800000001	DR	20.05.2016			1,450.00	CAD		
			1800000002	DR	15.05.2016			1,240.00	CAD		
			1800000003	DR	18.05.2016			7,890.00	CAD		
								12,580.00	CAD		
	Account 601256							12,580.00	CAD		
								12,580.00	CAD		

Customer 601256
Company Code SFE1
Name Showroom 1 for SFE1
City London

Fig 1

Let's assume the customer is making only a part payment against the invoice highlighted above. F-28 is the transaction code or the path to clear open items:

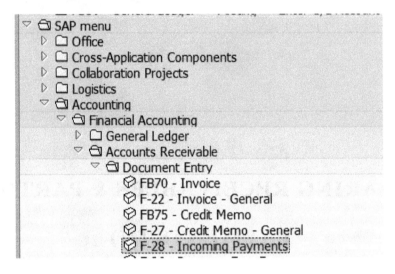

▽ 🗀 SAP menu
  ▷ 🗀 Office
  ▷ 🗀 Cross-Application Components
  ▷ 🗀 Collaboration Projects
  ▷ 🗀 Logistics
  ▽ 🗀 Accounting
    ▽ 🗀 Financial Accounting
      ▷ 🗀 General Ledger
      ▽ 🗀 Accounts Receivable
        ▽ 🗀 Document Entry
          ♡ FB70 - Invoice
          ♡ F-22 - Invoice - General
          ♡ FB75 - Credit Memo
          ♡ F-27 - Credit Memo - General
          ♡ F-28 - Incoming Payments

Fig 2

A few fields are mandatory but one should try to fill in as much as known:

Post Incoming Payments: Header Data

Process open items

Document Date	☑		Type	DZ	Company Code	SFE1
Posting Date	20.05.2016		Period	5	Currency/Rate	CAD
Document Number					Translatn Date	
Reference					Cross-CC no.	
Doc.Header Text					Trading part.BA	
Clearing text						

Bank data

Account	☑				Business Area	
Amount					Amount in LC	
Bank charges					LC bank charges	
Value date					Profit Center	
Text					Assignment	

Open item selection		Additional selections
Account		⦿ None
Account Type	D	☐ Other accounts	○ Amount
Special G/L ind		☑ Standard OIs	○ Document Number
Pmnt advice no.		○ Posting Date
☐ Distribute by age		○ Dunning Area
☐ Automatic search		○ Others

Fig 3

180

The document type DZ should be selected by default but if not, please enter DZ. The period should again be the current open posting period.

Document date is the date on which it is being entered, usually 'today'

Bank Data: Amount is the total amount on the check, Account is the Bank G/L account to which the posting will be made.

Post Incoming Payments: Header Data

Process open items					
Document Date	200516	Type	DZ	Company Code	SFE1
Posting Date	20.05.2016	Period	5	Currency/Rate	CAD
Document Number				Translatn Date	
Reference				Cross-CC no.	
Doc.Header Text				Trading part.BA	
Clearing text					

Bank data				
Account	107000	Business Area	
Amount	1250	Amount in LC	
Bank charges		LC bank charges	
Value date		Profit Center	
Text		Assignment	

Open item selection			Additional selections	
Account	601256		⦿ None	
Account Type	D	☐ Other accounts	◯ Amount	
Special G/L ind		☑ Standard OIs	◯ Document Number	
Pmnt advice no.			◯ Posting Date	
☐ Distribute by age			◯ Dunning Area	
☐ Automatic search			◯ Others	

Fig 4

In the section Open Items selection, the Account is the customer #.

Enter data as above and click on **Process open items** or simply Press Enter.

These lines in Fig 5 are the same as what we saw in the customer receivable report in Fig 1. As we also notice in Fig 5, there are cash discounts against invoices if the customer is paying on/before the date when he receives this discount for early payment. We will discuss the applicability of discounts later; here we simply adjust the amount that is being paid against the invoice. To do that we need to be able to 'isolate' the 2nd line from the rest.

First, deactivate all the line items by

(i)   selecting Select All button:

All lines will turn Blue:

Standard		Partial pmt		Res.items		Withhldg tax		

Account items 601256 Showroom 1 for SFE1

Document	D.	Docume	P.	Busi	Day	CAD Gross	Cash discnt	CashD.
1800000000	DR	10.05.2	01		4–	2,000.00	60.00	3.000
1800000001	DR	20.05.2	01		14–	1,450.00	43.50	3.000
1800000002	DR	15.05.2	01		14–	1,240.00	37.20	3.000
1800000003	DR	18.05.2	01		14–	7,890.00	236.70	3.000

Fig 5

(ii)   Next, click on Deactivate all items:

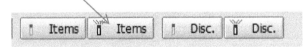

All lines will turn black:

182

Standard	Partial pmt	Res.items	Withhldg tax

Account items 601256 Showroom 1 for SFE1

Document	D	Docume	P	Busi	Day	CAD Gross	Cash discnt	CashD
1800000000	DR	10.05.2...	01		4-	2,000.00	60.00	3.000
1800000001	DR	20.05.2...	01		14-	1,450.00	43.50	3.000
1800000002	DR	15.05.2...	01		14-	1,240.00	37.20	3.000
1800000003	DR	18.05.2...	01		14-	7,890.00	236.70	3.000

Fig 6

(iii)   Position the cursor in the line to be adjusted (here, the 2nd line):

Standard	Partial pmt	Res.items	Withhldg tax

Account items 601256 Showroom 1 for SFE1

Document	D	Docume	P	Busi	Day	CAD Gross	Cash discnt	CashD
1800000000	DR	10.05.2...	01		4-	2,000.00	60.00	3.000
1800000001	DR	20.05.2...	01		14-	1,450.00	43.50	3.000
1800000002	DR	15.05.2...	01		14-	1,240.00	37.20	3.000
1800000003	DR	18.05.2...	01		14-	7,890.00	236.70	3.000

Fig 7

Then activate the line item with the activate item key:

Fig 8

Only that line (here, 2nd) will turn blue as below.

Note: Alternatively, double clicking the actual amount also works the same way. Double clicking toggles between blue and black. It is not necessary to first make all of them inactive and then active...it merely depends on how many lines there are. E.g. if there are just 2 lines, double click on the one you want or don't

183

want to select by toggling between Blue and Blank. As a general SAP process, Blue means active, Black means inactive. Practice this a few times to get a better understanding of it.

Since we are not allowing the cash discount on this payment, we simply clear out the amount in the cash discount column for this line:

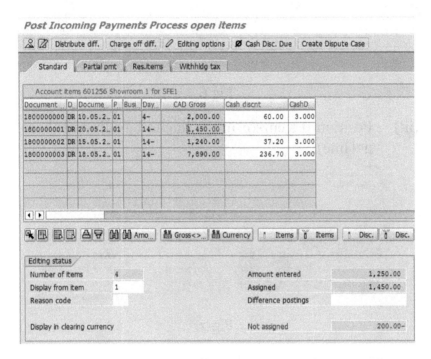

Fig 9

Note the difference between the invoice value and the payment as the Not Assigned amount at the bottom right. To balance it, we need to move this amount to the difference postings cell by double clicking in it:

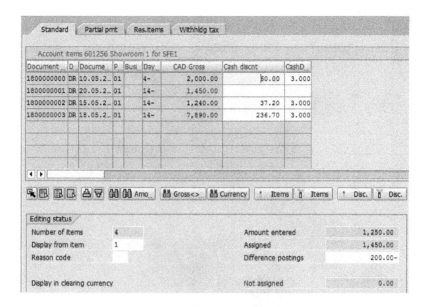

Fig 10

We can now either simulate this first or post directly. Simulation tells us:

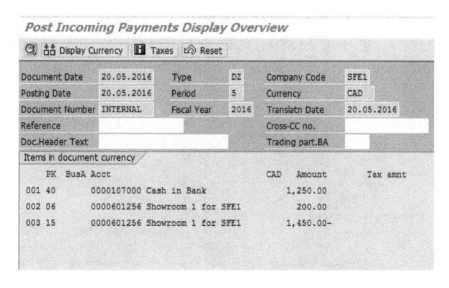

Fig 11

The balance of the receivable will be automatically put back in the AR of the customer via the posting key 06, which is:

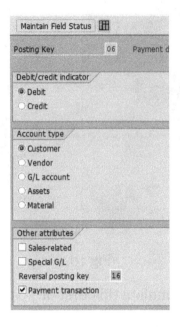

Fig 12

Usually, for the benefit of the auditors as well for our own memory, we put some notes. By double clicking on the line we find a spot to put this text in the notes:

Customer	601256	Showroom 1 for SFE1		G/L Acc	121000
Company Code	SFE1				
Shefaria Ent. Canada		London			
Item 3 / Incoming payment / 15					
Amount	1,450.00	CAD			
Bus. Area					
Bline Date	20.05.2016		Disc. amount	0.00	
Pmnt Block			Pmt Method		
Assignment					
Text	Partial payment of $1250 applied to this invoice				
Next line item					

Fig 13

If the above space is not sufficient for the notes, click on ![Long text] **Long text** and enter it there. Texts can be entered even after

186

the document has been posted by going back to it in a 'change' mode. While the amounts, G/Ls etc cannot be modified in an already posted document, the notes can be altered.

Post the document and SAP gives us the posting #:

Fig 14

When we look up the customers' receivables in FBL5N again, we find this invoice now has only the remaining balance:

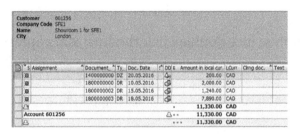

Fig 15

We can look up this document in transaction FB03:

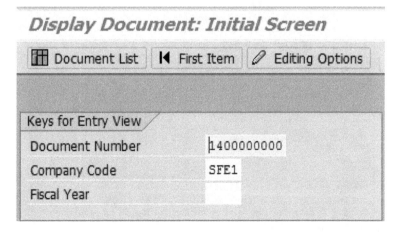

Fig 16

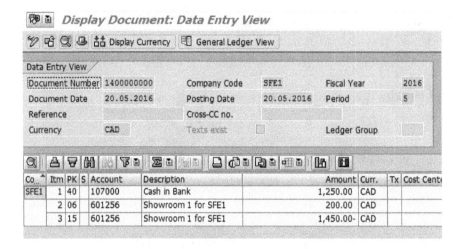

Fig 17

To see the notes, just double click the line that represents the full invoice:

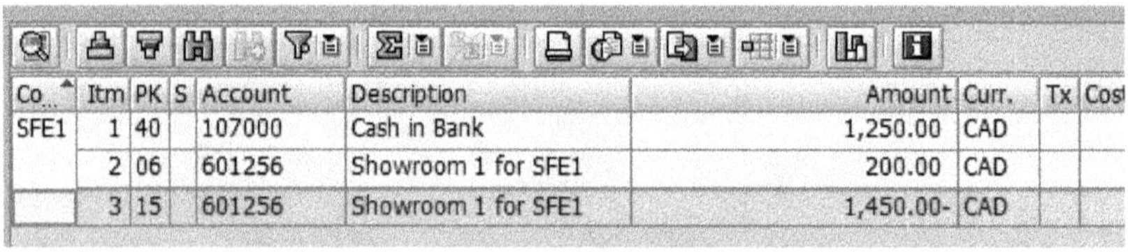

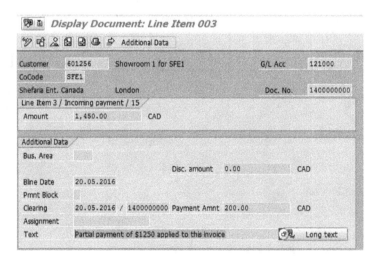

Fig 18

Fig 19

188

To look up documents in FB03: If we do not know the document #, then click on Document List,

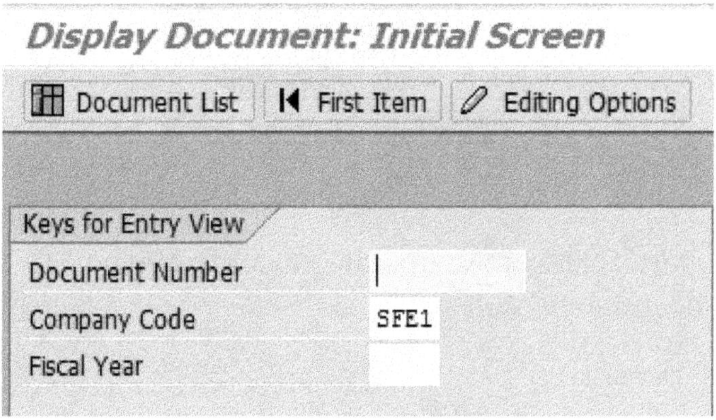

Fig 20

Enter as much data as you can on the screen and click Execute:

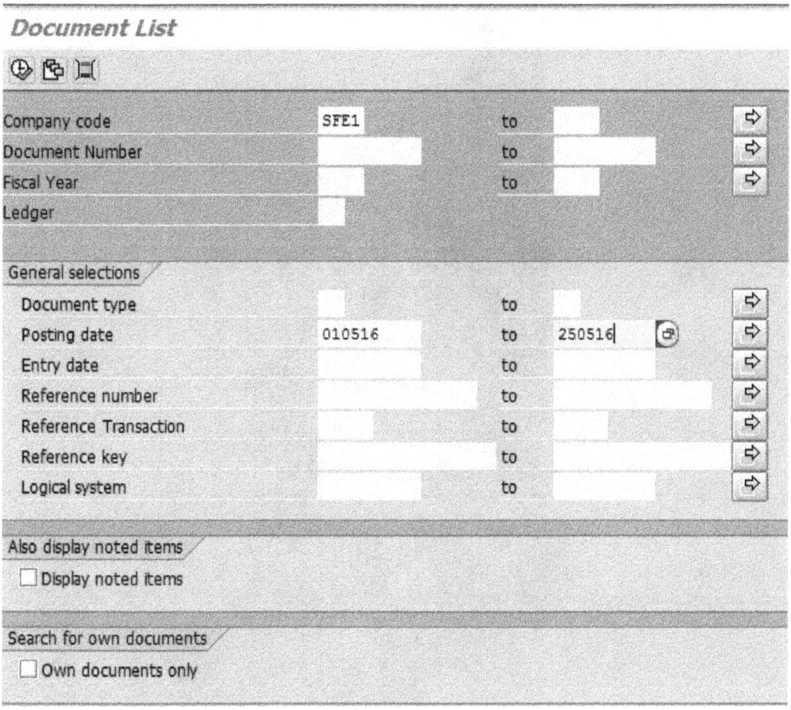

Fig 21

You can also ask it to display only those documents that you may have posted by clicking on:

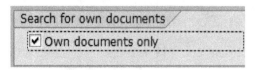

Fig 22

In the report that comes up, the document type DZ means a payment document:

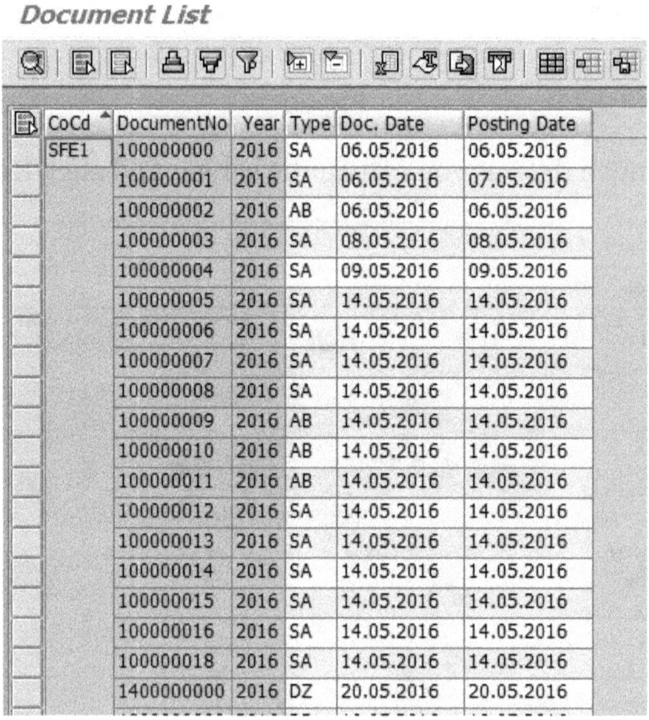

Document List

CoCd	DocumentNo	Year	Type	Doc. Date	Posting Date
SFE1	100000000	2016	SA	06.05.2016	06.05.2016
	100000001	2016	SA	06.05.2016	07.05.2016
	100000002	2016	AB	06.05.2016	06.05.2016
	100000003	2016	SA	08.05.2016	08.05.2016
	100000004	2016	SA	09.05.2016	09.05.2016
	100000005	2016	SA	14.05.2016	14.05.2016
	100000006	2016	SA	14.05.2016	14.05.2016
	100000007	2016	SA	14.05.2016	14.05.2016
	100000008	2016	SA	14.05.2016	14.05.2016
	100000009	2016	AB	14.05.2016	14.05.2016
	100000010	2016	AB	14.05.2016	14.05.2016
	100000011	2016	AB	14.05.2016	14.05.2016
	100000012	2016	SA	14.05.2016	14.05.2016
	100000013	2016	SA	14.05.2016	14.05.2016
	100000014	2016	SA	14.05.2016	14.05.2016
	100000015	2016	SA	14.05.2016	14.05.2016
	100000016	2016	SA	14.05.2016	14.05.2016
	100000018	2016	SA	14.05.2016	14.05.2016
	1400000000	2016	DZ	20.05.2016	20.05.2016

Fig 23

190

Double click on it to see more details:

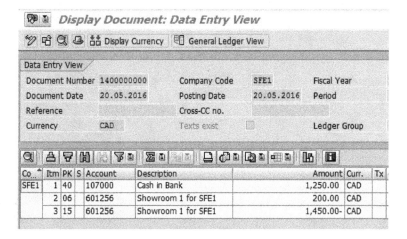

Fig 24

POSTING RESIDUAL PAYMENTS (U)

T Code FB70

Residual payments in SAP are regarded as disputed amounts. The intent is to record those as such pending decisions. The effect they have is that the customer's credit balance/limits are not affected since they are disputed. If not paid, then at the end of the financial period they may find their way to bad debts depending on the company's policy.

We will post a new customer invoice using transaction FB70.

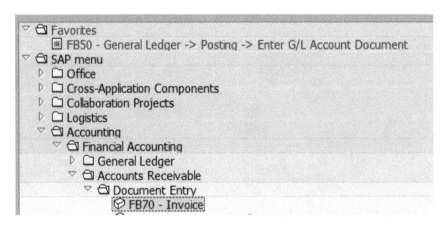

Fig 1

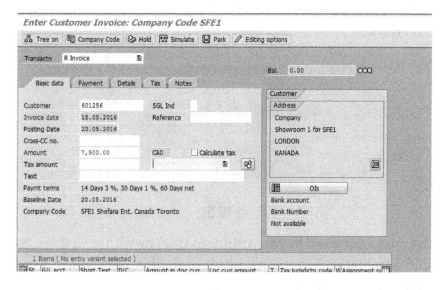

Fig 2

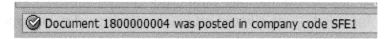

Document 1800000004 was posted in company code SFE1

Fig 3

This currently shows up in the customer's AR statements, FBL5N:

Customer	601256										
Company Code	SFE1										
Name	Showroom 1 for SFE1										
City	London										

S	Assignment	Document	Ty.	Posting Date	PayT	Net due date	Days net	Doc. Date	DD	Σ	Amount in local cur.	LCurr	Clrng doc.
		1400000000	DZ	20.05.2016		20.05.2016	0	20.05.2016			200.00	CAD	
		1800000000	DR	10.05.2016	0004	09.07.2016	60	10.05.2016			2,000.00	CAD	
		1800000002	DR	20.05.2016	0004	19.07.2016	60	15.05.2016			1,240.00	CAD	
		1800000003	DR	20.05.2016	0004	19.07.2016	60	18.05.2016			7,890.00	CAD	
		1800000004	DR	20.05.2016	0004	19.07.2016	60	18.05.2016			7,500.00	CAD	
										*	18,830.00	CAD	
Account 601256										**	18,830.00	CAD	
										***	18,830.00	CAD	

Fig 4

The net due date is being calculated based on posting date + days net due because in the customer master the payment terms defined are 60 days:

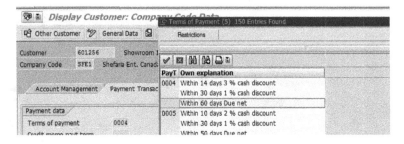

Fig 5

If the customer were to pay within 30 days or within 14 days, SAP would automatically apply 1% or 3% cash discounts, which we will see later in this course.

Let's say the customer has paid only partial amount and the remaining needs to be cleared off via this process. The transaction to do this is previously used F-28 or, we can look at a new one here, F-26 which leads up to the same result as F-28. The only difference is, in F-28 if you already know the document you are posting against, it makes it simpler and we don't have to search, deactivate and re-activate the document we need.

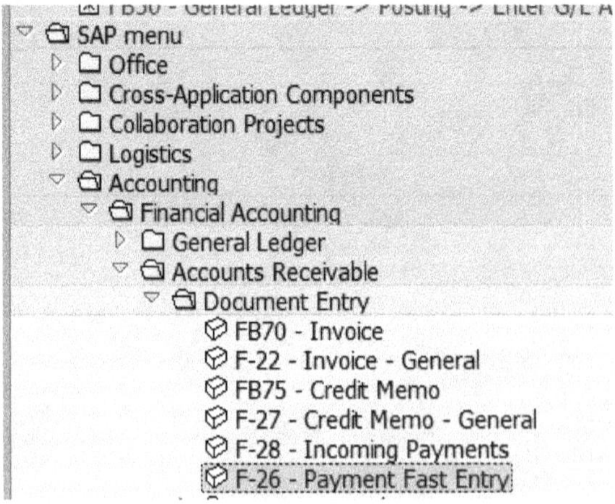

Fig 6

Enter the data as below for the bank account you will debit for this payment:

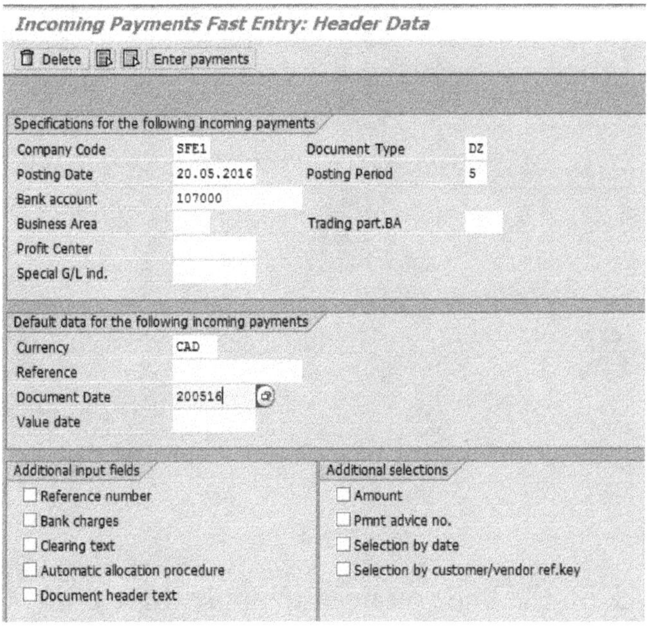

Incoming Payments Fast Entry: Header Data

🗑 Delete   Enter payments

Specifications for the following incoming payments

Company Code	SFE1	Document Type	DZ
Posting Date	20.05.2016	Posting Period	5
Bank account	107000		
Business Area		Trading part.BA	
Profit Center			
Special G/L ind.			

Default data for the following incoming payments

Currency	CAD
Reference	
Document Date	200516
Value date	

Additional input fields
- ☐ Reference number
- ☐ Bank charges
- ☐ Clearing text
- ☐ Automatic allocation procedure
- ☐ Document header text

Additional selections
- ☐ Amount
- ☐ Pmnt advice no.
- ☐ Selection by date
- ☐ Selection by customer/vendor ref.key

Fig 7

Now on **Enter payments** where you can enter the customer # and amount:

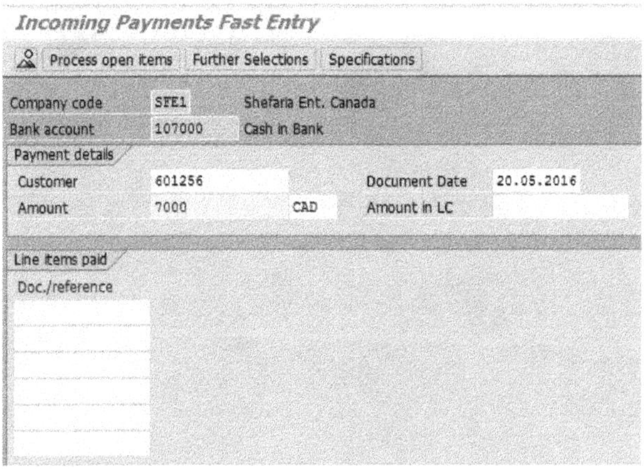

Incoming Payments Fast Entry

Process open items   Further Selections   Specifications

Company code	SFE1	Shefaria Ent. Canada
Bank account	107000	Cash in Bank

Payment details

Customer	601256		Document Date	20.05.2016
Amount	7000	CAD	Amount in LC	

Line items paid

Doc./reference

Fig 8

Then on Process open items to bring up the invoices open for payment of this customer:

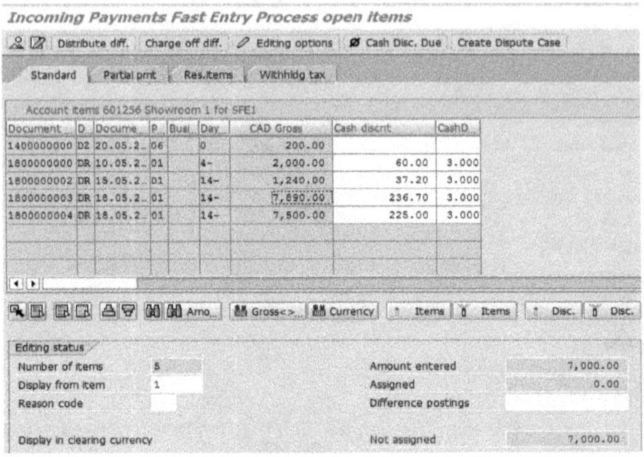

Incoming Payments Fast Entry Process open items

Fig 9

Double click on the line you need to apply this against to make it blue. Note that since the payment has come within 15 days, SAP has applied a cash discount automatically as done below in Fig 9.

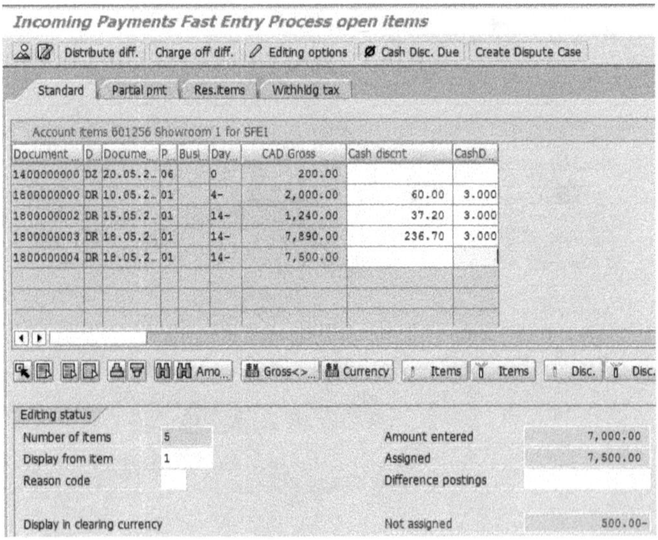

Fig 10

Since the customer has disputed the difference amount anyway, you have the choice of wiping out this discount by clearing out the line manually and then decide whether to give the discounts later once resolution for this difference happens. Therefore, we will clear the cash discounts (Fig 10) and apply the paid amount to the entire document.

We now need to account for this residual amount, we do this by going to the Residual items tab:

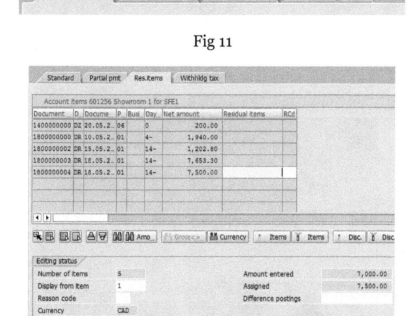

Fig 11

Fig 12

Either manually enter the amount in the cell Residual items next to the Net Amount or double click in it. and the Not Assigned amount at the bottom turns to 0 (Fig 13)

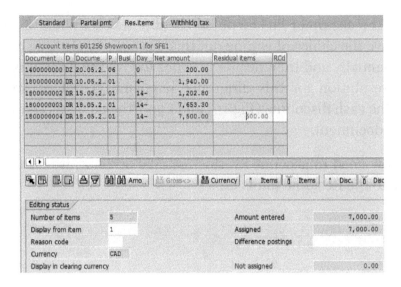

Fig 13

Simulate if you would like to:

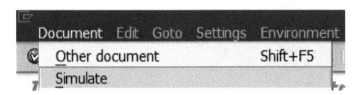

Fig 14

To see 3 lines:

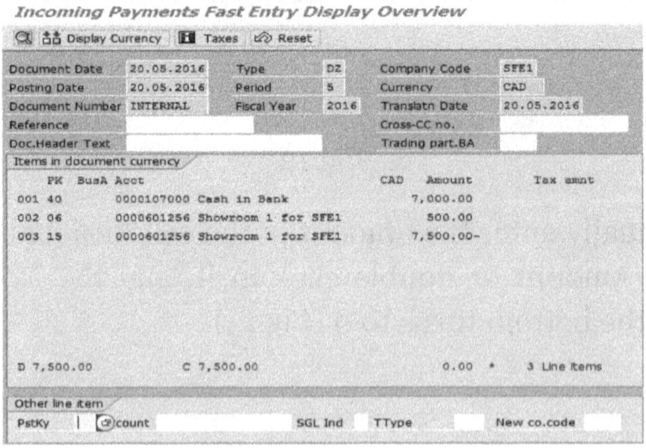

Incoming Payments Fast Entry Display Overview

Document Date	20.05.2016	Type	DZ	Company Code	SFE1
Posting Date	20.05.2016	Period	5	Currency	CAD
Document Number	INTERNAL	Fiscal Year	2016	Translatn Date	20.05.2016
Reference				Cross-CC no.	
Doc.Header Text				Trading part.BA	

Items in document currency

PK	BusA	Acct		CAD	Amount	Tax amnt
001	40		0000107000 Cash in Bank		7,000.00	
002	06		0000601256 Showroom 1 for SFE1		500.00	
003	15		0000601256 Showroom 1 for SFE1		7,500.00-	

D 7,500.00   C 7,500.00   0.00 *   3 Line items

Other line item

PstKy		@count		SGL Ind	TType		New co.code	

Fig 15

You may also want to make a note at this point to explain this remaining. To do that, double click on the difference line:

```
002 06      0000601256 Showroom 1 for SFE1           500.00
```

Fig 16

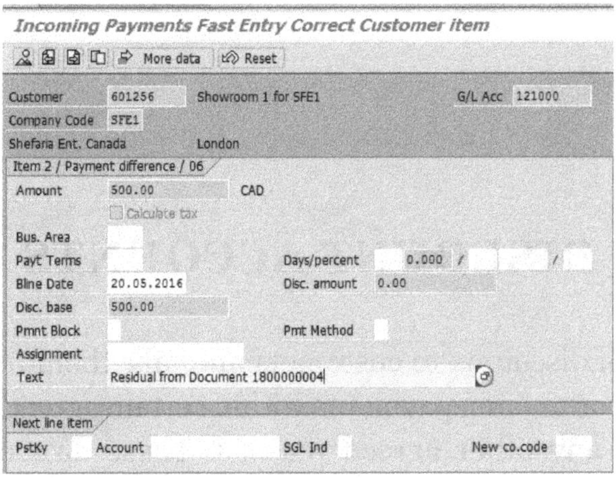

Fig 17

Then save it:

⊘ Document 1400000001 was posted in company code SFE1

Fig 18

Let us now check the customer balance in FBL5N or FD10N:

Thus, this balance remains on the customer account as payable:

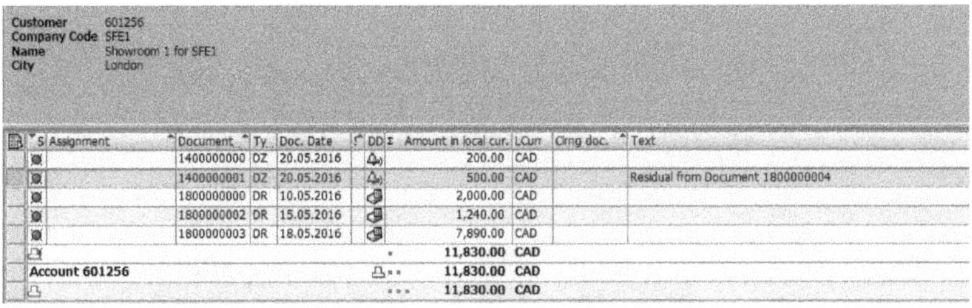

Customer   601256
Company Code   SFE1
Name   Showroom 1 for SFE1
City   London

S Assignment	Document	Ty	Doc. Date	DD Σ	Amount in local cur.	LCur	Clrng doc.	Text
	1400000000	DZ	20.05.2016		200.00	CAD		
	1400000001	DZ	20.05.2016		500.00	CAD		Residual from Document 1800000004
	1800000000	DR	10.05.2016		2,000.00	CAD		
	1800000002	DR	15.05.2016		1,240.00	CAD		
	1800000003	DR	18.05.2016		7,890.00	CAD		
				*	11,830.00	CAD		
Account 601256				**	11,830.00	CAD		
				***	11,830.00	CAD		

Fig 19

CASH DISCOUNT ACCOUNTS (C/U)

We give cash discounts to customers and take them from vendors by receiving or making payments within certain agreed to specified days or for any other agreed reasons. These discounts require expense or income accounts as part of the P & L accounts to post these discounts. Part of this set up is data (setting up of the accounts themselves in the CoA) and part configuration (to make the cash discount process pick up these accounts at times of posting via the automatic account assignment process of SAP).

As the first step, we need to define 2 G/L accounts of the P & L type for cash discount given and taken.

Select your numbering (here, 450600 and 460600 for cash discount given and taken respectively) for the two types and enter data for both as in Figs 1 and 2.

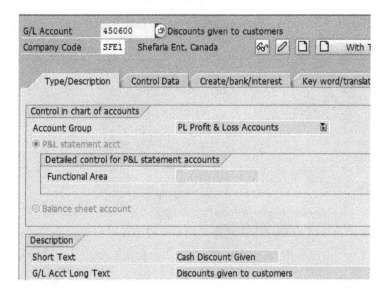

Fig 1

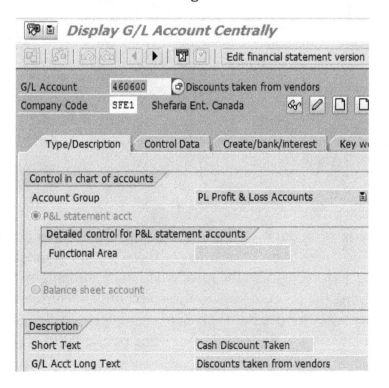

Fig 2

For both enter Control data and Create/Bank/Interest Data as:

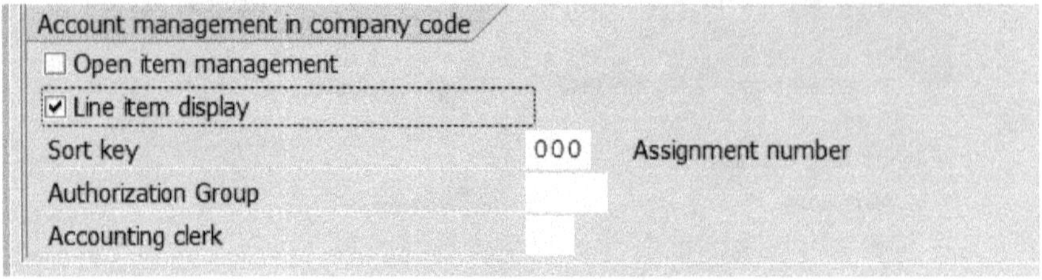

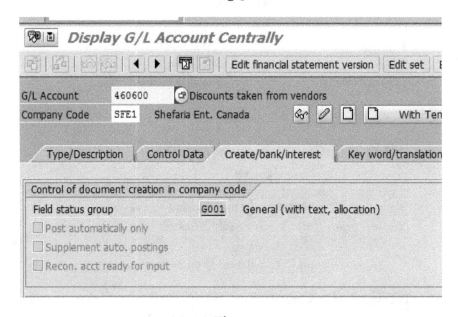

Fig 3

Fig 4

Once we have 450600 and 460600 setup, we need to make the system recognize to make postings to these accounts, much in the same way as it recognizes the reconciliation accounts. This is done by assigning the process keys to these accounts in configurations. The process key for discounts given to customers is called SKT and this configuration is done in the following path in SPRO (Fig 5)

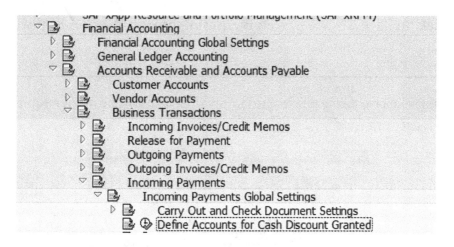

Financial Accounting
  ▷ Financial Accounting Global Settings
  ▷ General Ledger Accounting
  ▽ Accounts Receivable and Accounts Payable
     ▷ Customer Accounts
     ▷ Vendor Accounts
     ▽ Business Transactions
        ▷ Incoming Invoices/Credit Memos
        ▷ Release for Payment
        ▷ Outgoing Payments
        ▷ Outgoing Invoices/Credit Memos
        ▽ Incoming Payments
           ▽ Incoming Payments Global Settings
              ▷ Carry Out and Check Document Settings
              ⊕ Define Accounts for Cash Discount Granted

Fig 5

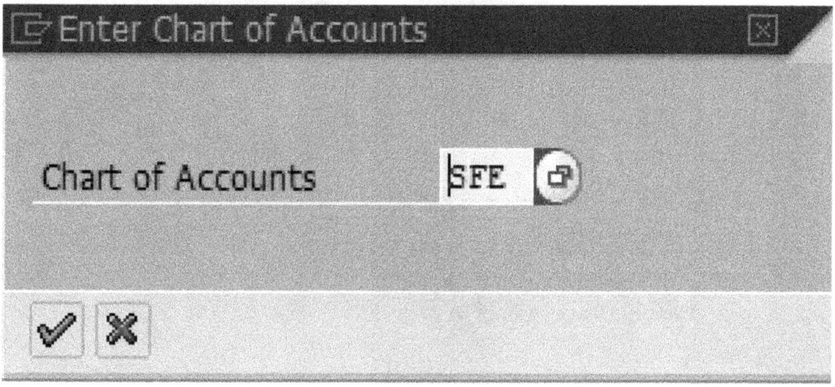

Enter Chart of Accounts   ☒

Chart of Accounts   SFE ⟳

✓ ✗

Fig 6

Ensure SKT exists on the screen:

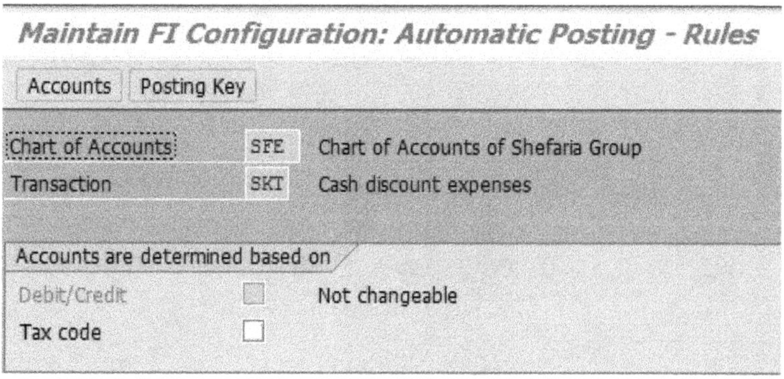

Maintain FI Configuration: Automatic Posting - Rules

| Accounts | Posting Key |

| Chart of Accounts | SFE | Chart of Accounts of Shefaria Group |
| Transaction | SKT | Cash discount expenses |

Accounts are determined based on

| Debit/Credit | ☐ | Not changeable |
| Tax code | ☐ | |

Fig 7

Click on Save to save this configuration linking the CoA SFE with SKT.

Next, click on 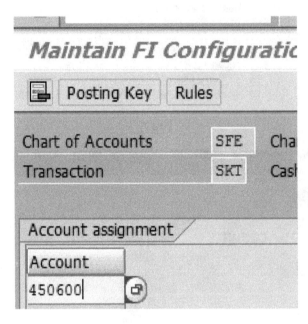 and enter the Cash discount given in the G/L account field:

Fig 8

Save:

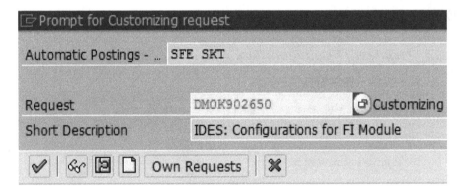

Fig 9

Repeat the same configuration for Cash Discount taken G/L account 460600 with process key SKE in the path

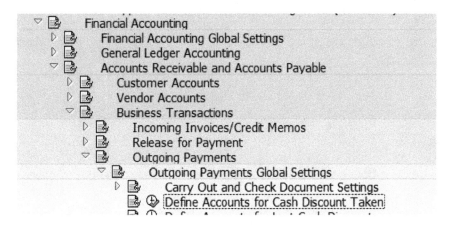

Fig 10

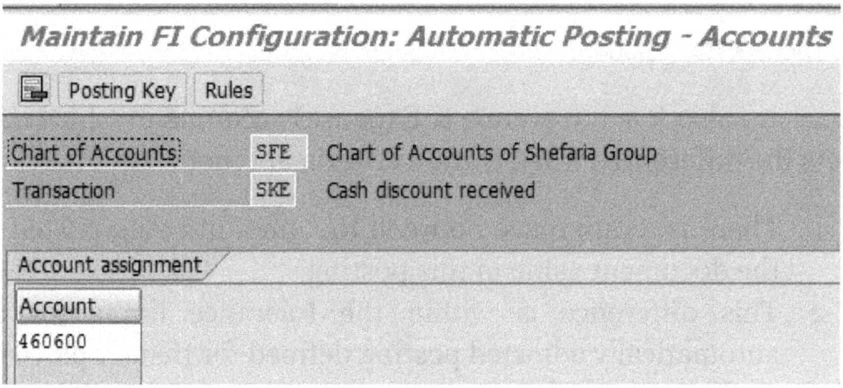

Maintain FI Configuration: Automatic Posting - Accounts

| Posting Key | Rules |

| Chart of Accounts | SFE | Chart of Accounts of Shefaria Group |
| Transaction | SKE | Cash discount received |

Account assignment

| Account |
| 460600 |

Fig 11

UNDER AND OVER PAYMENTS (C/U)

T Code SPRO, FS00

These are also P & L (revenue & Expense) accounts in which SAP posts the differences when certain criteria are met:

1. There is a difference between the amount being posted vs the document value in this posting
2. This difference is within the tolerance limits for an automatically adjusted posting defined for that employee
3. Cash discount adjustments can't take care of this difference

Since these under and over payments can occur from customers and to vendors alike, often companies prefer to have a sub-group of "Other" accounts under P & L to set up such accounts in that group. In our case, we will keep it simple and like for cash discount accounts set up 2 G/L accounts 900100 and 900200 under P & L group for one Under Payment Account and the other Over Payment Account. Enter data as in Fig 1

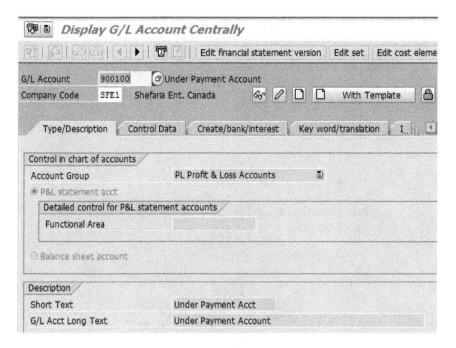

Fig 1

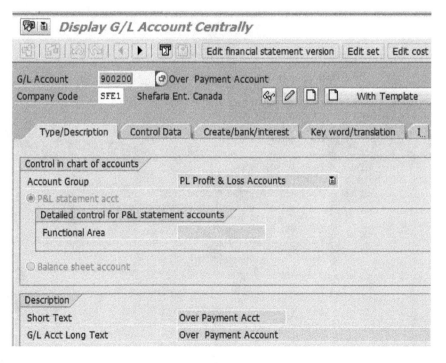

Fig 2

207

For both enter Control data and Create/Bank/Interest Data as:

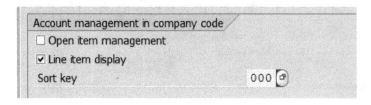

Fig 3

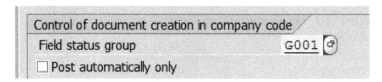

Fig 4

The next step is to make SAP recognize these 2 accounts 900100 and 900200 to post the Under and Over payments to via the process key ZDI:

The path to do that is:

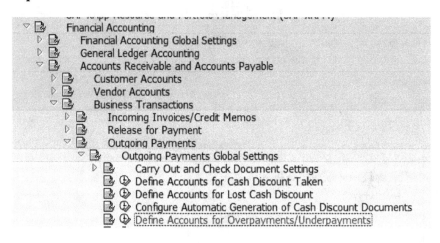

Fig 5

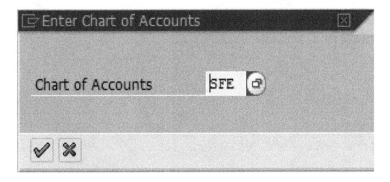

Fig 6

Ensure ZDI is present:

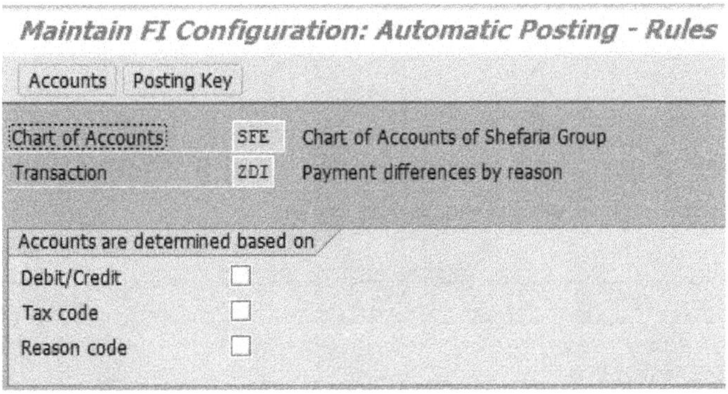

Maintain FI Configuration: Automatic Posting - Rules

Accounts	Posting Key

Chart of Accounts	SFE	Chart of Accounts of Shefaria Group
Transaction	ZDI	Payment differences by reason

Accounts are determined based on

Debit/Credit	☐
Tax code	☐
Reason code	☐

Fig 7

Click on the Debit/Credit Key and Save:

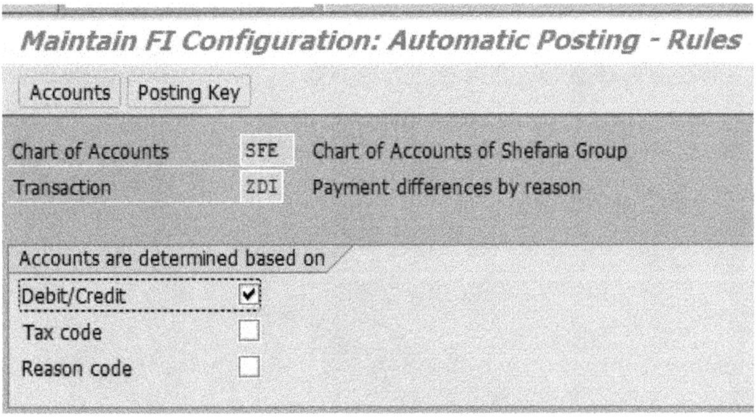

Maintain FI Configuration: Automatic Posting - Rules

Accounts	Posting Key

Chart of Accounts	SFE	Chart of Accounts of Shefaria Group
Transaction	ZDI	Payment differences by reason

Accounts are determined based on

Debit/Credit	☑
Tax code	☐
Reason code	☐

Fig 8

Along with the Save message at the bottom, a new window opens up to enter the 2 accounts:

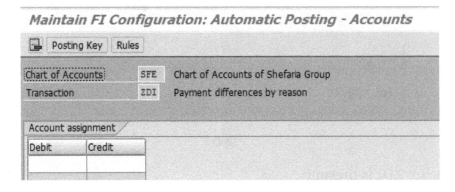

Fig 9

The under payment account in the Debit field and the over, payment account goes into Credit field:

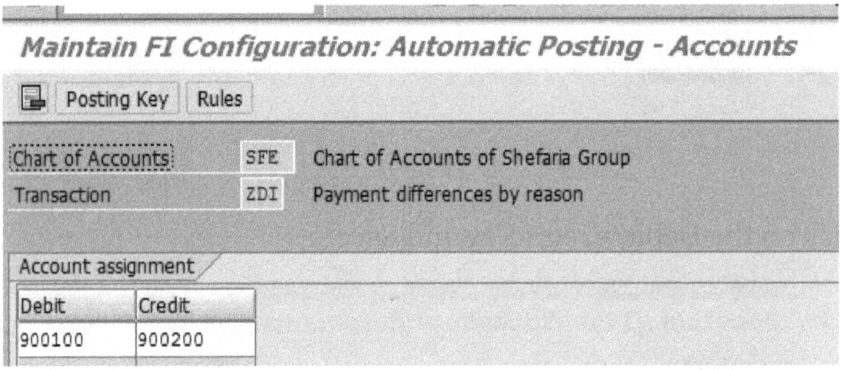

Fig 10

Save the configuration.

POSTING INCOMING UNDER/OVER PAYMENTS WITH, W/O DISCOUNTS (U)

Now that we have our over/under and discount G/Ls in place along with employee tolerances, we can see the effects of the same via actual postings with various scenarios.

T Code F-28

I. EFFECT OF TOLERANCE LIMITS

Let us try to first post an incoming payment *outside of tolerance limits* from a customer in F-28:

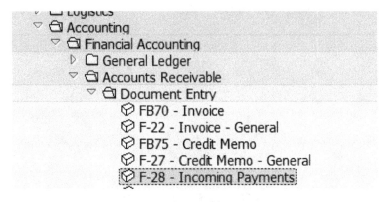

Fig 1

Ensure that account type D comes pre-entered. Enter the rest of the data in this by now familiar screen – Bank G/L account, amount, posting date, document date, value date, customer # etc:

Post Incoming Payments: Header Data

Process open items

Document Date	200516	Type	DZ	Company Code	SFE1
Posting Date	20.05.2016	Period	5	Currency/Rate	CAD
Document Number				Translatn Date	
Reference				Cross-CC no.	
Doc.Header Text				Trading part.BA	
Clearing text					

Bank data

Account	107000		Business Area	
Amount	1500		Amount in LC	
Bank charges			LC bank charges	
Value date			Profit Center	
Text			Assignment	

Open item selection			Additional selections	
Account	601256		◉ None	
Account Type	D	☐ Other accounts	○ Amount	
Special G/L ind		☑ Standard OIs	○ Document Number	
Pmnt advice no.			○ Posting Date	
☐ Distribute by age			○ Dunning Area	
☐ Automatic search			○ Others	

Fig 2

Again, select the appropriate line against which this amount needs to be adjusted. In our example, we will adjust it against line 3:

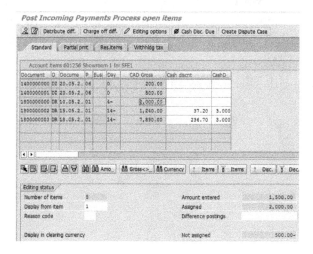

Fig 3

Note the Not assigned amount, the difference of the actual and the amount being posted. This amount needs to now be posted to the under payment account as the customer has underpaid us by this amount. To verify if it will work, simulate the document:

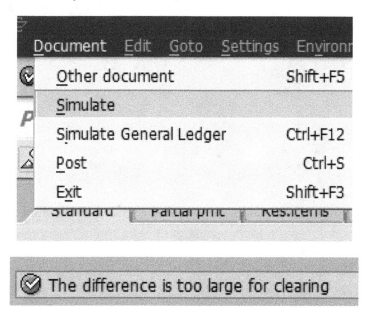

213

Fig 4

This means we have not told SAP what to do with the difference of and the difference being outside of the employee's tolerance limits that we defined earlier to be only $100, it will not post automatically. We do have the option to post it as partial payment and throwing this difference amount back into the customer's AR.

II. POSTING AN AMOUNT WITHIN THE TOLERANCE LIMITS

Post Incoming Payments: Header Data

Process open items

Document Date	200516	Type	DZ	Company Code	SFE1	
Posting Date	20.05.2016	Period	5	Currency/Rate	CAD	
Document Number				Translatn Date		
Reference				Cross-CC no.		
Doc.Header Text				Trading part.BA		
Clearing text						

Bank data

Account	107000	Business Area	
Amount	1960	Amount in LC	
Bank charges		LC bank charges	
Value date		Profit Center	
Text		Assignment	

Open item selection			Additional selections	
Account	601256	⊡	● None	
Account Type	D	☐ Other accounts	○ Amount	
Special G/L ind		☑ Standard OIs	○ Document Number	
Pmnt advice no.			○ Posting Date	
☐ Distribute by age			○ Dunning Area	
☐ Automatic search			○ Others	

Fig 5

Post Incoming Payments Process open items

👤 ▨ Distribute diff. | Charge off diff. | ✎ Editing options | ∅ Cash Disc. Due | Create Dispute Case

Standard | Partial pmt | Res.items | Withhldg tax

Account items 601256 Showroom 1 for SFE1

Document	D.	Docume	P	Busi	Day	CAD Gross	Cash discnt	CashD
1400000000	DZ	20.05.2...	06		0	200.00		
1400000001	DZ	20.05.2...	06		0	500.00		
1800000000	DR	10.05.2...	01		4-	2,000.00		
1800000002	DR	15.05.2...	01		14-	1,240.00	37.20	3.000
1800000003	DR	18.05.2...	01		14-	7,890.00	236.70	3.000

◄ ►

🔍 ▣ ▣ ▣ 🖶 ▽ ▥ ▥ Amo_ | ▦ Gross<>_ | ▦ Currency | ↑ Items | ↓ Items | ↑ Disc. | ↓ Disc.

Editing status

Number of items	5	Amount entered	1,960.00
Display from item	1	Assigned	2,000.00
Reason code		Difference postings	
Display in clearing currency		Not assigned	40.00-

Fig 6

215

When we try to simulate it this time, we find SAP determined the difference to post to the underpayment account from configuration as it is within $100:

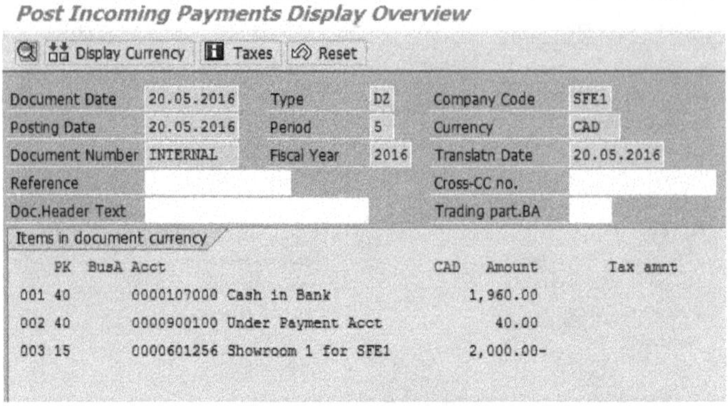

Post Incoming Payments Display Overview

Display Currency | Taxes | Reset

Document Date	20.05.2016	Type	DZ	Company Code	SFE1
Posting Date	20.05.2016	Period	5	Currency	CAD
Document Number	INTERNAL	Fiscal Year	2016	Translatn Date	20.05.2016
Reference				Cross-CC no.	
Doc.Header Text				Trading part.BA	

Items in document currency

PK	BusA	Acct		CAD Amount	Tax amnt
001	40	0000107000	Cash in Bank	1,960.00	
002	40	0000900100	Under Payment Acct	40.00	
003	15	0000601256	Showroom 1 for SFE1	2,000.00-	

Fig 7

Had there been any cash discounts associated with this, it would have first posted to that cash discount and then the remaining balance (subject to the balance being a max of $100, to this underpayment account) as in next section.

We can now post the document:

Document 1400000002 was posted in company code SFE1

Fig 8

When we run the payables again, note there is no balance for this invoice, which we posted against earlier as it wrote off the amount of $ 40

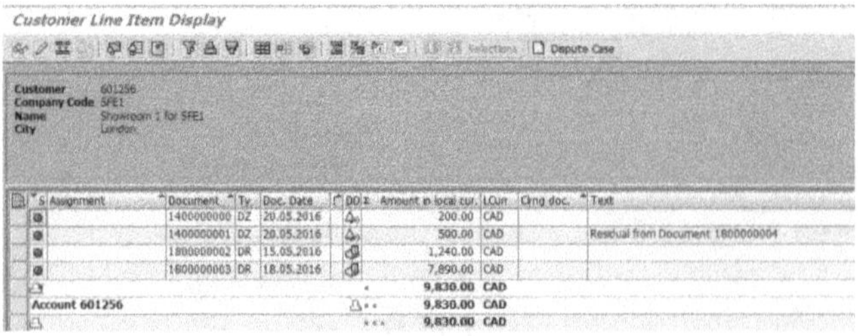

Customer Line Item Display

Customer	601256
Company Code	SFE1
Name	Showroom 1 for SFE1
City	London

S	Assignment	Document	Ty.	Doc. Date	DD	Amount in local cur.	LCur	Clrng doc.	Text
		1400000000	DZ	20.05.2016		200.00	CAD		
		1400000001	DZ	20.05.2016		500.00	CAD		Residual from Document 1800000004
		1800000002	DR	15.05.2016		1,240.00	CAD		
		1800000063	DR	18.05.2016		7,890.00	CAD		
						9,830.00	CAD		
	Account 601256					9,830.00	CAD		
						9,830.00	CAD		

Fig 9

216

III.   POSTING WITH A CASH DISCOUNT AND A DIFFERENCE WITHIN TOLERANCE LIMITS

Line 3 has applicable cash discounts and we can post an amount, which is within tolerance limits after the cash discount has been applied:

Customer	601256												
Company Code	SFE1												
Name	Showroom 1 for SFE1												
City	London												

S	Document	Ty.	Posting Date	PayT	Net due date	Days net	Doc. Date	DD	Σ	Amount in local cur.	Disc.1	Curr. cash disc. amt	Disc.2	LCurr	G/L Account
	1400000000	DZ	20.05.2016		20.05.2016	0	20.05.2016			200.00	0.000	0.00	0.000	CAD	121000
	1400000001	DZ	20.05.2016		20.05.2016	0	20.05.2016			500.00	0.000	0.00	0.000	CAD	121000
	1800000002	DR	20.05.2016	0004	19.07.2016	60	15.05.2016			1,240.00	3.000	37.20	1.000	CAD	121000
	1800000003	DR	20.05.2016	0004	19.07.2016	60	18.05.2016			7,890.00	3.000	236.70	1.000	CAD	121000
									*	9,830.00				CAD	
Account 601256									***	9,830.00				CAD	
									***	9,830.00				CAD	

Fig 10

Post Incoming Payments: Header Data

Process open items

Document Date	200516	Type	DZ	Company Code	SFE1	
Posting Date	20.05.2016	Period		Currency/Rate	cad	
Document Number				Translatn Date		
Reference				Cross-CC no.		
Doc.Header Text				Trading part.BA		
Clearing text						

Bank data

Account	107000	Business Area	
Amount	1150	Amount in LC	
Bank charges		LC bank charges	
Value date		Profit Center	
Text		Assignment	

Open item selection			Additional selections	
Account	601256		◉ None	
Account Type	D	☐ Other accounts	○ Amount	
Special G/L ind		☑ Standard OIs	○ Document Number	

Fig 11

217

As before, we select the appropriate line:

Post Incoming Payments Process open items

Document	D.	Docume	P.	Busi.	Day	CAD Gross	Cash discnt	CashD
1400000000	DZ	20.05.2...	06		0	200.00		
1400000001	DZ	20.05.2...	06		0	500.00		
1800000002	DR	15.05.2...	01		14-	1,240.00	37.20	3.000
1800000003	DR	18.05.2...	01		14-	7,890.00	236.70	3.000

Editing status

Number of items	4	Amount entered	1,150.00
Display from item	1	Assigned	1,202.80
Reason code		Difference postings	
Display in clearing currency		Not assigned	52.80-

Fig 12

Note the difference, which is still unaccounted for after applying the cash discount. However, since this is within the tolerance limits, let us try to simulate this after allocating the difference:

Amount entered	1,150.00
Assigned	1,202.80
Difference postings	52.80-
Not assigned	0.00

Fig 13

218

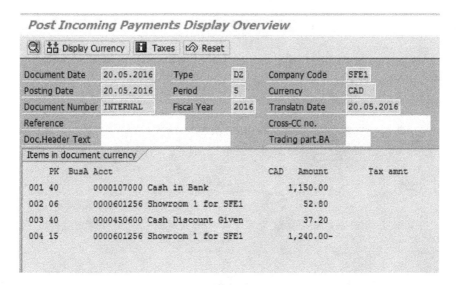

Fig 14

We now find SAP returning with the G/L for cash discount given and posts the balance back into the customer A/R.

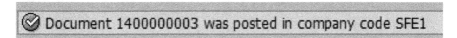

Fig 15

The invoice now has a balance of 52.80 still showing as receivable from the customer:

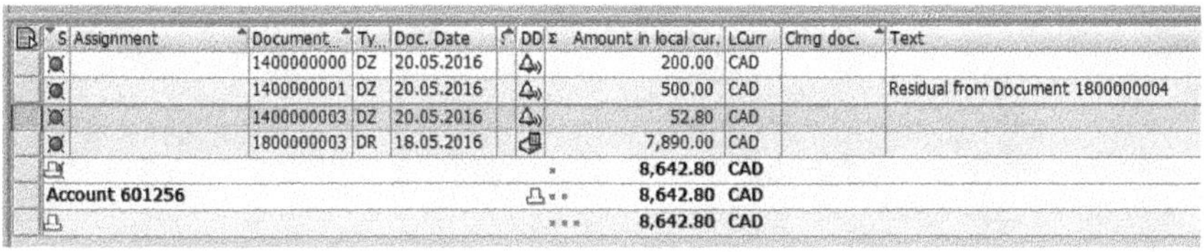

S	Assignment	Document	Ty	Doc. Date	DD	Σ Amount in local cur.	LCurr	Clrng doc.	Text
		1400000000	DZ	20.05.2016		200.00	CAD		
		1400000001	DZ	20.05.2016		500.00	CAD		Residual from Document 1800000004
		1400000003	DZ	20.05.2016		52.80	CAD		
		1800000003	DR	18.05.2016		7,890.00	CAD		
						8,642.80	CAD		
	Account 601256					8,642.80	CAD		
						8,642.80	CAD		

Fig 16

IV.   OVERPAYMENT WITH CASH DISCOUNT

Let us attempt to post against an invoice an amount that will leave a difference more than the max permissible after the applicable cash discount is applied:

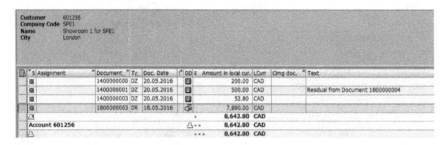

Fig 17

Post Incoming Payments: Header Data

| Process open items |

Document Date	250516	Type	DZ	Company Code	SFE1
Posting Date	25.05.2016	Period	5	Currency/Rate	CAD
Document Number				Translatn Date	
Reference				Cross-CC no.	
Doc.Header Text				Trading part.BA	
Clearing text					

Bank data

Account	107000	Business Area	
Amount	7900	Amount in LC	
Bank charges		LC bank charges	
Value date		Profit Center	
Text		Assignment	

Open item selection			Additional selections	
Account	601256		⦿ None	
Account Type	D	☐ Other accounts	○ Amount	
Special G/L ind		✔ Standard OIs	○ Document Number	
Pmnt advice no.			○ Posting Date	
☐ Distribute by age			○ Dunning Area	
☐ Automatic search			○ Others	

Fig 18

220

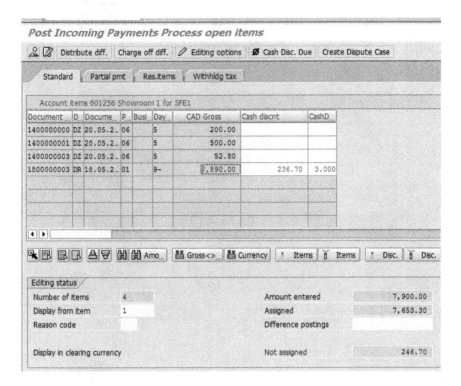

Fig 19

When we try to simulate this:

Fig 20

Once again, the difference being over the employee tolerance we have defined, we cannot post this over payment.

We reduce the amount that is being paid so that the not assigned amount is reduced to under the tolerance:

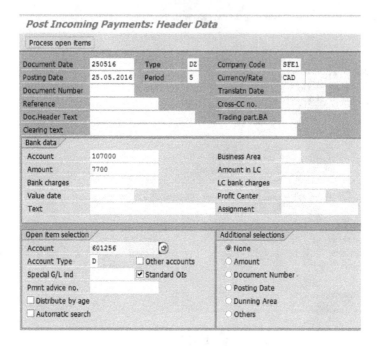

Fig 21

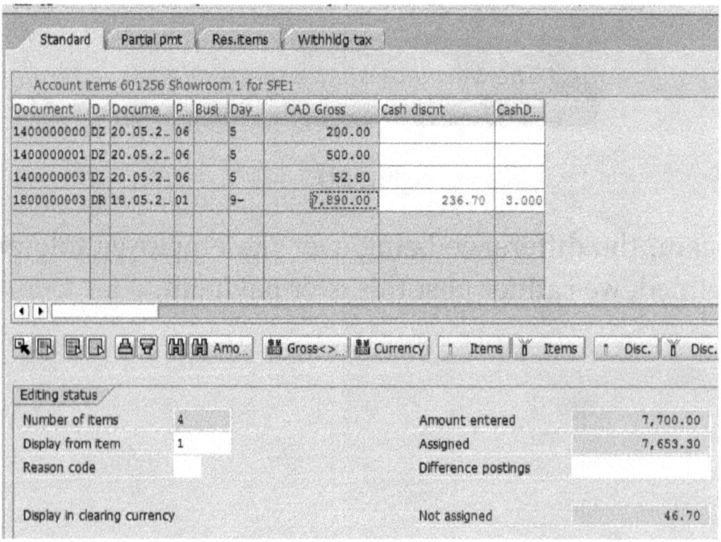

Fig 22

We notice the unassigned difference after adjusting the cash discount is being posted to the over payment account

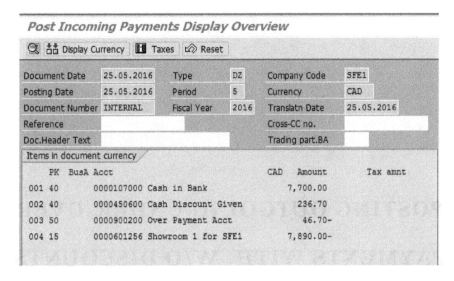

Fig 23

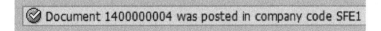

Fig 24

POSTING OUTGOING UNDER/OVER PAYMENTS WITH, W/O DISCOUNTS (U)

T Code F-53

Let us now post an outgoing payment to a vendor within tolerance limits using F-53:

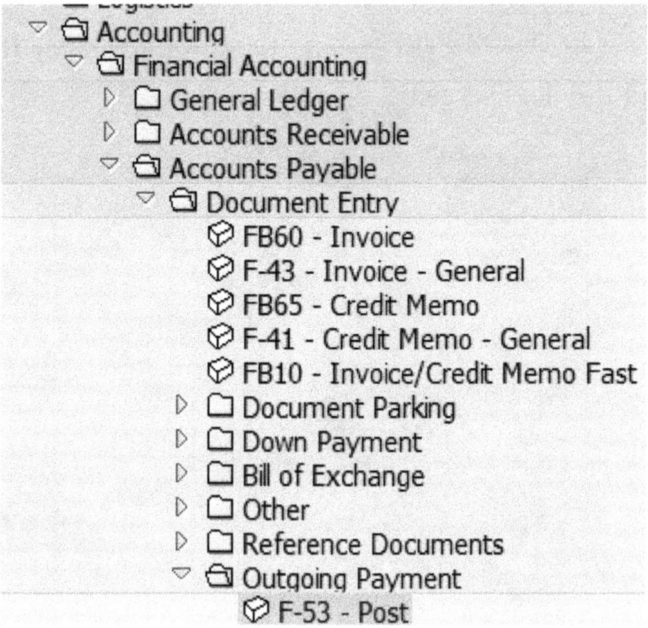

Fig 1

I. EFFECT OF TOLERANCE LIMITS:

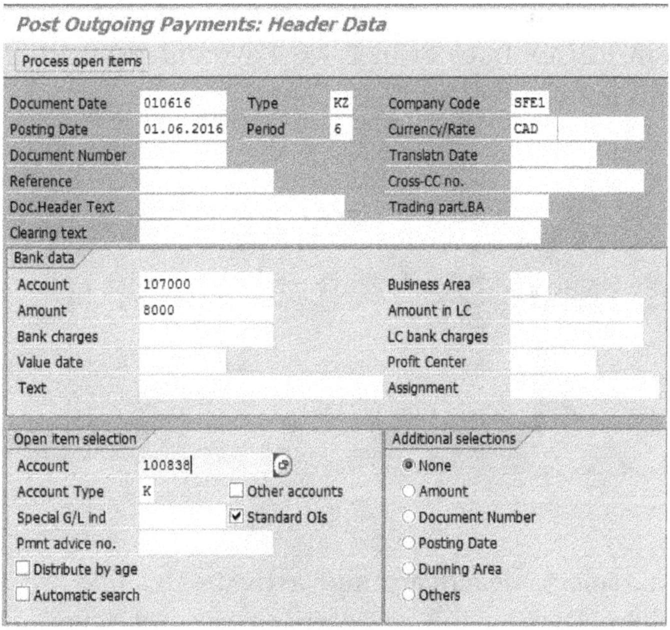

Fig 2

Click on Process open items and the vendor's open line items come up in the next screen:

Post Outgoing Payments Process open items

Distribute diff. | Charge off diff. | Editing options | Cash Disc. Due

Standard | Partial pmt | Res.items | Withhldg tax

Account items 100838 Wood vendor for SFE1

Document	D	Docume	P	Busi	Day	CAD Gross	Cash discnt	CashD
1900000000	KR	10.05.2..	31		12-	1,500.00-	30.00-	2.000
1900000001	KR	10.05.2..	31		12-	1,200.00-	24.00-	2.000
1900000002	KR	10.05.2..	31		12-	1,100.00-	22.00-	2.000
1900000004	KR	28.05.2..	31		28-	1,450.00-	30.81-	2.125
1900000011	KR	28.05.2..	31		28-	1,230.00-	26.14-	2.125
1900000016	KR	10.01.2..	31		143	8,500.00-		
1900000017	KR	20.01.2..	31		133	12,800.00-		
1900000018	KR	15.01.2..	31		138	4,500.00-		

Amo... | Gross<> | Currency | Items | Items | Disc. | Disc

Editing status

Number of items	10	Amount entered	8,000.00-
Display from item	1	Assigned	35,847.05-
Reason code		Difference postings	
Display in clearing currency		Not assigned	27,847.05

Fig 3

Once again, this is reflective of the vendor line item balance in FBL1N, except documents that may have already been selected in a payment run but have not yet processed. In that case, they still show up in FBL1N but not in F-53. Payment runs are discussed later in this manual.

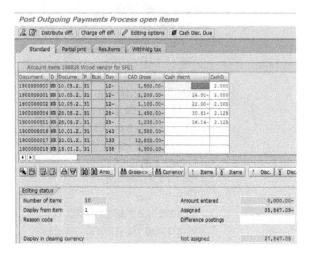

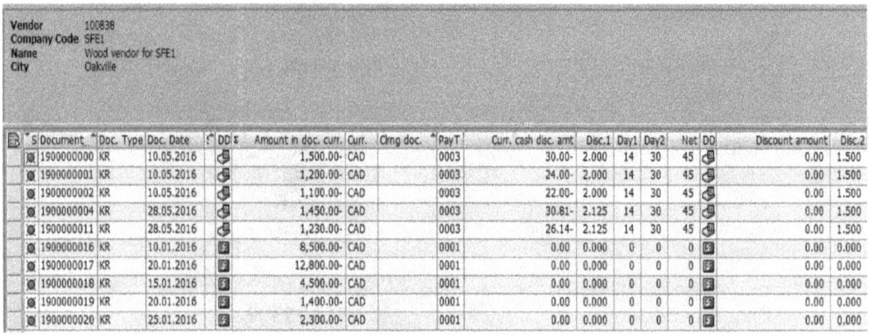

Vendor 100838
Company Code SFE1
Name Wood vendor for SFE1
City Oakville

S	Document	Doc. Type	Doc. Date	DD	Amount in doc. curr.	Curr.	Clrng doc.	PayT	Curr. cash disc. amt	Disc.1	Day1	Day2	Net	DD	Discount amount	Disc.2
	1900000000	KR	10.05.2016		1,500.00-	CAD		0003	30.00-	2.000	14	30	45		0.00	1.500
	1900000001	KR	10.05.2016		1,200.00-	CAD		0003	24.00-	2.000	14	30	45		0.00	1.500
	1900000002	KR	10.05.2016		1,100.00-	CAD		0003	22.00-	2.000	14	30	45		0.00	1.500
	1900000004	KR	28.05.2016		1,450.00-	CAD		0003	30.81-	2.125	14	30	45		0.00	1.500
	1900000011	KR	28.05.2016		1,230.00-	CAD		0003	26.14-	2.125	14	30	45		0.00	1.500
	1900000016	KR	10.01.2016		8,500.00-	CAD		0001	0.00	0.000	0	0	0		0.00	0.000
	1900000017	KR	20.01.2016		12,800.00-	CAD		0001	0.00	0.000	0	0	0		0.00	0.000
	1900000018	KR	15.01.2016		4,500.00-	CAD		0001	0.00	0.000	0	0	0		0.00	0.000
	1900000019	KR	20.01.2016		1,400.00-	CAD		0001	0.00	0.000	0	0	0		0.00	0.000
	1900000020	KR	25.01.2016		2,300.00-	CAD		0001	0.00	0.000	0	0	0		0.00	0.000

Fig 4

As always, select, deactivate and activate the line we will post against, here the line of 5,500 that does not have a discount available for early payments:

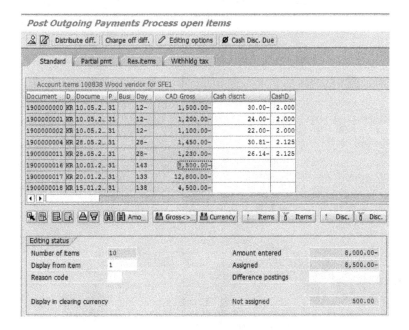

Fig 5

Since we are paying a lesser amount than the amount on the invoice, this must be an under payment to the vendor. Let us confirm by trying to simulate the document:

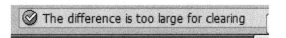

Fig 6

The above message tells us we do not have the authorization to post this document because the difference between the vendor's invoice and the payment we are making is more than what we are authorized for.

II. POSTING AN AMOUNT WITHIN TOLERANCE LIMITS:

Let us attempt the same posting with a bigger amount closer to the invoice amount:

Post Outgoing Payments Process open items

   | Distribute diff. | Charge off diff. | ✎ Editing options | Ø Cash Disc. Due

| Standard | Partial pmt | Res.items | Withhldg tax |

Account items 100838 Wood vendor for SFE1

Document	D	Docume	P	Busi	Day	CAD Gross	Cash discnt	CashD
1900000000	KR	10.05.2...	31		12–	1,500.00–	30.00–	2.000
1900000001	KR	10.05.2...	31		12–	1,200.00–	24.00–	2.000
1900000002	KR	10.05.2...	31		12–	1,100.00–	22.00–	2.000
1900000004	KR	28.05.2...	31		28–	1,450.00–	30.81–	2.125
1900000011	KR	28.05.2...	31		28–	1,230.00–	26.14–	2.125
1900000016	KR	10.01.2...	31		143	8,500.00–		
1900000017	KR	20.01.2...	31		133	12,800.00–		
1900000018	KR	15.01.2...	31		138	4,500.00–		

| Amo... | Gross<>... | Currency | ↑ Items | ↥ Items | ↑ Disc. | ↥ Disc. |

Editing status				
Number of items	10		Amount entered	8,450.00–
Display from item	1		Assigned	8,500.00–
Reason code			Difference postings	
Display in clearing currency			Not assigned	50.00

Fig 7

Simulate the posting:

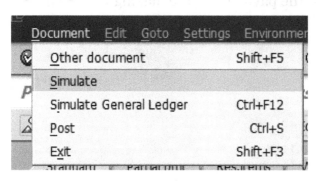

Document	Edit	Goto	Settings	Environmen
Other document				Shift+F5
Simulate				
Simulate General Ledger				Ctrl+F12
Post				Ctrl+S
Exit				Shift+F3

Fig 8

Post Outgoing Payments Display Overview

🔍 ⊟⊟ Display Currency ⬛ Taxes ↺ Reset

Document Date	01.06.2016	Type	KZ	Company Code	SFE1
Posting Date	01.06.2016	Period	6	Currency	CAD
Document Number	INTERNAL	Fiscal Year	2016	Translatn Date	01.06.2016
Reference				Cross-CC no.	
Doc.Header Text				Trading part.BA	

Items in document currency

	PK	BusA	Acct		CAD Amount	Tax amnt
001	50		0000107000	Cash in Bank	8,450.00-	
002	50		0000900200	Over Payment Acct	50.00-	
003	25		0000100838	Wood vendor for SFE	8,500.00	

D 8,500.00   C 8,500.00   0.00 *   3 Line items

Other line item

PstKy		@count		SGL Ind	TType		New co.code	

Fig 9

We see the difference is being posted to the over payment account as a credit (posting key 50) to the over payment account it determined from the configuration. This is counter intuitive – it hits the over payment account because it is a 'profit' to the customer i.e. SFE1 (same as an overpayment would be to us from our customer).

Post the document and the vendor's payable report clears this document completely:

✓ Document 1500000000 was posted in company code SFE1

Fig 10

Vendor   100838
Company Code   SFE1
Name   Wood vendor for SFE1
City   Oakville

S Document	Doc. Type	Doc. Date	DD E.	Amount in doc. curr.	Curr.	Clrng doc.	PayT	Curr. cash doc. amt	Disc.1	Day1	Day2	Net DD	Discount amount	Disc.2
1900000090	KR	10.05.2016		1,300.00-	CAD		0003	30.60-	2.000	14	30	45	0.00	1.500
1900000091	KR	10.05.2016		1,200.00-	CAD		0003	24.00-	2.000	14	30	45	0.00	1.500
1900000092	KR	18.05.2016		1,100.00-	CAD		0003	22.00-	2.000	14	30	45	0.00	1.500
1900000094	KR	18.05.2016		1,450.00-	CAD		0003	30.81-	2.125	14	30	45	0.00	1.500
1900000011	KR	18.05.2016		1,230.00-	CAD		0003	26.14-	2.125	14	30	45	0.00	1.500
1900000017	KX	20.01.2016		12,800.00-	CAD		0001	0.00	0.000	0	0	0	0.00	0.000
1900000018	KR	15.01.2016		4,500.00-	CAD		0001	0.00	0.000	0	0	0	0.00	0.000
1900000019	KR	20.01.2016		1,400.00-	CAD		0001	0.00	0.000	0	0	0	0.00	0.000
1900000020	KR	25.01.2016		2,300.00-	CAD		0001	0.00	0.000	0	0	0	0.00	0.000
				27,480.00- CAD										

Fig 11

III. POSTING WITH CASH DISCOUNT AND UNDERPAYING THE VENDOR

In F-53 enter the amount we will pay the vendor:

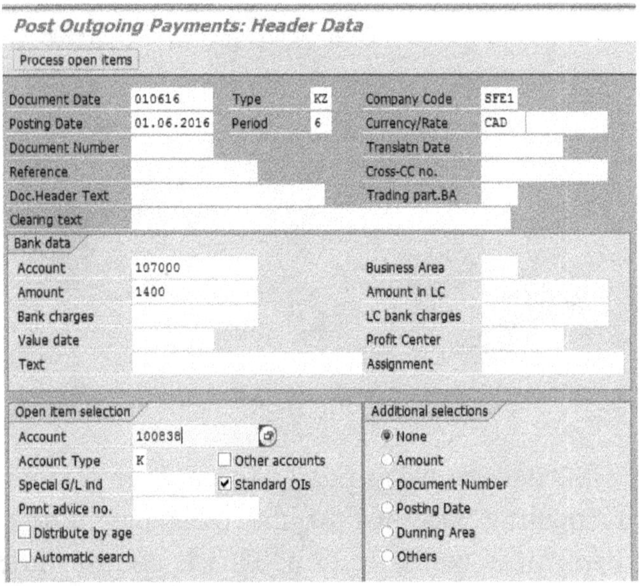

Post Outgoing Payments: Header Data

Process open items

Document Date	010616	Type	KZ	Company Code	SFE1	
Posting Date	01.06.2016	Period	6	Currency/Rate	CAD	
Document Number				Translatn Date		
Reference				Cross-CC no.		
Doc.Header Text				Trading part.BA		
Clearing text						

Bank data

Account	107000	Business Area	
Amount	1400	Amount in LC	
Bank charges		LC bank charges	
Value date		Profit Center	
Text		Assignment	

Open item selection

		Additional selections
Account	100838	● None
Account Type	K ☐ Other accounts	○ Amount
Special G/L ind	☑ Standard OIs	○ Document Number
Pmnt advice no.		○ Posting Date
☐ Distribute by age		○ Dunning Area
☐ Automatic search		○ Others

Fig 12

Process Open Items:

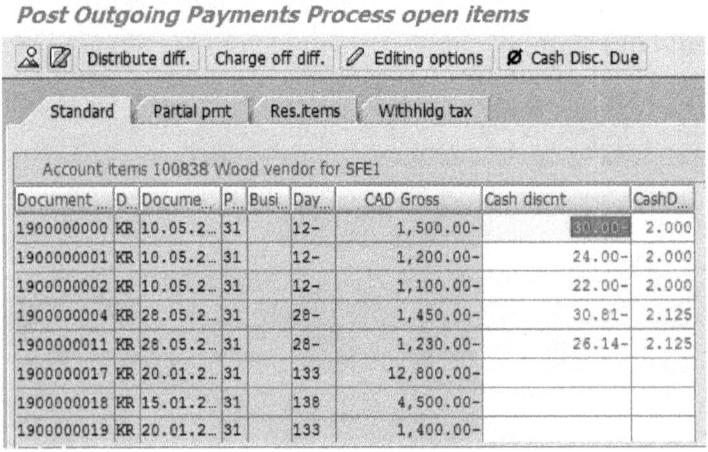

Post Outgoing Payments Process open items

👤 📝 Distribute diff. | Charge off diff. | ✏ Editing options | ∅ Cash Disc. Due

Standard | Partial pmt | Res.items | Withhldg tax

Account items 100838 Wood vendor for SFE1

Document	D	Docume	P	Busi	Day	CAD Gross	Cash discnt	CashD
1900000000	KR	10.05.2...	31		12-	1,500.00-	30.00-	2.000
1900000001	KR	10.05.2...	31		12-	1,200.00-	24.00-	2.000
1900000002	KR	10.05.2...	31		12-	1,100.00-	22.00-	2.000
1900000004	KR	28.05.2...	31		28-	1,450.00-	30.81-	2.125
1900000011	KR	28.05.2...	31		28-	1,230.00-	26.14-	2.125
1900000017	KR	20.01.2...	31		133	12,800.00-		
1900000018	KR	15.01.2...	31		138	4,500.00-		
1900000019	KR	20.01.2...	31		133	1,400.00-		

Fig 13

Let us assume the first invoice below is being paid off with this amount of $1,400 The invoice is $1,500 and since we are paying within 30 days, as per the terms, we are also entitled to a cash discount of 2 % = $30.

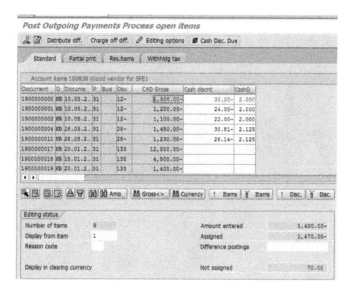

Fig 14

The Not Assigned amount of $70.00 will then be required to post to the over payment account. Let us simulate this event:

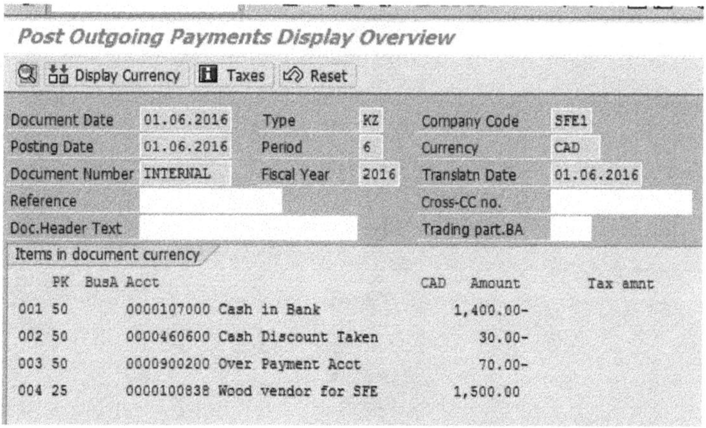

Post Outgoing Payments Display Overview

Display Currency | Taxes | Reset

Document Date	01.06.2016	Type	KZ	Company Code	SFE1
Posting Date	01.06.2016	Period	6	Currency	CAD
Document Number	INTERNAL	Fiscal Year	2016	Translatn Date	01.06.2016
Reference				Cross-CC no.	
Doc.Header Text				Trading part.BA	

Items in document currency

PK	BusA	Acct		CAD	Amount	Tax amnt
001 50		0000107000	Cash in Bank		1,400.00-	
002 50		0000460600	Cash Discount Taken		30.00-	
003 50		0000900200	Over Payment Acct		70.00-	
004 25		0000100838	Wood vendor for SFE		1,500.00	

Fig 15

Post:

Document 1500000001 was posted in company code SFE1

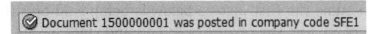

Fig 16

The AP statement removes the line altogether:

Vendor 100838
Company Code SFE1
Name Wood vendor for SFE1
City Oakville

S	Document	Doc. Type	Doc. Date	DD	Amount in doc. curr.	Curr.	Clrng doc.	PayT	Curr. cash disc. amt	Disc.1	Day1	Day2	Net
	1900000001	KR	10.05.2016		1,200.00-	CAD		0003	24.00-	2.000	14	30	45
	1900000002	KR	10.05.2016		1,100.00-	CAD		0003	22.00-	2.000	14	30	45
	1900000004	KR	28.05.2016		1,450.00-	CAD		0003	30.81-	2.125	14	30	45
	1900000011	KR	28.05.2016		1,230.00-	CAD		0003	26.14-	2.125	14	30	45
	1900000017	KR	20.01.2016		12,800.00-	CAD		0001	0.00	0.000	0	0	0
	1900000018	KR	15.01.2016		4,500.00-	CAD		0001	0.00	0.000	0	0	0
	1900000019	KR	20.01.2016		1,400.00-	CAD		0001	0.00	0.000	0	0	0
	1900000020	KR	25.01.2016		2,300.00-	CAD		0001	0.00	0.000	0	0	0
					25,980.00-	**CAD**							
	Account 100838				**25,980.00-**	**CAD**							
					25,980.00-	**CAD**							

Fig 17

HANDLING DOWN PAYMENTS TO

VENDORS (C/U)

Down payments (aka advance payments) are often used to pay vendors for turnkey projects or asset purchases. These are treated differently in SAP compared to normal vendor payments for trade payables. Down payments made to vendors remain on the book as current assets till adjusted/cleared against the actual invoice.

    I.   Define Reconciliation Account for Vendor Down Payment
    II.   Making the Down Payment to Vendor
    III.   Displaying the Balances for confirmation of postings
    IV.   Receiving the Invoice against Down Payment made
    V.   Displaying the balances
    VI.   Clearing the Down Payment made
   VII.   Displaying the Balances for confirmation of postings
VIII.   Clear the Vendor's Account

I is a one- time configuration, the rest are all transactions. II, IV, VI and VIII are the actual postings in the process. III, V and VII are included only to confirm the process is going well.

All are discussed in sequence.

I.   DEFINE RECONCILIATION ACCOUNT FOR VENDOR DOWN PAYMENT (C)

T Code SPRO

They require their own reconciliation account, under the normal payables one for reporting separately on the Balance sheet.

Like the customer or vendor reconciliation accounts, this down payment reconciliation, account is also a configuration; to do that, follow the path:

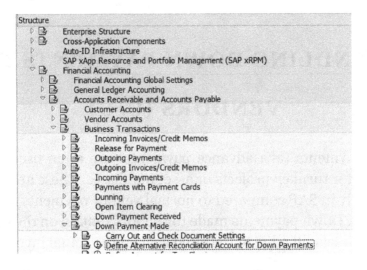

Fig 1

Maintain Accounting Configuration : Special G/L - List

Acct Type	SGL Ind.	Name	Description
K	1	Down pa	Down pyt req
K	A	Dwn p...	Down payment on current assets
K	B	Financi	Financial assets down payment
K	F	Pmt req	Down payment request
K	I	Dwn p...	Intangible asset down payment
K	M	Dwn p...	Tangible asset down payment
K	O	Amortiz	Amortization down payment
K	R	Revenue	Revenue Vendors - Reco
K	V	Dwn p...	Stocks down payment
K	Z	Dwn p...	Dwn Pmt for Order/Project

Fig 2

234

Double click on the line corresponding to the current assets (the only one we will define here) and enter your CoA in the window that pops up:

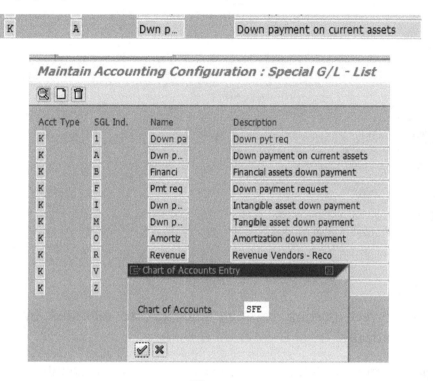

Fig 3

Let's say we use 213000 as this sp G/L account to capture these down payments:

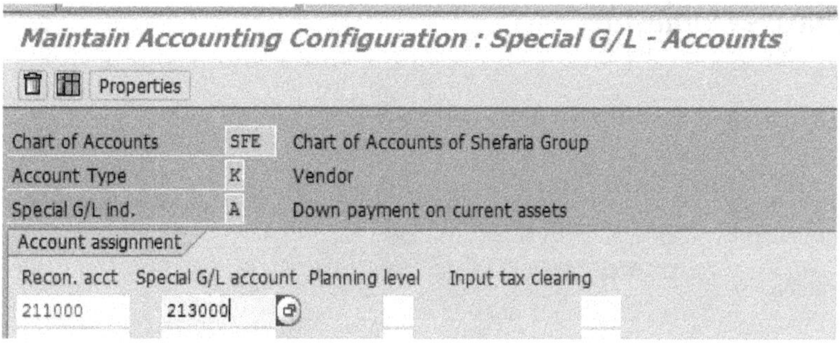

Fig 4

Save the data in the transport.

Next, to ensure it is properly configured, click on Properties:

Properties to verify the correct posting keys are there:

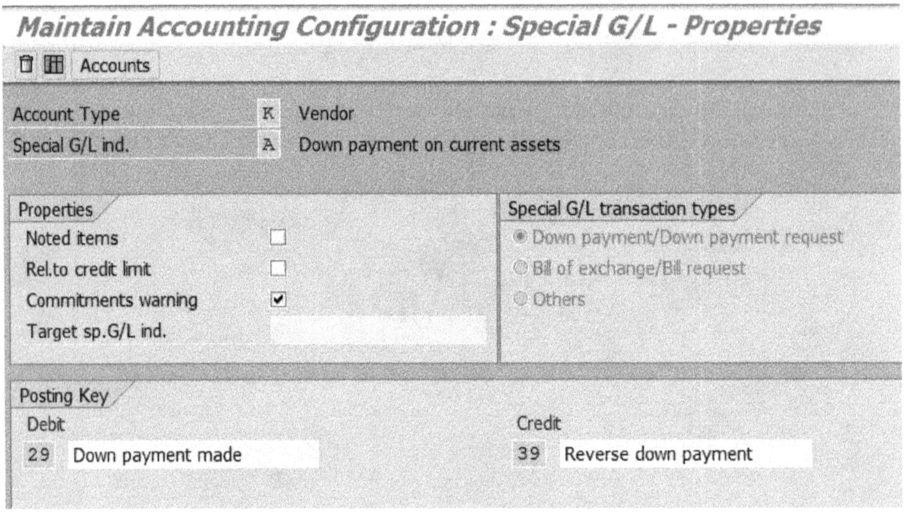

Maintain Accounting Configuration : Special G/L - Properties

⎌ ▦ Accounts

Account Type	K	Vendor
Special G/L ind.	A	Down payment on current assets

Properties		Special G/L transaction types
Noted items	☐	◉ Down payment/Down payment request
Rel.to credit limit	☐	○ Bill of exchange/Bill request
Commitments warning	☑	○ Others
Target sp.G/L ind.		

Posting Key		
Debit		Credit
29 Down payment made		39 Reverse down payment

Fig 5

The correct posting keys 29 and 39 are allocated by SAP automatically.

Next step is to define these reconciliation G/L accounts 211000 and 213000 in your co code as you did the other G/L accounts, bearing in mind these are Balance sheet accounts. Both will be reconciliation accounts, we will use 213000 as the account for *Trade Payables - Special purchases* and 211000 for *Trade Payables – Domestic.*

236

II. MAKING THE DOWN PAYMENT TO THE VENDOR (U)

T Code F-48

Now that we have configured the down payment account, we are ready to make a down payment to a vendor – that down payment will be held as a current assets till settled.

The T Code to make down payments is F-48 or follow the menu path:

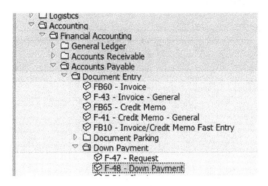

Fig 6

The screen opens like this:

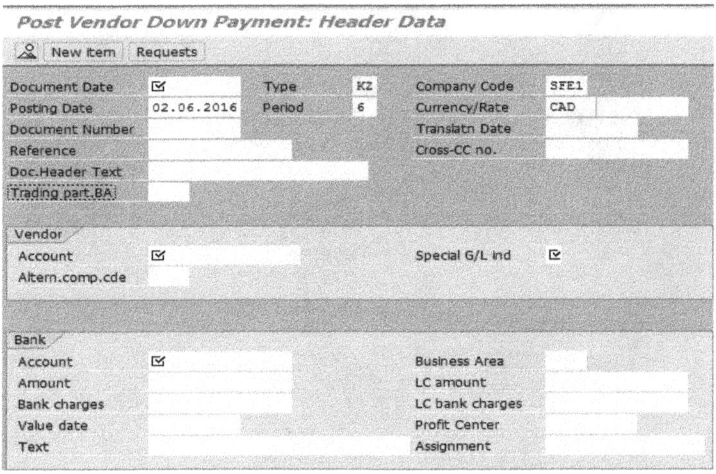

Fig 7

Enter the following information:

- Date
- Vendor account
- Bank GL account # which will hold this down payment and the value date if mandatory. This date belongs to Treasury to monitor cash requirements and availability
- CC
- Amount and currency
- The Spl acct indicator will be 'A' which is SAP standard for Down Payment:

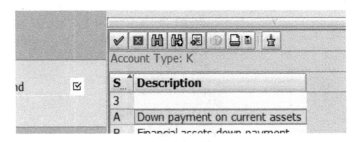

Fig 8

Enter the data as below to post this down payment. Notes can also be entered to describe the nature/reason for this payment.

Post Vendor Down Payment: Header Data

New Item   Requests

Document Date	010616	Type	KZ	Company Code	SFE1
Posting Date	02.06.2016	Period	6	Currency/Rate	CAD
Document Number				Translatn Date	
Reference				Cross-CC no.	
Doc.Header Text					
Trading part.BA					

Vendor
| Account | 100838 | | | Special G/L ind | A |
| Altern.comp.cde | | | | | |

Bank
Account	107000			Business Area	
Amount	10000			LC amount	
Bank charges				LC bank charges	
Value date				Profit Center	
Text	Down Payment for HVAC system			Assignment	

Fig 9

Hit Enter and the system takes us to the next screen:

Enter the amount or a * which is all this screen requires:

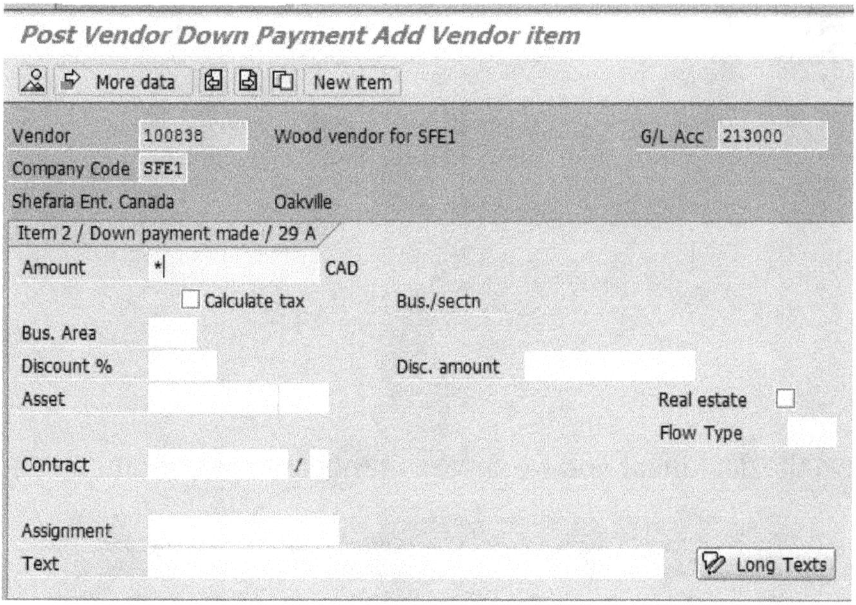

Post Vendor Down Payment Add Vendor item

  More data   New item

| Vendor | 100838 | Wood vendor for SFE1 | G/L Acc | 213000 |

Company Code SFE1

Shefaria Ent. Canada   Oakville

Item 2 / Down payment made / 29 A

| Amount | *| | CAD |

☐ Calculate tax   Bus./sectn

Bus. Area

| Discount % | | Disc. amount | |

Asset   Real estate ☐

                                   Flow Type

Contract   /

Assignment

Text   Long Texts

Fig 10

Note how SAP found the G/L account 213000 by itself to post to for reconciliation. It found it from the configuration we did earlier.

Now we have the option again to simulate this document for any errors before posting it:

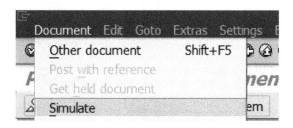

Fig 11

239

If everything looks fine:

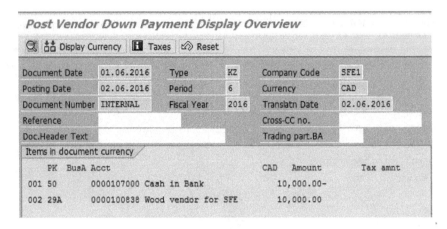

Fig 12

Save the document and we get the number at the bottom:

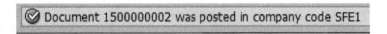

Fig 13

III. DISPLAYING THE BALANCES FOR CONFIRMATION OF POSTINGS (U)

T Code FK10N

We can now display the balances in the vendor account via the transaction FK10N or the path:

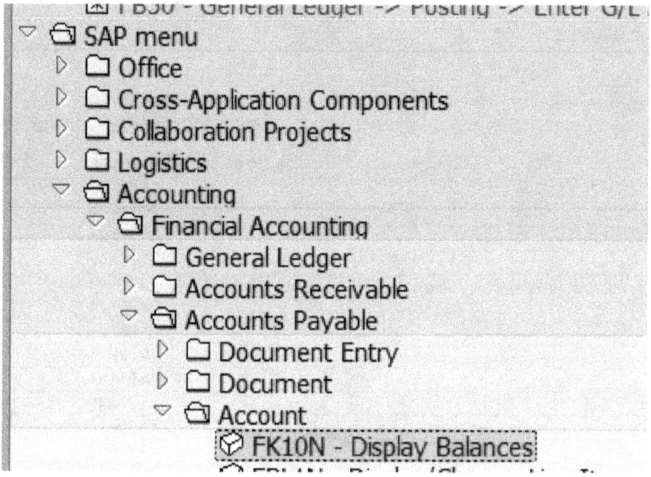

Fig 14

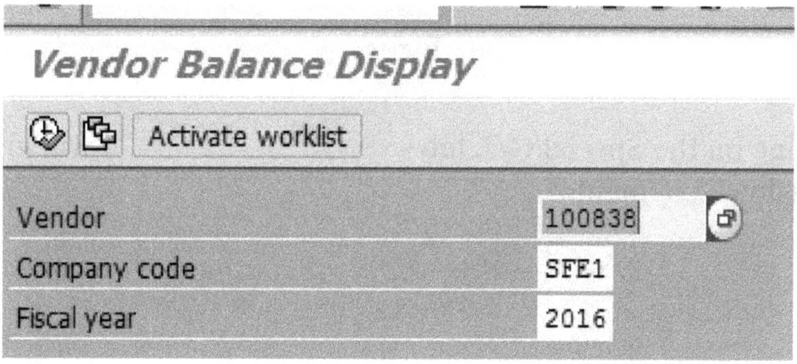

Fig 15

Execute and the results give all the balances against this vendor:
The default screen will show the normal transaction balances:

	Vendor Balance Display

Vendor   100838   Wood vendor for SFE1
Company Code   SFE1   Shefaria Ent. Canada
Fiscal Year   2016
Display crrncy CAD

| Bals | Special G/L |

Period	Debit	Credit	Balance	Cumulative balance	Sales/Purchases
Balance Car.					
1		29,500.00	29,500.00-	29,500.00-	29,500.00-
2				29,500.00-	
3				29,500.00-	
4				29,500.00-	
5		6,480.00	6,480.00-	35,980.00-	6,480.00-
6	10,000.00		10,000.00	25,980.00-	
7				25,980.00-	
8				25,980.00-	
9				25,980.00-	
10				25,980.00-	
11				25,980.00-	
12				25,980.00-	
13				25,980.00-	
14				25,980.00-	
15				25,980.00-	
16				25,980.00-	
Total	10,000.00	35,980.00	25,980.00-	25,980.00-	35,980.00-

Fig 16

Clicking on the Special G/L tab - | Bals | Special G/L | will give us
these down payments:

Vendor   100838   Wood vendor for SFE1
Company Code   SFE1   Shefaria Ent. Canada
Fiscal Year   2016
Display crrncy CAD

| Bals | Special G/L |

Transaction	Bal.Carried Fwd	Debit	Credit	Balance
Down payment on current assets		10,000.00		10,000.00
Total		10,000.00		10,000.00
Account balance		10,000.00	35,980.00	25,980.00-
Total		20,000.00	35,980.00	15,980.00-

Fig 17

As usual, double click on the Total line and you see the detailed breakdown of that balance:

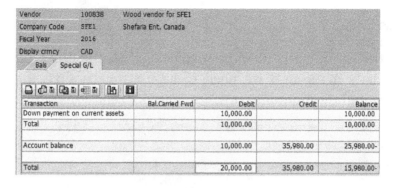

Fig 18

Fig 19

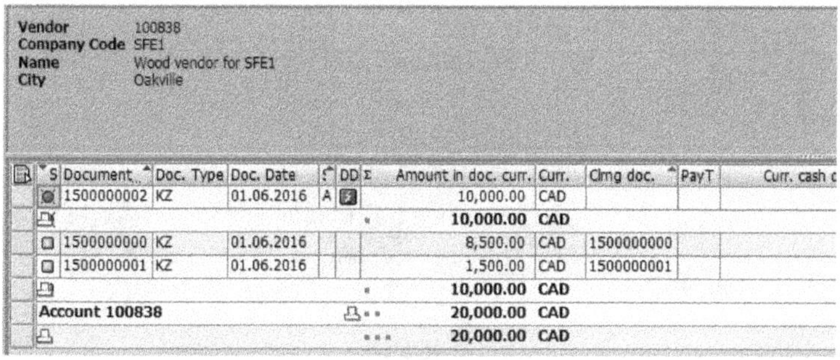

Note the document # we just entered at the top as document type KZ. The letter A is symbolic of the Spl G/L indicator

IV. RECEIVING/BOOKING THE INVOICE AGAINST THE DOWN PAYMENT MADE (U)

T Code FB60

Now, the vendor provides the invoice against the down payment we already made and we need to adjust that against the debit balance in the vendor account.

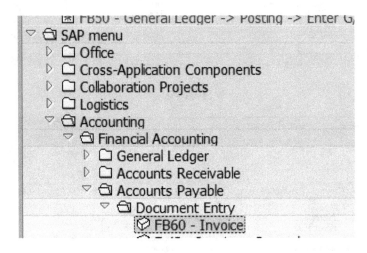

Fig 20

We debit the purchase account

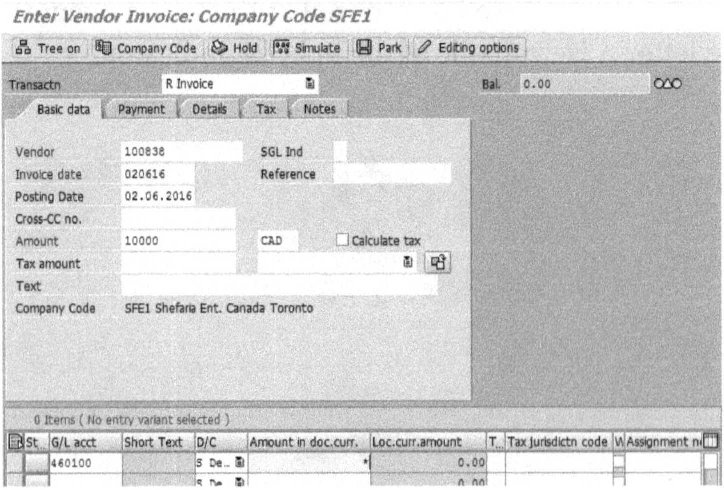

Fig 21

On hitting Enter, we get an information message:

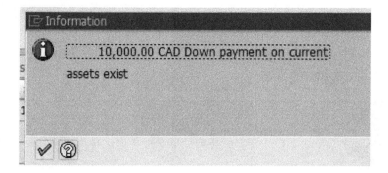

Fig 22

*** This amount shown in the message can be different if multiple down payments have been posted to the vendor account, which have not been cleared yet.

Hit Enter again:

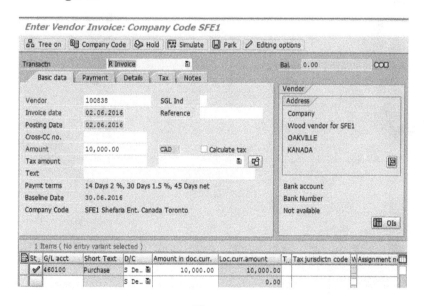

Fig 23

and save it:

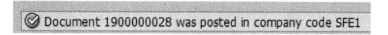

V. DISPLAYING THE BALANCES (U)

T Code FK10N

If you check FK10N again, we notice the payables having gone up with this invoice:

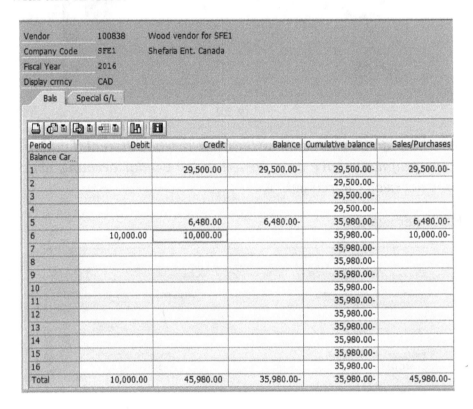

Period	Debit	Credit	Balance	Cumulative balance	Sales/Purchases
Balance Car...					
1		29,500.00	29,500.00-	29,500.00-	29,500.00-
2				29,500.00-	
3				29,500.00-	
4				29,500.00-	
5		6,480.00	6,480.00-	35,980.00-	6,480.00-
6	10,000.00	10,000.00		35,980.00-	10,000.00-
7				35,980.00-	
8				35,980.00-	
9				35,980.00-	
10				35,980.00-	
11				35,980.00-	
12				35,980.00-	
13				35,980.00-	
14				35,980.00-	
15				35,980.00-	
16				35,980.00-	
Total	10,000.00	45,980.00	35,980.00-	35,980.00-	45,980.00-

Vendor 100838 Wood vendor for SFE1
Company Code SFE1 Shefaria Ent. Canada
Fiscal Year 2016
Display crrncy CAD
Bals | Special G/L

Fig 24

VI. Clearing the Down Payment made to Vendor (U)

T Code F-54

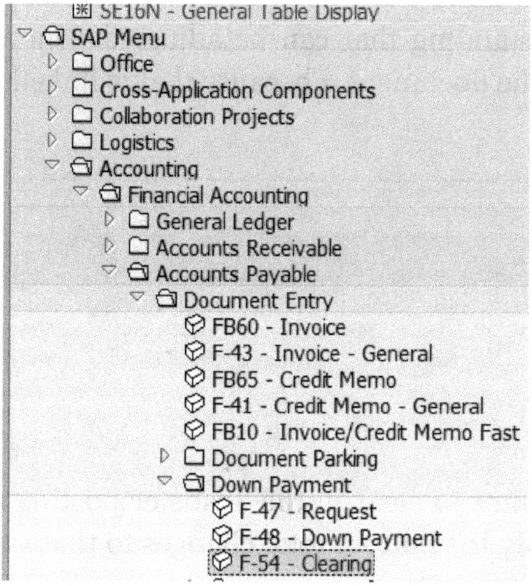

Fig 25

Enter the relevant data:

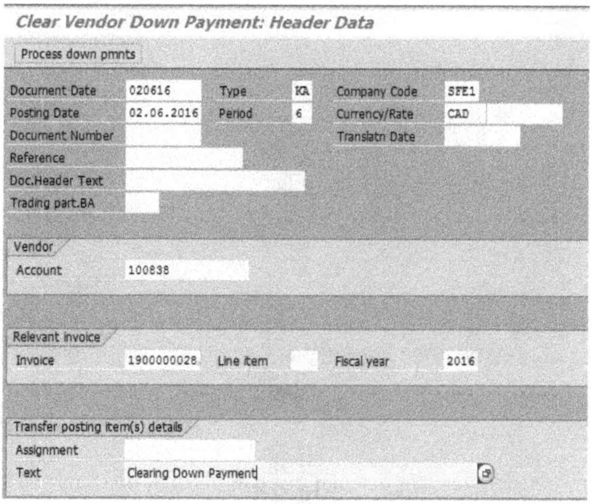

Fig 26

Note the # we use – the posting # we got earlier to say that we will be clearing against this internal document #.

Click on the button 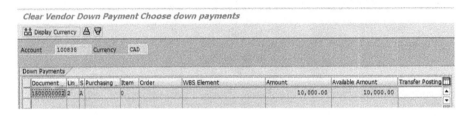 to display the down payments outstanding that can be adjusted – note SAP got the posting from the document # because that is linked to the original document #

Clear Vendor Down Payment Choose down payments

ㅁㅁ Display Currency 🖨 🔽

| Account | 100838 | Currency | CAD | | | | | |

Down Payments

Document	Lin	S	Purchasing	Item	Order	WBS Element	Amount	Available Amount	Transfer Posting
1500000002	2	A		0				10,000.00	10,000.00	

Fig 27

Enter the amount to clear in the Transfer posting column, press Enter and verify the bottom total changes to that same amount in blue:

Clear Vendor Down Payment Choose down payments

ㅁㅁ Display Currency 🖨 🔽

| Account | 100838 | Currency | CAD | | | | | |

Down Payments

Lin	S	Purchasing	Item	Order	WBS Element	Amount	Available Amount	Transfer Posting
2	A		0				10,000.00	10,000.00	10,000.00

| Display item | ▌ / 1 | | Total | 10,000.00 |

Fig 28

248

Again, we can simulate the document:

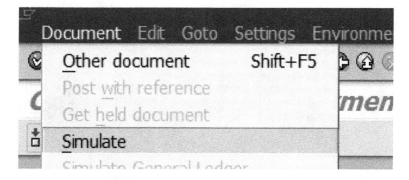

Fig 29

Clear Vendor Down Payment Display Overview

Document Date	02.06.2016	Type	KA	Company Code	SFE1		
Posting Date	02.06.2016	Period	6	Currency	CAD		
Document Number	INTERNAL	Fiscal Year	2016	Translatn Date	02.06.2016		
Reference				Cross-CC no.			
Doc.Header Text				Trading part.BA			

Items in document currency

PK	BusA	Acct		CAD	Amount	Tax amnt
001	39A	0000100838	Wood vendor for SFE		10,000.00-	
002	26	0000100838	Wood vendor for SFE		10,000.00	

Fig 30

If everything looks right, post it by saving it:

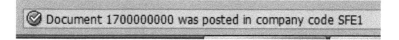

Document 1700000000 was posted in company code SFE1

VII. CHECKING THE BALANCES (U)

T Code FK10N

Click on the tab Special G/L:

Vendor	100838	Wood vendor for SFE1
Company Code	SFE1	Shefaria Ent. Canada
Fiscal Year	2016	
Display crrncy	CAD	

Transaction	Bal.Carried Fwd	Debit	Credit	Balance
Down payment on curre...		10,000.00	10,000.00	
Total		10,000.00	10,000.00	
Account balance		20,000.00	45,980.00	25,980.00-
Total		30,000.00	55,980.00	25,980.00-

Fig 31

We notice that the amount of $10,000 has now moved from the column Balance to Credit in the vendor.

Double click on the Total line:

Vendor	100838
Company Code	SFE1
Name	Wood vendor for SFE1
City	Oakville

S	Document	Doc. Type	Doc. Date	DD	Σ	Amount in doc. curr.	Curr.	Clrng doc.	P
	1700000000	KA	02.06.2016			10,000.00	CAD		
					▪	10,000.00	CAD		
	1500000000	KZ	01.06.2016			8,500.00	CAD	1500000000	
	1500000001	KZ	01.06.2016			1,500.00	CAD	1500000001	
	1500000002	KZ	01.06.2016	A		10,000.00	CAD	1700000000	
					▪	20,000.00	CAD		
Account 100838					▪▪	30,000.00	CAD		
					▪▪▪	30,000.00	CAD		

Fig 32

The 2 highlighted cancelling entries of 10,000 each are revealed above. Note the reference of the clearing document 1700000000 in the document No 1500000002.

VIII. Clearing the Vendor's Account (U)

T Code F-44

This is the last step in the process of down payments – to clear the vendor account. F-44 or follow the path:

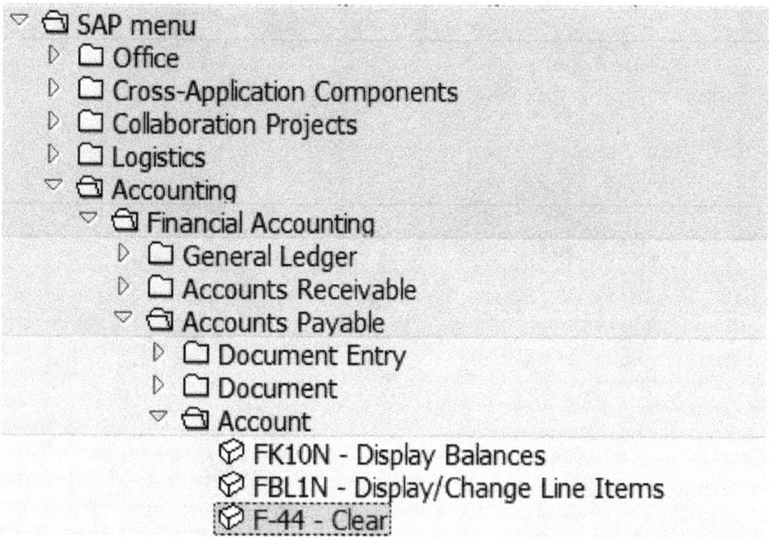

```
▽ 📁 SAP menu
    ▷ 🗀 Office
    ▷ 🗀 Cross-Application Components
    ▷ 🗀 Collaboration Projects
    ▷ 🗀 Logistics
    ▽ 📁 Accounting
        ▽ 📁 Financial Accounting
            ▷ 🗀 General Ledger
            ▷ 🗀 Accounts Receivable
            ▽ 📁 Accounts Payable
                ▷ 🗀 Document Entry
                ▷ 🗀 Document
                ▽ 📁 Account
                    ⊘ FK10N - Display Balances
                    ⊘ FBL1N - Display/Change Line Items
                    ⊘ F-44 - Clear
```

Fig 33

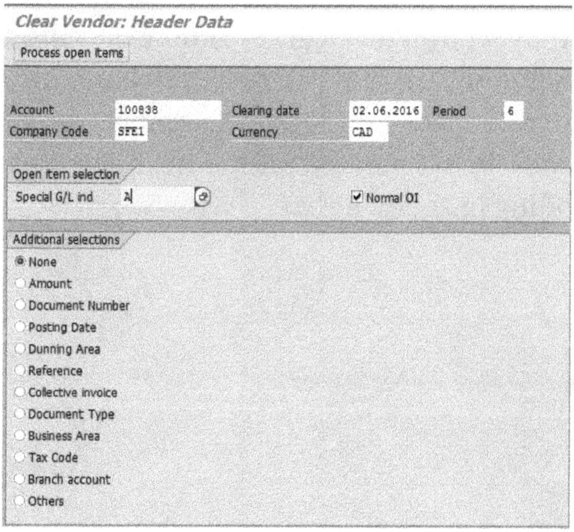

Clear Vendor: Header Data

Process open items

Account	100838	Clearing date	02.06.2016	Period	6
Company Code	SFE1	Currency	CAD		

Open item selection

Special G/L ind	A			☑ Normal OI

Additional selections
- ⦿ None
- ○ Amount
- ○ Document Number
- ○ Posting Date
- ○ Dunning Area
- ○ Reference
- ○ Collective invoice
- ○ Document Type
- ○ Business Area
- ○ Tax Code
- ○ Branch account
- ○ Others

Fig 34

251

Enter the vendor account # as above and click on the tab

Process open items

To display all the invoices pending in the vendor account for clearing.

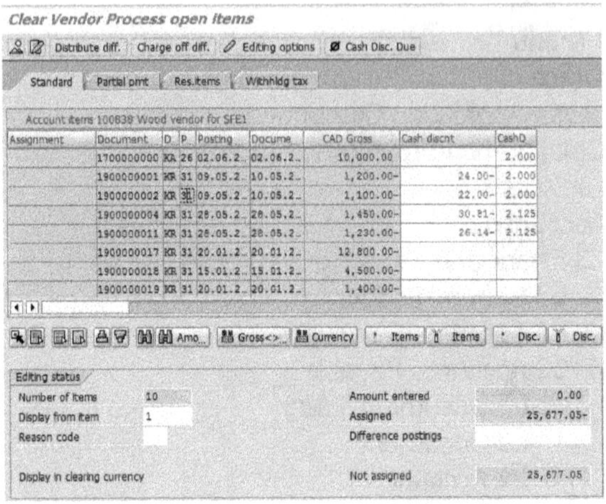

Fig 35

Since there are many entries here, we first need to choose our correct ones that we want to clear. We know they are 1900000028 from the vendor's invoice reference document (FB60) and 1700000002 from clearing (F-54). Therefore, we need to select them first. Some items may be on the next screen so have to be found by scrolling in the right bar.

Select the ones you need to square off:

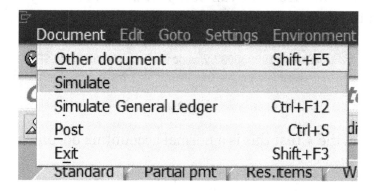

Assignment	Document	D	P	Posting	Docume	CAD Gross	Cash discnt	CashD
	1700000000	KA	26	02.06.2	02.06.2	10,000.00		2.000
	1900000028	KR	31	02.06.2	02.06.2	10,000.00-		

Amo... Gross<> Currency ↑ Items ↓ Items ↑ Disc. ↓ Disc.

Editing status

Number of items	10		Amount entered	0.00
Display from item	9		Assigned	0.00
Reason code			Difference postings	
Display in clearing currency			Not assigned	0.00

Fig 36

Ensure that the not assigned amount is 0 as above.

At this point, we are ready to clear these 2 by saving the posting. This is a special posting, which does not post any line item #s but merely takes them out of the pending reports. This clearing once done, cannot be reversed either and the down payment process needs to begin again if required to. Again, SAP gives us the option to simulate the document:

Document	Edit	Goto	Settings	Environment
Other document				Shift+F5
Simulate				
Simulate General Ledger				Ctrl+F12
Post				Ctrl+S
Exit				Shift+F3
Standard	Partial pmt		Res.items	W

Fig 37

As stated, this simulation screen will have no line items like all the others we saw:

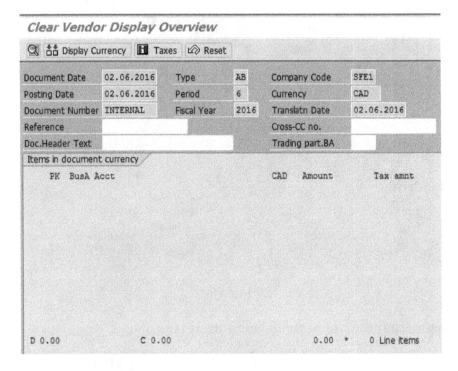

Fig 38

This screen is blank because it creates no line items as the 2 lines are being netted off completely with each other. If there were to be differences of any kind, line items would be created for them. Since SAP showed no errors, we can now post the document by saving it. We get the posting number at the bottom:

Fig 39

Note from the # that this is a normal accounting document.

To verify the posting indeed took place and that the down payment was adjusted against the vendor invoice, we can look up FBL1N:

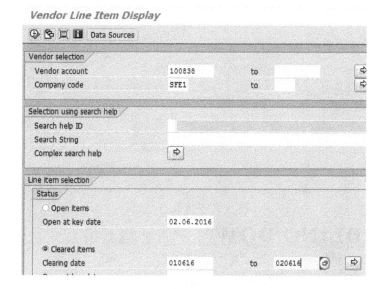

Fig 40

In addition, execute. We see both our documents here:

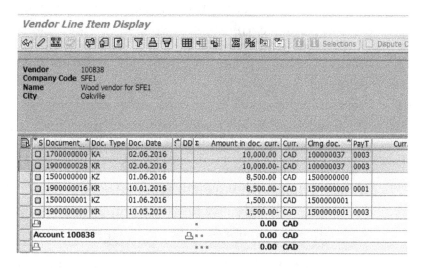

Fig 41

HANDLING DOWN PAYMENTS FROM CUSTOMERS (C/U)

The same way as we pay vendors down payments, customers may also pay us down payments for products like machinery, automobiles etc., primarily the capital expense type purchases.

I. Define Reconciliation Account for Customer Down Payment
II. Receiving the Down Payment from the customer
III. Displaying the Balances for confirmation of postings
IV. Sending the Invoice against Down Payment received
V. Displaying the balances
VI. Clearing the Down Payment received
VII. Displaying the Balances for confirmation of postings
VIII. Clear the Customer's Account

I is a one- time configuration, the rest are all transactions. II, IV, VI and VIII are the actual postings in the process. III, V and VII are included only to confirm the process is going well.

All are discussed in sequence.

I. DEFINE RECONCILIATION ACCOUNT FOR CUSTOMER DOWN PAYMENT (C)

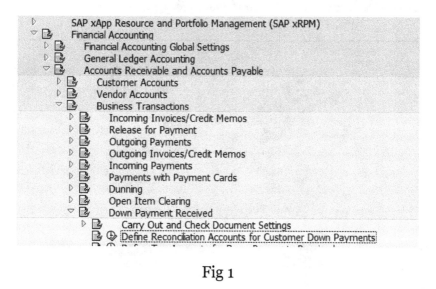

Fig 1

Again the Sp G/L indicator is A:

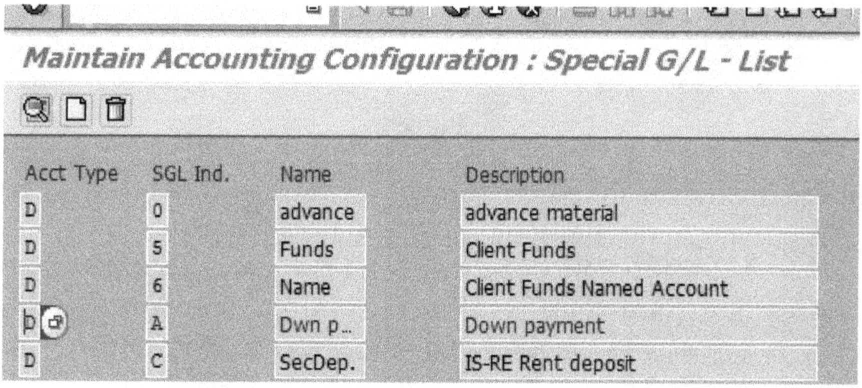

Maintain Accounting Configuration : Special G/L - List

Acct Type	SGL Ind.	Name	Description
D	0	advance	advance material
D	5	Funds	Client Funds
D	6	Name	Client Funds Named Account
D	A	Dwn p..	Down payment
D	C	SecDep.	IS-RE Rent deposit

Fig 2

Double click on it:

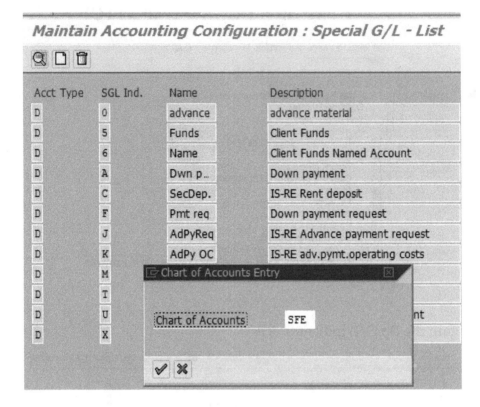

Fig 3

Hit Enter with the following data:

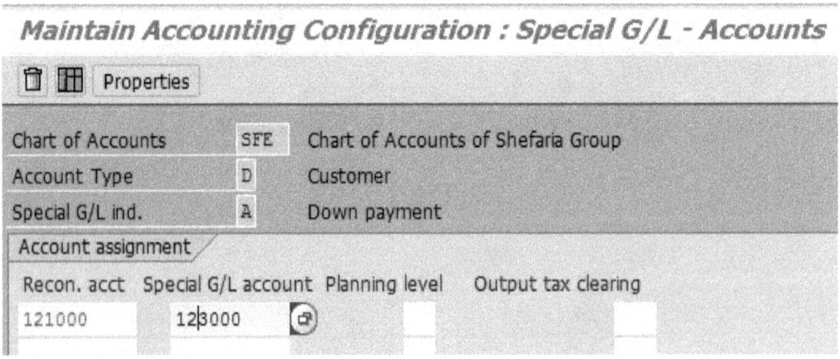

Fig 4

At this point, it is important to ensure the posting keys defined in these accounts are correct. Save the configuration and click on

Properties

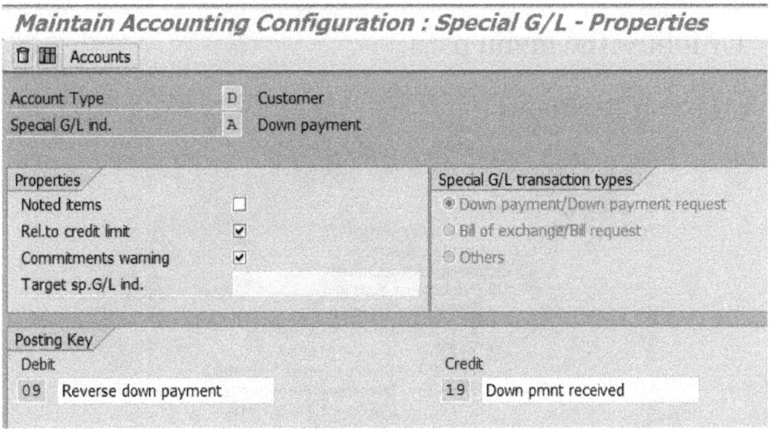

Maintain Accounting Configuration : Special G/L - Properties

Accounts

Account Type	D	Customer
Special G/L ind.	A	Down payment

Properties

Noted items	☐
Rel.to credit limit	☑
Commitments warning	☑
Target sp.G/L ind.	

Special G/L transaction types

- ◉ Down payment/Down payment request
- ○ Bill of exchange/Bill request
- ○ Others

Posting Key

Debit		Credit	
09	Reverse down payment	19	Down pmnt received

Fig 5

We notice that the posting keys are from the range defined for customers. Ensure the 2 G/L accounts 121000 and 123000 exist in the company code in FS00.

II. RECEIVING/BOOKING THE DOWN PAYMENT FROM THE CUSTOMER (U)

T Code F-29

Or follow the menu path:

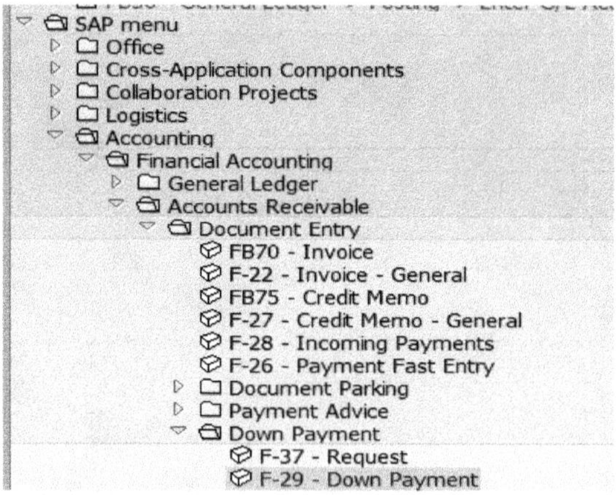

Fig 6

Enter the necessary data as below, notes can also be entered to describe the reason of this payment:

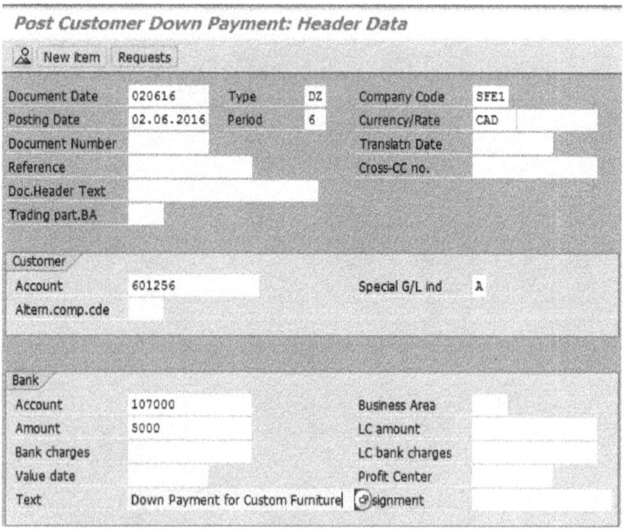

Fig 7

Hit Enter and on the next screen enter the amount again for the contra entry. Note how SAP fetches the G/L account 123000 on it's own based on the configuration we did in the previous step:

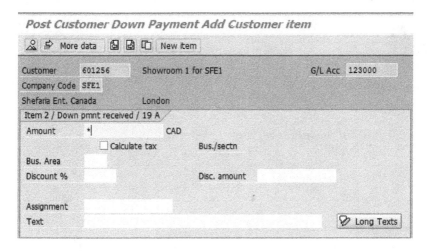

Fig 8

As always, we can simulate the document before posting:

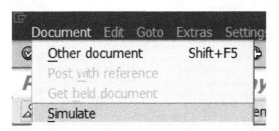

Fig 9

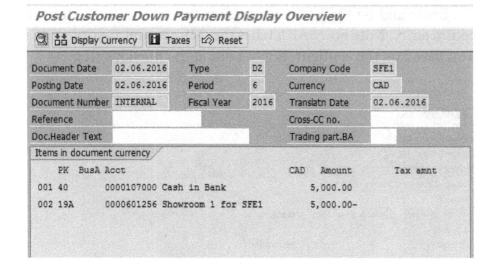

Fig 10

If the document looks good, post it by saving it to get the document #:

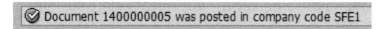

Fig 11

III. DISPLAYING THE BALANCES FOR CONFIRMATION OF POSTINGS (U)

T Code FD10N or:

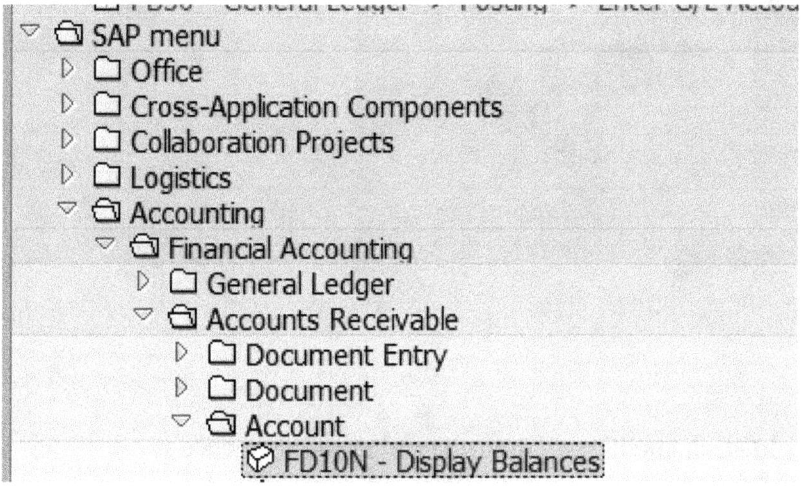

SAP menu
- ▷ Office
- ▷ Cross-Application Components
- ▷ Collaboration Projects
- ▷ Logistics
- ▽ Accounting
  - ▽ Financial Accounting
    - ▷ General Ledger
    - ▽ Accounts Receivable
      - ▷ Document Entry
      - ▷ Document
      - ▽ Account
        - FD10N - Display Balances

Fig 12

Put the customer number and CC and the year and execute:

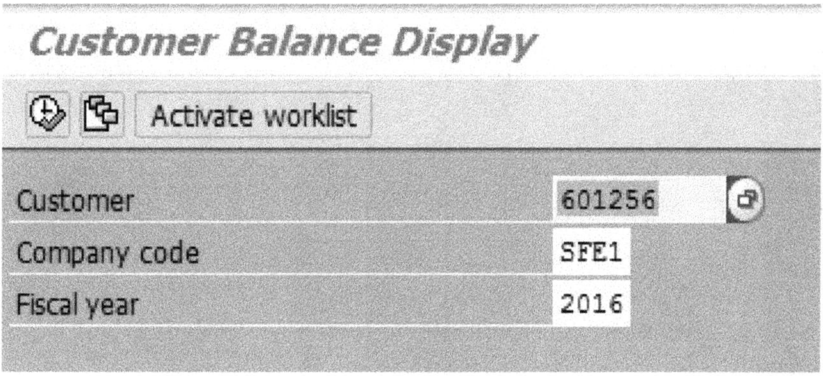

Customer Balance Display

Activate worklist

Customer	601256
Company code	SFE1
Fiscal year	2016

Fig 13

The down payment balances are under the special GL tab:

Customer	601256	Showroom 1 for SFE1
Company Code	SFE1	Shefaria Ent. Canada
Fiscal Year	2016	
Display crrncy	CAD	

Balances / Special general ledger

Transaction	Bal.Carried Fwd	Debit	Credit	Balance
Down payment			5,000.00	5,000.00-
Total			5,000.00	5,000.00-
Account balance		26,932.80	20,080.00	6,852.80
Total		26,932.80	25,080.00	1,852.80

Fig 14

Double click the Total line to see the latest entry:

Customer Line Item Display

Customer	601256
Company Code	SFE1
Name	Showroom 1 for SFE1
City	London

S	Assignment	Document	Ty	Doc. Date	DD	Σ Amount in local cur.	LCurr	Clrng doc.	Text
		1400000000	DZ	20.05.2016		200.00	CAD		
		1400000001	DZ	20.05.2016		500.00	CAD		Residual from Document 1800000004
		1400000003	DZ	20.05.2016		52.80	CAD		
		1400000005	DZ	02.06.2016	A	5,000.00-	CAD		
		1800000005	DR	28.05.2016		3,100.00	CAD		
		1800000010	DR	28.05.2016		3,000.00	CAD		
						1,852.80	CAD		
		1400000000	DZ	20.05.2016		1,450.00-	CAD	1400000000	Partial payment of $1250 applied to this invoice
		1800000001	DR	20.05.2016		1,450.00	CAD	1400000000	
		1400000001	DZ	20.05.2016		7,500.00-	CAD	1400000001	
		1800000004	DR	18.05.2016		7,500.00	CAD	1400000001	
		1400000002	DZ	20.05.2016		2,000.00-	CAD	1400000002	
		1800000000	DR	10.05.2016		2,000.00	CAD	1400000002	
		1400000003	DZ	20.05.2016		1,240.00-	CAD	1400000003	
		1800000002	DR	15.05.2016		1,240.00	CAD	1400000003	
		1400000004	DZ	25.05.2016		7,890.00-	CAD	1400000004	
		1800000003	DR	18.05.2016		7,890.00	CAD	1400000004	
						0.00	CAD		
	Account 601256					1,852.80	CAD		

Fig 15

IV. SENDING THE INVOICE AGAINST THE DOWN PAYMENT RECEIVED (U)

T Code FB70 or:

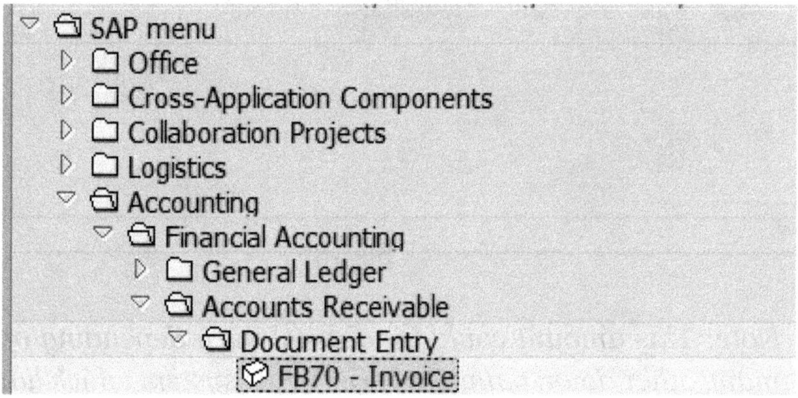

Fig 16

Enter the important data as below to credit the appropriate G/L account for sales against this down payment received:

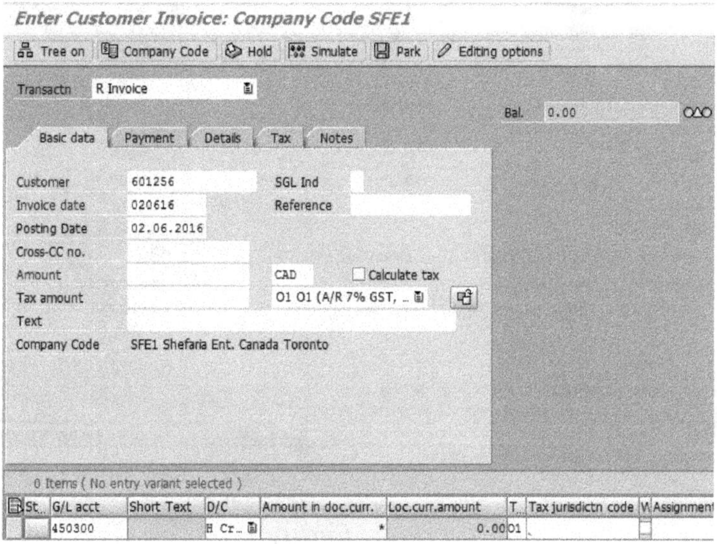

Fig 17

Hit Enter to ensure zero balance at top right in Green:
An info message will pop up:

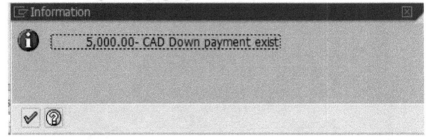

Fig 18

Note: This amount could (and does) vary depending on how many other down payments exist in the system which have not been settled yet.

Enter Customer Invoice: Company Code SFE1

🖧 Tree on 🏢 Company Code 🕙 Hold 🎛 Simulate 💾 Park ✏ Editing options

Transactn	R Invoice		

Bal. 0.00

Basic data	Payment	Details	Tax	Notes

Customer 601256   ⓒ SGL Ind

Invoice date 02.06.2016   Reference

Posting Date 02.06.2016

Cross-CC no.

Amount 5,000.00   CAD   ☐ Calculate tax

Tax amount

Text

Paymt terms 14 Days 3 %, 30 Days 1 %, 60 Days net

Baseline Date 02.06.2016

Company Code SFE1 Shefaria Ent. Canada Toronto

Customer
Address
Company
Showroom 1 for SFE1
LONDON
KANADA

OIs
Bank account
Bank Number
Not available

1 Items (No entry variant selected)

St	G/L acct	Short Text	D/C	Amount in doc.curr.	Loc.curr.amount	Tax code	Tax jurisdictn code	W	Assign
✔	450300	Sales	H Cr...	5,000.00	5,000.00				

Fig 19

266

Again, we can simulate this document if we wish to verify the entries or want to make corrections before posting:

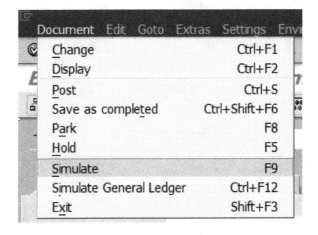

Fig 20

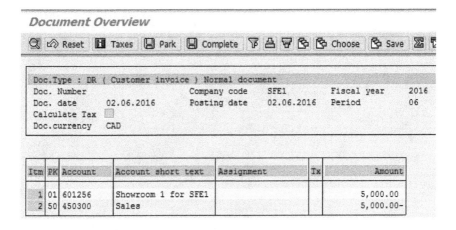

Fig 21

We can now save this document:

Fig 22

V. DISPLAYING THE BALANCES (U)

T Code FD10N:

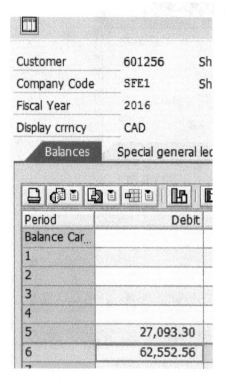

Customer	601256	Sh
Company Code	SFE1	Sh
Fiscal Year	2016	
Display crrncy	CAD	

Balances   Special general led

Period	Debit
Balance Car...	
1	
2	
3	
4	
5	27,093.30
6	62,552.56

Fig 23

Customer   601256
Company Code   SFE1
Name   Showroom 1 for SFE1
City   Toronto

S	Assignment	Document	Ty	Doc. Date	DD	Amount in local cur.	LCurr	Clmg doc.	Text
☐	0080015370	90000000	RV	08.06.2016		2,675.00	CAD	90036688	
☐	0080015370	90036689	RV	08.06.2016		2,675.00	CAD	90036690	
☐		90036692	RV	08.06.2016		2,407.50	CAD	90036695	
☐		90036702	RV	13.06.2016		1,926.00	CAD	90036705	
☐		90036701	RV	13.06.2016		4,012.50	CAD	90036706	
☐	0080015370	90036691	RV	08.06.2016		2,675.00	CAD	90036707	
☐	0080015372	90036697	RV	11.06.2016		2,675.00	CAD	90036708	
☐	0080015373	90036700	RV	11.06.2016		267.50	CAD	90036709	
☐	0080015374	90036699	RV	11.06.2016		802.50	CAD	90036710	
☐		90036696	RV	08.06.2016		160.50	CAD	90036711	
☐		90036698	RV	13.06.2016		16,050.00	CAD	90036712	
☐		1800000014	DR	02.06.2016		5,000.00	CAD	100000038	

Fig 24

VI. CLEARING DOWN PAYMENT MADE BY THE CUSTOMER (U)

T Code F-39 or:

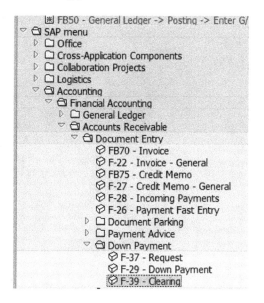

Fig 25

Enter the data as below including the invoice #, which is being cleared:

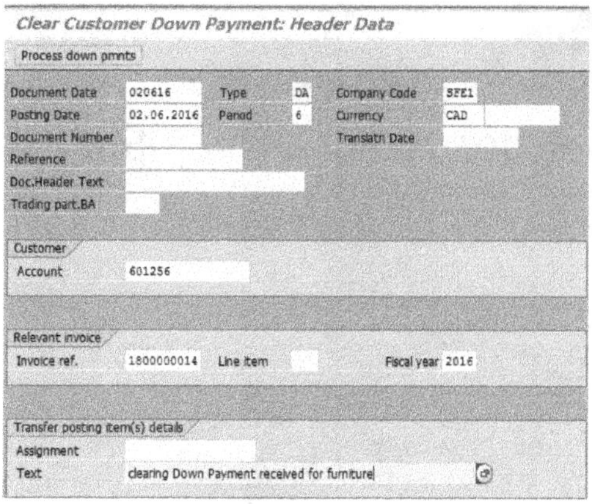

Fig 26

Click on 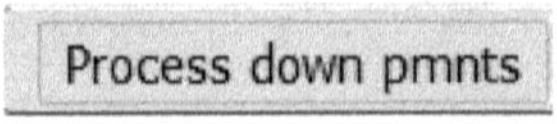
Process down pmnts

Now choose the relevant line by doc # (if multiple lines show op) and enter the amount being cleared in the last column:

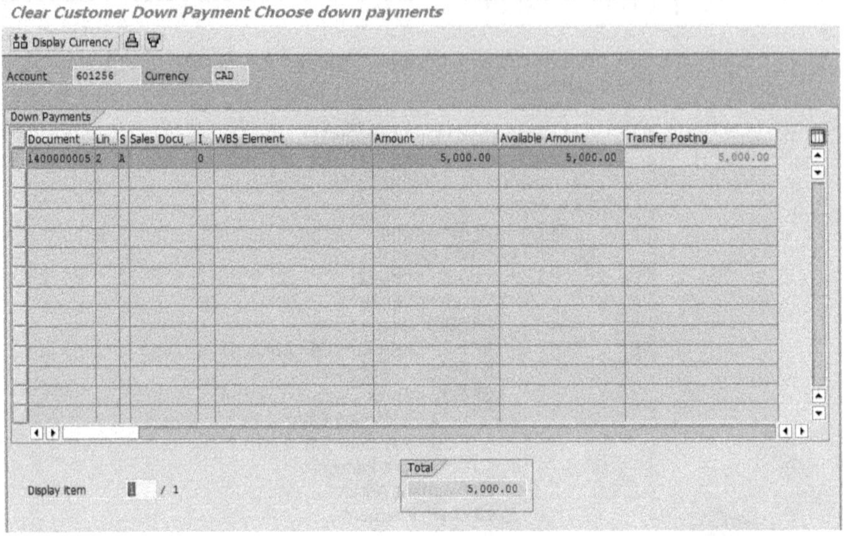
Clear Customer Down Payment Choose down payments
Display Currency
Account 601256
Currency CAD
Down Payments
Document
Lin
S
Sales Docu
I
WBS Element
Amount
Available Amount
Transfer Posting
1400000005 2 A 0 5,000.00 5,000.00 5,000.00
Total
5,000.00
Display item / 1

Fig 27

Ensure that the total at the bottom is same as the amount being cleared:

Again, we can simulate it:

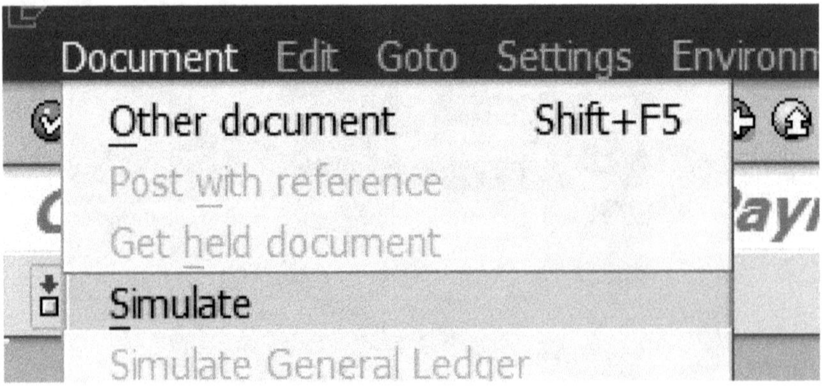
Document
Edit
Goto
Settings
Other document
Shift+F5
Post with reference
Get held document
Simulate
Simulate General Ledger

Fig 28

If it looks good, then save it:

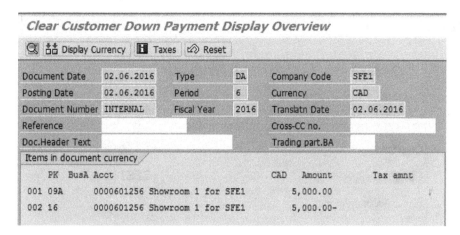

Fig 29

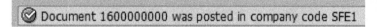

VII. CHECKING THE CUSTOMER BALANCE (U)

T Code: FD10N

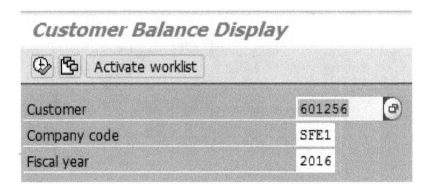

Fig 30

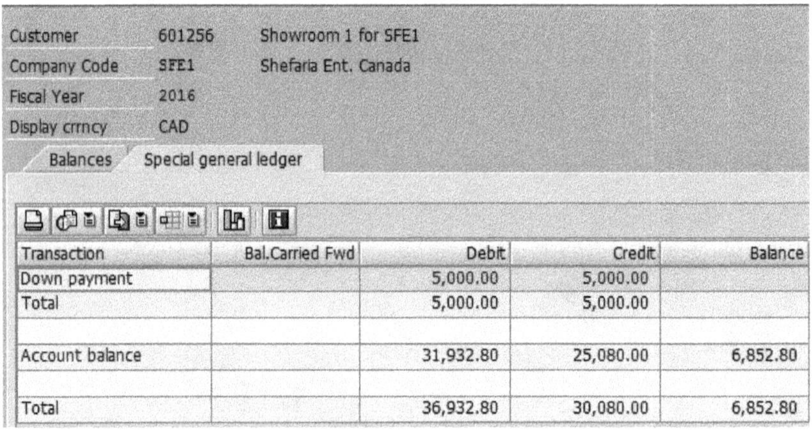

Customer	601256	Showroom 1 for SFE1
Company Code	SFE1	Shefaria Ent. Canada
Fiscal Year	2016	
Display crrncy	CAD	

Balances / Special general ledger

Transaction	Bal.Carried Fwd	Debit	Credit	Balance
Down payment		5,000.00	5,000.00	
Total		5,000.00	5,000.00	
Account balance		31,932.80	25,080.00	6,852.80
Total		36,932.80	30,080.00	6,852.80

Fig 31

Double click on Total again to confirm the document is cleared.

The 2 highlighted cancelling entries of 5,000 each are revealed above. Note the reference of the clearing document 1600000000 in the document No 1800000014 (Fig 32)

Customer   601256
Company Code   SFE1
Name   Showroom 1 for SFE1
City   London

S	Assignment	Document	Ty	Doc. Date	DD	Σ	Amount in local cur.	LCurr	Clrng doc.	Text
		1400000003	DZ	20.05.2016			52.80	CAD		
		1600000000	DA	02.06.2016			5,000.00-	CAD		clearing Down Payment received for furniture
		1800000005	DR	28.05.2016			3,100.00	CAD		
		1800000010	DR	28.05.2016			3,000.00	CAD		
		1800000014	DR	02.06.2016			5,000.00	CAD		
							6,852.80	CAD		
		1400000000	DZ	20.05.2016			1,450.00-	CAD	1400000000	Partial payment of $1250 applied to this invoice
		1800000001	DR	20.05.2016			1,450.00	CAD	1400000000	
		1400000001	DZ	20.05.2016			7,500.00-	CAD	1400000001	
		1800000004	DR	18.05.2016			7,500.00	CAD	1400000001	
		1400000002	DZ	20.05.2016			2,000.00-	CAD	1400000002	
		1800000000	DR	10.05.2016			2,000.00	CAD	1400000002	
		1400000003	DZ	20.05.2016			1,240.00-	CAD	1400000003	
		1800000002	DR	15.05.2016			1,240.00	CAD	1400000003	
		1400000004	DZ	25.05.2016			7,890.00-	CAD	1400000004	
		1800000003	DR	18.05.2016			7,890.00	CAD	1400000004	
		1400000005	DZ	02.06.2016	A		5,000.00-	CAD	1600000000	
		1600000000	DA	02.06.2016	A		5,000.00	CAD	1600000000	clearing Down Payment received for furniture
							0.00	CAD		

Fig 32

273

VIII. CLEARING THE CUSTOMER ACCOUNT (U)

T Code: F-32 or:

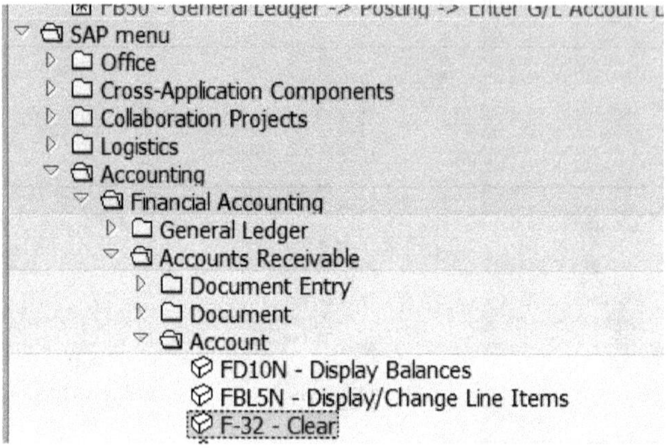

Fig 33

Enter the data as below:

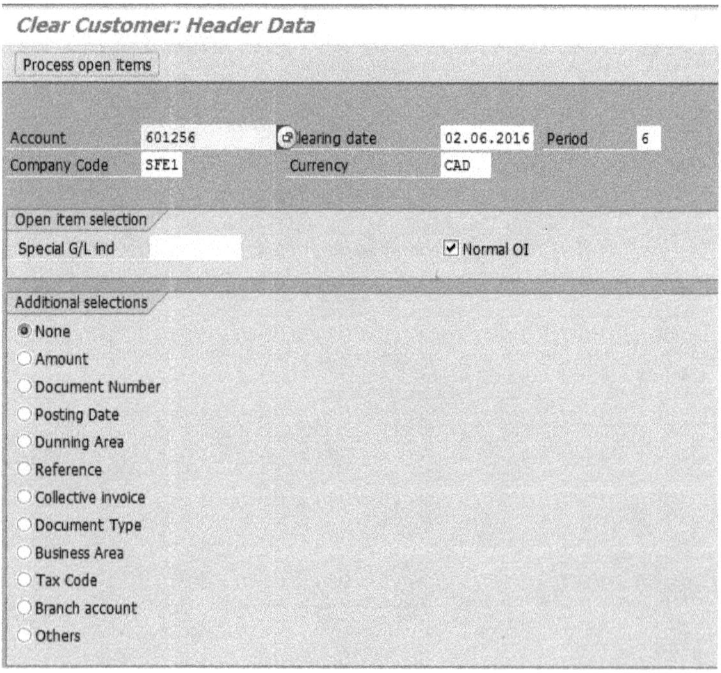

Fig 34

Click on 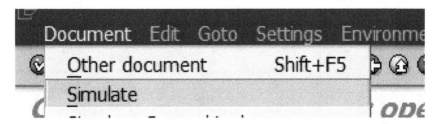 Process open items

Clear Customer Process open items

👤 📝	Distribute diff.	Charge off diff.	✏ Editing options	Ø Cash Disc. Due	Create Dispute Case		

Standard	Partial pmt	Res.items	Withhldg tax

Account items 601256 Showroom 1 for SFE1

Assignment	Document	D	P	Posting	Docume	CAD Gross	Cash discnt	CashD
	1400000000	DZ	06	20.05.2	20.05.2	200.00		
	1400000001	DZ	06	20.05.2	20.05.2	500.00		
	1400000003	DZ	06	20.05.2	20.05.2	52.80		
	1600000000	DA	16	02.06.2	02.06.2	5,000.00-		
	1800000005	DR	01	28.05.2	28.05.2	3,100.00	93.00	3.000
	1800000010	DR	01	28.05.2	28.05.2	3,000.00	90.00	3.000
	1800000014	DR	01	02.06.2	02.06.2	5,000.00		

🔍 ▣	▣ ▣	🖨 ▽	▦ ▦ Amo	▦ Gross<>	▦ Currency	↑ Items	Y Items	↑ Disc.	Y Disc

Editing status

Number of items	7	Amount entered	0.00
Display from item	1	Assigned	0.00
Reason code		Difference postings	
Display in clearing currency		Not assigned	0.00

Fig 34

Again, follow the process of selecting/deselecting the required line and ensure the not assigned amount is 0 as above.

Simulate:

Document Edit Goto Settings Environme

Other document   Shift+F5

Simulate

Fig 35

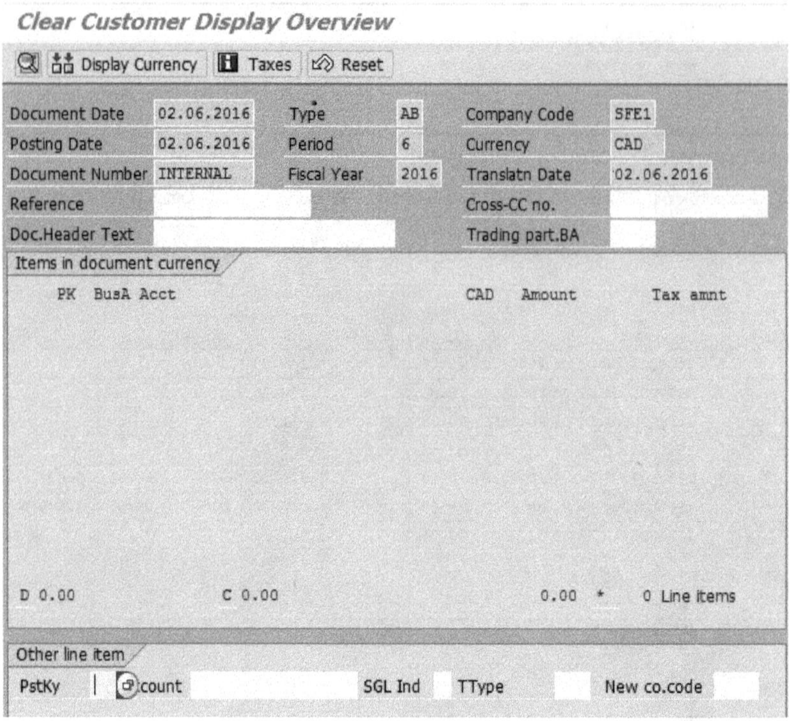

Clear Customer Display Overview
Display Currency
Taxes
Reset
Document Date
02.06.2016
Type
AB
Company Code
SFE1
Posting Date
02.06.2016
Period
6
Currency
CAD
Document Number
INTERNAL
Fiscal Year
2016
Translatn Date
02.06.2016
Reference
Cross-CC no.
Doc.Header Text
Trading part.BA
Items in document currency
PK BusA Acct
CAD Amount
Tax amnt
D 0.00
C 0.00
0.00 *
0 Line items
Other line item
PstKy
count
SGL Ind
TType
New co.code

Fig 36

Again, there are no line items in this clearing. If everything is good, Save it:

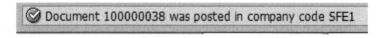

Document 100000038 was posted in company code SFE1

Fig 37

Check FD10N again:

Customer Line Item Display
Dispute Case
Customer
601256
Company Code
SFE1
Name
Showroom 1 for SFE1
City
London
Account 601256

Fig 38

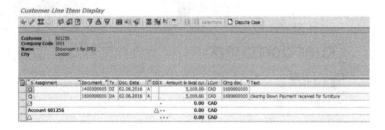

GOODS RECEIPT (U)

T Code: MIGO

One of the most important transactions and the cusp between Materials Management (MM) and FI, the T Code MIGO is used very frequently in goods based organizations, which buy components or raw materials from vendors. The vendor masters drive how the goods will be received by the company – whether a GR (goods receipt) document must exist before a vendor's invoices can be received in the system or not. Normally this transaction is done by purchasing who verify the goods are in order before receiving them in the system and thereby *indirectly* approving the vendor invoice.

A goods receipt can occur via many ways as an initial transfer of stock, receipt of goods from a vendor, returns from customers etc. For our purpose, to understand the relationship between Materials and Finance, we will cause the GR to create from a Purchase Order (PO) that we will create on a vendor. While the actual detailed creation of the PO, being part of MM, is out of scope of the FI course, we will review some data in the vendor master, which is applicable to this transaction including Purchasing data. In XK01, create vendor, let us use the existing vendor to create purchasing views for it:

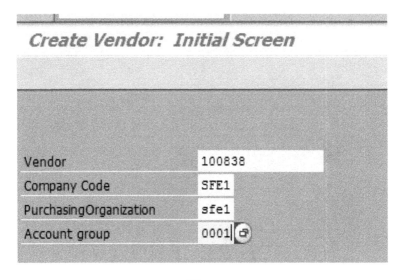

Fig 1

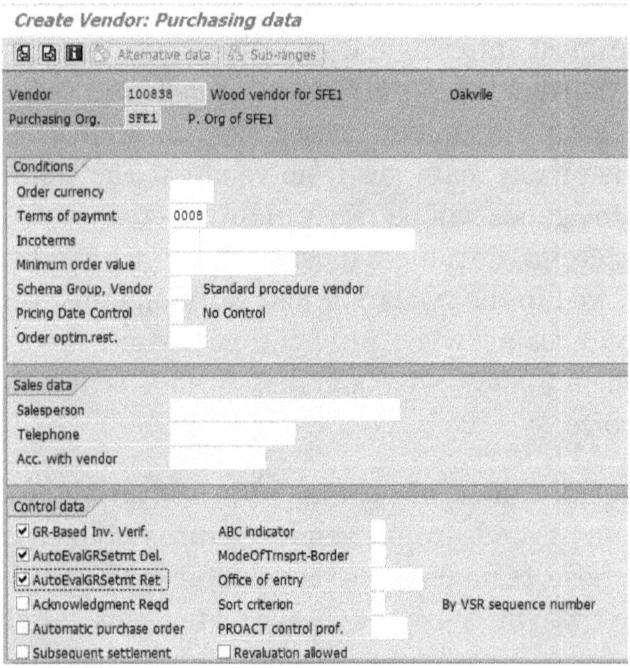

Fig 2

The ordering currency – used rarely, normally the customer or purchaser decides the ordering currency though this option is available in case the vendor is located overseas and insists on any certain currency that is different from the currency of the buying company. It can be over written in the PO.

The payment terms field in purchasing will take precedence over the payment terms in the accounting screen at time of PO creation.

GR-Based Inv. Verify. Means until the MIGO transaction has been done (effectively approving the payment for the goods and/or services having been received), the accounting department can't book this invoice (it can be held as an accrual, but not converted into a payable till MIGO is done).

The other buttons are also relevant to accounting depending on what the organization does with the vendor's invoices and how it pays or accrues them. The 2 main ones often used are the ERS (evaluated receipt settlement) in which accruals can be automatically converted to payables and Automatic PO whereby POs can be generated automatically from Purchase requisitions.

For our purpose, we have created a simple PO on an external vendor for material in transaction ME21N the details of which are out of scope of this manual though some of it has been covered in a later section on Framework POs.

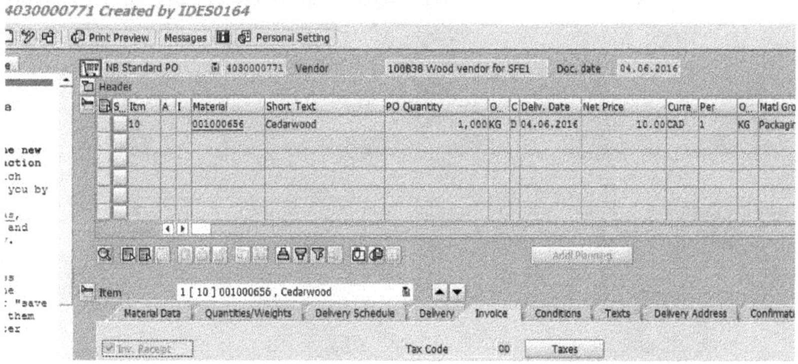

Fig 3

The PO can be displayed in ME23N

Fig 4

by entering the PO # in the open field by clicking on

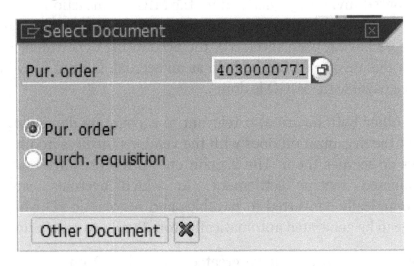

Fig 5

Click on 'Other Document' to view the PO.

From FI perspective, the primary tab of importance at the line item level is Invoice:

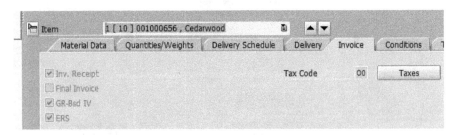

Fig 6

This data, Inv Receipt and GR-Bsd IV as we saw, has defaulted from the vendor master.

Since the PO requires a GR/IR, let us do the GR first via the transaction **MIGO:**

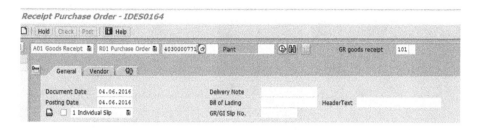

Fig 7

Enter the PO # at the top.

- A crucial field on this screen is the Movement type at the top right. In Materials Management, the entire process of inventory control and movements is driven by Movement type. The SAP standard Movement type for GR from vendors is 101 (for reversals, 102). It is important to note that this 101 default on the MIGO screen is based on the Movement type the user last used. It may be necessary to correct it to the required one. We do have the ability to define our own default values for this screen:

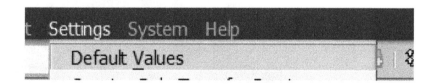

Fig 8

On clicking Enter, the PO number disappears from the top field and all it's associated data flows into the line item levels at the bottom of the screen:

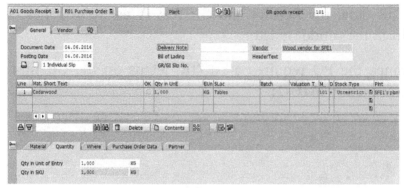

Fig 9

On the Quantity tab above, you have the option to 'part receive' the goods in case all were not shipped by the vendor. Let us assume we received only 100 out of the 1000 kg ordered. Change the quantity from 1000 to 100 and click on 'Item OK:

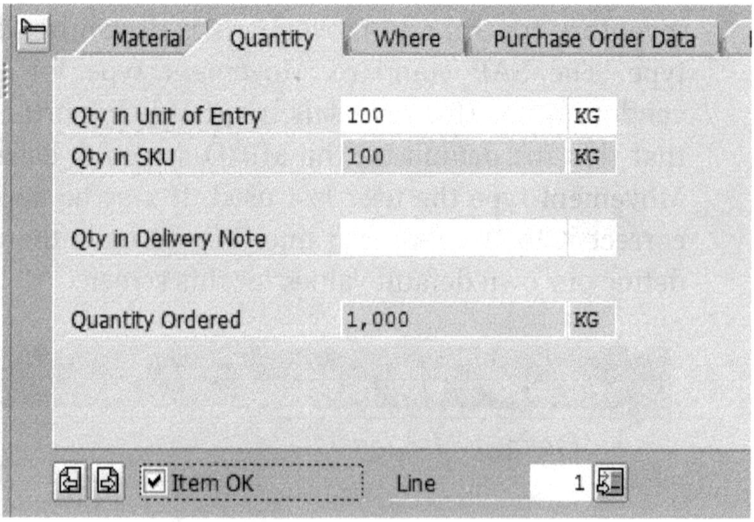

Material	Quantity	Where	Purchase Order Data	

Qty in Unit of Entry	100	KG	
Qty in SKU	100	KG	
Qty in Delivery Note			
Quantity Ordered	1,000	KG	

☑ Item OK   Line   1

Fig 10

Save to post the document:

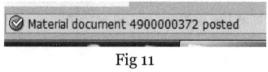

Fig 11

This material document would also have posted an accounting document, which can be viewed by going to the material document in MB03:

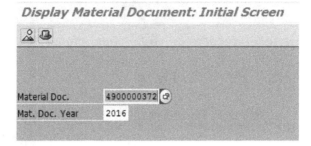

Fig 12

Alternatively, going back to the PO in ME23N in which a PO History tab would now have appeared at the line item level. This tab is not available unless a subsequent document is posted against the line item.

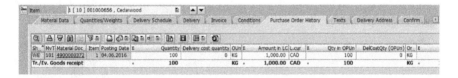

Fig 13

Click on the hyperlink (on the Material Doc number) and it takes us into the material document:

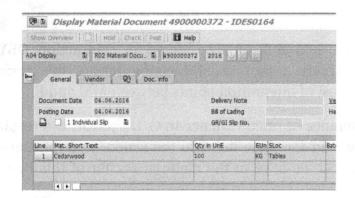

Fig 14

Click on the Doc info tab:

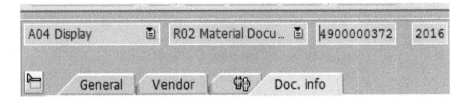

Fig 15

And then on the

Revealing the accounting document behind it:

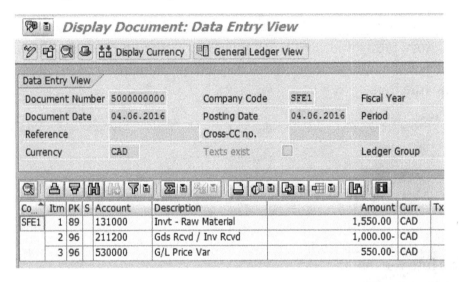

Fig 16

These G/L accounts are configured in transaction OBYC and though strictly a part of MM configuration, this transaction decides most of integration points between MM and FI.

The difference of price variance to G/L 530000 is a result of the price we paid for these items to the vendor and the standard or variable cost we have in the material master of this item in our system.

The details of this calculation are explained next.

Price on the PO is $10.00 per kg which translates to $1,000 as the amount of the goods received that we will pay the vendor:

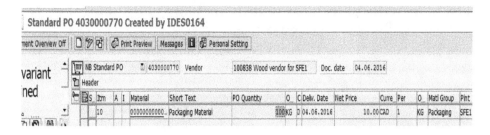

Fig 17

Price in Material Master is 15.50 per kg which translates to a value of 1,550 for 100 kg of goods received:

Display Material 000000000001000656 (Raw material)

⇒ Additional data   Organizational levels

Plant data / stor. 2   Accounting 1   Accounting 2   Costing 1   C.

Material	000000000001000656	Cedarwood
Plant	SF01	SFE1's plant in Toronto

General data

Base Unit of Measure	KG	Kilogram	Valuation Category	
Currency	CAD		Current period	11 2017
Division			Price determ.	☐ ML act.

Current valuation

Valuation Class	3000		
VC: Sales order stk		Proj. stk val. class	
Price control	S	Price Unit	1
Moving price	17.87	Standard price	15.50

Fig 18

The difference, thus, is the price variance of 550 for buying from this vendor i.e. in this case, a benefit to SFE1 since the goods bought for 1,000 are actually valued at 1,550 in the system.

INVOICE VERIFICATION (U)

T Code: MIRO

Unlike MIGO which is primarily performed by the purchasing dept., MIRO is done by Finance/Accounting, as this is the equivalent of booking of vendor invoices for AP based on how the vendor master data is set up.

To explain this process, we will continue working with the same PO. Since MIGO had already occurred, Purchasing has freed up this transaction for FI to take over to book the vendor invoice when it is available against the same PO we did MIGO against – we will use the highlighted line below:

Sh	MvT	Material Doc	Item	Posting Date	Σ	Quantity	Delivery cost quantity	OUn	Σ	Amount in LC	L.cur	Σ
WE	101	4900000375	1	07.06.2016		150	0	KG		1,500.00	CAD	
WE	102	4900000374	1	04.06.2016		100-	0	KG		1,000.00-	CAD	
WE	101	4900000373	1	04.06.2016		200	0	KG		2,000.00	CAD	
WE	101	4900000372	1	04.06.2016		100	0	KG		1,000.00	CAD	
Tr./Ev. Goods receipt					▪	350		KG	▪	3,500.00	CAD	▪
RE-L		5105608953	2	05.06.2016		200	0	KG		2,000.00	CAD	
Tr./Ev. Invoice receipt					▪	200		KG	▪	2,000.00	CAD	▪

Item 1 [10] 001000656 , Cedarwood

Material Data | Quantities/Weights | Delivery Schedule | Delivery | Invoice | Conditions | Purchase Order History

Fig 1

For the purpose of this we will assume the vendor submits the invoice equal to the PO we created which is more than the actual Goods received (100 vs 1,000). Go to screen for T Code MIRO and enter the Invoice date, amount of the vendor invoice and the PO number as below and Hit Enter:

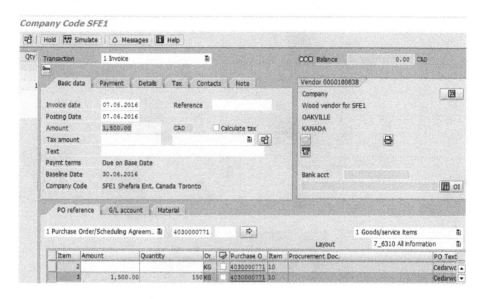

Fig 2

Select the line as above against which this payment has been made and post it by clicking Save. We can choose multiple lines also to post against the same vendor invoice if the invoice is for multiple deliveries made to us.

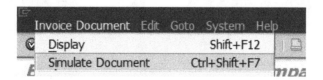

Fig 3

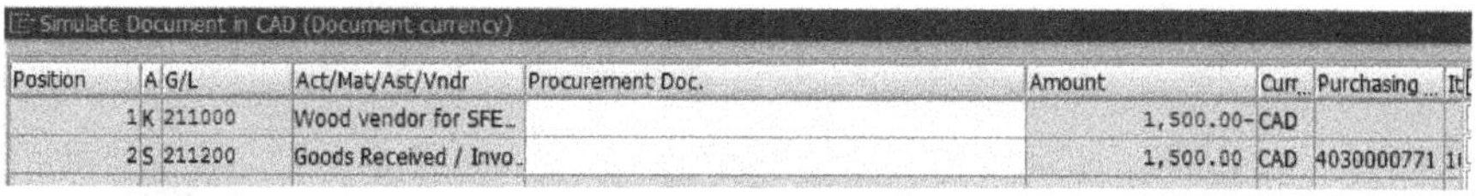

Fig 4

It tells us that the vendor will be credited and the GR/IR account debited for the same amounts.

Since it looks good, we can go back to the previous screen and save the document or post, it directly from the simulation screen via the Post button at the bottom left:

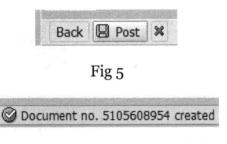

Fig 5

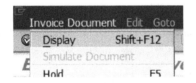

Fig 6

We can view this document by:

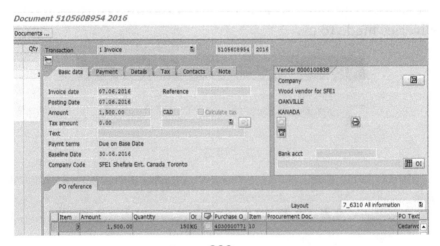

Fig 7

Or in transaction MIR4:

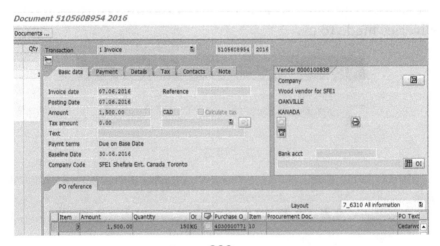

Fig 8

Click on the tab Follow-On Documents ...

To see the details of the actual accounting document:

Data Entry View									
Document Number	5100000001		Company Code	SFE1		Fiscal Year		2016	
Document Date	07.06.2016		Posting Date	07.06.2016		Period		6	
Reference			Cross-CC no.						
Currency	CAD		Texts exist	☐		Ledger Group			

Co.	Itm	PK	S	Account	Description	Amount	Curr.	Tx	Cost Cent
SFE1	1	31		100838	Wood vendor for SFE1	1,500.00-	CAD	00	
	2	86		211200	Gds Rcvd / Inv Rcvd	1,500.00	CAD	00	

Fig 9

Note that it credited the vendor and cleared the amount in 211200 with a debit, which had earlier been credited when we did the MIGO (goods receipt).

This amount should now show up in the accounts payable to this vendor, which we can look up via FBL1N:

Vendor	100838
Company Code	SFE1
Name	Wood vendor for SFE1
City	Oakville

S	Document	Doc. Type	Doc. Date	DD	Σ	Amount in doc. curr.	Curr.	Clrng doc.	PayT	Curr. cash disc. amt	Disc.1	Day1	Day2	Net	DD
	1900000002	KR	10.05.2016			1,100.00-	CAD		0003	22.00-	2.000	14	30	45	
	1900000004	KR	28.05.2016			1,450.00-	CAD		0003	30.81-	2.125	14	30	45	
	1900000011	KR	28.05.2016			1,230.00-	CAD		0003	26.14-	2.125	14	30	45	
	1900000017	KR	20.01.2016			12,800.00-	CAD		0001	0.00	0.000	0	0	0	
	1900000019	KR	20.01.2016			1,400.00-	CAD		0001	0.00	0.000	0	0	0	
	1900000020	KR	25.01.2016			2,300.00-	CAD		0001	0.00	0.000	0	0	0	
	1900000029	KR	10.05.2016			2,000.00-	CAD		0003	40.00-	2.000	14	30	45	
	5100000000	RE	04.06.2015			2,000.00-	CAD		0008	0.00	0.000	0	0	0	
	5100000001	RE	07.06.2015			1,500.00-	CAD		0008	0.00	0.000	0	0	0	
	5100000002	RE	07.06.2015			100.00-	CAD		0008	0.00	0.000	0	0	0	
						25,880.00-	CAD								
Account 100838						25,880.00-	CAD								
						25,880.00-	CAD								

Fig 10

EVALUATED INVOICE RECEIPT (U)

T Code MRRL

Often there are vendors whose invoices are converted into payables directly from accruals or after goods have been received, i.e. the company does not wait for the vendor to submit the invoices for the goods or services. SAP has a concept of Evaluated Invoice Receipt (ERS) to enable this. The pre-requisite for this is the check on 2 fields in the vendor master in purchasing data:

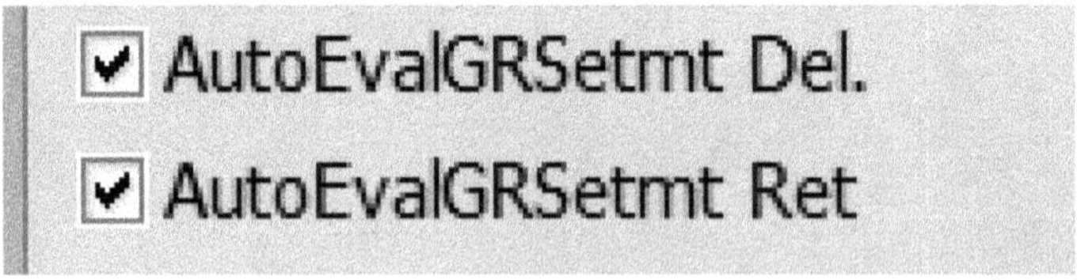

Fig1

Alternatively, this check can be put in the PO on the line item invoice tab at time of creation or modification. In MM there are purchase info records that are material specific settings, and they over ride what is in the vendor master – in the PIR, we must also ensure that the indicator – No ERS – is NOT set else, that will over ride this setting.

The Goods receipt must exist before this GR can be converted into a payable. Let us do a GR (MIGO) against an existing PO:

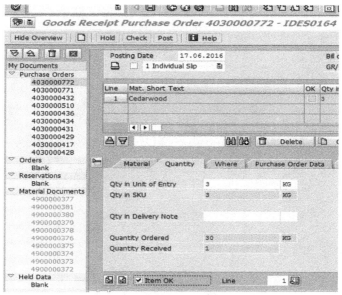

Fig 2

Fig 3

The PO shows the GRs of the quantity but there is no Invoice Receipt (IR) yet.

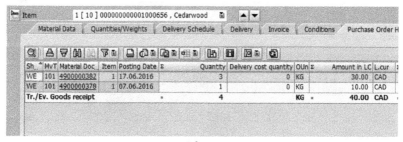

Fig 4

Since the vendor is set up for ERS, we should be able to create the IR without the vendor actually having submitted the invoice. The transaction to run ERS is MRRL. Enter the selection data as necessary and run the transaction. It also gives the ability to first run it in test mode to verify the contents of the documents that will get processed:

Evaluated Receipt Settlement (ERS) with Logistics Invoice Verification

Document Selection				
Company Code	SFE1	to		⇨
Plant		to		⇨
Posting Date of Goods Receip		to		⇨
Goods Receipt Document		to		⇨
Fiscal Year of Goods Receipt		to		⇨
Vendor	100838	to		⇨
Purchasing Document		to		⇨
Item		to		⇨

Processing Options		
Doc. selection	3	Document selection per order item
Test Run	✔	
☐ Settle Goods Items + Planned Delivery Costs		

Fig 5

Execute to view in this test mode and we find the lines of our PO along with some others are ready to create IRs:

Evaluated Receipt Settlement (ERS) with Logistics Invoice Verification

	Pstable	Vendor	Ref. Doc.	FYrRef	RfIt	Purch.Doc.	Item	Reference	Doc. N.	Ye.	InfoTe.	FI Doc.	DC	B/Lac
	X	100838	4900000372	2016	1	4030000771	10							
	X	100838	4900000373	2016	1		10							
	X	100838	4900000375	2016	1		10							
	X	100838	4900000376	2016	1		10							
	X	100838	4900000377	2016	1		10							
	X	100838	4900000381	2016	1		10							
	X	100838	4900000378	2016	1	4030000772	10							
	X	100838	4900000382	2016	1		10							

Fig 6

The X indicator in the Postable field means this line item will be posted when not run in test mode. The field Info text blank is an indicator that all is well with this line. Any error would have been reflected in this field.

Now we can go back, remove the test flag, and post it by executing again. If we want to restrict only to one PO, we can enter that in the selection criteria also and post only for that:

Evaluated Receipt Settlement (ERS) with Logistics Invoice Verification

Document Selection

Company Code	SFE1	to		⇨
Plant		to		⇨
Posting Date of Goods Receip		to		⇨
Goods Receipt Document		to		⇨
Fiscal Year of Goods Receipt		to		⇨
Vendor	100838	to		⇨
Purchasing Document	4030000772	to		⇨
Item		to		⇨

Processing Options

Doc. selection	3	Document selection per order item
Test Run	☐	
☐ Settle Goods Items + Planned Delivery Costs		

Fig 7

This time, in the real run, it gives the actual Invoice doc # and the FI document #:

Evaluated Receipt Settlement (ERS) with Logistics Invoice Verification

	Pstable	Vendor	Ref. Doc.	FYrRef	RfIt	Purch.Doc.	Item	Reference	Inv. Doc. No.	Year	InfoText	FI Doc.	D
	X	100838	4900000378	2016	1	4030000772	10		5105608960	2016		5100000006	
		100838	4900000382	2016	1	4030000772	10		5105608960	2016		5100000006	

Fig 8

The PO history for that line item will now reflect this number:

Sh	MvT	Material Doc.	Item	Posting Date	Σ	Quantity	Delivery cost quantity	OUn	Σ	Amount in LC	L.cur	Σ	Qty
WE	101	4900000382	1	17.06.2016		3	0	KG		30.00	CAD		
WE	101	4900000378	1	07.06.2016		1	0	KG		10.00	CAD		
Tr./Ev. Goods receipt					≡	4		KG	≡	40.00	CAD	≡	
RE-L		5105608960	1	17.06.2016		1	0	KG		10.00	CAD		
RE-L		5105608960	2	17.06.2016		3	0	KG		30.00	CAD		
Tr./Ev. Invoice receipt					≡	4		KG	≡	40.00	CAD	≡	

Fig 9

As will the AP of the vendor in FBL1N:

Vendor 100838
Company Code SFE1
Name Wood vendor for SFE1
City Oakville

S	Document	Doc. Type	Doc. Date	DD	Σ	Amount in doc. curr.	Curr.	Clrng doc.	PayT	Curr. cash disc. amt	Disc.1	Day1	Day2	Net	DD
⬛	1900000002	KR	10.05.2016			1,100.00-	CAD		0003	16.50-	2.000	14	30	45	
⬛	1900000004	KR	28.05.2016			1,450.00-	CAD		0003	30.81-	2.125	14	30	45	
⬛	1900000011	KR	28.05.2016			1,230.00-	CAD		0003	26.14-	2.125	14	30	45	
⬛	1900000017	KR	20.01.2016			12,800.00-	CAD		0001	0.00	0.000	0	0	0	
⬛	1900000019	KR	20.01.2016			1,400.00-	CAD		0001	0.00	0.000	0	0	0	
⬛	1900000020	KR	25.01.2016			2,300.00-	CAD		0001	0.00	0.000	0	0	0	
⬛	1900000029	KR	10.05.2016			2,000.00-	CAD		0003	30.00-	2.000	14	30	45	
⬛	5100000000	RE	04.06.2016			2,000.00-	CAD		0008	0.00	0.000	0	0	0	
⬛	5100000001	RE	07.06.2016			1,500.00-	CAD		0008	0.00	0.000	0	0	0	
⬛	5100000002	RE	07.06.2016			100.00-	CAD		0008	0.00	0.000	0	0	0	
⬛	5100000003	RE	11.06.2016			120.00-	CAD		0008	0.00	0.000	0	0	0	
⬛	5100000004	RE	11.06.2016			6,280.00-	CAD		0008	0.00	0.000	0	0	0	
⬛	5100000005	RE	11.06.2016			6,280.00-	CAD		0008	0.00	0.000	0	0	0	
⬛	5100000006	RE	17.06.2016			40.00-	CAD		0008	0.00	0.000	0	0	0	
					≡	26,040.00-	CAD								
Account 100838						26,040.00-	CAD								
						26,040.00-	CAD								

Fig 10

Reversing an ERS is done by creating a credit memo via MIRO. The GR can also be reversed after that if necessary.

E.g if we now want to reverse this ERS, in MIRO, we choose:

Fig 11

Fig 12

Enter the amount in the Amount column that is being reversed, Hit Enter and the 2 lines against which we have the IR will come up:

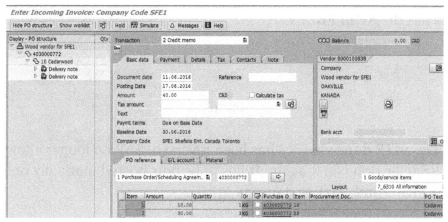

Fig 13

We have the option to select only one and reverse only that amount or if we just save this, it will reverse both:

Fig 14

If we go back to the PO, we find that the IR has been reversed for both the instances:

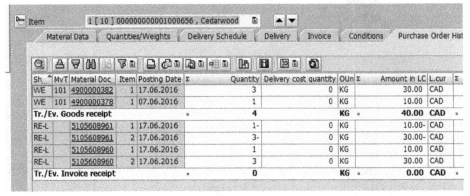

Fig 15

As has the AP in FBL1N:

Fig 16

Once an IR done via ERS has been reversed, SAP no longer allows ERS to be done on it again. It has to be now posted manually only via MIRO and can't be done via MRRL.

ERS is very useful to post AP of vendors who provide shipping services; in most cases, the number of invoices is large even though amounts may be small. ERS comes in very handy to prevent manual work and can be run as background jobs to post the AP from the accruals of shipment costs and other service costs.

PURCHASE ORDER CREATION (U)

T Code ME21N

Purchase Orders for raw materials will usually be created by the Purchasing department, and are a part of the MM Module. Certain kind of POs like Framework POs, also referred to as 'Open', 'Blanket', or 'Standing' POs may fall under the purview of Finance. These would typically be POs like for electricity, insurance etc and invoices thus coming in from such vendors, can be paid against these POs bypassing MIGO as there is nothing to *receive*. The POs help track the monies spent on such purchases and make the audit trail clear.

The code to create POs is ME21N. The key is to select the correct PO type, and the main 3 ones are:

1. NB – standard PO used for external vendors and intercompany Purchases
2. UB – stock transport orders used to move material from the same company's one plant to another plant

3. FO – Framework order which is what we will discuss here

Create Purchase Order
Document Overview On
NB Standard PO
FO Framework order

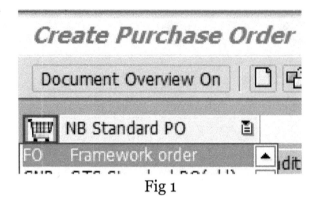

Fig 1

We will use the vendor electricity company for this purpose. This vendor need not be set as a GR/IR based payment, as there is no tracking need for the electricity received by the MM department.

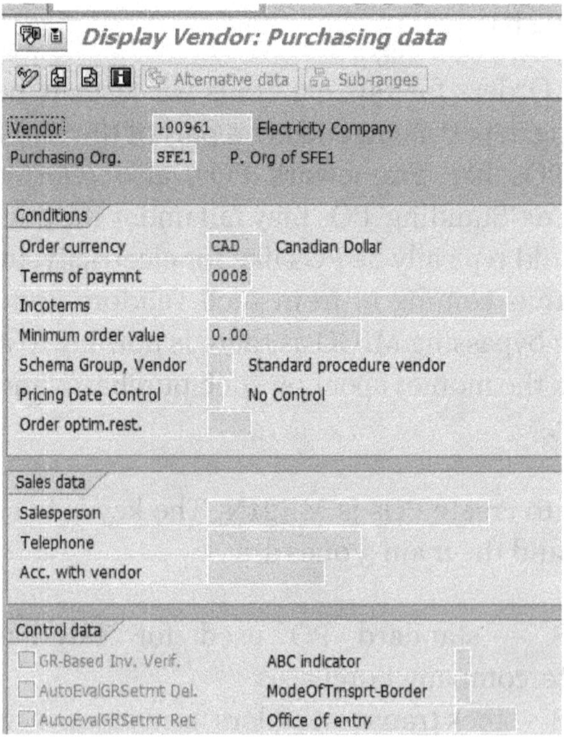

Display Vendor: Purchasing data
Alternative data
Sub-ranges
Vendor
100961
Electricity Company
Purchasing Org.
SFE1
P. Org of SFE1
Conditions
Order currency
CAD
Canadian Dollar
Terms of paymnt
0008
Incoterms
Minimum order value
0.00
Schema Group, Vendor
Standard procedure vendor
Pricing Date Control
No Control
Order optim.rest.
Sales data
Salesperson
Telephone
Acc. with vendor
Control data
GR-Based Inv. Verif.
ABC indicator
AutoEvalGRSetmt Del.
ModeOfTrnsprt-Border
AutoEvalGRSetmt Ret
Office of entry

Fig 2

On the main ME21N screen, choose FO as the PO type and enter the vendor # as below along with the period this PO will be valid for, normally made yearly but there are no restrictions.

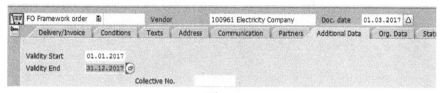

Fig 3

Since the service really is not inventor able or requires any costing etc, one can freely enter it as the material – here we use – Electricity. The important field is the Account Assignment group – here we say it is K i.e. a cost center must be allocated to this purchase. Further, the plant (SF01) and Material group are mandatory fields. The PO must have a value – e.g. here, 100,000; the quantity is meaningless – has been entered as 1 EA.

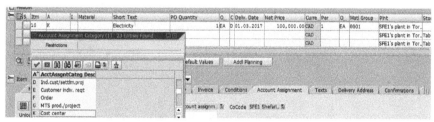

Fig 4

In the line item data, the appropriate cost center is entered:

Fig 5

And the required tax under the Invoice tab:

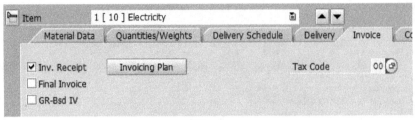

Fig 6

Save the PO:

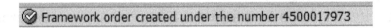

The payment of this PO can be made the same way in MIRO as any other goods based PO.

AUTOMATIC PAYMENT RUNS (C/U)

Automatic payment programs (t code F110) can be set up in SAP to issue checks to vendors and rebates to customers w/o manual intervention to a large extent. It cuts down the time for processing as well as by automating the process; the companies are able to stay on schedules for making payments.

I. Bank Setup in SAP (C)

T Code SPRO

The first step to enable auto payments is to define from where they will be paid from i.e. the bank accounts. To set up a bank in a CC, follow the path in configuration in Fig 1

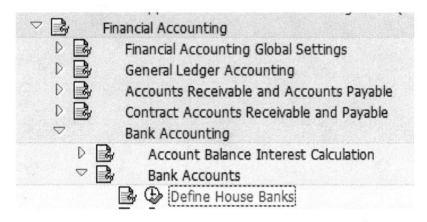

Fig 1

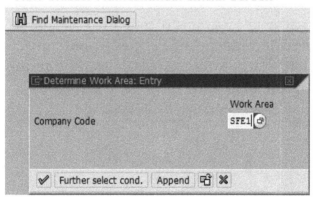

Fig 2

Click Enter and in the new window enter the details of the bank after clicking on New Entries:

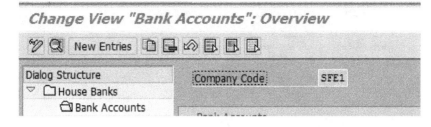

Change View "Bank Accounts": Overview

New Entries

Dialog Structure	Company Code	SFE1
▽ ☐ House Banks		
☐ Bank Accounts		

Fig 3

New Entries: Details of Added Entries

Dialog Structure	Company Code	SFE1	Shefaria Ent. Canada
▽ ☐ House Banks	House Bank	TD	TD Bank
☐ Bank Accounts			

House Bank Data

Bank Country	CA	Canada	Create
Bank Key	123456		Change

Communications data

Telephone 1		Tax Number 1	
Contact Person	John Doe		

Address

Address	
Bank name	TD Bank
Region	ON
Street	4120 Yonge Street
City	North York
Bank Branch	Yonge Street and York Mills

Fig 4

The House Bank is the abbreviation for your bank as TD above.

The bank key is the routing # of your bank

Enter telephone and contact person and other details in the address if you wish to and save.

Now double click on Bank Accounts to enter more details:

New Entries: Details of Added Entries

Dialog Structure	Company Code	SFE1	Shefaria Ent. Canada
▽ ☐ House Banks	House Bank	TD	TD Bank
☐ Bank Accounts			

Fig 5

Enter more details relevant to this account:

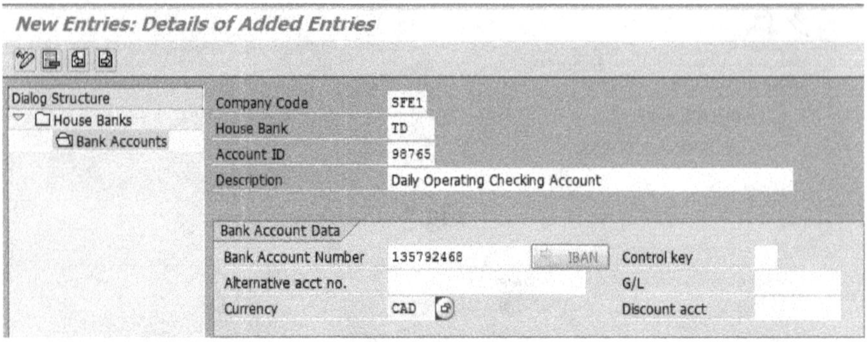

Fig 6

Save the data:

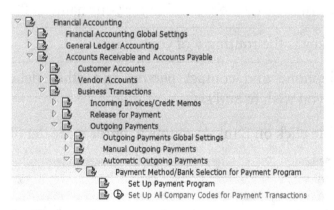

Fig 7

The next configuration step is to set up the Company Codes that will be able to make payments via automatic payment runs. The steps for that are in the path:

Fig 8

Click on New Entries and set up the CC in this table:

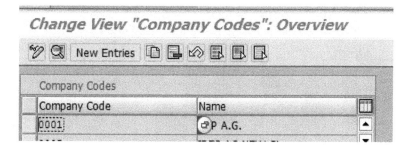

Fig 9

Set up the sending and paying with your CC.

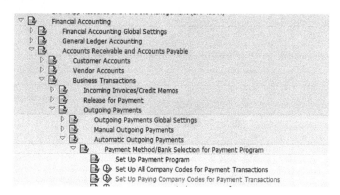

Fig 10

Save.

Now we are required to do some configurations about the details of the paying CC:

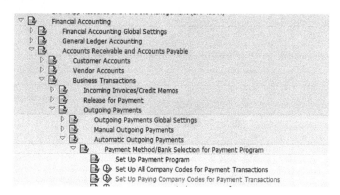

Fig 11

Click on New Entries:

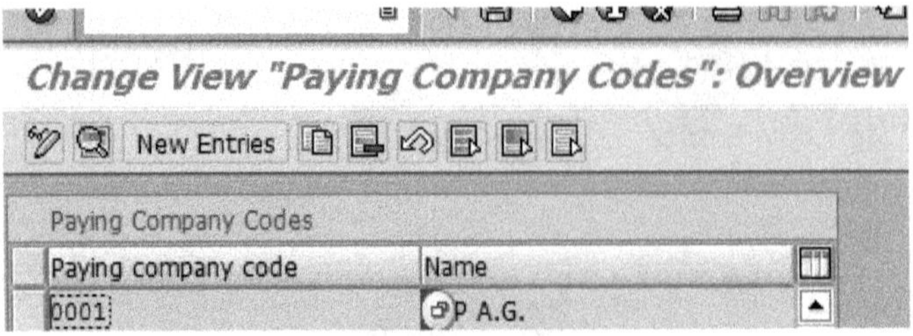

Change View "Paying Company Codes": Overview

New Entries

Paying Company Codes

Paying company code	Name	
0001	IP A.G.	▲

Fig 12

New Entries: Details of Added Entries

Paying co. code SFE1 Shefaria Ent. Canada

Control Data

Minimum amount for incoming payment	1.00	CAD
Minimum amount for outgoing payment	1.00	CAD

☐ No exchange rate differences
☐ No Exch.Rate Diffs. (Part Payments)
☐ Separate payment for each ref.
☐ Bill/exch pymt

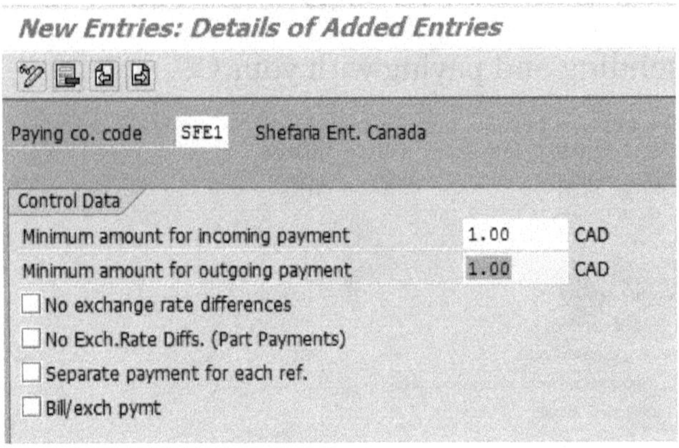

Fig 13

Save.

Next, we set up the methods by which our CC can make payments in the step:

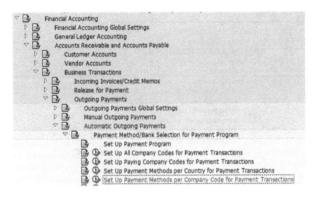

Fig 14

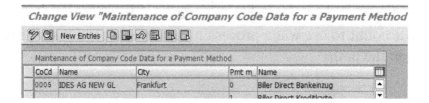

Fig 15

Click on New Entries again in the above screen:

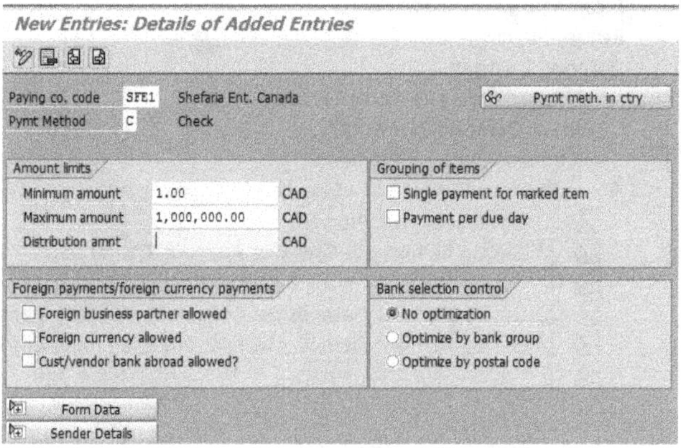

Fig 16

We define that we can make a minimum payment and max payment by Check as above in this CC. Save the configuration.

If you want to allow this CC to make transfers also, then make the relevant entry like for Check:

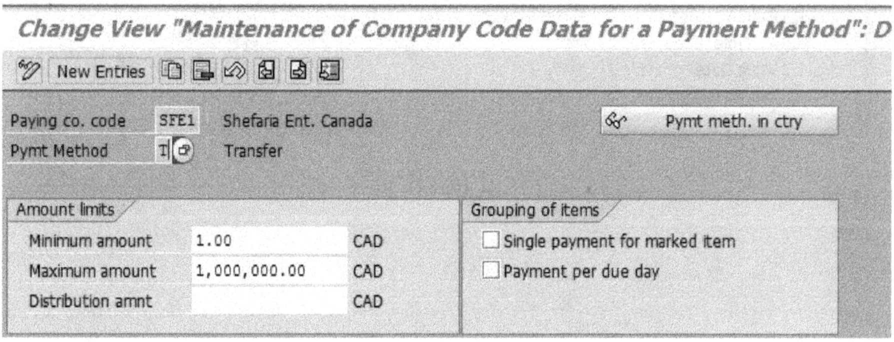

Fig 17

Next step would be to enable the program to understand which bank account to use when processing automatic payments. This is done in the path:

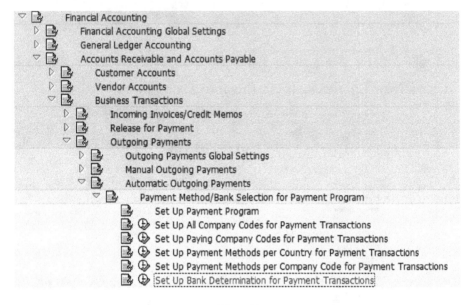

Fig 18

Find your CC:

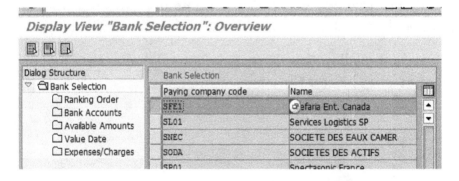

Fig 18

Double click on the step – Ranking Order as above after highlighting your CC.

The display mode changes to Change mode.

Click on New Entries:

Enter the relevant data for your methods of payment as below:

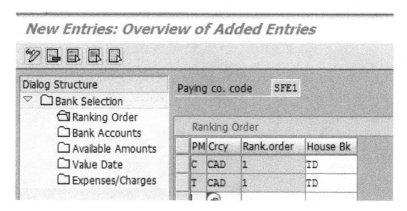

Fig 19

In the above configuration, we are telling SAP program to use this bank as the first priority for cutting checks or sending the payments by transfer.

Save the configuration.

Step back and select the CC again:

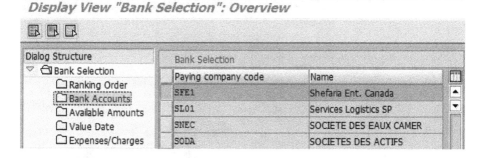

Fig 20

Double click on Bank Accounts:

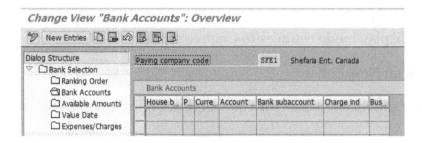

Fig 21

Click on New Entries and make the entries relating to the actual bank that will make the payments; basically, we are selecting what we have already configured:

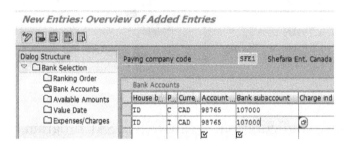

Fig 22

The only exception is the Bank sub-account, which is really the G/L account in the CC that needs to be debited or credited when payments are made to and from it.

Save the data and proceed similarly to the next step of Available Amounts.

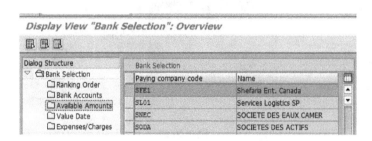

Fig 23

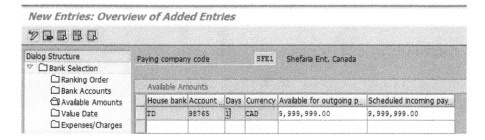

New Entries: Overview of Added Entries

Fig 24

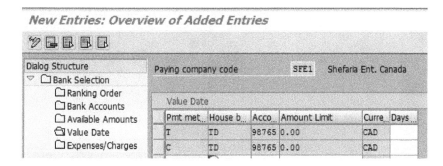

New Entries: Overview of Added Entries

Fig 25

Save.

All the above configuration steps can also be achieved in one area menu related to setting up the CC for auto payments. The t code for that area menu is FBZP:

Customizing: Maintain Payment Program

All company codes

Paying company codes

Pmnt methods in country

Pmnt methods in company code

Bank determination

House banks

II. CREATING CHECK LOTS (U)

T Code FCHI

Finally, define the check #s in the transaction code FCHI for the house bank and bank account that you will use for making the payments:

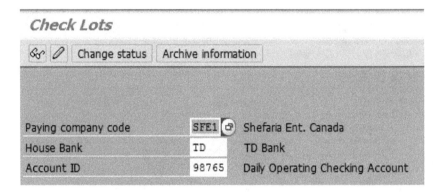

Fig 26

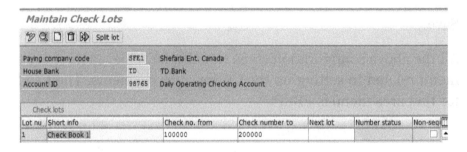

Fig 27

III. PAYMENT RUN (U)

T Code F110

To execute the actual payment run for your CC, use transaction F110 or follow the path in the SAP menu:

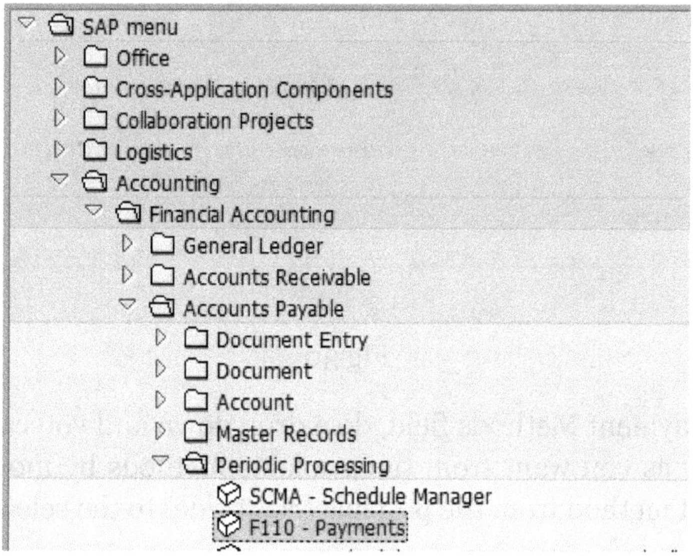

Fig 28

The Identification (Fig 29) is a free text field used to identify the particular run. It can be the name of the person or region or group creating it or anything else the company may prefer as nomenclature.

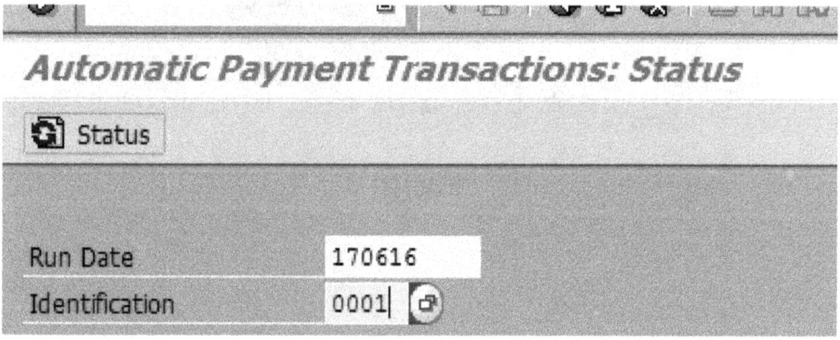

Fig 29

Enter the parameters in each tab as below or your own data:

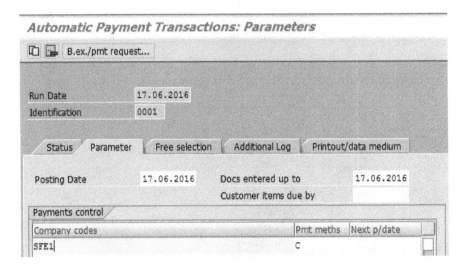

Fig 30

In the Payment Methods field, do a drop down and you can select as many as you want from the available methods by moving the payment method from the possible (right side) to the selected (left side):

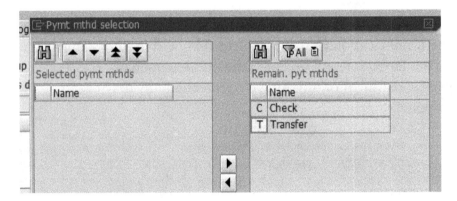

Fig 31

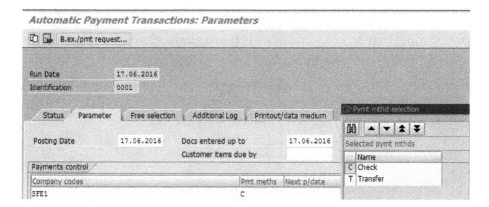

Fig 32

Click on the green arrow for OK:

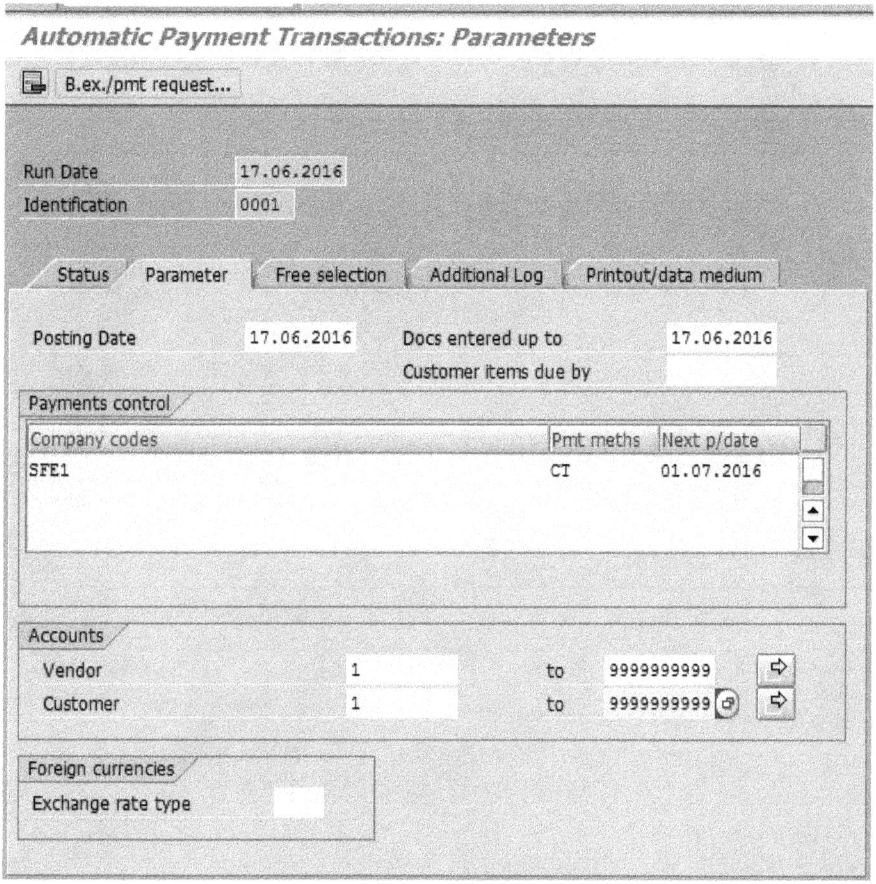

Fig 33

The above tells us that this payment run will make payments for all the due invoices of vendors and/or rebate checks of customers and will make the payments by Check or Transfer as the case may be (usually this value is set in the transaction from the master data from the vendor or customer). You can also restrict the vendors and/or customers to specific ones or ranges here.

Save the payment run.

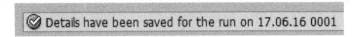

Fig 34

Click on the tab Proposal:

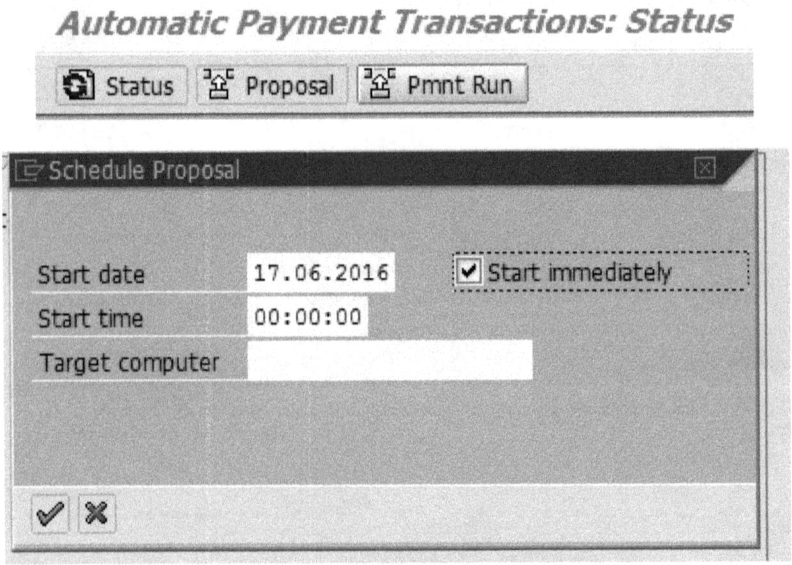

Automatic Payment Transactions: Status

Status	Proposal	Pmnt Run

Schedule Proposal

Start date	17.06.2016	☑ Start immediately
Start time	00:00:00
Target computer	

✓ ✗

Fig 35

We can either give a future date when this run will take place in the background or we can request it to begin immediately by checking the Start immediately button as above:

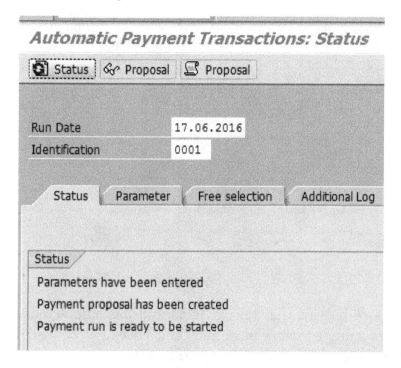

Fig 36

Click on Status refresh after every action to see what status it is at.

Fig 37

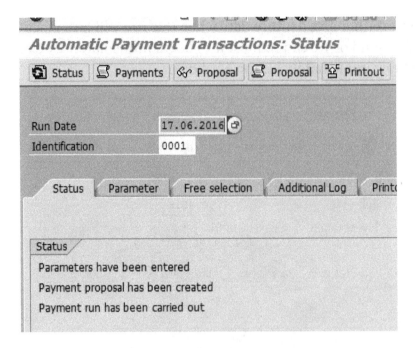

Automatic Payment Transactions: Status

🔁 Status 🗐 Payments 👓 Proposal 🗐 Proposal 👥 Printout

Run Date   17.06.2016

Identification   0001

| Status | Parameter | Free selection | Additional Log | Print… |

Status

Parameters have been entered

Payment proposal has been created

Payment run has been carried out

Fig 38

The above tells us that the payment run has completed and all vendors and customers have had their check cut or instructions sent to the bank to send their amounts by transfer.

To verify what was actually done, click on the Proposal button:

🗐 Proposal

Fig 39

Date	Time	Message text	Message class	Messa
23.11.2016	00:25:04	Job started	00	5
23.11.2016	00:25:04	Step 001 started (program SAPF110S, variant &000000001767, user ID IDES0164)	00	5
23.11.2016	00:25:04	Log for proposal run for payment on 22.11.2016, identification 00001	FZ	4
23.11.2016	00:25:04	>	FZ	6
23.11.2016	00:25:04	> Additional log for vendor 100838 company code SFE1	FZ	6
23.11.2016	00:25:04	>	FZ	6
23.11.2016	00:25:04	> ———— Due date determination additional log	FZ	7
23.11.2016	00:25:04	> Document 1500000026 line item 002 via CAD 2.68	FZ	7
23.11.2016	00:25:04	> Terms of payment: 05.11.2016 0 0.000 % 0 0.000 % 0	FZ	7
23.11.2016	00:25:04	> Item is clearable from 05.11.2016 with payments	FZ	7
23.11.2016	00:25:04	> Posting date for this run is 22.11.2016, for next run 23.11.2016	FZ	7
23.11.2016	00:25:04	> Item should be paid now	FZ	7
23.11.2016	00:25:04	> Item is due with 0.000 % cash discount	FZ	7
23.11.2016	00:25:04	>	FZ	6
23.11.2016	00:25:04	> ———— Due date determination additional log	FZ	7
23.11.2016	00:25:04	> Document 1500000028 line item 002 via CAD 250.00	FZ	7
23.11.2016	00:25:04	> Terms of payment: 05.11.2016 0 0.000 % 0 0.000 % 0	FZ	7
23.11.2016	00:25:04	> Item is clearable from 05.11.2016 with payments	FZ	7
23.11.2016	00:25:04	> Posting date for this run is 22.11.2016, for next run 23.11.2016	FZ	7
23.11.2016	00:25:04	> Item should be paid now	FZ	7
23.11.2016	00:25:04	> Item is due with 0.000 % cash discount	FZ	7

Fig 4

GOODS ISSUE AND IT'S EFFECT ON

ACCOUNTING (U)

T Code VL02N

In the same way as GR has an effect on accounting, goods issue, which is done when finished goods are shipped out to customers also has an effect too. This effect occurs through the Sales & Distribution module when orders are received and processed by companies. When deliveries are made, they relieve inventory and debit the COGS. Again, since creation of sales orders and deliveries is outside the scope of FI (being part of the SD module), we will limit our understanding to the cusp where SD and FI meet. Some of this will be covered when we do Billing later in this manual.

To understand the implications of master data, we will look at the customer master briefly for the data on the SD side that is important to Finance, apart from what we already constructed when we created the customers. The entire sales activity in SD takes place in a 'sales area', which strictly belongs to the SD module. Every sales area is attached to a CC via the sales organization. When AR is created, it is handed off to

Accounting under the CC as a current asset. For the most part, in the sales area data in XD01, only the billing tab is relevant to accounting. We will create our customer now in the sales area of our company:

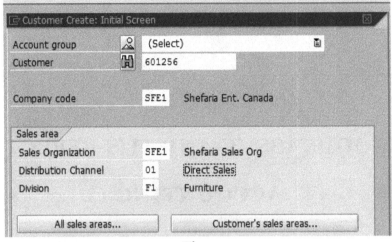

Fig 1

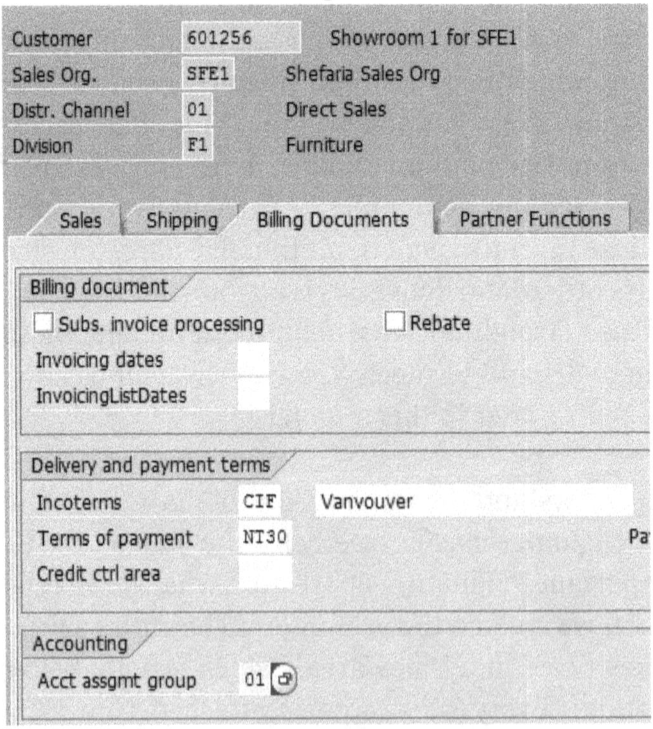

Fig 2

To keep our process simple, we restrict ourselves only to the terms of payment, Incoterms and Acct assignment group. The invoicing dates drive the base line date, which in turn drives the time from which the credit terms kick in. One could have an arrangement with the customer to send invoices only once a month, at EOM in which case, a calendar representing that would need to be entered in this field. Often, customers who receive a very high number of invoices may insist on having only an invoice list i.e. a list of invoices; in those scenarios, an appropriate calendar would need to be put in the Invoicing List Dates field.

For the purpose of this manual, a sales order (of order type OR) and a delivery have already been created and the process brought to the point of posting the goods from the delivery. The detailed creation f sales orders and deliveries, being a part of SD, is outside the scope of this manual. The delivery is goods issued (i.e. it's stocks relieved) in a transaction VL02N by pushing the button Post Goods Issue:

Fig 3

A message at the bottom says

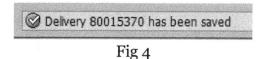

Fig 4

Click on the document flow button 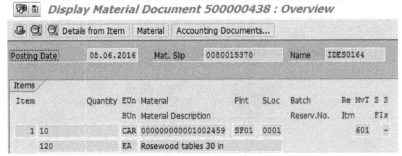 (Fig 3)

Business partner 0000601256 Showroom 1 for SFE1

Document	On	Status
▽ 🗎 Standard Order 0000012416	08.06.2016	Being processed
▽ 🗎 ➡ Delivery 0080015370	08.06.2016	Being processed
🗎 Picking request 20160608	08.06.2016	Completed
🗎 GD goods issue:delvy 0500000438	08.06.2016	complete

Fig 5

Click on the GD goods issue delivery line and then on

:us overview &ᵞ Display document Servi

·tner 0000601256 Showroom 1 for SFE1

	On
·d Order 0000012416	08.06.20
Delivery 0080015370	08.06.20
Picking request 20160608	08.06.20
GD goods issue:delvy 0500000438	08.06.20

Fig 6

Display Material Document 500000438 : Overview

Details from Item Material Accounting Documents...

Posting Date	08.06.2016	Mat. Slip	0080015370	Name	IDES0164

Items

Item	Quantity	EUn	Material	Plnt	SLoc	Batch	Re MvI	S	S
		BUn	Material Description			Reserv.No.	Itm		FIs
1	10	CAR	000000000001002459	SF01	0001		601	-	
	120	EA	Rosewood tables 30 in						

Fig 7

322

Click on the Accounting Documents tab:

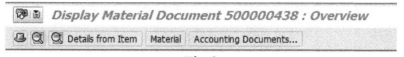

Fig 8

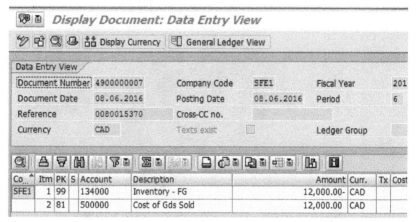

Fig 9

We notice how SAP credited the inventory and debited the COGS. This COGS will form a part of our P & L statement while calculating the periodic profits.

The goods issue in SAP language means the goods now belong to the customer under the custody of the shipper/transporter. Once the inventory is relieved, it is time to invoice the customer. Normally, invoicing is a function that has traditionally been performed by the finance or accounting dept. though in SAP, it falls under the SD module.

BILLING (U)

Billing in SAP is a function performed in Sales and Distribution. However, in many companies, billing is in reality, done by the Finance or Accounting department. Thus, we will cover billing to some extent in this manual.

In SAP, Billing is a very large sub-module and the term is used as a very generic term to encompass all invoicing, credit/debit memos, pro-forma invoices, inter-company invoicing etc. There are many kinds of billing documents that are set up in SAP to represent different requirements. Further, depending on the process, billing may be done with reference to a delivery where actual physical goods are invoiced or directly from a sales order in cases of services or debit/credit memos.

We will go through in some detail with 2 kinds of billing:

1. Invoicing with reference to deliveries i.e. when tangible, physical goods are sold
2. Invoicing wrf services when services are provided

We will also see how pro-forma invoices are created and debit or credit memos processed in SAP. As also, how data is passed from the SD module to the FI module once billing has taken place.

There are many transactions to do billing. Billing for a single or a few transactions can be done by VF01. Large-scale billing i.e. for many customer and/or documents is done in VF04. VF06 is utilized for creating background jobs for high volume billing. Depending on need, invoicing jobs are set up to run in the background or the users themselves do invoicing.

In the Order to Cash transaction cycle in the SD/FI modules, a transaction typically begins with a sales order or a credit/debit memo request. This sales order may be converted directly into an invoice if it is a services business of via a delivery into invoice if it is shipment of tangible products.

I.   CUSTOMER MASTER DATA WITH RESPECT TO BILLING (U)

T Code VD01 or XD01

Here, we will understand the order and the customer master's invoicing tab under sales area data in more detail.

A customer master has the following fields under the Sales Area data which are significant for accounting:

Fig 1

Invoicing dates - sometimes customers may insist on getting one invoice for the entire period if there are many transactions. This field can be populated with a calendar that will define the billing date of the invoices. This date will then default into every sales order and invoicing will take place with that same billing date for all the sales orders. The billing date is a precursor to the Baseline date from where the credit terms of the customer begin. Normally it is kept the same as the billing date though it can be altered. Every invoice in standard SAP leads to an accounting document which is what is reflected in a customer's AR. Usually companies prefer to keep it the same as the invoice number though it can be kept different as per need.

InvoiceListDates – invoices, for convenience, when in a high number can be combined into an invoice list. An invoice list is merely a 'list' of the invoices. It is not an accounting document. While pricing can be done in an invoice list and it becomes useful in cases of rebate processing, most organizations will prefer not to do it as it is double maintenance. A calendar similar to the one described earlier is maintained in this field to combine the invoices on that date.

Incoterms - Incoterms are internationally agreed shipping terms and have a strong bearing on the freight of the product. Depending on the Inco terms, the freight costs may or may not be a part of the invoice. Thus, these terms get to play a role in the invoking module.

Terms of Payment – When defined, these are the credit terms of the customer. The invoice will be due based on these terms, which will be used to calculate the baseline date. Baseline date is the date from which the actual credit clock begins. Usually it will be same as Billing date but need not be.

Credit control area – when set, this CCA is the umbrella under which the customer's credit limits are set up. The exposure of open AR, orders not yet executed or in the pipeline, all may together be a part of these credit limits, which will be depleted as more, and more invoicing takes place. Credit notes will, in the reverse way, release more credit limits of the customers.

Account Assignment group – is often used to define the G/L accounts to which the revenue relating to product sales, freight, surcharges/discounts etc will be directed to.

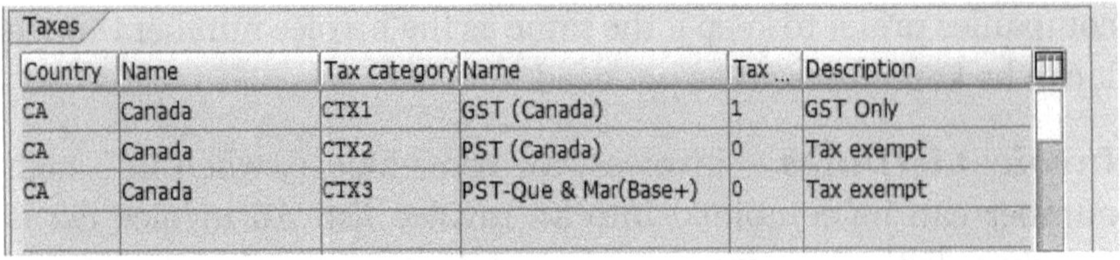

Taxes						
Country	Name	Tax category	Name	Tax ...	Description	
CA	Canada	CTX1	GST (Canada)	1	GST Only	
CA	Canada	CTX2	PST (Canada)	0	Tax exempt	
CA	Canada	CTX3	PST-Que & Mar(Base+)	0	Tax exempt	

Fig 2

The implication of the tax setup will be discussed in the section of Taxes separately later.

Among the check buttons, one is important:

Fig 3

If this is not checked, the customer will not be entitled to rebates.

Partner Functions. Standard SAP has 4 different partner functions or roles that a customer can play in the transaction. The 4 are defined below. They can be, and often are, different in one customer set up. For Finance, the only one relevant is the Payer – the function which will clear the AR.

The sold to is the highest of them all in hierarchy and can quadruple up as all 4 as in our case.

PF	Partner Function	Number	Name
SP	Sold-to party	601256	Showroom 1 for SFE1
BP	Bill-to party	601256	Showroom 1 for SFE1
PY	Payer	601256	Showroom 1 for SFE1
SH	Ship-to party	601256	Showroom 1 for SFE1

Fig 4

- Sold to party; the party that usually is the main customer that drives the purchases
- Ship to party; the location of the customer where goods are shipped to or services performed at
- Bill to; where the invoice is sent
- Payer; the one who pays and in whose name the AR is created

II. DIFFERENT TYPES OF BILLINGS AND BILLING TYPES (U)

The Billing type defines the purpose and behavior of how the transaction will get billed. Standard SAP has many billing types and they can be made to follow different numbering sequences. Many companies may also prefer to have this numbering sequence set up by CCs only for the purpose of identification and separation. The more common billing types in SAP are:

F2 Invoice (F2)
F5 Pro Forma for Order
F8 Pro Forma Inv f Dlv
G2 Credit Memo
IG Internal Credit Memo
IV Intercompany billing
L2 Debit Memo
LG Credit memo list
LR Invoice list
LRS Cancel invoice list
S1 Invoice Cancellation

We will look at F2, G2 and F5, the 3 satisfying different purposes.

F2 invoice can be created from a goods issued delivery only or from a sales order only. In the former case, the Actual goods issue date in the delivery serves to become the billing date in the invoice. In the latter case, the billing date flows from the sales order itself.

III.   INVOICING FROM A DELIVERY (U)

T Code VF01

The billing date that the invoice of this delivery will assume is under the Goods movement tab in the delivery in transaction VL03N – the Actual gds mvt date (Fig 4) goes on to become the billing date.

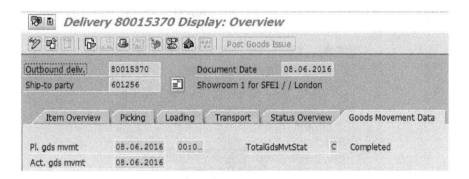

Fig 5

Using the transaction VF01 we will create the invoice from this delivery. In the VF01 screen, enter this delivery number:

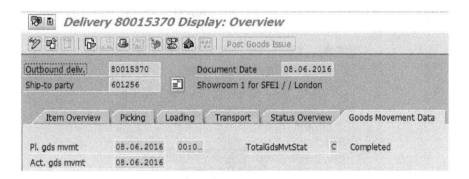

Fig 6

There is normally no need to enter the Billing type unless a billing type different from the system proposed one is required and in that case, certain configurations must be set up already for the billing to happen.

The open fields are the default criteria that can be changed and/or applied to all the deliveries being invoiced in this transaction.

A drop down of the Billing type will give the choices available:

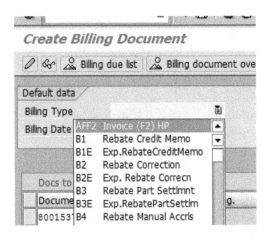

Fig 7

We can enter any dates in the other 3 fields though the billing data must be in the open period for the document to post to accounting. There is no need to define any of this data as it comes from the sales order and/or from the delivery into this invoice.

Multiple deliveries can be entered in the screen at the same time and depending on the configuration set up, some of them may combine to create one invoice e.g. if the customers, billing dates, pricing etc are the same.

Fig 8

If there are multiple lines on the delivery and we need to create separate invoices for each line or a combination of lines, or we simply want to invoice only a limited number now and the rest later, the button 📋 Selection list can be used to 'select' the line items we want to invoice now.

In our example, we will invoice the entire delivery. With the delivery # entered in the screen, Hit Enter:

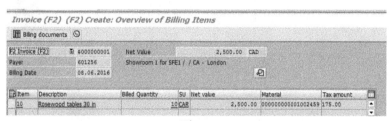

Fig 9

The invoice will get most of the data from the delivery and/or order and may re-determine some depending on how configurations are set up.

Save and the invoice # will show at the bottom:

333

IV. INVOICING FROM AN ORDER (U)

T Code VF01

In businesses, which do not sell any tangible goods but provide services, orders are created and invoiced directly when the services are completed or based on any other billing plan/schedule. The order is created in the transaction VA01 – use order type OR. We create a sales order for service materials:

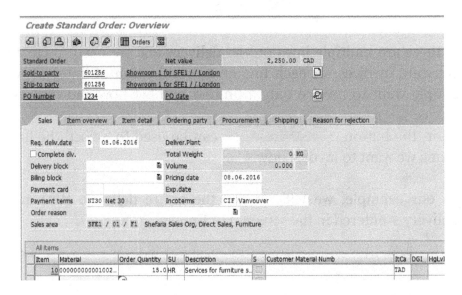

Fig 10

Save the order:

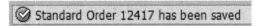

Fig 11

Now this order can be invoiced directly in VF01 bypassing a delivery (because there are no tangible goods to deliver for a service) as we did the delivery earlier:

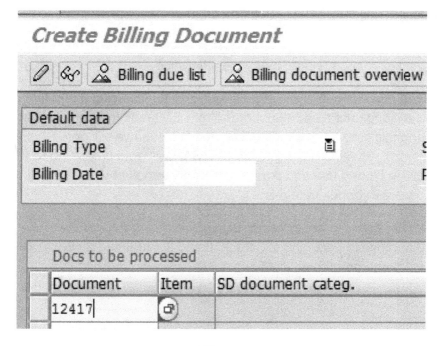

Fig 12

Save:

Fig 13

V. CREATING CREDIT MEMOS

T Code VF01

Credit memos may have (at least) 2 origins:

1. Return of goods from the customer
2. Non goods related e.g. price difference

The process will be exactly the same as for invoicing. If the former, it will originate as a returns order from SD leading up to a delivery and this time, instead of Posting goods issue, we will post *Goods receipt*, thus increasing the stocks. SAP will auto determine which billing type to use and create the credit memo wrt to delivery which has been goods receipted.

If the latter, the debit memo request will be created for the difference in price and the credit memo will create directly wrt the credit memo request itself as for issues like price difference, deliveries have no role to play since no material is being returned.

VI. IMPORTANT FIELDS ON A BILLING DOCUMENT

Most of the header data in the billing document defaults from the customer master and most of the line item data, from the material master.

VF02 is the transaction to make any changes in the existing billing document. VF03 is the transaction to display the billing document.

Payer:

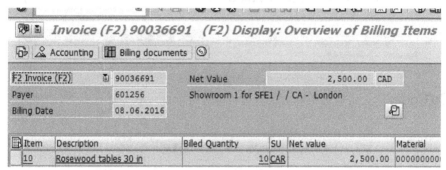

Fig 14

As far as Accounting is concerned, the Payer is the only significant customer. A customer master has 4 primary partner functions as we discussed earlier:

- Sold to party
- Ship to party
- Bill to
- Payer

Billing Date:

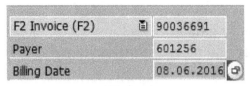

Fig 15

This is the date when the baseline date usually begins i.e. when the credit terms of the customer begin.

Under the section Header>Header:

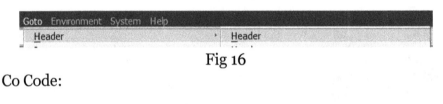

Fig 16

Co Code:

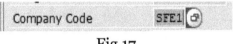

Fig 17

This is the CC responsible for the sales organization that did the transaction. This CC holds the AR and the receivables will form a part of it's current assets. On the Conditions tab, once can see the value of the document along with the taxes:

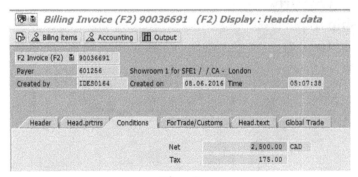

Fig 18

338

At the line item level, the important fields are:

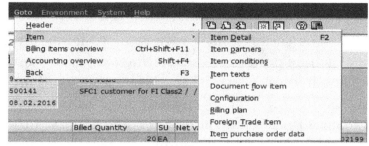

Fig 19

Service Rendered Date:

Fig 20

This is the date on which taxes are calculated i.e. the taxes existing on that date in SAP (or external systems) are the valid taxes for this transaction. It is independent of the billing date or date when the order created.

Calculation of taxes is discussed in the next section.

VII. PRO-FORMA INVOICES (U)

T Code VF01

Occasionally the customer may require a pro-forma invoice for purpose of getting prior approvals for imports, or for customs or bank funding in cases of capital goods etc. 2 standard pro-forma invoices exist in SAP – the F5 created from a sales order and F8 with reference to a delivery. The delivery does not have to be goods issued for this purpose. Pro-forma invoices do not create accounting entries i.e. they never hit AR. Neither can they be cancelled.

From order, type F5:

Create the sales order (order type called OR) in VA01, all that is needed to enter are the customer, material and quantity and SAP can determine everything else if the configurations and data re set up correctly.

Fig 21

Save

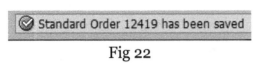

Fig 22

In VF01, enter the order # in the Document field and choose F5:

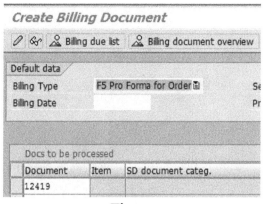

Fig 23

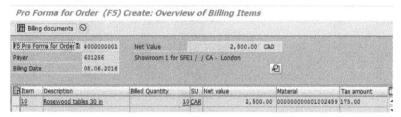

Fig 24

Save

Fig 25

From delivery, F8:

Sometimes information relating to shipping needs to be given on the pro-forma invoice like palletizing, gross weights, net weights, transporter etc and some of it may be available only in the delivery. In those cases, a delivery is created from the sales order and the pro-forma created wrt to that delivery instead of from the order.

Unlike the real invoice, for a pro-forma invoice the delivery need not be goods issued for the pro-forma to be created from it.

Create the order (type OR) in VAo1 and then the delivery in VLo1N using that sales order.

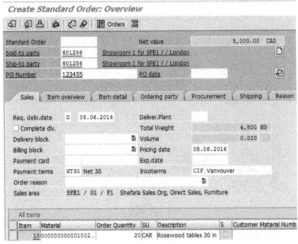

Fig 26

Fig 27

In VLo1N create a delivery from this sales order:

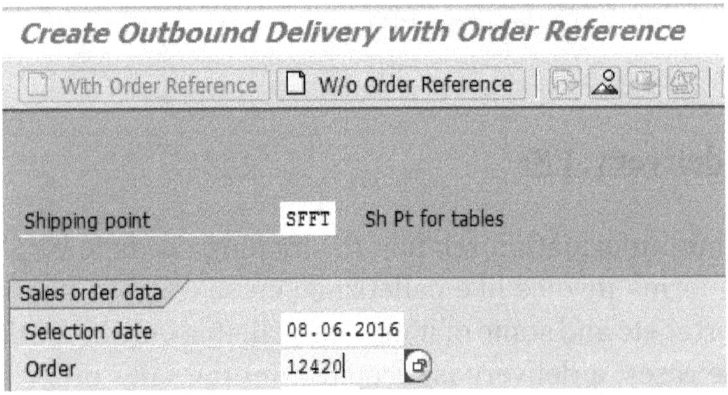

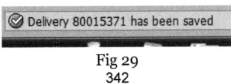

Fig 28

Delivery 80015371 has been saved

Fig 29

Use this delivery # in VF01, choosing F8 as the Billing type:

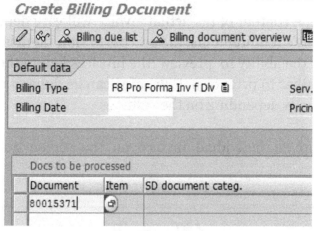

Fig 30

Hit Enter:

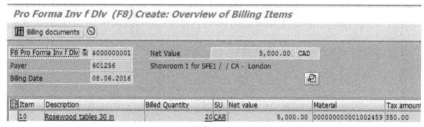

Fig 31

Save:

Fig 32

VIII. VIEWING AN INVOICE (U)

T Code VF03

Although the content of the actual invoice will vary depending on the company's requirements, the process to view them is the same. SAP offers the ability to 'preview' the invoices before the user can decide whether to print or not. Printing can be done in mass scale or individually depending on the volumes.

To look up an individual invoice on the screen go to VF03 (display):

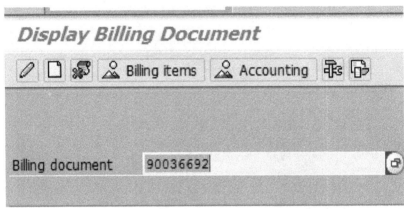

Fig 33

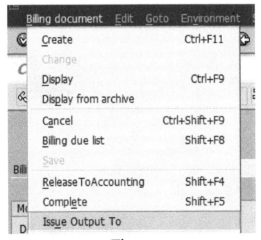

Fig 34

344

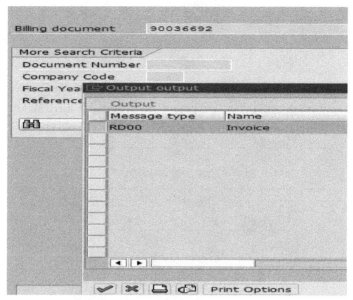

Fig 35

Every company will have it's own Message type (also called Outputs) and often there will be multiple (usually different formats and reasons thereof).

With the appropriate Output highlighted, click on the button

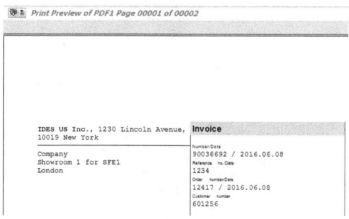

Fig 36

Use scrolling keys to see all the pages if there are multiple.

IX. Cancelling a Billing Document (U)

T Code VF11

This is done in transaction VF11 which looks like VF01 except for a different header and that here you have to enter the billing document that needs to be cancelled instead of the order # or delivery #:

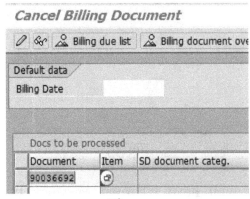

Fig 37

Hit Enter and Save.

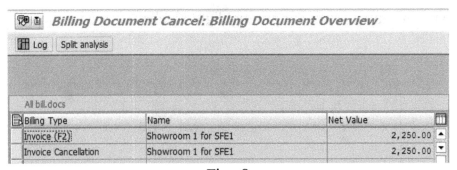

Fig 38

Fig 39

Once an existing billing document is cancelled, it releases the order or the delivery to get billed again. For the most part, in SAP, it is not possible to cancel a preceding document without first cancelling the subsequent document. Thus, it is very important that the data is good from the origin itself, as SAP can be very unforgiving if the data is wrong.

X. RELEASING BILLING DOCUMENTS TO ACCOUNTING (U)

T Code VFX3

With Billing over, Sales & Distribution hands off the data to accounting. At this cusp is a transaction VFX3 that has to be regularly monitored. Most billing documents will lead up to an accounting document (pro-forma invoices being a notable exception). However, due to various reasons these billing documents get stuck and have to be manually fixed by the users so they can make their way to AR. Some reasons for this are:

1. Old document, billing date is in a closed period.
2. Customer was not extended in the CC i.e. does not have CC data
3. Pricing was not correct
4. G/L account determination for revenue/freight etc. does not exist or is incorrect
5. For exports, certain mandatory foreign trade related data is missing
6. Tax calculations are not correct

And some more that may occur due to company specific custom transactions and data. This data will need to be fixed before these documents can be posted and in some cases, documents will need to be cancelled to re-create them with the correct data.

XI. ACCOUNTING DOCUMENT

Most invoices will lead to an accounting document if all the data was good in the invoice. The exceptions are special invoices like pro-forma invoices.

In VF03 we can view the invoice we created and it's accounting document:

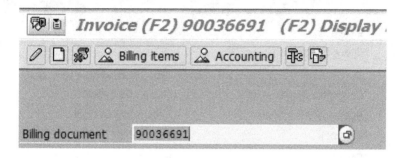

Fig 40

Click on ![Accounting]

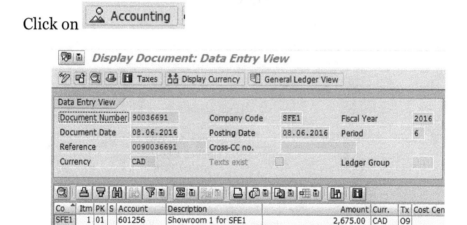

Fig 41

An accounting document is what one sees in the customer's receivables – normally most companies prefer to keep it same as the billing document # to avoid confusion though in SAP it is possible to have both of them as different.

XII. RELATIONSHIP BROWSER

T Code VF03, FB03

A very powerful tool to view the entire chain of transactions is a Relationship browser can be accessed from the accounting document

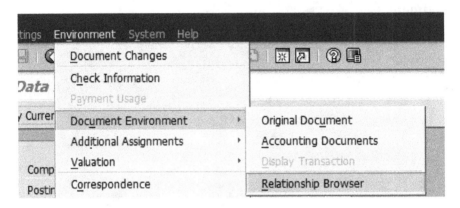

Fig 42

Document Relationship Browser

Relationship Tree	Descriptn
▽ Accounting document	SFE1 0090036691 2016
▽ CustIndivBillingDoc	0090036691
▽ Outbound Delivery	0080015370
Sales Order	0000012416
▽ CustIndivBillingDoc	0090036687
▽ CustIndivBillingDoc	0090036688
Accounting document	SFE1 0090036688 2016
Accounting document	SFE1 0090000000 2016
▽ CustIndivBillingDoc	0090036689
▽ CustIndivBillingDoc	0090036690
Accounting document	SFE1 0090036690 2016
Accounting document	SFE1 0090036689 2016
▽ Material Document	0500000438 2016
Accounting document	SFE1 4900000007 2016

Fig 43

350

TAXES IN SAP (U)

I.   PROCESS (C/U)

T Code SPRO, FTXP

Taxes in SAP are a setup of 3 modules - FI, SD and MM, the main structure and configurations are set up in FI and it is worthwhile to look at the user/functional aspect of this set up. The tax procedure in SAP is set up for each country; it is independent of the CC i.e. all CCs in any certain country can have only one tax procedure.

While not going into the details of the configurations because they are not CC specific, it is important to understand what these tax procedures are and how they are actually implemented in SAP.

Taxes in North America and Europe are calculated in different ways. We will concentrate on the Canadian taxes here which, though calculated the same way as the US ones, are far less complex than US taxation because in Canada it is a 2 tiered structure of Federal and Provincial taxes only while in the US, it is 4 tiered depending on industry, though generally most will fall under 3 tiers. The 4 tiers are state, city, county and district. Very few industries will get the district tax applied. Europe is straight forward with a single VAT being applied.

For this complex taxation and rates, corporations in the US also depend on external services, the 2 most popular being Vertex and Thomson Reuters (also called Sabrix). Often these external systems also keep track of the taxes applied and prepare reports for audits and compliance as well as for filing with the appropriate authorities.

There are 2 primary kinds of taxes in SAP:

- Input tax, used for purchases
- Output tax, used for sales

Depending on the complexity of the company's taxation i.e. based on the customer base and product offering, it may decide to:

- Follow a simple tax procedure whereby all calculations in SAP are done in a standard fashion, not dependent on the exact location of the customer. In Canada or US, this would typically apply to companies, which do business only in the same one province.

- May use the location of the customer if the business is done across provinces or states as the federal tax also will now come into play. This procedure uses Jurisdiction codes, which are provided by the govt. or can be created in SAP and are based on exact locations of the customers since taxes are always applied based on the place of consumption. However, the calculation of them still, would take place within SAP

-

- If the requirement is complex in terms of product and service offerings, which may be subject to different rates of taxation, the company may decide to connect to an external system like Vertex as noted above. The taxes here too, are calculated based on the jurisdiction code however; the calculation does not take place within SAP. Instead, the pertinent data is sent out to the external system via a transmission and the taxation numbers are returned back by that system and applied in SAP. This is usually real time.

Within SAP, the process is driven by tax procedures, tax codes and tax classifications. The mechanism is as follows:

WHO: Ship to customer for output tax or purchasing plant for input tax. Taxes are generally applied based on the place of service provided/consumption/use.

IF: If tax will be applied. Tax classifications are master data and the customers are given the appropriate tax class in their customer master. Alike, for vendors in the vendor master. The tax classifications are usually simple – 0 means customer is non-taxable and 1 means taxable. Occasionally we may have something additional also, like partial taxation. A similar indicator exists in the material master, which decides if the product or service is taxable, or not. Only when both, customer and material are set as taxable, is the tax applied.

HOW: The tax procedure decides this. How will the tax be applied i.e. directly as intra provincial, via jurisdiction codes internally in SAP or from an external system. As we know, we can configure only one tax procedure per country so before SAP is implemented this choice is generally made.

HOW MUCH: This is decided by the tax codes or external systems. In a typical taxation setup, the Finance or accounting department sets up these tax codes in a transaction FTXP that replicates the tax procedure being used and sets up the correct tax rates. SD replicates the same for sales and MM for purchases in their respective tax pricing conditions.

To set up taxes in a tax code. Go to transaction FTXP, in the pop up window, say CA (for Canada):

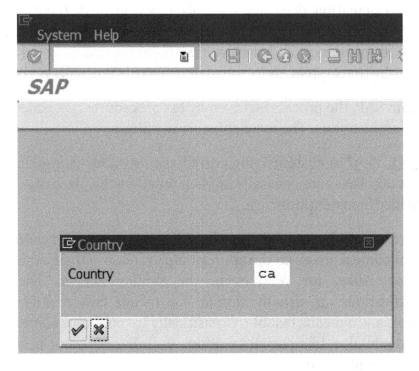

Fig 1

In the window that comes up:

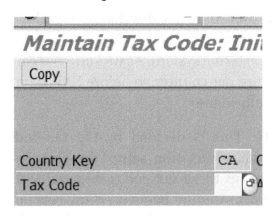

Fig 2

Place the cursor in the Tax code field and hit F4 or ask for the drop down:

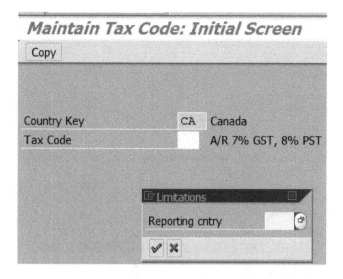

Fig 3

Hit Enter again without entering CA and all the tax codes set up for Canada will come up:

Tx	Description
00	0 input tax
10	TAXCANN
I0	A/P 0% GST, 0%PST
I1	A/P 7% GST, 8% Ont PST distributed
I2	A/P 7% GST, 7% BC PST distributed
I3	A/P 7% GST, 11% NB PST distributed
I4	A/P 7% GST, 6.5% PST Quebec distributed
I5	A/P 7% GST, 6.5% QST, separate
I6	A/P 7% GST, 7% PST Manitoba distributed
I7	A/P 7% GST, 9% PST Saskatchewan, distributed
I8	A/P 7% GST, 12% NFLD PST distributed
I9	A/P GST 7%, no PST
IN	A/P 7% GST, 11% NS PST distributed
IP	A/P 7% GST, 10% PEI PST distributed
M0	New tax code
N0	No tax
O0	A/R 0% GST, 0% PST
O1	A/R 7% GST, 8% PST Ontario
O2	A/R 7% GST, 7% MST Manitoba
O3	A/R 7% GST, 9% SST Saskatchewan
O4	A/R 7% GST, 7% BCST British Columbia
O9	A/R GST 7%, No PST
P0	A/P GST exempt, PST 12% NewFoundland

Fig 4

355

Let us choose O9 as the one we will set up taxation in. Double click on it and Hit Enter:

Maintain Tax Code: Tax Rates

Properties | Tax accounts | Deactivate line

Country Key	CA	Canada
Tax Code	O9	A/R GST 7%, No PST
Procedure	TAXCA	
Tax type	A	Output tax

Percentage rates

Tax Type	Acct Key	Tax Percent. Rate	Level	From Lvl	Cond. Type
*			0	0	
Base Amount			100	0	BASB
***********			105	0	
A/P and MM			106	0	
Federal Taxes (US):			107	0	
*	VSC		110	100	GTI1
*	TR1		112	100	TRA1
A/P Sales Tax 1 Inv.	NVV		115	100	AP1I
*	NVV		120	100	GTI2
Subtotal			199	0	
Subtotal			200	0	
Provincial Taxes (Ca			210	0	
*	NVV		220	100	PTI1
*	VST		230	100	PTI2

Fig 5

Percentage rates

Tax Type	Acct Key	Tax Percent. Rate	Level	From Lvl	Cond. Type
*	TR2		232	100	TRA2
*			250	0	
Separate G/L posting			251	0	
*	NVV		260	199	PTI3
*	VST		270	199	PTI4
*	TR3		272	199	TRA3
Subtotal			298	0	
*			299	0	
Self assessed:			300	0	
*	VSC		310	100	GTI3
*	VST		320	100	PTI5
*	VST		330	199	PTI6
*************			399	0	
Self assess Prov.			410	0	

Fig 6

356

Tax Type	Acct Key	Tax Percent. Rate	Level	From Lvl	Cond. Type
*	MW1			420	100	PTU1
*	MW2		430	200	PTU2
*			498	0	
**********			499	0	
A/R and SD			600	0	
*	MWS		610	100	GTO0
*			698	0	
Subtotal			700	0	
*	MWS		710	100	GTO1
*	MW1		720	700	GTO2
Subtotal			750	0	
*	MW2		830	100	PST1
*	MW2		840	750	PST2

Percentage rates

Fig 7

The above is the tax procedure TAXCA being used in our system in Canada. Thus, all CCs in Canada are using this. The main columns denote:

-   Tax type – input, output. Though we have called for tax code O9, the procedure is common to both, input and output.

-   Account key. This key is a determining factor of how the tax values are going to post to GLs

-   Tax percent rate. You would be most concerned about this field. This is where the actual numbers relating to tax percentages will be entered.

Click on the tax 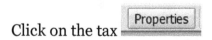 Properties

Here we can alter/enter the description of what this tax code represents. Let us say we retain this and our customers are charged 7% GST when we sell them the products. Just having 7% in the description does not mean it will get charged. We now need to enter this 7% in the field relating to MWS as the account key.

357

Maintain Tax Code: Tax Rates

| Properties | Tax accounts | Deactivate line |

Country Key	CA	Canada	
Tax Code	09	A/R GST 7%, No PST	
Procedure	TAXCA		
Tax type	A	Output tax	

Percentage rates

Tax Type	Acct Key	Tax Percent. Rate	Level	From Lvl	Cond. Type
*			0	0	

Properties

Tax Code	09	A/R GST 7%, No PST
Tax type	A	Output tax
CheckID	☐	
EU code		
Target tax code		
Tgt Tax Code: Output		
Tgt Tax Code: Input		
Tol.per.rate		
Reporting cntry		

Fig 8

Maintain Tax Code: Tax Rates

| Properties | Tax accounts | Deactivate line |

Country Key	CA	Canada	
Tax Code	09	A/R GST 7%, No PST	
Procedure	TAXCA		
Tax type	A	Output tax	

Percentage rates

Tax Type	Acct Key	Tax Percent. Rate	Level	From Lvl	Cond. Type
*	MW1		420	100	PTU1
*	MW2		430	200	PTU2
*			498	0	
**********			499	0	
A/R and SD			600	0	
*	MWS	7.000	610	100	GTO0
*			698	0	
Subtotal			700	0	
*	MWS		710	100	GTO1
*	MW1		720	700	GTO2
Subtotal			750	0	
*	MWZ		830	100	PST1
*	MWZ		840	750	PST2

Fig 9

358

In our case we are not using the jurisdiction based tax procedure so configurations are missing and we don't want to alter that because it will affect all CCs of others also that have been created in Canada. However, the above must be maintained if we use a JC based procedure.

Click on   Tax accounts

It asks for the CoA:

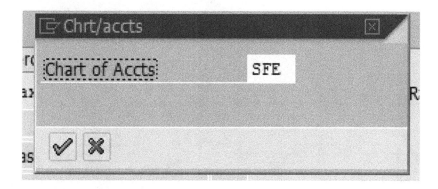

Fig 10

In this field, we have the ability to define the tax G/L accounts where we want the GST/PST/HST etc postings to be made. Again, these become relevant only when using a JC based procedure.

We will, however, see how tax can be applied to a sales document only via SD because the tax postings still flow to some G/L. There are 3 steps, all 3 of them are master data.

II. MASTER DATA (U)

T Code XD01/XD02, MM01/MM02, VK11/VK12

Let us ensure our customer is taxable first i..e it has tax class as 1 for GST:

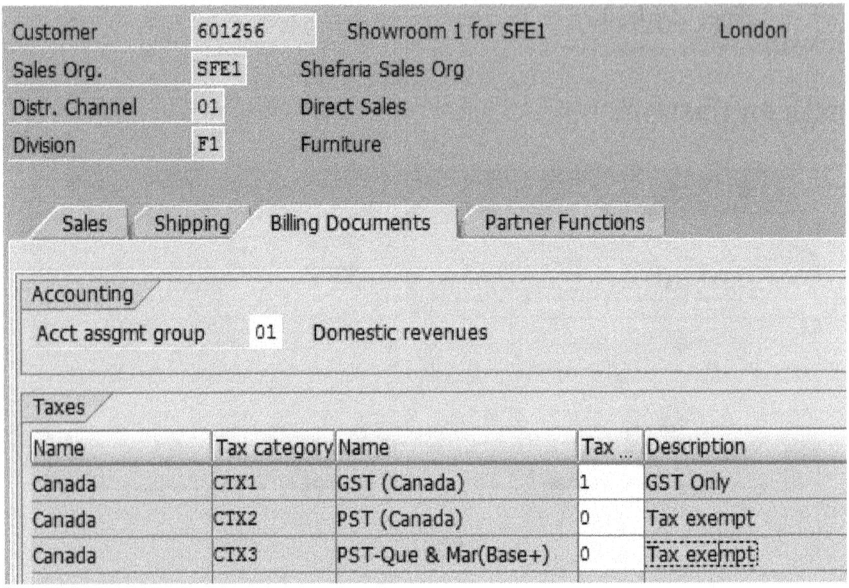

Customer	601256	Showroom 1 for SFE1		London
Sales Org.	SFE1	Shefaria Sales Org		
Distr. Channel	01	Direct Sales		
Division	F1	Furniture		

Sales | Shipping | Billing Documents | Partner Functions

Accounting

Acct assgmt group   01   Domestic revenues

Taxes

Name	Tax category	Name	Tax ...	Description
Canada	CTX1	GST (Canada)	1	GST Only
Canada	CTX2	PST (Canada)	0	Tax exempt
Canada	CTX3	PST-Que & Mar(Base+)	0	Tax exempt

Fig 11

Our material also to taxable as we know taxes get applied only when both are set to taxable in MM02

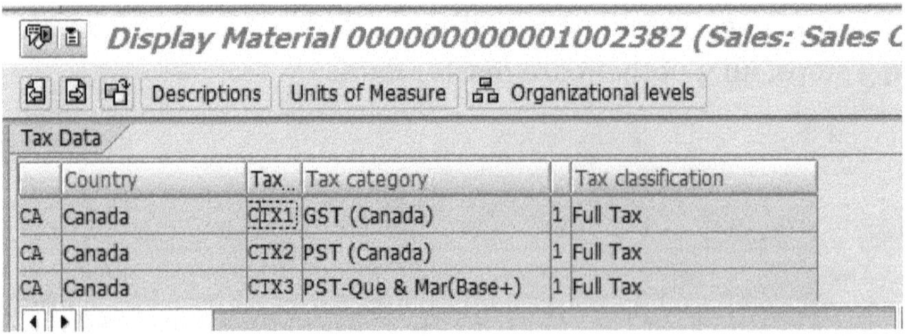

Display Material 000000000001002382 (Sales: Sales C

Descriptions | Units of Measure | Organizational levels

Tax Data

	Country	Tax ...	Tax category		Tax classification
CA	Canada	CTX1	GST (Canada)	1	Full Tax
CA	Canada	CTX2	PST (Canada)	1	Full Tax
CA	Canada	CTX3	PST-Que & Mar(Base+)	1	Full Tax

Fig 12

360

Next, we set a tax pricing condition only on the SD side. This is done in transaction VK11:

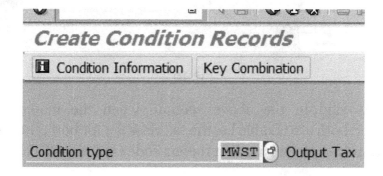

Fig 13

Hit Enter and choose the 2nd sequence as we are doing domestic sales here:

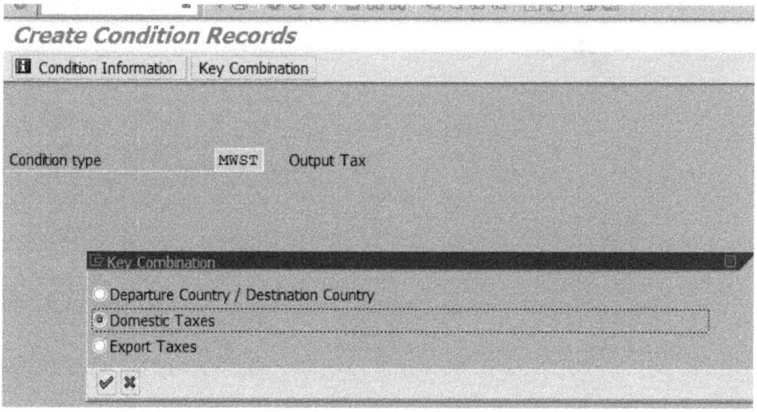

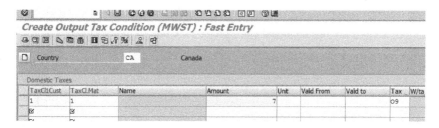

Fig 14

Enter data as below:

Fig 15

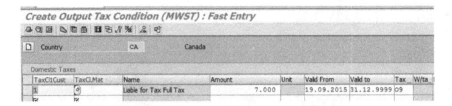

Fig 16

Save. As said in the above section, when the material and customer, both are taxable i.e. the tax class is 1 for both, then apply a domestic tax of 7% based on the tax code O9 (only GST).

III.   EFFECT ON DOCUMENT CREATION (U)

T Code VA01

Let us create a sales order and see the effect:

We see on the pricing screen that the system has now applied the 7% tax we set up:

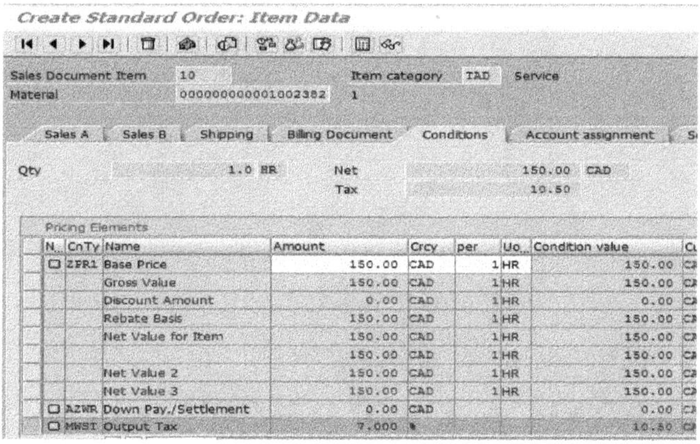

Fig 17

Next, we take this order to invoicing and see what happens with the taxes:

The accounting document of the invoice so created has a separate line for tax:

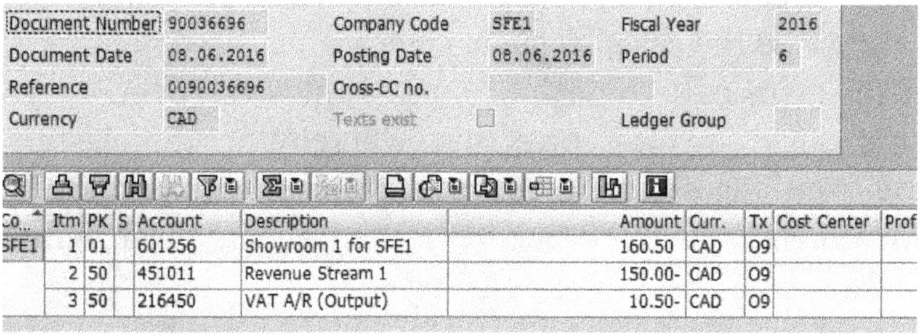

Fig 18

We noticed the amount got posted to the G/L 216450 and the customer got charged to pay this amount.

INVOICE CORRECTION (U)

T Code VA01, VF01

Occasionally, we will have a situation when taxes were charged on an invoice when the customer was actually nontaxable due to their status and/or location or any other reason. If the invoice was created in the current open period, then the simplest way is to cancel and re-create a correct one without taxes. However, this may not always be the case; as such, things often become known only when the invoices become due for payment later. In SAP there is a process called 'invoice correction' whereby for the existing transaction from a closed period, we can re-create an invoice by netting off only the taxes if the period in which the original document was posted, is now closed.

Let us say we have an invoice on which we charged taxes as in the highlighted invoice below:

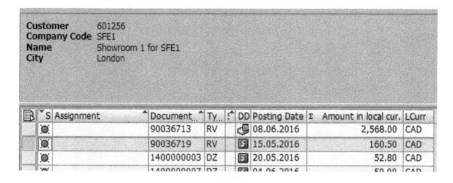

Fig 1

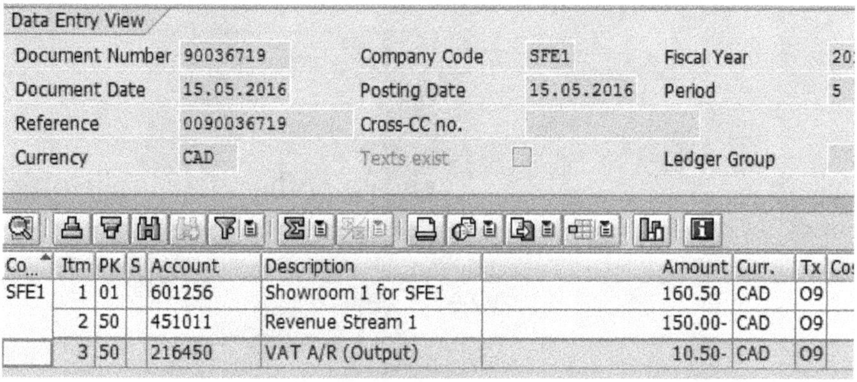

Fig 2

The customer was in fact nontaxable and so will pay only the net amount instead of with taxes so we need to adjust the tax amount in SAP. One way of course, is to simply post a manual JE for this amount. However, since the transaction has actually originated from the SD side in SAP, the correct procedure would also be to originate the correction from SD. Besides, often tax authorities and auditors do not like to see manual JEs.

Order Creation

To originate this from SD, we create an order of type RK in transaction VA01 wrt this invoice:

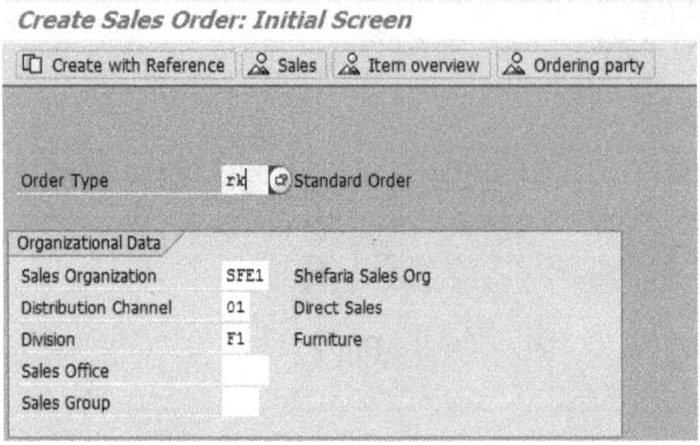
Create Sales Order: Initial Screen
Create with Reference
Sales
Item overview
Ordering party
Order Type
rk
Standard Order
Organizational Data
Sales Organization
SFE1
Shefaria Sales Org
Distribution Channel
01
Direct Sales
Division
F1
Furniture
Sales Office
Sales Group

Fig 3

Click on 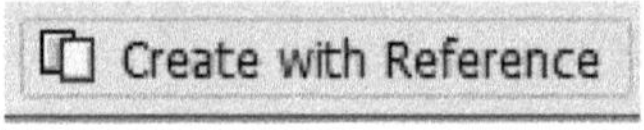
Create with Reference
and enter the reference invoice as below:

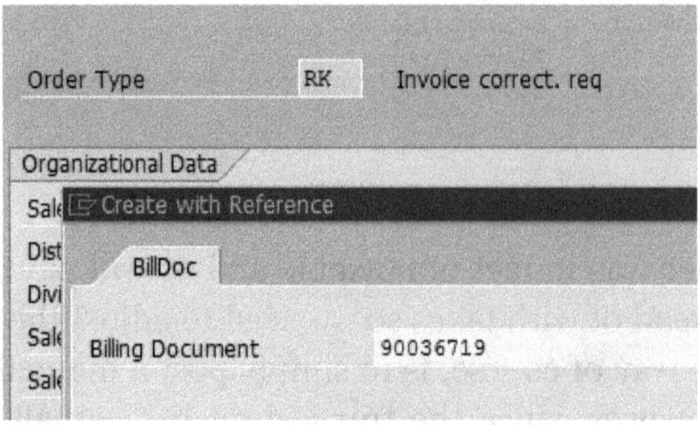
Order Type
RK
Invoice correct. req
Organizational Data
Create with Reference
BillDoc
Billing Document
90036719

Fig 4

Click on Copy:

Copy
Item Selection

Fig 5

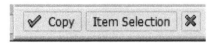

We find that SAP pulls in 2 lines, one positive value and the other negative:

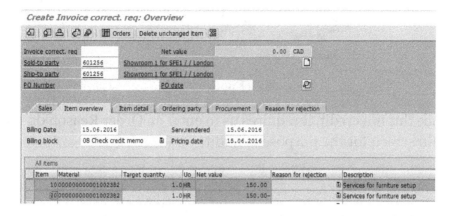

Fig 6

Left as it is, the system will create an invoice of 0 value. However, since we need to post a credit entry only for the taxes, we need to change the tax indicators at the line item level for the 2nd line on this order under the Billing tab. Note that SAP will not allow to change anything on the first line anyway as that is a copy of what already occurred in the invoice and is thus, greyed out.

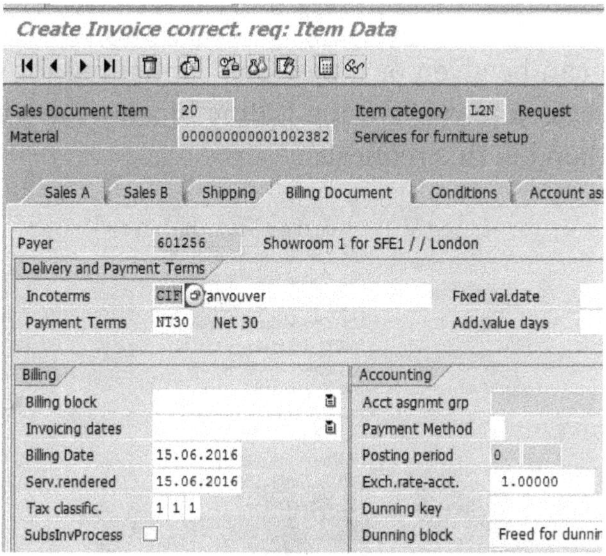

Fig 7

The indicators in the Tax Classific. fields need to be made to 0 as below:

Serv.rendered 15.06.2016
Tax classific. 0 0 0
SubsInvProcess

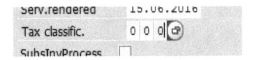

Fig 8

Since this is a credit, it requires us to enter an Order Reason on the main screen for the purpose of audit:

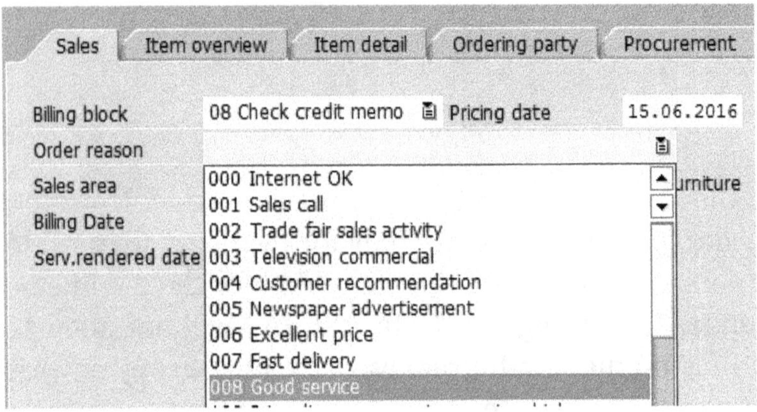

Sales
Item overview
Item detail
Ordering party
Procurement
Billing block
08 Check credit memo
Pricing date
15.06.2016
Order reason
Sales area
Billing Date
Serv.rendered date
000 Internet OK
001 Sales call
002 Trade fair sales activity
003 Television commercial
004 Customer recommendation
005 Newspaper advertisement
006 Excellent price
007 Fast delivery
008 Good service

Fig 9

Any reason can be given or a new one configured for such cases. We will also need to remove the Billing block we see in the print above and then bill this request:

Billing block
08 Check credit memo
Order reason
Sales area
Billing Date
01 Calculation missing
02 Compl Confirm Missng
03 Prices incomplete
04 Check terms of paymt
05 Check delivery terms
08 Check credit memo
09 Check debit memo
41 not yet completed
42 no price agreement
43 new price as of....
50 Authorisation Req
51 Rejected
All items
Item

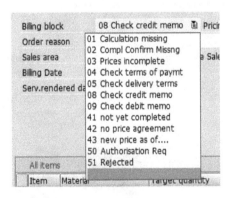

Fig 10

Billing

Credit Memo (G2) Create: Overview of Billing Items

Billing documents

G2 Credit Memo	6000000001	Net Value		0.00 CAD		
Payer	601256	Showroom 1 for SFE1 / / CA - London				
Billing Date	15.06.2016					

Item	Description	Billed Quantity	SU	Net value	Material	Tax amount
10	Services for furniture setup	1.0	HR	150.00	000000000001002382	10.50
20	Services for furniture setup	1.0	HR	150.00-	000000000001002382	0.00

Fig 11

As we see above, SAP will be posting a credit memo for the tax amount dollars only. Save the document. The accounting document tells us the customer is being credited and tax G/L account being debited with this tax amount.

Data Entry View

Document Number	90036720	Company Code	SFE1	Fiscal Year	20
Document Date	15.06.2016	Posting Date	15.06.2016	Period	6
Reference	0090036719	Cross-CC no.			
Currency	CAD	Texts exist		Ledger Group	

Co.	Itm	PK	S	Account	Description	Amount	Curr.	Tx	Cc
SFE1	1	11		601256	Showroom 1 for SFE1	10.50-	CAD	**	
	2	40		451011	Revenue Stream 1	150.00	CAD	09	
	3	40		216450	VAT A/R (Output)	10.50	CAD	09	
	4	50		451011	Revenue Stream 1	150.00-	CAD		

Fig 12

The customer's AR statement now reads this tax amount being netted off. So, when the customer pays only the net amount the AR will be reflective of that too:

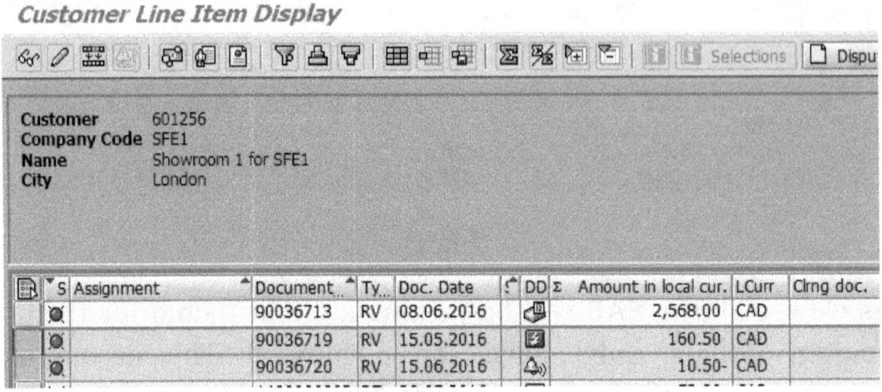
Customer Line Item Display
Selections
Customer 601256
Company Code SFE1
Name Showroom 1 for SFE1
City London
S Assignment Document Ty.. Doc. Date DD Σ Amount in local cur. LCurr Clrng doc.
90036713 RV 08.06.2016 2,568.00 CAD
90036719 RV 15.05.2016 160.50 CAD
90036720 RV 15.06.2016 10.50- CAD

Fig 13

CUSTOMER STATEMENTS IN SAP (U)

T Code FBL5N, F.27

Most companies send customers' open AR statements at end of the month, quarter or year as the policy may be. Though for the most part, the feel and look of these statements will be specific to the company, with their logos, formatting, information etc, the basic process of running the transaction in SAP to generate statements will likely be the same. In some cases, the companies may also have their own transaction code to run statements en masse for all customers in a Co Code all together. However, standard SAP also does offer the ability to print an individual account statement or multiple statements. Since we will actually not be printing any, we can see the transaction that enables us to see an individual account statement as a pdf document within SAP.

Go to customer AR statement, FBL5N and enter the customer #/s and the date, as on which you want to see the statements:

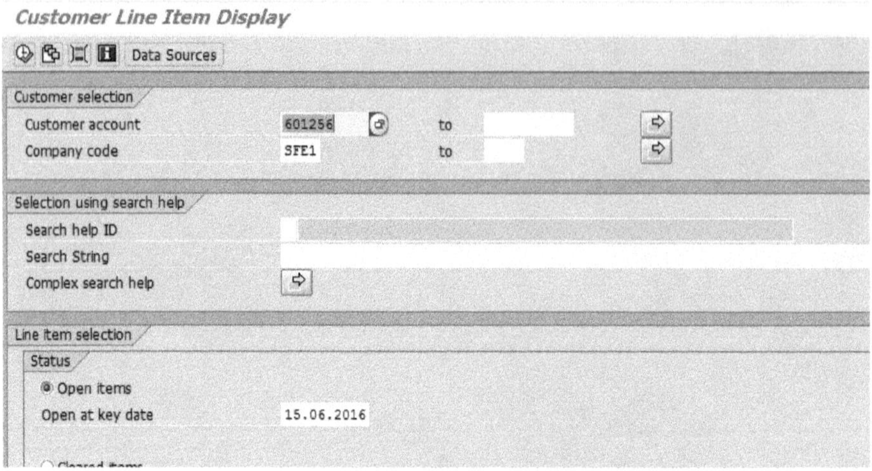

Customer Line Item Display

Data Sources

Customer selection
Customer account	601256	to			
Company code	SFE1	to			

Selection using search help
Search help ID
Search String
Complex search help

Line item selection
Status
● Open items
Open at key date   15.06.2016

Fig 1

Execute to get to the detailed line items.

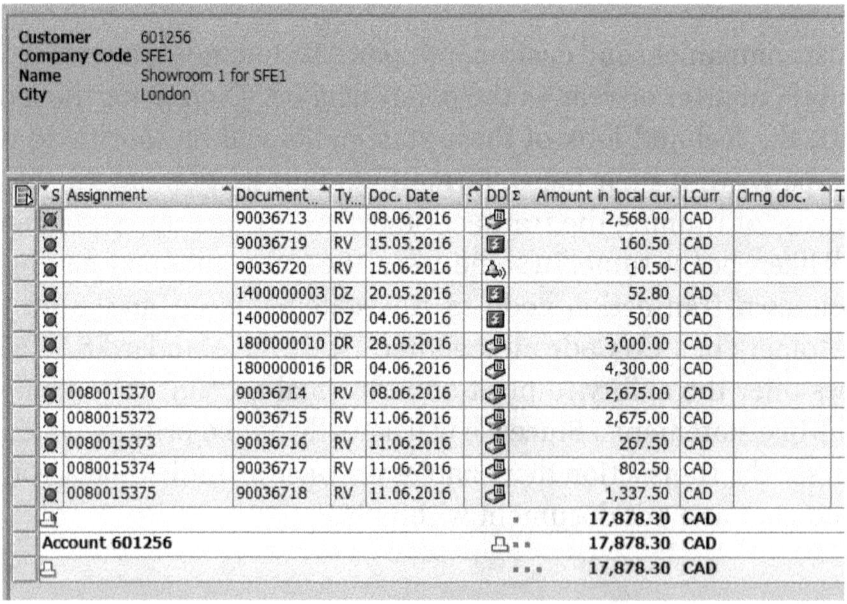

Customer	601256
Company Code	SFE1
Name	Showroom 1 for SFE1
City	London

S	Assignment	Document	Ty	Doc. Date	DD	Σ	Amount in local cur.	LCurr	Clrng doc.	T
		90036713	RV	08.06.2016			2,568.00	CAD		
		90036719	RV	15.05.2016			160.50	CAD		
		90036720	RV	15.06.2016			10.50-	CAD		
		1400000003	DZ	20.05.2016			52.80	CAD		
		1400000007	DZ	04.06.2016			50.00	CAD		
		1800000010	DR	28.05.2016			3,000.00	CAD		
		1800000016	DR	04.06.2016			4,300.00	CAD		
	0080015370	90036714	RV	08.06.2016			2,675.00	CAD		
	0080015372	90036715	RV	11.06.2016			2,675.00	CAD		
	0080015373	90036716	RV	11.06.2016			267.50	CAD		
	0080015374	90036717	RV	11.06.2016			802.50	CAD		
	0080015375	90036718	RV	11.06.2016			1,337.50	CAD		
						•	17,878.30	CAD		
Account 601256						••	17,878.30	CAD		
						•••	17,878.30	CAD		

Fig 2

Click on any line item and follow the path below to request a statement:

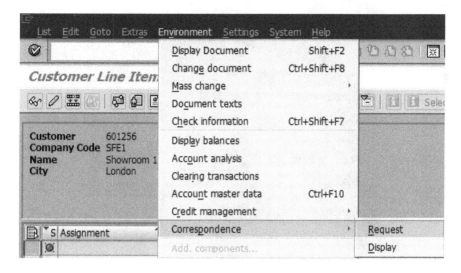

Fig 3

Double click on the SAP06 option. This is the tankard SAP one, likely the actual organization may have it's own.

Corr.	Type of correspondence
SAP06	Account statement
SAP07	Bill of exchange charges statement
SAP08	Open item list
SAP09	Internal document
SAP10	Individual correspondence
SAP11	Customer credit memo
SAP13	Customer statement (single statement)
SAP14	Open item list with pmnt advice (single)
SAP15	Open item list (association)
SAP16	Open item list with pmnt advice (assoc.)

Fig 4

373

In the window that comes, enter the posting dates of the range of documents you need the statement for:

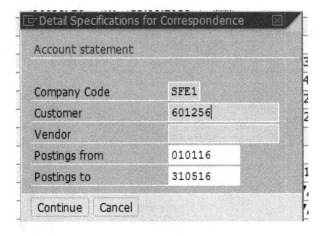

Fig 5

And click on the Continue Button.

A message at the bottom says:

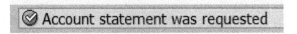

Fig 6

Go back to the same path, this time, asking to Display the statement:

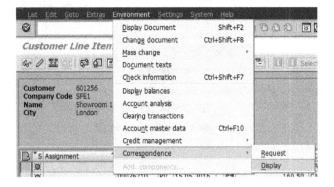

Fig 7

Enter the correct Printer when the window pops up and Click on continue:

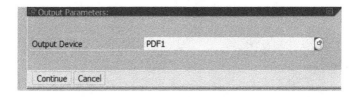

Fig 8

The statement comes up as a Preview:

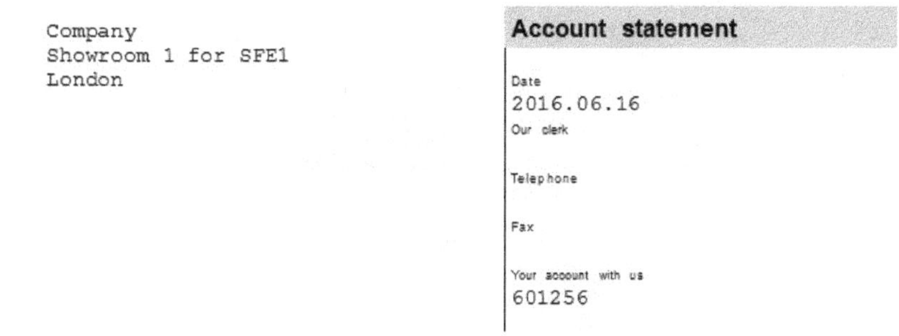

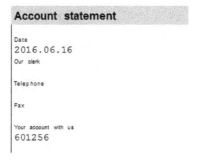

Fig 9

You can scroll up and down the pages using the keys

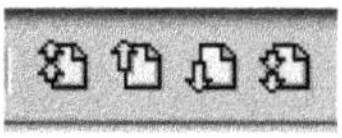

In the real world, when printers are connected in SAP, we can print the statement out using the actual printer. Scroll down to see the actual statement numbers:

Account statement from 2016.01.01 to 2016.05.31

Doc Number	Doc Date	Trans-action	Curr-ency	Amount	Clearing
Balance carried forward 2016.01.01:				0.00	
1800000000	2016.05.10	DR	CAD	2,000.00	1400000002
0090036719	2016.05.15	RV	CAD	160.50	
1800000002	2016.05.15	DR	CAD	1,240.00	1400000003
1800000003	2016.05.18	DR	CAD	7,890.00	1400000004
1800000004	2016.05.18	DR	CAD	7,500.00	1400000001
1400000000	2016.05.20	DZ	CAD	200.00	1400000006
1400000000	2016.05.20	DZ	CAD	1,450.00-	1400000000
1400000001	2016.05.20	DZ	CAD	500.00	1400000014
1400000001	2016.05.20	DZ	CAD	7,500.00-	1400000001
1400000002	2016.05.20	DZ	CAD	2,000.00-	1400000002
1400000003	2016.05.20	DZ	CAD	52.80	
1400000003	2016.05.20	DZ	CAD	1,240.00-	1400000003
1800000001	2016.05.20	DR	CAD	1,450.00	1400000000
1400000004	2016.05.25	DZ	CAD	7,890.00-	1400000004
1800000005	2016.05.28	DR	CAD	3,100.00	1400000015
1800000010	2016.05.28	DR	CAD	3,000.00	
Final balance 2016.05.31:			CAD	7,013.30	

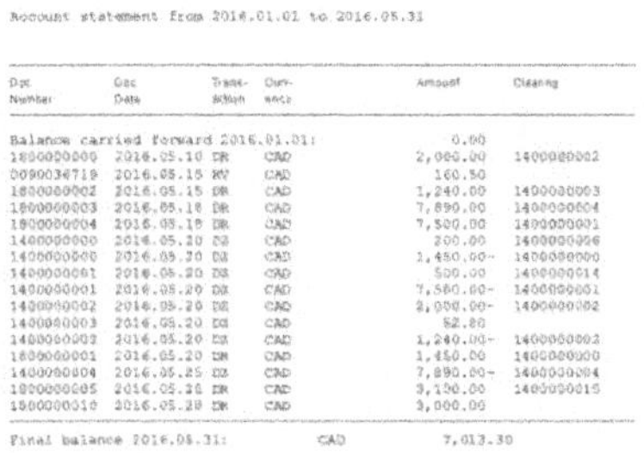

Fig 10

We could also choose all postings, not just open AR if in FBL5N, we choose the Posting Dates option instead of the Open as on option:

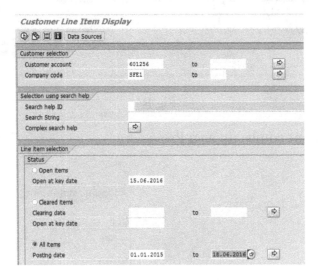

Fig 11

Executing it, we can see the same transactions as we see in the statement plus more though not in chronological order:

S	Assignment	Document	Ty	Doc. Date	DD	Σ Amount in local cur.	LCurr	Clrng doc.	Text
		90036713	RV	08.06.2016		2,568.00	CAD		
		90036719	RV	15.05.2016		160.50	CAD		
		90036720	RV	15.06.2016		10.50-	CAD		
		1400000003	DZ	20.05.2016		52.80	CAD		
		1400000007	DZ	04.06.2016		50.00	CAD		
		1800000010	DR	28.05.2016		3,000.00	CAD		
		1800000016	DR	04.06.2016		4,300.00	CAD		
	0080015370	90036714	RV	08.06.2016		2,675.00	CAD		
	0080015372	90036715	RV	11.06.2016		2,675.00	CAD		
	0080015373	90036716	RV	11.06.2016		267.50	CAD		
	0080015374	90036717	RV	11.06.2016		802.50	CAD		
	0080015375	90036718	RV	11.06.2016		1,337.50	CAD		
						17,878.30	CAD		
	0080015370	90000000	RV	08.06.2016		2,675.00	CAD	90036688	
	0080015370	90036688	RV	08.06.2016		2,675.00-	CAD	90036688	
	0080015370	90036689	RV	08.06.2016		2,675.00	CAD	90036690	
	0080015370	90036690	RV	08.06.2016		2,675.00-	CAD	90036690	
		90036692	RV	08.06.2016		2,407.50	CAD	90036695	
		90036695	RV	08.06.2016		2,407.50-	CAD	90036695	

Fig 12

They can be made to show up chronologically by sorting them by Doc. date as below. Place the cursor on that heading and click on the first button in the pair ![sort buttons] to sort them by dates:

Customer   601256
Company Code   SFE1
Name   Showroom 1 for SFE1
City   London

S.	Assignment	DocumentNo	Ty.	Doc. Date	S	DD	Σ	Amount in local cur.	LCurr	Clng doc.	Text
☐		1800000000	DR	10.05.2016				2,000.00	CAD	1400000002	
☐		1800000015	DR	10.05.2016				1,500.00	CAD	1400000007	
✿		90036719	RV	15.05.2016	☑			160.50	CAD		
☐		1800000002	DR	15.05.2016				1,240.00	CAD	1400000003	
☐		1800000004	DR	18.05.2016				7,500.00	CAD	1400000001	
☐		1800000003	DR	18.05.2016				7,890.00	CAD	1400000004	
✿		1400000003	DZ	20.05.2016	☑			52.80	CAD		

Fig 13

Other than this, we can also use transaction F.27 to directly print or preview statements:

Periodic Account Statements

General selections

Company code	SFE1	to
Account type	D	to
Account		to
Indicator in master record	2	
Key dates for acct statement		
Accounting clerks		to

Fig 14

The data in the above screen will get validated with the data in the customer master's correspondence tab and gets pulled into the program to create the statements for e.g. this customer has WR as accounting clerk and 2 in the bank statement field:

Customer
601256
Showroom 1 for SFE1
London
Company Code
SFE1
Shefaria Ent. Canada
Account Management
Payment Transactions
Correspondence
Insurance
Dunning data
Dunn.Procedure
SFE1
Dunning block
Dunn.recipient
Leg.dunn.proc.
Last dunned
Dunning level
4
Dunning clerk
Grouping key
Dunning areas..
Correspondence
Acctg clerk
WR
Acct statement
2

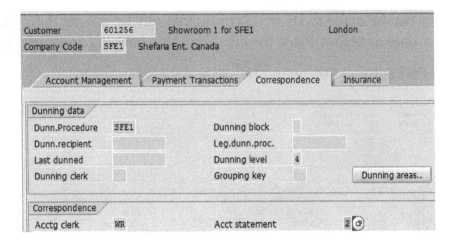

Fig 15

Thus, this customer will get pulled up in the statement (since the variant has asked for all accounting clerks). We could have restricted the data by specific accounting clerk/s.

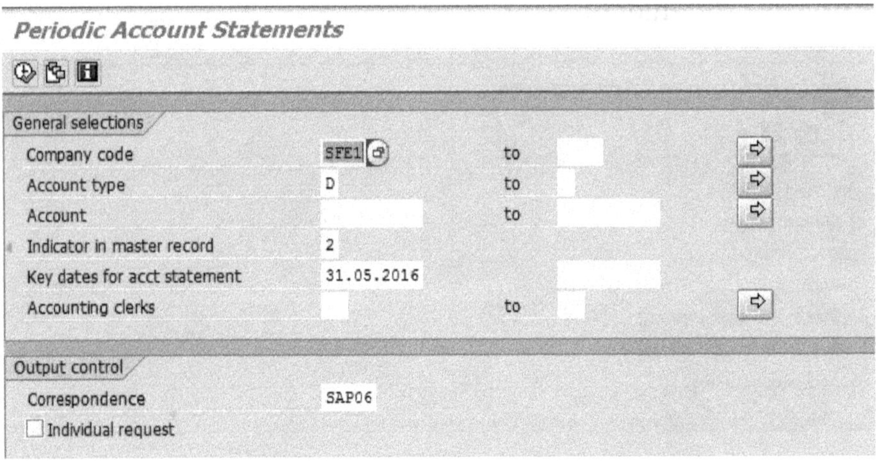

Periodic Account Statements
General selections
Company code
SFE1
to
Account type
D
to
Account
to
Indicator in master record
2
Key dates for acct statement
31.05.2016
Accounting clerks
to
Output control
Correspondence
SAP06
Individual request

Fig 16

Executing on this screen, we get the message:

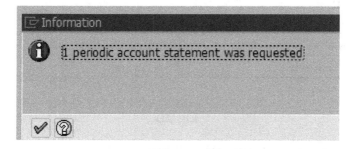

Fig 17

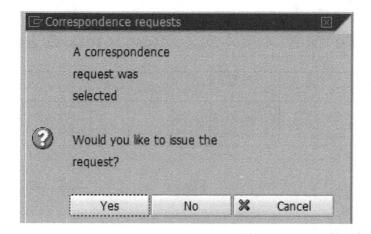

Fig 18

Hit Enter:

Enter the output device in the new screen:

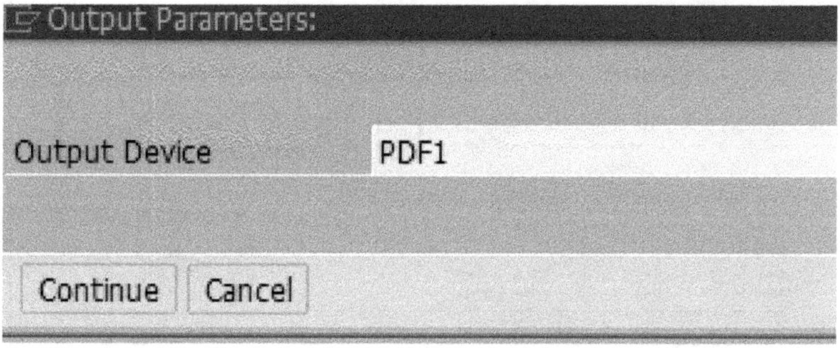

Fig 19

When you see the screen below, you know statements have been generated:

CoCd	Type of correspondence	Spool no.	Name	Suf1	Suffix 2	Pages	Fax/e
SFE1	Account statement	22,334	SAP06		SFE1	1	

Fig 20

They can be seen in transaction SP02:

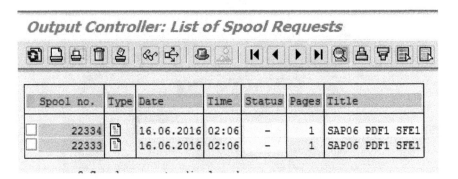

Output Controller: List of Spool Requests

Spool no.	Type	Date	Time	Status	Pages	Title
22334		16.06.2016	02:06	-	1	SAP06 PDF1 SFE1
22333		16.06.2016	02:06	-	1	SAP06 PDF1 SFE1

Fig 21

Click on 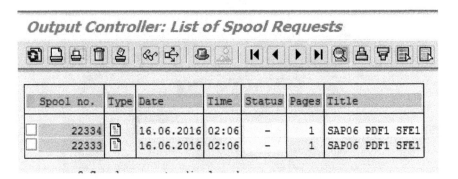 for your spool #:

Company	Account statement
Showroom 1 for SFE1	
London	Date
	2016.06.16
	Our clerk
	Telephone
	Fax
	Your account with us
	601256

Account statement from 2016.05.31 to 2016.05.31

Doc. Number	Doc. Date	Trans- action	Curr- ency	Amount	Clearing

Balance carried forward 2016.05.31:   CAD   7,013.30
No postings in account statement period.

Fig 22

DUNNING (C/U)

T Code SPRO, F150

Invoices and statements sometimes do not get payments from difficult customers. This is where dunning steps in. Simply stated, dunning is a reminder to the customer that payments from them are overdue and they should remit the same to the vendor. The dunning process can also keep track of a customer's payment habits, which can be used in reporting, and decision making on the credit policies a company should adopt to keep receivables in control. There may be customers who buy a lot, pay slow but do pay and do not default. In those cases, the company may want to retain the business, increase the prices marginally to cover for the lost interest and give more than normal credit so their receivables do not affect overdue AR.

Further, this process can also be taken a step forward and this information sent to collection agencies. This is a useful feature for high volume mass product selling companies like cell phone providers, utility companies etc.

While the language on a dunning letter will be company specific like in statements, the process of generating dunning letters in SAP is the same. It involves some configuration set up and master data in the customer's CC data view.

The standard dunning system in SAP covers 4 different customer transactions:

> 1. Open A/R invoices, including invoices that are partially credited or partially paid
> 2. Invoices that include installments
> 3. A/R credit memos
> 4. Incoming payments that are not based on invoices

I.   DUNNING SETUP (C)

I.   SETUP DUNNING AREA:

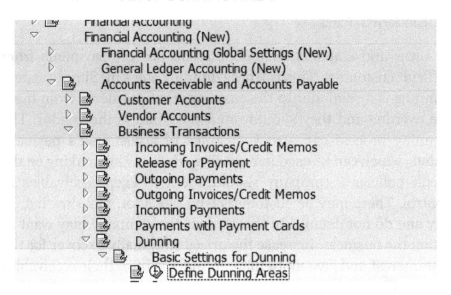

Fig 1

Dunning areas can be a sales area, a certain profit center, a business area, or can also set up a dunning area for domestic customers or foreign customers etc., the idea really being as to who is responsible for this dunning set up in SAP.

We will set up a generic dunning area for the co code:

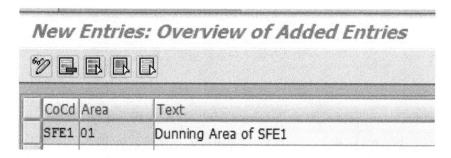

Fig 2

II.   DUNNING KEY:

A dunning key defines the levels of dunning that can take place.

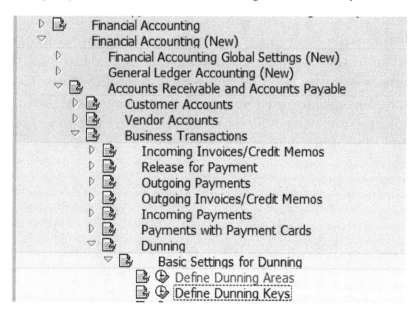

Fig 3

There are pre-defined dunning keys given by SAP, which are normally used.

Check All and Save:

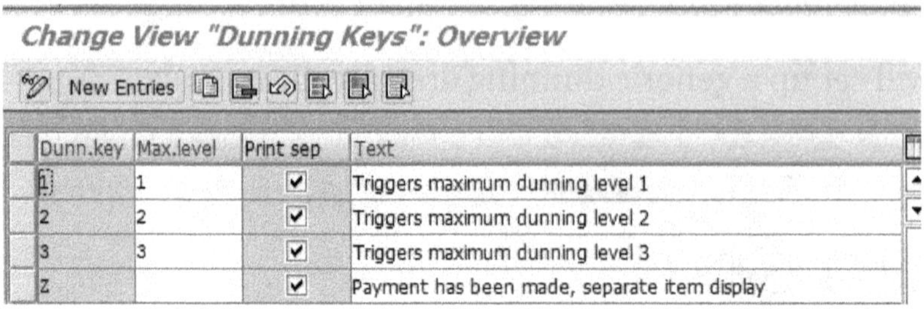

Dunn.key	Max.level	Print sep	Text
1	1	☑	Triggers maximum dunning level 1
2	2	☑	Triggers maximum dunning level 2
3	3	☑	Triggers maximum dunning level 3
Z		☑	Payment has been made, separate item display

Change View "Dunning Keys": Overview

New Entries

Fig4

With this, we triggered all the dunning levels possible in standard SAP i.e. multiple reminders if necessary can go to the customers so set up to receive them.

III.   DUNNING BLOCKING REASONS:

Certain customers regardless of their payment schedules are too important and are not sent dunning letters to avoid bad unpleasantness. We can define dunning reasons in configuration and then in the customer master, in Correspondence tab, those customers can be assigned some reason or the other for not dunning them. Those customers will then be bypassed during the dunning run and will not be sent letters. They are put on a 'dunning block'.

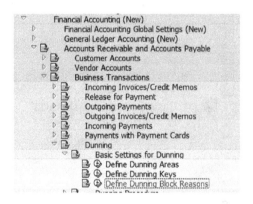

Fig 5

384

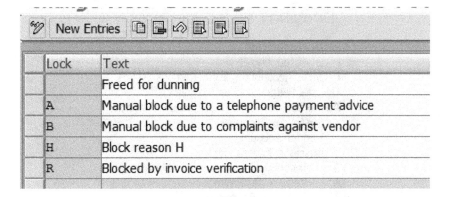

Fig 6

Any of the above reasons, A, B, H or R (users can define their own also) can then be assigned in the customer master in the field

Dunning Block:

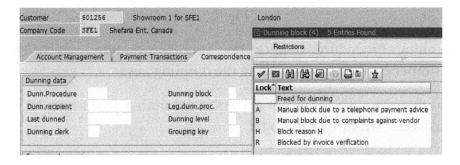

Fig 7

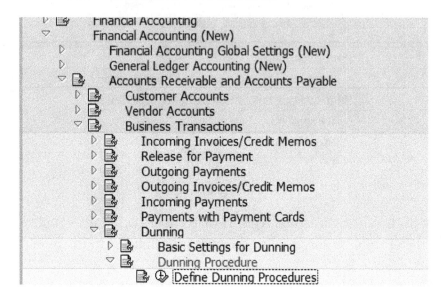

Fig 8

Dunning Procedure defines the process whereby which the customers will be dunned using the dunning keys.

To understand the different drivers in a dunning procedure, let us make our own for our co code:

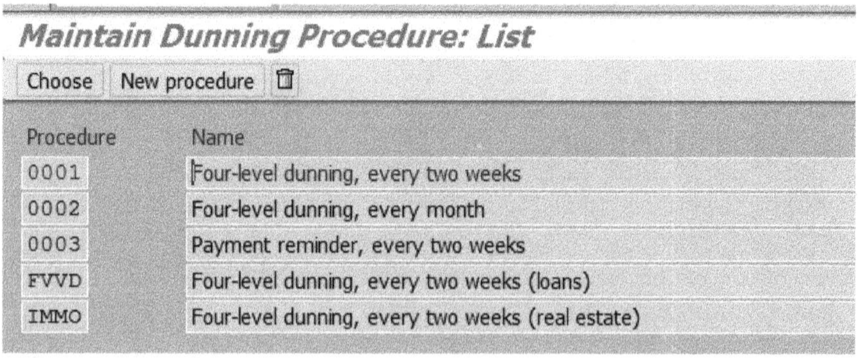

Maintain Dunning Procedure: List

| Choose | New procedure | 🗑 |

Procedure	Name
0001	Four-level dunning, every two weeks
0002	Four-level dunning, every month
0003	Payment reminder, every two weeks
FVVD	Four-level dunning, every two weeks (loans)
IMMO	Four-level dunning, every two weeks (real estate)

Fig 9

Click on New Procedure to give it a name and Code:

Maintain Dunning Procedure: Overview

Dunning levels	Charges	Minimum amounts	Dunning texts	Sp. G/L indicator

Dunn.Procedure	SFE1
Name	Dunning Procedure of SFE1

General data

Dunning Interval in Days	14
No.of dunning levels	4
Total due items from dunning level	
Min.days in arrears (acct)	5
Line item grace periods	2
Interest indicator	01 Standard itm int.cal
Public hol.cal.ID	CA
☑ Standard transaction dunning	
☐ Dun special G/L transactions	

Reference data

Ref.Dunning Procedure for Texts	0001 Four-level dunning, every two weeks

Fig 10

(a) The field Dunning Interval in Days defines the # of days in between when the customer receives the next dunning letter. When the dunning job runs, the system checks if this many # of days have passed when the last dunning took place

(b) Dunning levels – the max number of levels of dunning that can be done. 4 is currently the max number in SAP. Normally, if 4 reminders don't lead to results, there is a good chance to write off the amount or pass to a collection agency. However, a company may decide to set up more levels if it feels it will help.

(c) Days in arrears, which at least one item in this account, must have for a dunning notice to be created. These minimum days in arrears have no influence on calculating the days overdue

(d) Line item grace period – if you want to give a grace period of any kind due to delays in post etc. This would then add to the days set in (c) when SAP looks for customers who need to be sent letters in the specific dunning run.

(e) Interest indicator - optional field, we would enter an interest calculation indicator here if we want dunning interest to be calculated for this customer

(f) Check the field Standard Transaction dunning

V. DEFINE DUNNING CHARGES

Define the Dunning charges to Dunning Procedures Click on the tab Charges

Enter the currency CAD and Hit Enter and enter data as below:

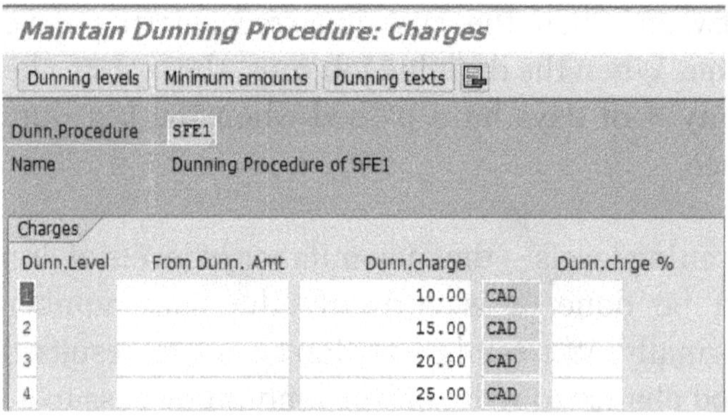

Maintain Dunning Procedure: Charges

| Dunning levels | Minimum amounts | Dunning texts |

| Dunn.Procedure | SFE1 |
| Name | Dunning Procedure of SFE1 |

Charges

Dunn.Level	From Dunn. Amt	Dunn.charge		Dunn.chrge %
1		10.00	CAD	
2		15.00	CAD	
3		20.00	CAD	
4		25.00	CAD	

Fig 11

Dunning charges can be defined in 2 different ways:

(i) As an absolute amount as in the above case
(ii) As a % amount. This % amount is calculated by multiplying this % with the total of all overdue items in the dunning notice. The result is the dunning charge in dunning currency.

VI. Minimum Amounts

Minimum amounts

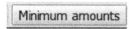

The objective of defining Min Amounts is to cover administrative charges associated with dunning the customers.

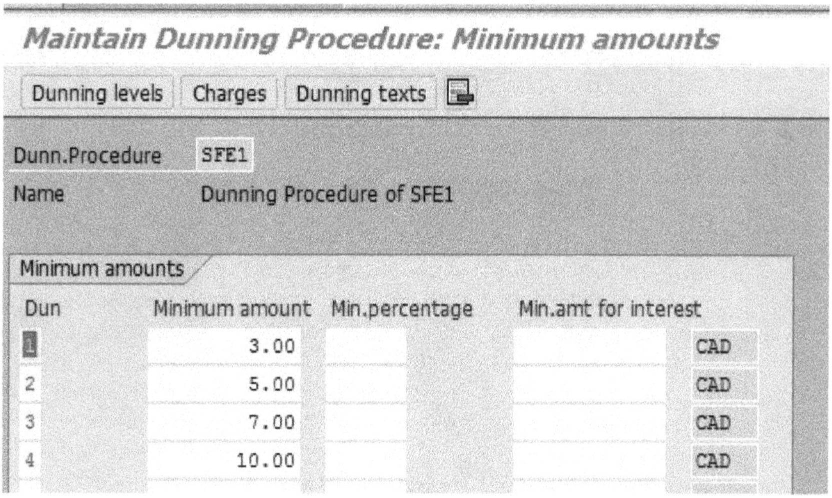

Maintain Dunning Procedure: Minimum amounts
Dunning levels
Charges
Dunning texts
Dunn.Procedure
SFE1
Name
Dunning Procedure of SFE1
Minimum amounts
Dun
Minimum amount
Min.percentage
Min.amt for interest
1
3.00
CAD
2
5.00
CAD
3
7.00
CAD
4
10.00
CAD

Fig 12

VII. Dunning Texts

Next, we assign what text/letters we will be sent to the customers when we dun them.

Click on
Dunning texts

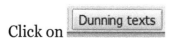

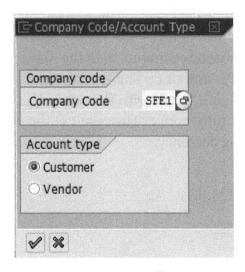

Fig 13

Choose Customer and Click OK

Click on 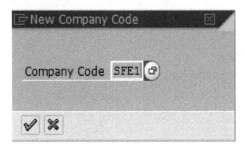 to set our CC in the list

Company Code SFE1

Fig 14

Select the 2 options – Dunning by dunning area and Separate Notice per dunning level:

Maintain Dunning Procedure: Company code data

New company code 🔣

Company code	Dunning by dunning area	Separate notice per dunning level	Ref.comp.code for texts
SFE1	☑	☑	SFE1

Fig 15

Save the data:

VIII. DUNNING LEVELS

The next step is to maintain the actual dunning levels in the dunning procedure. Click on Dunning levels :

Let's assume we want to calculate interest only at the 3rd and 4th level of dunning and give grace of interest on the 1st and 2nd duns:

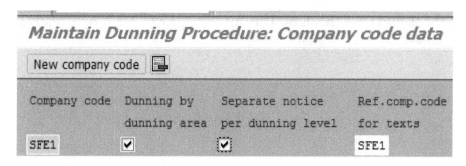

Dunn.Procedure	SFE1
Name	Dunning Procedure of SFE1

Dunning level	1	2	3	4

Days in arrears/interest				
Days in arrears	2	16	30	44
Calculate interest?	☐	☐	☑	☑

Print parameters				
Always dun?	☐	☐	☐	☑
Print all items	☐	☐	☑	☑
Payment deadline				

Legal dunning procedure
☐ Always dun in legal dunning proc.

Fig 16

Note the difference of 14 days – this 14 is coming from the time period we defined earlier as the gap between the different duns.

Go back and save the data. The dunning procedure is now ready to be used.

II.   DUNNING THE CUSTOMER (U)

T Code FD02, F150

First, we set up the appropriate master data. Go to transaction FD02 (change customer's CC data) and add the dunning procedure in the Correspondence tab:

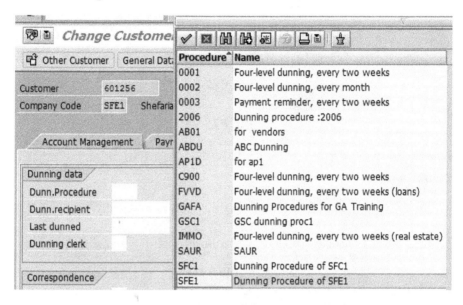

Fig 17

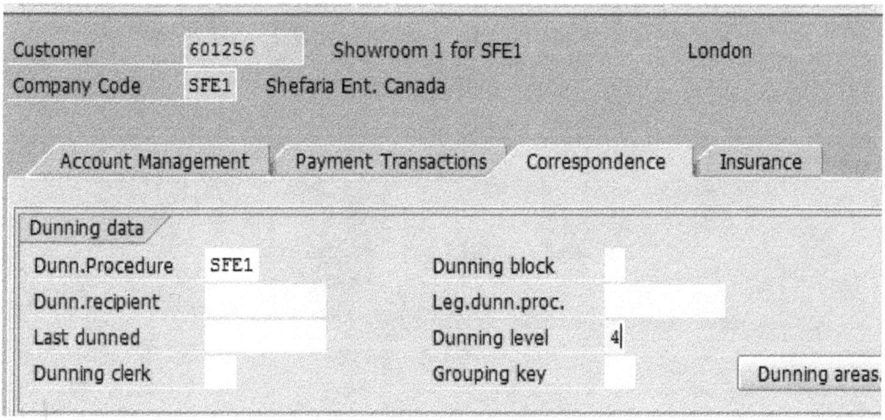

Fig 18

Save.

Once the customer is set up, we are ready to test the dunning process. The t code is F150 for setting up dunning runs for customers collectively or dun individually, or follow the path:

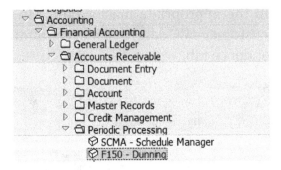

Fig 19

Give the dunning run an ID and the date on which you want it to occur:

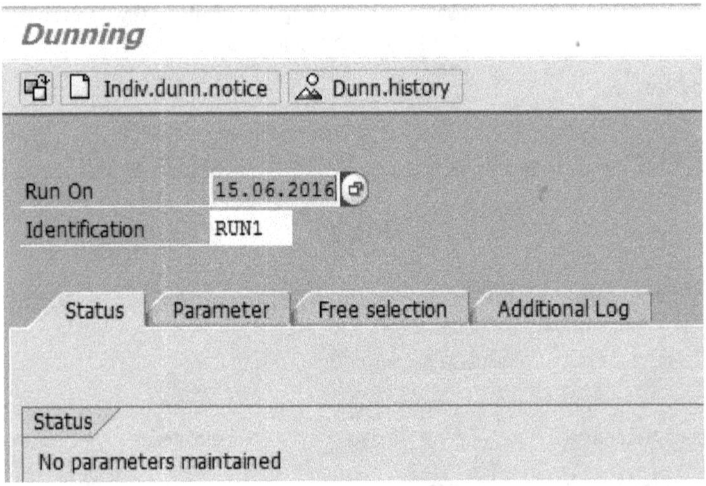

Dunning

Run On   15.06.2016

Identification   RUN1

Status   Parameter   Free selection   Additional Log

Status

No parameters maintained

Fig 20

Enter the other necessary data:

Run On	15.06.2016			
Identification	RUN1			

Status	Parameter	Free selection	Additional Log

Date

Dunning date	☑	
Docmnts posted up to	☑	

Company Code

Company Code		to	

Account Restrictions

Customer		to		
Vendor		to		

Fig 21

The dunning date is the date of issue and also the date from which the arrears are calculated. Documents posted upto date will include all the documents posted till that date.

Account restrictions enable you to exclude or include accounts that should not be dunned or should be dunned. This is different from the exclusions that come in due to data not set in the customer or vendor masters. SAP checks for both – those excluded in the customer master will be excluded as well as those listed here for exclusion will also be excluded. If you want only a few customers to be dunned, then set them up here and SAP will pick up only those for dunning provided they have been set up appropriately in the customer master to be dunned. If a customer is excluded in the customer master then inclusion here will not create dunning letters for them.

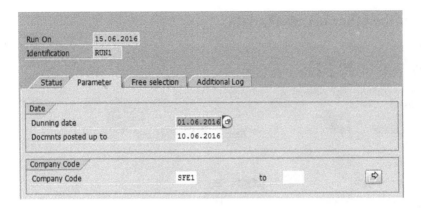

Fig 22

Save the run.

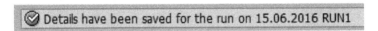

Fig 23

Now, a background job will kick in on 15.06.2016 in this case and create dunning notices for all the appropriately set up customers.

III. Individual Dunning Notices (U)

T Code F150

We can also see individual notices for any particular customer/s instead of all customers in one run.

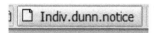

Enter the PDF printer in the window that comes up:

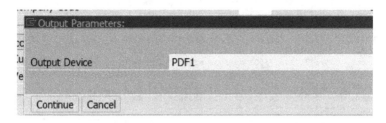

Fig 24

Enter data as:

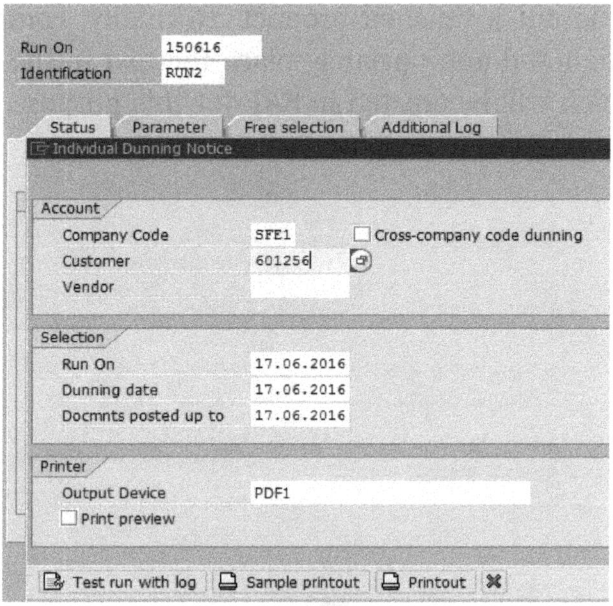

Fig 25

Click on

A very crude letter comes up:

```
  Dunning Data

FI Dunning - Modules
_____
============================================================
> Account D 0000601256 , company code SFE1 is being processed
> _____ Reading account data and document information ___ Phase 0 ___
> Account D 0000601256 read items: 12
> _____ Processing and completing dunning lines _____ Phase I ___
> Document 0090036713/2016/001 days in arrears 21- <= 0
> Document 0090036719/2016/001 has new dunning level 1 .
> Document 1400000003/2016/002 has new dunning level 1 .
> Document 1400000007/2016/002 has new dunning level 1 .
> Document 1800000010/2016/001 days in arrears 40- <= 0
> Document 1800000016/2016/001 days in arrears 47- <= 0
> Document 0090036714/2016/001 days in arrears 21- <= 0
> Document 0090036715/2016/001 days in arrears 24- <= 0
> Document 0090036716/2016/001 days in arrears 24- <= 0
> Document 0090036717/2016/001 days in arrears 24- <= 0
> Document 0090036718/2016/001 days in arrears 24- <= 0
> _____ Check legal dunning procedure and credit memos ___ Phase II -
> Credit memo 0090036720/2016/001 has new dunning level 1 . Without invoice refere
```

Fig 26

This letter is not a finished product. Normally, companies will develop, align and appropriately place the text in the forms and layouts, which will be created in SAP for this purpose. Here, it is only for demonstration purpose.

CASH MANAGEMENT – CASH JOURNAL

Cash Management is used to monitor cash flows and to ensure that you have sufficient liquidity to cover your payment obligations.

The cash journal is a sub ledger of Bank Accounting. It is used to manage a company's cash transactions. The system automatically calculates and displays the opening and closing balances, and the receipts and payments totals. User can run several cash journals for each company code. The user can also carry out postings to G/L accounts, as well as vendor and customer accounts.

I. CREATE GENERAL LEDGER ACCOUNT (U):

T Code FS01

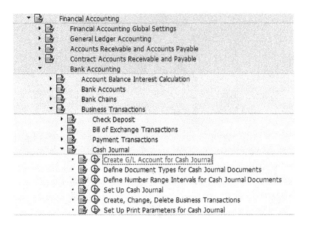

Fig 1

Petty Cash G/L A/C 107100 was created in FS01: we have 3 G/Ls relating to cash:

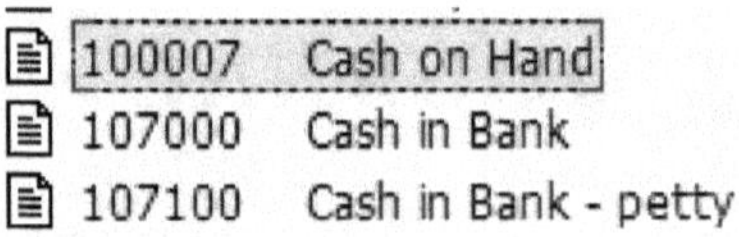

📄	100007	Cash on Hand
📄	107000	Cash in Bank
📄	107100	Cash in Bank - petty

Fig 2

These GL Accounts will later be used for cash journal postings.

II. DEFINING CORRESPONDENCE TYPES (C)

T Code SPRO

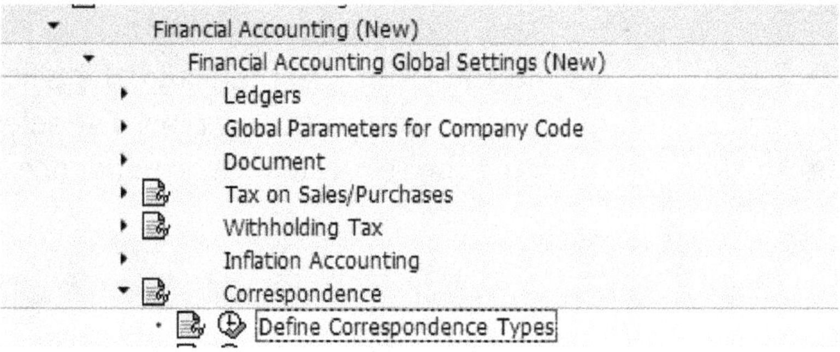

Fig 3

A correspondence type is set up for Company Code : SFE1

Enter New Entries

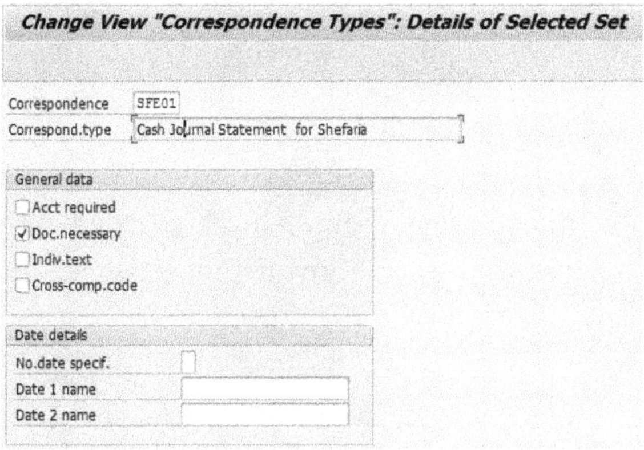

Fig 4

Fill up the required fields as shown above and press to save the settings. The system will confirm creation of new correspondance type by this message display:

Fig 5

III. ASSIGNING PROGRAMS FOR CORRESPONDENCE TYPES (C)

T Code SPRO

In this activity, we define the print program and the selection variant corresponding to each correspondence type. The selection variant is used when printing the requested correspondence.

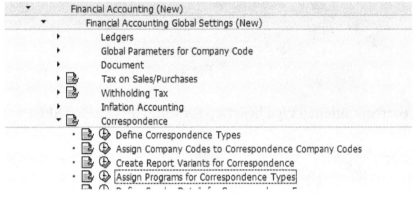

Fig 6

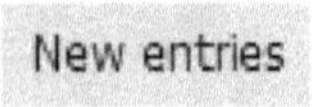

New entries In the Change View "Allocate program for automatic correspondence": overview screen, make the new entries :

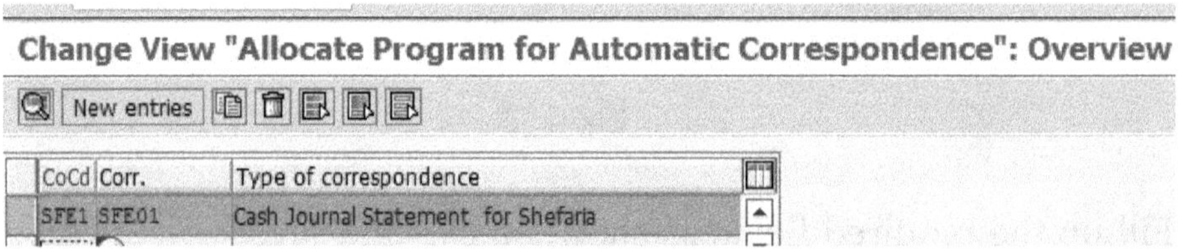

Change View "Allocate Program for Automatic Correspondence": Overview

CoCd	Corr.	Type of correspondence
SFE1	SFE01	Cash Journal Statement for Shefarla

Fig 7

Enter the following details :

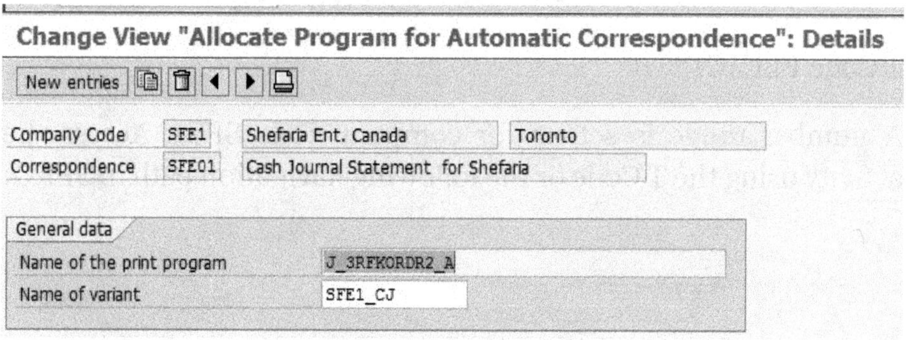

Change View "Allocate Program for Automatic Correspondence": Details

New entries

| Company Code | SFE1 | Shefaria Ent. Canada | Toronto |
| Correspondence | SFE01 | Cash Journal Statement for Shefaria | |

General data

| Name of the print program | J_3RFKORDR2_A |
| Name of variant | SFE1_CJ |

Fig 8

Save the entries.

IV. DEFINING NUMBER RANGE INTERVALS FOR CASH JOURNAL DOCUMENTS (C)

T Code FBCJC1

A number range is set up for company code SFE1. Access the activity using the T Code or the following navigation path in SPRO:

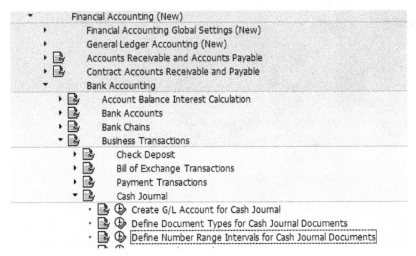

Fig 9

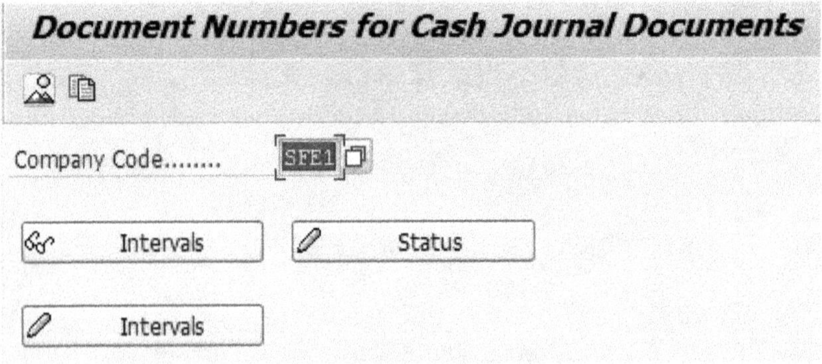

Fig 10

Click 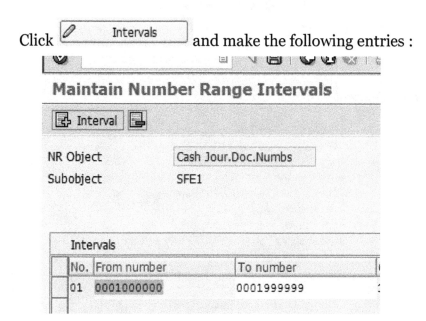 and make the following entries :

Fig 11

Save your entries.

V. DEFINE DOCUMENT TYPE FOR CASH JOURNAL DOCUMENTS (C)

T Code OBA7

Or follow the path below in SPRO:

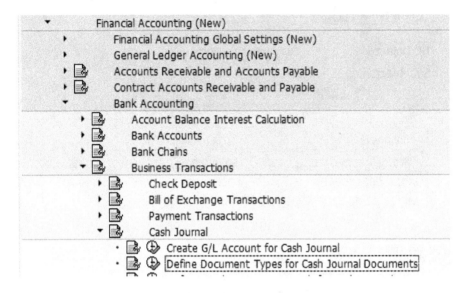

Fig 12

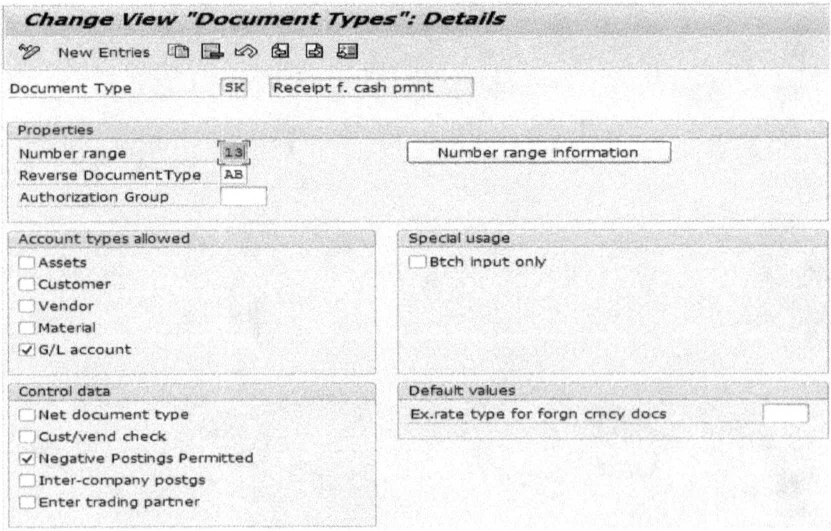

Fig 13

VI. SETTING UP CASH JOURNAL (C)

T Code FBCJC0

Finally, we need to set up Cash Journal itself. In this set up we will assign GL Account, Document type to the Cash Journal for GL Postings .

In SPRO follow the path below:

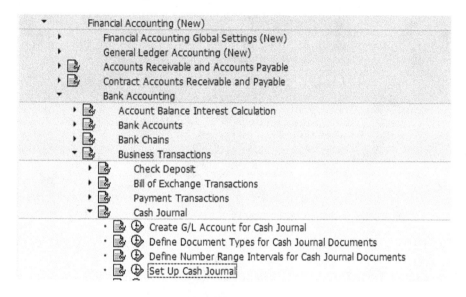

Fig 14

Make the following entries:

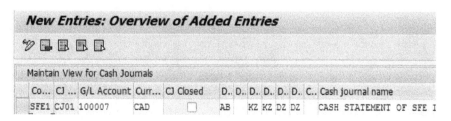

Fig 15

Save the Entries.

VII. CREATING, CHANGING AND DELETING BUSINESS TRANSACTIONS (C)

T Code FBCJC2

In this activity, we create, change and delete business transactions for the cash journal. In SPRO:

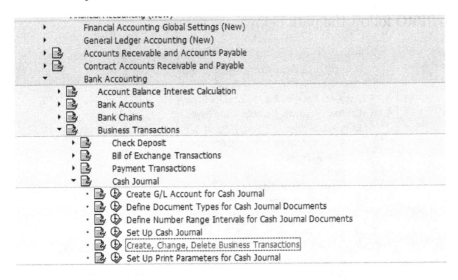

Fig 16

Make the following entries:

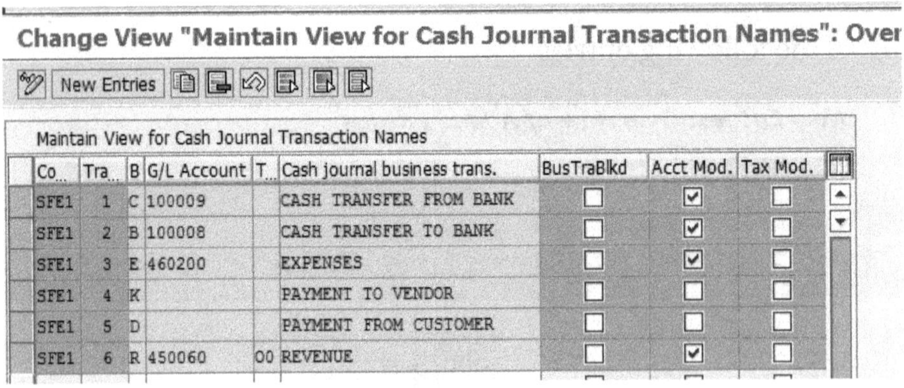

Change View "Maintain View for Cash Journal Transaction Names": Over

New Entries

Maintain View for Cash Journal Transaction Names

Co	Tra	B	G/L Account	T	Cash journal business trans.	BusTraBlkd	Acct Mod.	Tax Mod.	
SFE1	1	C	100009		CASH TRANSFER FROM BANK	☐	☑	☐	
SFE1	2	B	100008		CASH TRANSFER TO BANK	☐	☑	☐	
SFE1	3	E	460200		EXPENSES	☐	☑	☐	
SFE1	4	K			PAYMENT TO VENDOR	☐	☐	☐	
SFE1	5	D			PAYMENT FROM CUSTOMER	☐	☐	☐	
SFE1	6	R	450060	00	REVENUE	☐	☑	☐	

Fig 17

VIII. Setting up Print Parameters for Cash Journal (C)

T Code FBCJC3

To print the cash journal and the cash journal receipts, we have to set up the corresponding print program parameters per company code. SAP standard is used. In SPRO:

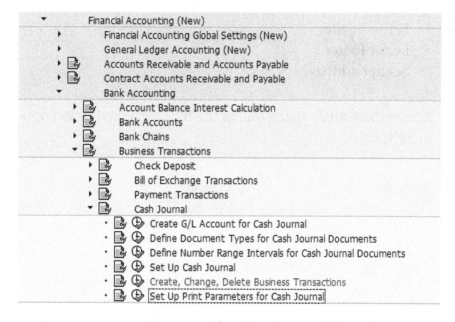

Fig 18

Choose New Entries option and make the following entries :

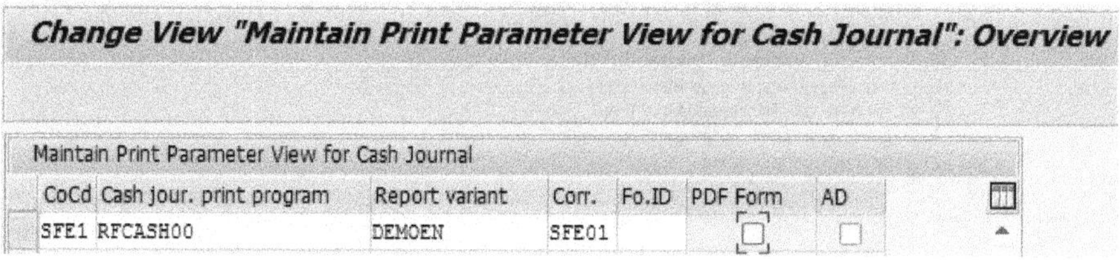

CoCd	Cash jour. print program	Report variant	Corr.	Fo.ID	PDF Form	AD	
SFE1	RFCASH00	DEMOEN	SFE01				

Change View "Maintain Print Parameter View for Cash Journal": Overview

Maintain Print Parameter View for Cash Journal

Fig 19

Save the entries.

IX. DEFINING SENDER DETAILS FOR CORRESPONDENCE FORM(C)

T Code SPRO

In this activity, you define which texts are to be used in the letter window and the signature line for each company code. This applies to the following:

- Letter header
- Letter footer
- Sender address

Access the activity using one of the following navigation option in SPRO:

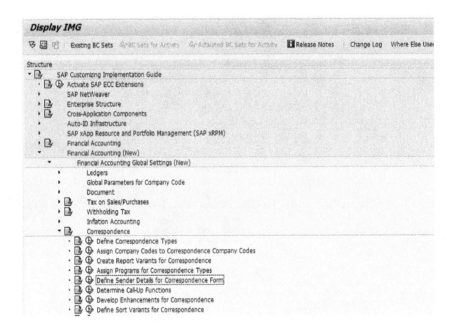

Fig 20

Make the following entries and save:

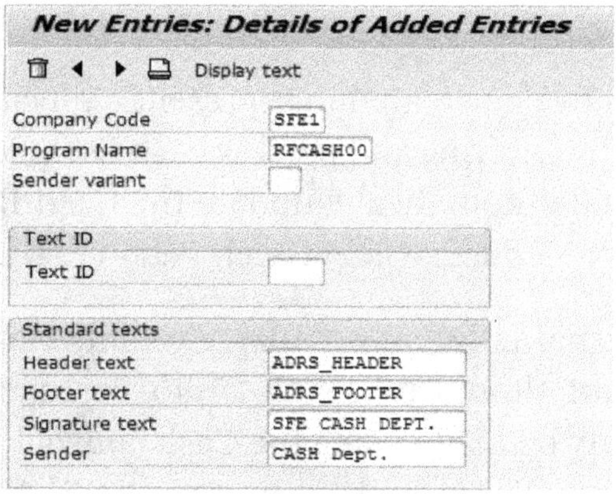

New Entries: Details of Added Entries

🗑 ◀ ▶ 🖨 Display text

Company Code	SFE1
Program Name	RFCASH00
Sender variant	

Text ID

Text ID	

Standard texts

Header text	ADRS_HEADER
Footer text	ADRS_FOOTER
Signature text	SFE CASH DEPT.
Sender	CASH Dept.

Fig 21

X.   Cash Journal – User Manual (U)

T Code FBCJ

A Cash Journal can be created to represent a physical "Petty Cash Box" and then, by entering and posting each Cash Payment or Cash Receipt, SAP will automatically update the Cash Balance thereby allowing an easy reconciliation of each Petty Cash box.

Each Cash Journal is linked to a GL Account via Configuration. This GL Account should be set to "Auto Postings only" so that postings can only be made using the Cash Journal and in this way the balance on the GL Account always agrees with the Cash Journal balance. Postings are made according to pre-defined Business Transactions.

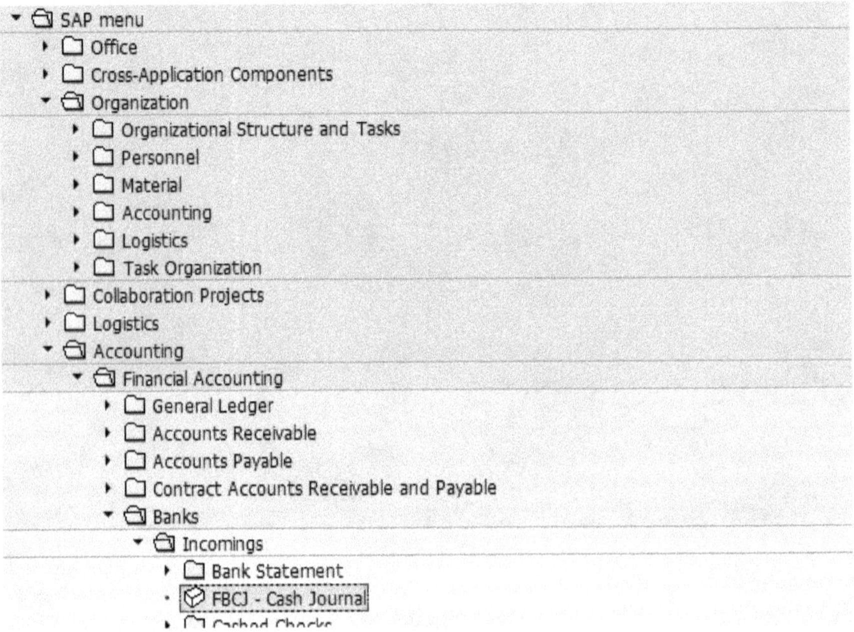

Fig 22

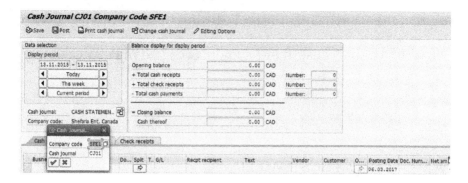

Fig 23

Click 🔲 to update Company Code : SFE1
Cash Journal   : CJ01

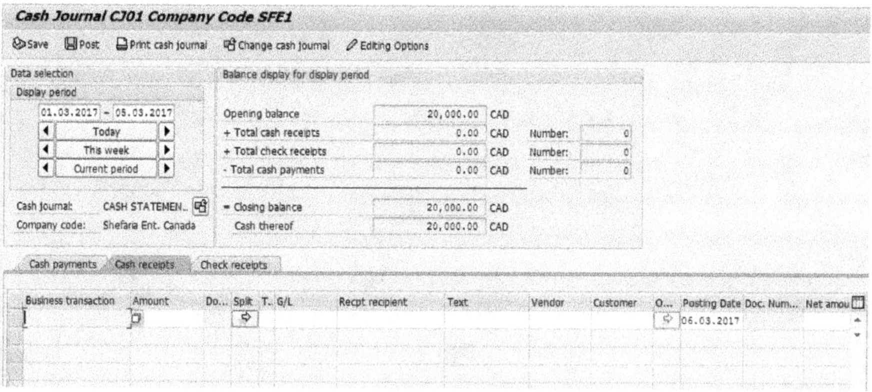

Fig 24

Enter the Period for which you are going to run the cash journal

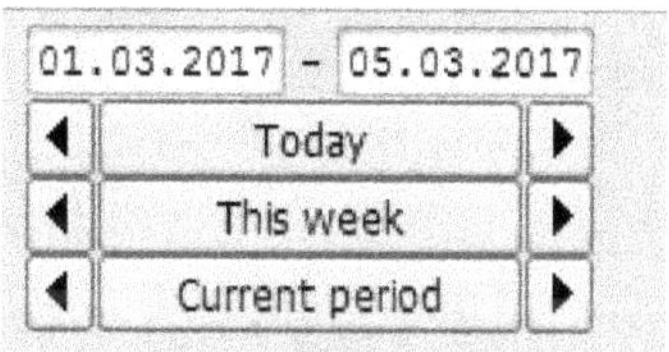

Fig 25

Based on the Period Opening and Closing Balance will be updated.

If we wan to book a customer payment received in Petty cash. Then enter we the following :

Under Cash receipts Select Business Transaction via F4 function:

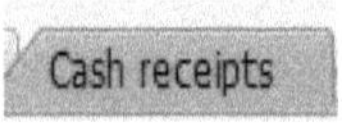

PAYMENT FROM CUSTOMER
Amount : 1500
Text :   Description of Payment
Customer :   601288
Posting Date :   Date e.g. 06.03.2017 [Date of payment received]

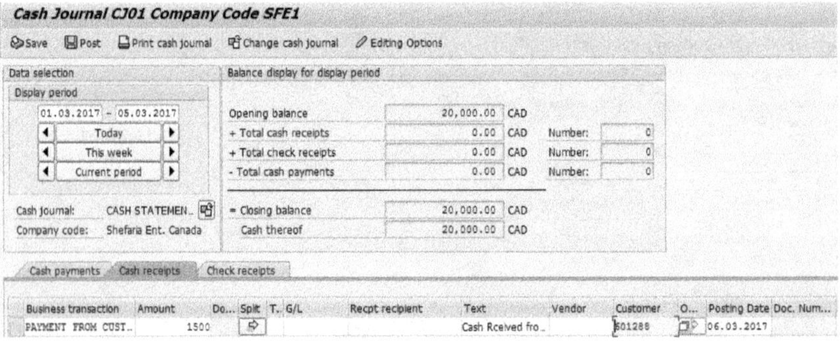

Fig 26

Similary for making payment to a vendor choose the following under Cash payments :

Business Transaction : Payment to Vendor

Fig 27

After doing Necessary Cash Journal entries, select the entry and

Choose 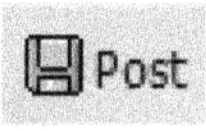
Post

Entry will turn into Green showing it is posted succesfully (Fig 28)

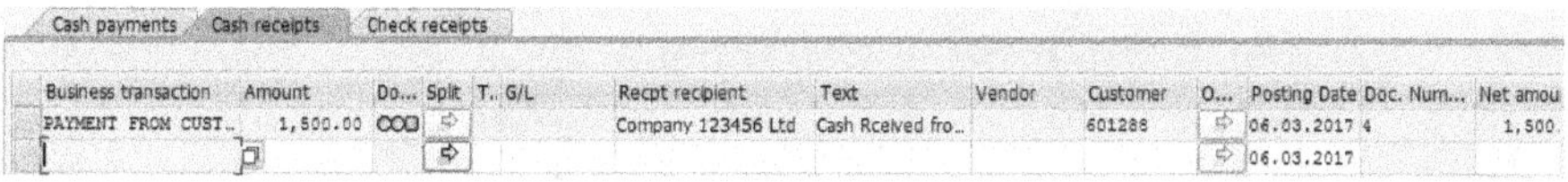
Cash payments
Cash receipts
Check receipts
Business transaction
Amount
Do...
Split
T..
G/L
Recpt recipient
Text
Vendor
Customer
O...
Posting Date
Doc. Num...
Net amou
PAYMENT FROM CUST..
1,500.00
Company 123456 Ltd
Cash Rceived fro...
601288
06.03.2017
4
1,500.
06.03.2017

Fig 28

Print Cash Journal : Choose 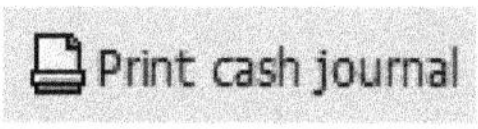
Print cash journal

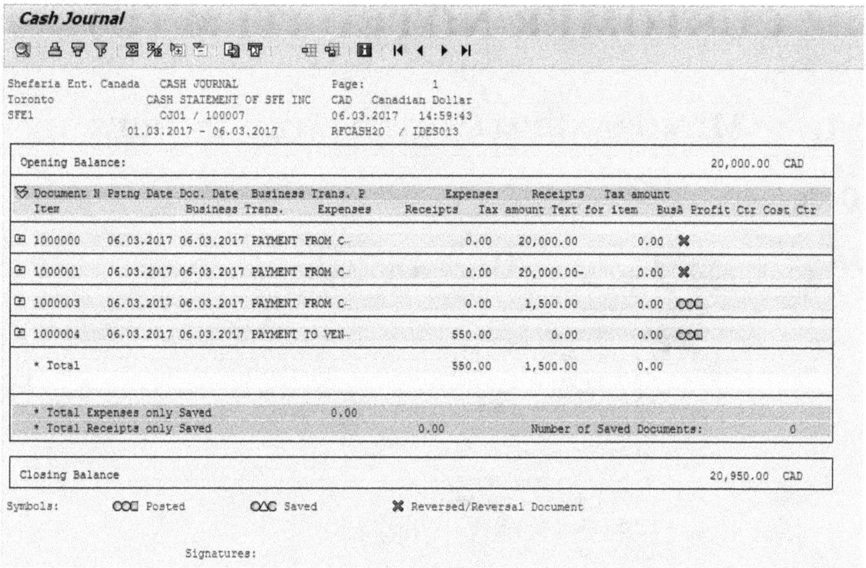
Cash Journal
Shefaria Ent. Canada CASH JOURNAL Page: 1
Toronto CASH STATEMENT OF SFE INC CAD Canadian Dollar
SFE1 CJ01 / 100007 06.03.2017 14:59:43
01.03.2017 - 06.03.2017 RFCASH20 / IDES013
Opening Balance: 20,000.00 CAD
Document N Pstng Date Doc. Date Business Trans. P Expenses Receipts Tax amount
Item Business Trans. Expenses Receipts Tax amount Text for item BusA Profit Ctr Cost Ctr
1000000 06.03.2017 06.03.2017 PAYMENT FROM C.. 0.00 20,000.00 0.00
1000001 06.03.2017 06.03.2017 PAYMENT FROM C.. 0.00 20,000.00- 0.00
1000003 06.03.2017 06.03.2017 PAYMENT FROM C.. 0.00 1,500.00 0.00
1000004 06.03.2017 06.03.2017 PAYMENT TO VEN.. 550.00 0.00 0.00
* Total 550.00 1,500.00 0.00
* Total Expenses only Saved 0.00
* Total Receipts only Saved 0.00 Number of Saved Documents: 0
Closing Balance 20,950.00 CAD
Symbols: Posted Saved Reversed/Reversal Document
Signatures:

The Fig 29

Here we see Opening and Closing Balance getting updated following Cash Journal Posting.

CUSTOMER NOTED ITEM (U)

I.   MEMORANDUM (NOTED) ITEM ENTRIES

T Code F-49

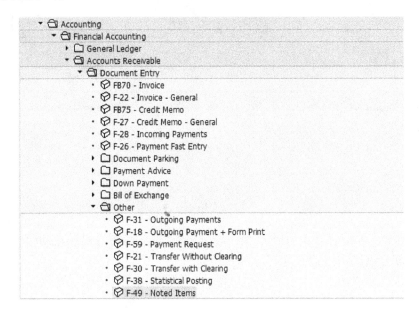

Fig 1

These can be used for recording Bank Guarantee or any other entries which do not need to be posted to the customer Account and the general ledger A/c. It creates a one line entry only. These entries will have no effect on the Financial Books. We use them only for the purpose of recording and after the purpose is over we can reverse the same.

Create the transaction with the posting key as 09 or 19 using either of the following Special GL Indicators:

L : Letter of Credit
G: Bank Gurantee

Customer Account Number and Amount is to be filled.
Fill in the Bank Guarantee Due Dates so that on the Maturity Date we can reverse it later on.

Scenario : Customer provides bank gurantee. Now to get the payment encashed in real it may take some time. We can record the transaction in a form of entry without impacting the book of accounts. This entry is just for information purposes only.

In the following screen fill up the required details :

Account : Customer Account No.
Reference : We can put Sales Order no or Bank Gurantee ref No
Amount : Bank Gurantee Amount
Text : Free Field for Description

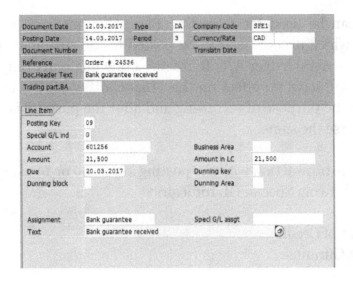

Fig 2

Save:

Fig 3

System saved the entry as NOTED Item :

We can also view the entry in FBL5N with choosing the option 'Noted Items':

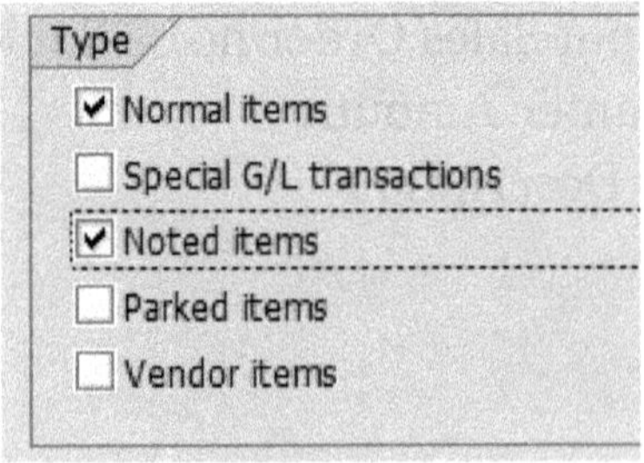

Fig 4

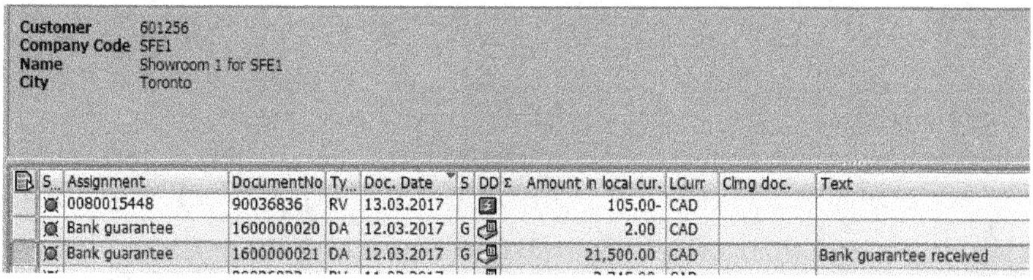

Customer	601256
Company Code	SFE1
Name	Showroom 1 for SFE1
City	Toronto

S	Assignment	DocumentNo	Ty	Doc. Date	S	DD	Σ	Amount in local cur.	LCurr	Clmg doc.	Text
☼	0080015448	90036836	RV	13.03.2017				105.00-	CAD		
☼	Bank guarantee	1600000020	DA	12.03.2017	G			2.00	CAD		
☼	Bank guarantee	1600000021	DA	12.03.2017	G			21,500.00	CAD		Bank guarantee received

Fig 5

419

II. REVERSAL OF NOTED ITEM ENTRIES (U)

T Code FB08

We generally use this option in order to cancel the initial entry/postings or those, which are found to be incorrect. That can be due to many reasons in practical scenarios. SAP provides a list of Reason codes to be selected during reversal; we can choose as applicable:

Reason	Text
01	Reversal in current period
02	Reversal in closed period
03	Actual reversal in current period
04	Actual reversal in closed period
05	Accrual
06	Asset transaction reversal
07	Incorrect document date
08	Accrual/defferal posting fot itcs
11	Real/Defferral Reversal reaon for AML
12	ACCRUL/DEFERRAL REV REASON FOR REVERSAL
13	ACCRUL/DEFERRAL REV REASON FOR REVERSAL
1R	Reversal, incorrect original date aml
1S	Accrual/defferal posting for soda
ER	Posting Error - C900
RE	Reversal, incorrect original date
WE	Wrong Entry

Fig 6

As we reverse the normal documents, we can, in the same way, reverse the Noted Entries also in FB08

Provide the Noted Item Document Number, Company Codes, Fiscal Year and Reversal Reason.

Accounting
Financial Accounting
General Ledger
Posting
Document
FB02 - Change
FB09 - Change Line Items
FB03 - Display
FB04 - Display Changes
FBRA - Reset Cleared Items
Parked Documents
Reference Documents
Cross-Company-Code Transaction
Reverse
FB08 - Individual Reversal

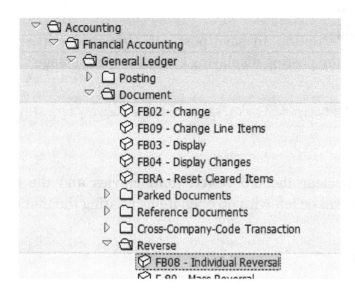

Fig 7

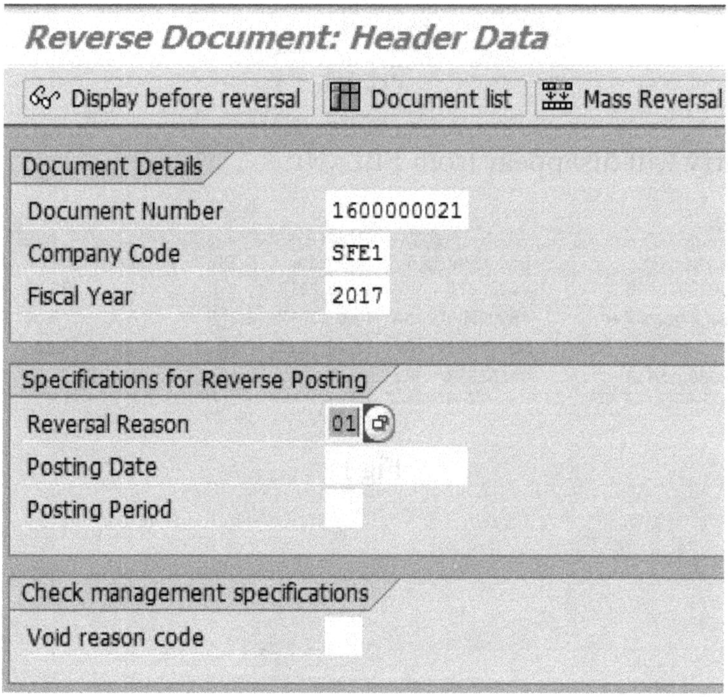

Reverse Document: Header Data
Display before reversal
Document list
Mass Reversal
Document Details
Document Number
1600000021
Company Code
SFE1
Fiscal Year
2017
Specifications for Reverse Posting
Reversal Reason
01
Posting Date
Posting Period
Check management specifications
Void reason code

Fig 8

Select 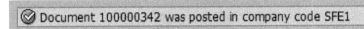 option to save/post the reversal entries. System confirms the posting displaying the following message :

Fig 9

This will clear the old Noted Item entries and the Customer Account will be left with no open items relating tho that entry.

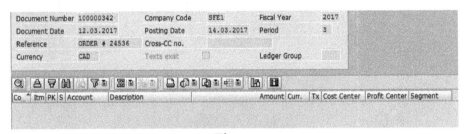

Document Number	100000342	Company Code	SFE1	Fiscal Year	2017
Document Date	12.03.2017	Posting Date	14.03.2017	Period	3
Reference	ORDER # 24536	Cross-CC no.			
Currency	CAD	Texts exist	☐	Ledger Group	

Co	Itm	PK	S	Account	Description		Amount	Curr.	Tx	Cost Center	Profit Center	Segment

Fig 10

The entry will disappear from FBL5N:

S.	Assignment	DocumentNo	Ty	Doc. Date	S	DD	Σ	Amount in local cur.	LCurr	Clr
☀	0080015448	90036836	RV	13.03.2017		☒		105.00-	CAD	
☀	Bank guarantee	1600000020	DA	12.03.2017	G	◿		2.00	CAD	
☀		90036823	RV	11.03.2017		◿		3,745.00	CAD	
☀	0080015444	90036833	RV	11.03.2017		◿		16,050.00	CAD	

Fig 11

FOREIGN CURRENCY VALUATION

(C/U)

Some companies maintain accounting reports like financial statements in a currency different from the local currency because they are subsidiaries of companies in other countries that have a different currency. Foreign currency valuation is done for preparing the financial statements at a key date. Documents posted in foreign currencies have to be converted to company code currency for preparing the company's financial statements as the company's financial statement can include only those transactions which are posted in company code's operational currency. Hence all the posings which are open items and items which are posted in GL accounts with foreign currency have to be valuated in company code currency. Valuation is performed at the exchange rate on the valuation date. In that way gain or loss is calculated and posted to exchange rate gain/loss accounts. Another scenario where this may be used is when the original invoice to the customer or from a vendor is in one currency but got paid in the other.

Scenario:

- Company Code (Local) currency : CAD$ (Canadian Dollar)
- Foreign Currency   : USD$ (US Dollar)

Pre-requisites:

- Create G/L Accounts for Foreign Currency Valuation Gain & Loss Posting Account
- Maintain Exchange Rate
- Define Valuation Methods
- Foreign Currency Valuation – Automatic Postings for curreign valuation

The report Foreign Currency Valuation (New) (T Code FAGL_FC_VAL) provides us with the following functions:

Valuation of foreign currency balance sheet accounts
Valuation of open items in foreign currencies
Saving the exchange rate differences determined from the valuation document Performing the adjustment postings required

I. CREATE G/L ACCOUNTS FOR FOREIGN CURRENCY VALUATION GAIN & LOSS POSTING ACCOUNT (U)

Transaction Code : FS00

We need to create this account to assign for Automatic posting during the realization of Gain or Loss derived from Foreign Currency revaluation.

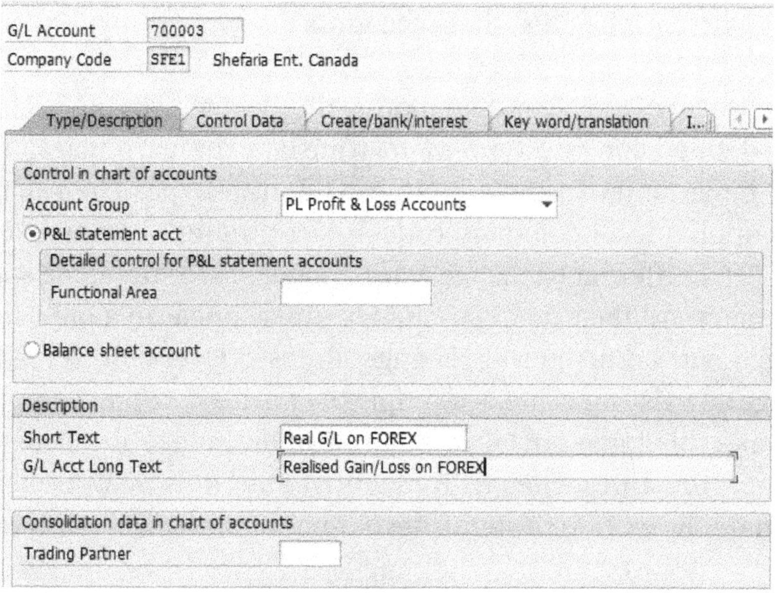

| G/L Account | 700003 | |
| Company Code | SFE1 | Shefaria Ent. Canada |

Type/Description | Control Data | Create/bank/interest | Key word/translation | I... | ◀ | ▶

Control in chart of accounts

| Account Group | PL Profit & Loss Accounts ▾ |

⦿ P&L statement acct

Detailed control for P&L statement accounts

| Functional Area | |

○ Balance sheet account

Description

| Short Text | Real G/L on FOREX |
| G/L Acct Long Text | Realised Gain/Loss on FOREX |

Consolidation data in chart of accounts

| Trading Partner | |

Fig 1

II. MAINTAIN EXCHANGE RATE (C/U)

Transaction Code : OB08

Exchange rates are required to:

- Translate foreign currency amounts when posting or clearing
- Determine the gain and loss from exchange rate differences
- Evaluate open items in foreign currency and the foreign currency balance sheet accounts

When we post and clear documents, the system uses the exchange rates defined for rate type **M** to translate the currencies. There must be an entry in the system for this rate type. The exchange rates apply for all company codes i.e. 2 different company codes can't get 2 different exchange rates applicable for the same set of 2 currencies. All the existing exchange rates appear in a table in the Change View Currency Exchange Rates : Overview screen. To change an existing value, we simply overwrite it. Often, companies will take this table out of configuration and make it master data because the rates change frequently and it is not feasible to originate the ex rate from the development system all the time.

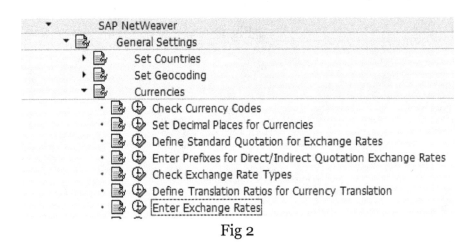

Fig 2

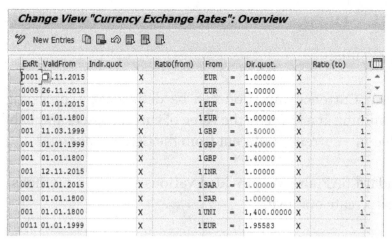

ExRt	ValidFrom	Indir.quot		Ratio(from)	From		Dir.quot.		Ratio (to)	
0001	□.11.2015		X		EUR	=	1.00000	X		▲
0005	26.11.2015		X		EUR	=	1.00000	X		▼
001	01.01.2015		X		1 EUR	=	1.00000	X	1	
001	01.01.1800		X		1 EUR	=	1.00000	X	1	
001	11.03.1999		X		1 GBP	=	1.50000	X	1	
001	01.01.1999		X		1 GBP	=	1.40000	X	1	
001	01.01.1800		X		1 GBP	=	1.40000	X	1	
001	12.11.2015		X		1 INR	=	1.00000	X	1	
001	01.01.2015		X		1 SAR	=	1.00000	X	1	
001	01.01.1800		X		1 SAR	=	1.00000	X	1	
001	01.01.1800		X		1 UNI	=	1,400.00000	X	1	
0011	01.01.1999		X		1 EUR	=	1.95583	X	1	

Fig 3

Click **New Entries** to update the following:

ExRt	ValidFrom	Indir.quot		Ratio(from)	From		Dir.quot.		Ra...	To
M	01.01.2016		X		1 CAD	=	0.74000	X	1	USD
M	01.01.2016		X		USD	=	1.35	X		CAD

Fig 4

Click 🖫 to save the entries

✅ Data was saved

Fig 5

III. Define Valuation Methods (C)

T Code OB59

Foreign Currency valuation can be defined as a procedure for determining at a key date the value of current assets and liabilities posted in a currency different from the CC currency.

Standard SAP already provided various valuation methods. Also we can create our own.

'M' is the average rate of any foreign currency. SAP uses exchange rate type 'M' to value all foreign currency items.

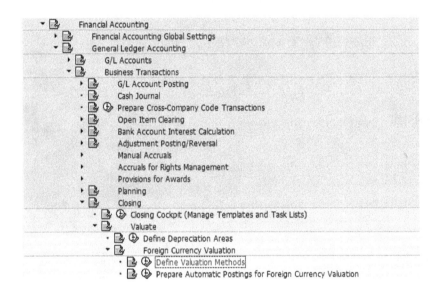

Fig 6

Click on New Entries and update the following :

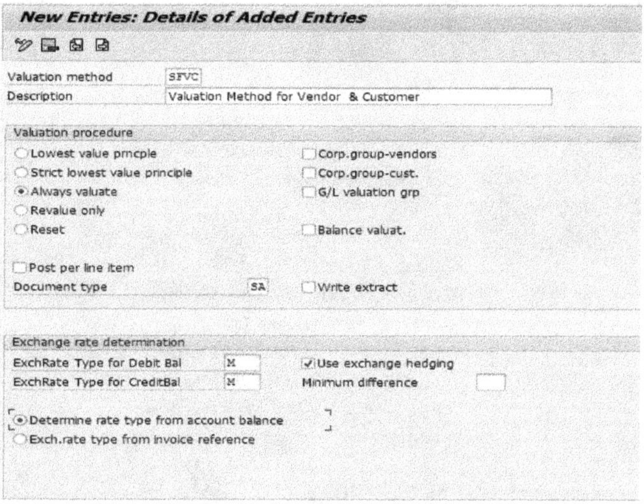

Fig 7

Various Exchange rate type is available with M being the most frequently used.

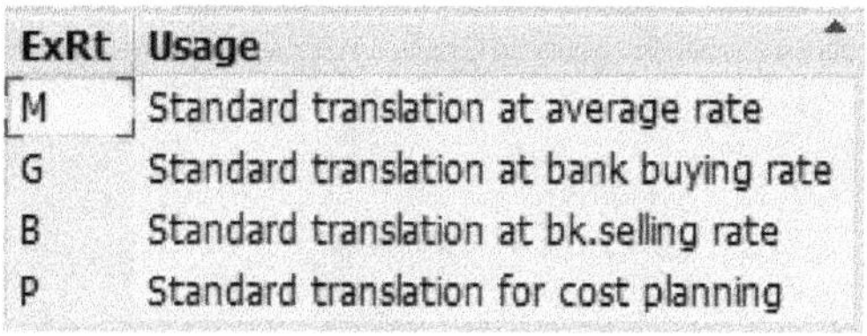

ExRt	Usage
M	Standard translation at average rate
G	Standard translation at bank buying rate
B	Standard translation at bk.selling rate
P	Standard translation for cost planning

Fig 8

Click ⊟ to Save all entries relating to Valuation Method

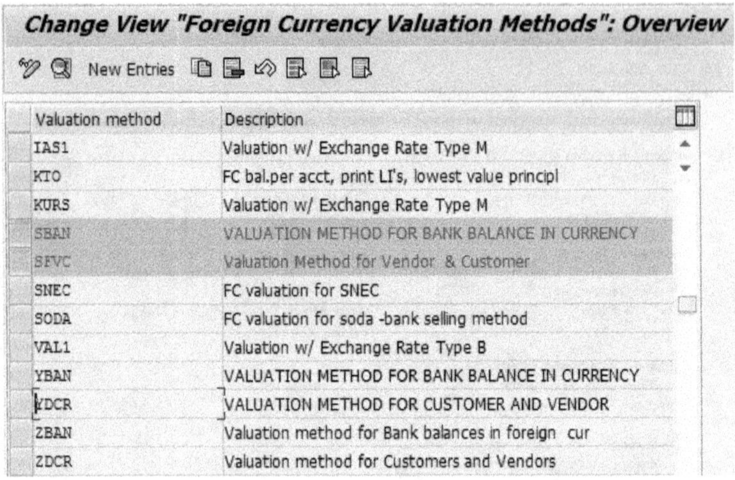

Change View "Foreign Currency Valuation Methods": Overview

New Entries

Valuation method	Description
IAS1	Valuation w/ Exchange Rate Type M
KTO	FC bal.per acct, print LI's, lowest value principl
KURS	Valuation w/ Exchange Rate Type M
SBAN	VALUATION METHOD FOR BANK BALANCE IN CURRENCY
SFVC	Valuation Method for Vendor & Customer
SNEC	FC valuation for SNEC
SODA	FC valuation for soda -bank selling method
VAL1	Valuation w/ Exchange Rate Type B
YBAN	VALUATION METHOD FOR BANK BALANCE IN CURRENCY
YDCR	VALUATION METHOD FOR CUSTOMER AND VENDOR
ZBAN	Valuation method for Bank balances in foreign cur
ZDCR	Valuation method for Customers and Vendors

Fig 9

430

IV. AUTOMATIC POSTING : ASSIGN GL ACCOUNTS FOR FOREIGN CURRENCY VALUATION (C)

T Code OBA1

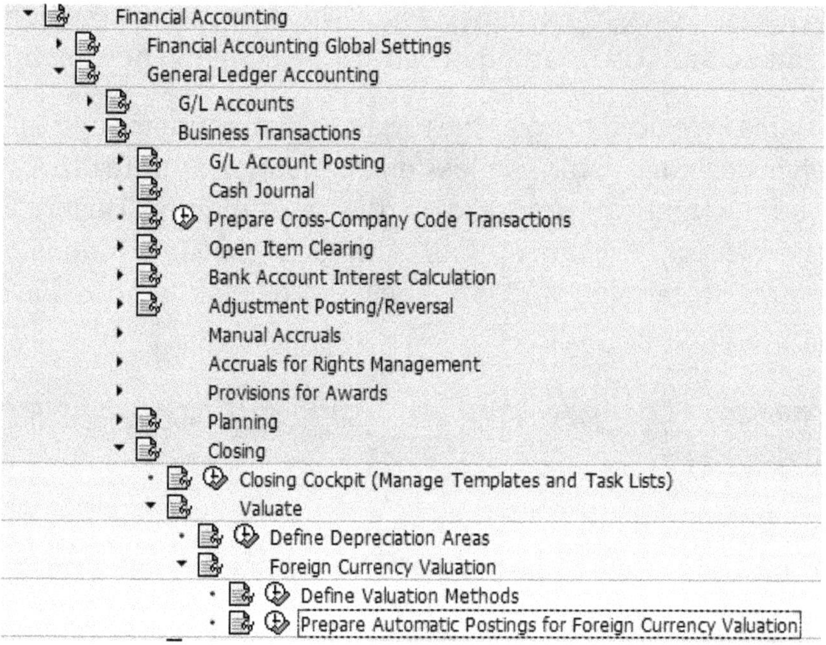

Fig 10

Here the gain and loss account assigned to accounting key KDB and KDF for automatic posting.

Procedures			
Description	Transaction	Account determ.	
Document Split for Currency Exchange	CEX	☑	▲
Exch. Rate Diff. using Exch. Rate Key	KDB	☑	▼
Exchange Rate Dif.: Open Items/GL Acct	KDF	☑	
Payment difference for altern.currency	KDW	☑	
Payment diff.for altern.curr.(offset)	KDZ	☑	
Internal currencies rounding differences	RDF	☑	

Fig 11

Enter the Chart of Accounts as

Chart of Accounts SFE and update the following under Transaction Key KDB by double clicking on it.

Expense Account: We need to enter the GL Account Code for Unrealized Foreign Exchange loss. The loss on revaluation is unrealized and will be automatically reversed in the next month.

ER Gains : We need to enter the revenue GL Account for unrealized foreign exchange gain. The loss on revaluation is unrealized and wil be automaticaly reversed in the next month. This is also applicable for Exchange Rate difference in open items e.g. Accounts Receivable and Accounts Payable or we can have a separate account.

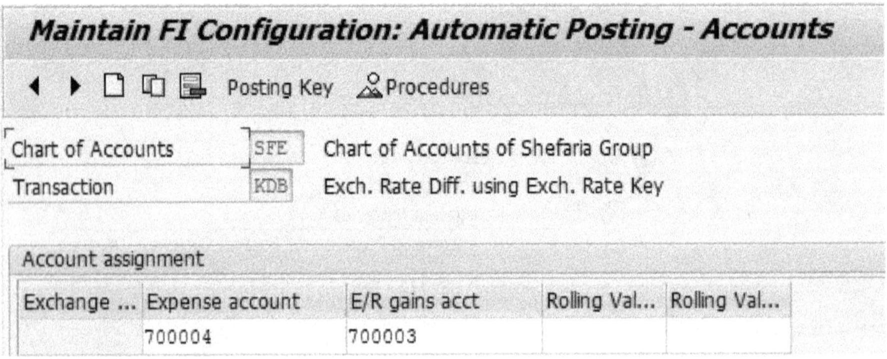

Maintain FI Configuration: Automatic Posting - Accounts

◀ ▶ ☐ ☐ ☐ Posting Key ⚲ Procedures

| Chart of Accounts | SFE | Chart of Accounts of Shefaria Group |
| Transaction | KDB | Exch. Rate Diff. using Exch. Rate Key |

Account assignment

Exchange ...	Expense account	E/R gains acct	Rolling Val...	Rolling Val...
	700004	700003		

Fig 12

Save all entries

Update Transaction Key KDF
Here we update GL Account Code for Accounts receivable and payable (reconcilliation account)

Enter 'SFE' as Chart of Accounts in the pop up and Click New Entries to update the following:

G/L Account : Balance Sheet Account (AP , AR, Bank G/L)
Loss   : G/L Account for Forex Loss
Gain   : G/L Account for Forex gain

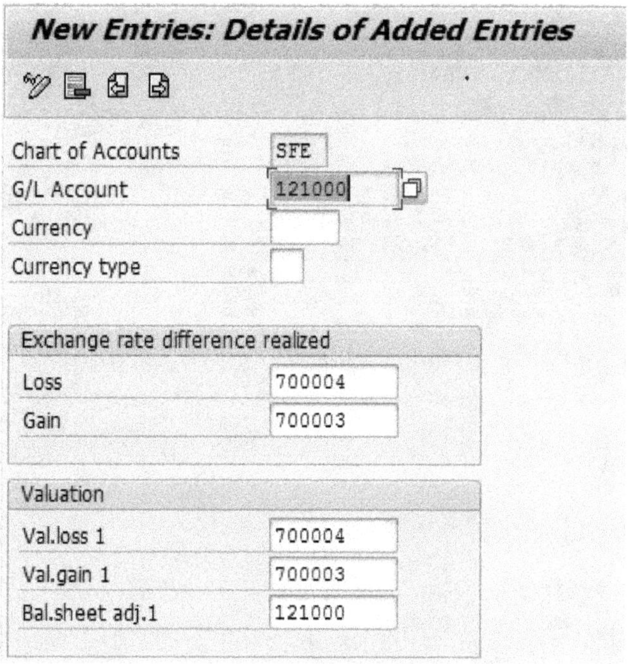

New Entries: Details of Added Entries

Chart of Accounts	SFE
G/L Account	121000
Currency	
Currency type	

Exchange rate difference realized

Loss	700004
Gain	700003

Valuation

Val.loss 1	700004
Val.gain 1	700003
Bal.sheet adj.1	121000

Fig 13

V.   REALISED GAIN LOSS (U)

T Code FB60

Now we can do a transaction to see how this will work:

- Booking Vendor Invoice in Foreign Currency . e.g. in EUR

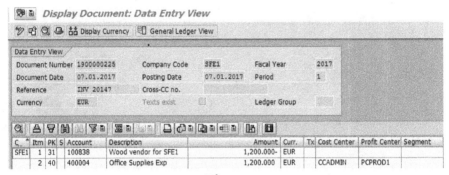

Fig 14

VI. MAKING PAYMENT IN FOREIGN CURRENCY (U)

T Code F-53

Post Outgoing Payments Display Overview

| 🔍 ⚏ Display Currency | 🔳 Taxes | ↩ Reset |

Document Date	11.02.2017	Type	KZ	Company Code	SFE1	
Posting Date	11.02.2017	Period	2	Currency	EUR	0.69700
Document Number	INTERNAL	Fiscal Year	2017	Translatn Date	11.02.2017	
Reference	1900000225			Cross-CC no.		
Doc.Header Text				Trading part.BA		

Items in document currency

PK	BusA	Acct		EUR	Amount	Tax amnt
001	50	0000100062	HSBC Bank (Outgoing		1,200.000-	
002	25	0000100838	Wood vendor for SFE		1,200.000	
003	50	0000700003	Real Gain on FOREX		0.000	

Fig 15

Click Display Currency to view exchange rate gain/loss on the payment transaction (U)

Click ⚏ Display Currency   to see the payment amount in local currency : CAD

Post Outgoing Payments Display Overview

| 🔍 ⚏ Display Currency | 🔳 Taxes | ↩ Reset |

Document Date	11.02.2017	Type	KZ	Company Code	SFE1	
Posting Date	11.02.2017	Period	2	Currency	EUR	0.69700
Document Number	INTERNAL	Fiscal Year	2017	Translatn Date	11.02.2017	
Reference	1900000225			Cross-CC no.		
Doc.Header Text				Trading part.BA		

Items in local currency

PK	BusA	Acct		CAD	Amount	Tax amnt
001	50	0000100062	HSBC Bank (Outgoing		836.40-	
002	25	0000100838	Wood vendor for SFE		2,064.00	
003	50	0000700003	Real Gain on FOREX		1,227.60-	

Fig 16

VII. Unrealized Gain or Loss (U)

T Code : FAGL_FC_VAL

Or Navigate below:

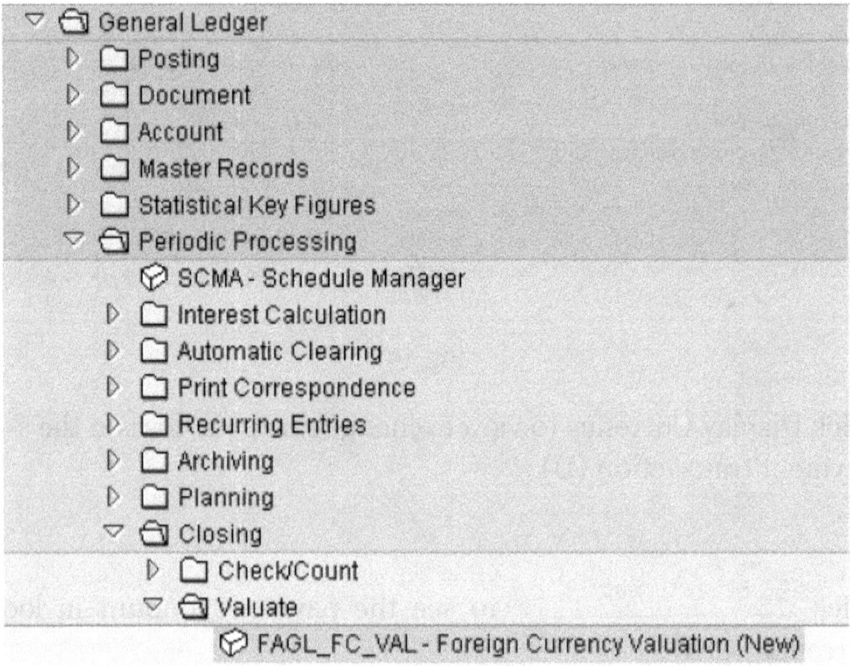

```
▽ 🗁 General Ledger
  ▷ 🗀 Posting
  ▷ 🗀 Document
  ▷ 🗀 Account
  ▷ 🗀 Master Records
  ▷ 🗀 Statistical Key Figures
  ▽ 🗁 Periodic Processing
      ⊘ SCMA - Schedule Manager
    ▷ 🗀 Interest Calculation
    ▷ 🗀 Automatic Clearing
    ▷ 🗀 Print Correspondence
    ▷ 🗀 Recurring Entries
    ▷ 🗀 Archiving
    ▷ 🗀 Planning
    ▽ 🗁 Closing
        ▷ 🗀 Check/Count
        ▽ 🗁 Valuate
            ⊘ FAGL_FC_VAL - Foreign Currency Valuation (New)
```

Fig 17

Usage:

All open items in foreign currency are valuated as part of the foreign currency valuation:

- The individual open items of an account in foreign currency form the basis of the valuation i.e. every open item of an account in foreign currency is valuated individually.

- The total difference from all the open items in an account is posted to a financial statement adjustment account.

436

- The exchange rate profit or loss from the valuation is posted to a separate expense or revenue account for exchange rate differences as an offset posting.

Features :

- Unrealized exchange rate differences - When we valuate open items in foreign currency, the exchange rate difference determined is posted as an unrealized exchange rate difference.

- Realized exchange rate differences - For an incoming payment, when we are clear open items, the current exchange rate is determined. Since the exchange differences that were not realized are reversed, the full exchange rate difference is now posted as realized.

- Reversing exchange rate difference postings - On the specified reversal date or in the reversal period, the posted exchange rate differences are automatically reversed by a reverse posting after the valuation run.

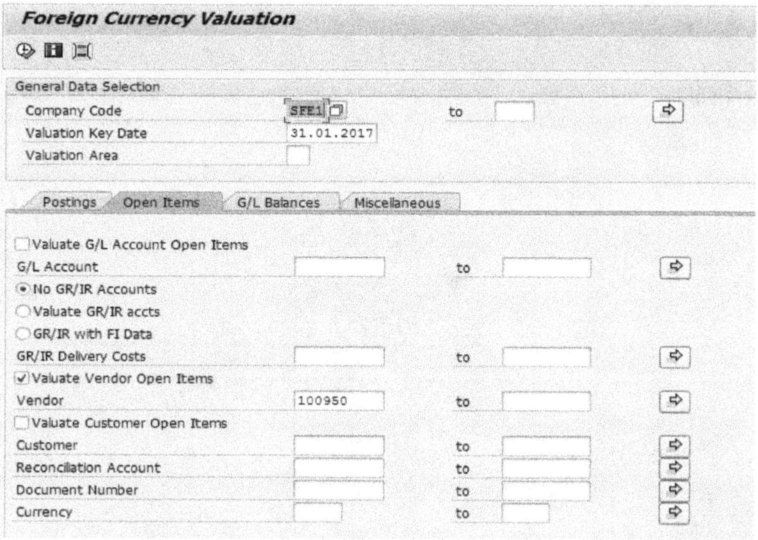

Fig 18

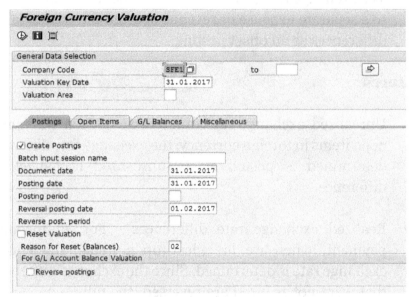

Fig 19

Click Execute

Fig 20

438

BILL OF EXCHANGE (C/U)

Bills of exchange are a form of short-term finance. If the customer pays by bill of exchange, it does not make payment immediately, but only once the maturity period specified on the bill has elapsed (three months, for example). Bills of exchange can be passed on to third parties for refinancing (bill of exchange usage). A bill of exchange can be discounted at a bank in advance of its due date (discounting). The bank buys the bill of exchange from us. Since it does not receive the amount until the date recorded on the bill, it charges us interest (discount) to cover the period between receiving the bill of exchange and its eventual payment. Some form of handling charge is also usually levied.

- Posting procedure of Bill of Exchange Receivable

There are 3 basic events for which bill of exchange can actually take place.

1. Payment by Bill of Exchange :
   Firstly, the payment by bill of exchange is posted and used to clear the receivable against the customer. There is a now

439

a bill of exchange receivable, which is recorded on the customer account and the special G/L account.

2. Bill of Exchange Usage
   If the bill of exchange is used for refinancing and is passed on to a bank, then the bill of exchange usage must be posted. The bill of exchange liability (liability to recourse) that you now have is recorded on special accounts in the system until it has expired.

3. Cancel the Bill of Exchange Liability
   Once the due date of the bill of exchange has elapsed, including any country-specific period for the bill of exchange protest, you can cancel the bill of exchange receivable for your customer and the bill of exchange liability.

I. Bill of Exchange Configuration (C)

T Code OBYN

Define Alternative Reconciliation account for Account type ' D' and assign the reconciliation and alternative reconciliation GL's –

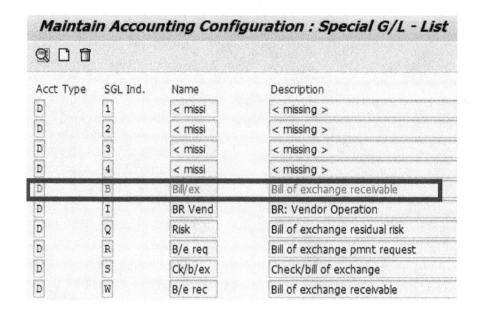

Fig 1

Enter Chart of Accounts :

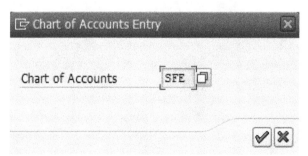

Fig 2

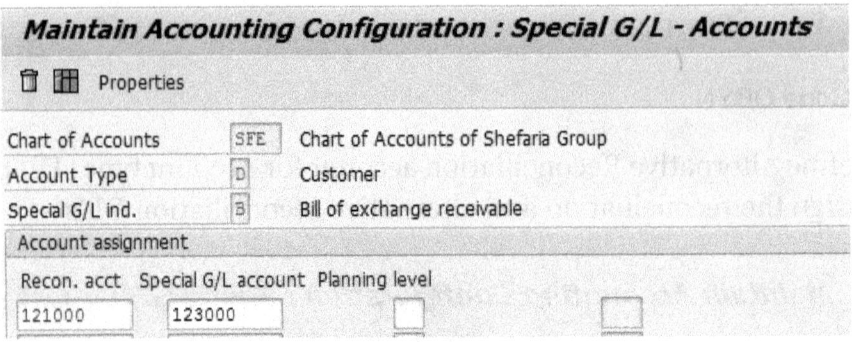

Maintain Accounting Configuration : Special G/L - Accounts

🗑 ▦ Properties

Chart of Accounts	SFE	Chart of Accounts of Shefaria Group
Account Type	D	Customer
Special G/L ind.	B	Bill of exchange receivable

Account assignment

Recon. acct	Special G/L account	Planning level	
121000	123000		

Fig 3

Save the entries

II. SETUP OF G/L ACCOUNT FOR BILL OF EXCHANGE (C/U)

T Code OBYK

Under Balance Sheet group of Accounts create the accounts as needed:

G/l Account : 100068 – Deutsche Bank Bill of exchange discount liability
100069 - Deutsche Bank - Collection of bills of exchange

Next, we link the Bank account and bank discounting account and reconciliation account together:

Change View "Bill Of Exchange Usage Bank SubAccounts": Overview

New Entries

ChAc	Bank acct	Usage	SGL In	Customer recon. acct	Bank subaccount for lab.
CAES	572000	D Discounting ▾ D		430000	520800
CAES	572000	D Discounting ▾ D		430100	520800
CAES	572000	D Discounting ▾ W		430000	520800
CAES	572000	F Forfeiting ▾ W		430000	520800
CAES	572000	I Collection ▾ W		430000	520900
CAFR	511300	I Collection ▾ W			413101
CAFR	511301	I Collection ▾ W			413101
CAFR	511302	I Collection ▾ W			413101
CAFR	511400	D Discounting ▾ W			413102
CAFR	511401	D Discounting ▾ W			413102
CAFR	511402	D Discounting ▾ W			413102
CAFR	512100	D Discounting ▾ B			512200
CAFR	512100	F Forfeiting ▾ B			512200
CAFR	512100	I Collection ▾ B			512200
CAFR	512101	▾ W			511802
CAFR	512102	▾ W			511804
CAJP	111207	D Discounting ▾ W			111370

Fig 4

Click **New Entries** to update the following:

ChAc	Bank acct	Usage		SGL In	Customer recon. acct	Bank subaccount for liab.
SFE	100066	D Discounting	B			100068
SFE	100066	D Discounting	W			100068
SFE	100066	F Forfeiting	B			100068
SFE	100066	F Forfeiting	W			100068
SFE	100066	I Collection	B			100069
SFE	100066	I Collection	W			100069

Fig 5

III. ACCEPTANCE OF BILL OF EXCHANGE

T Code F-36

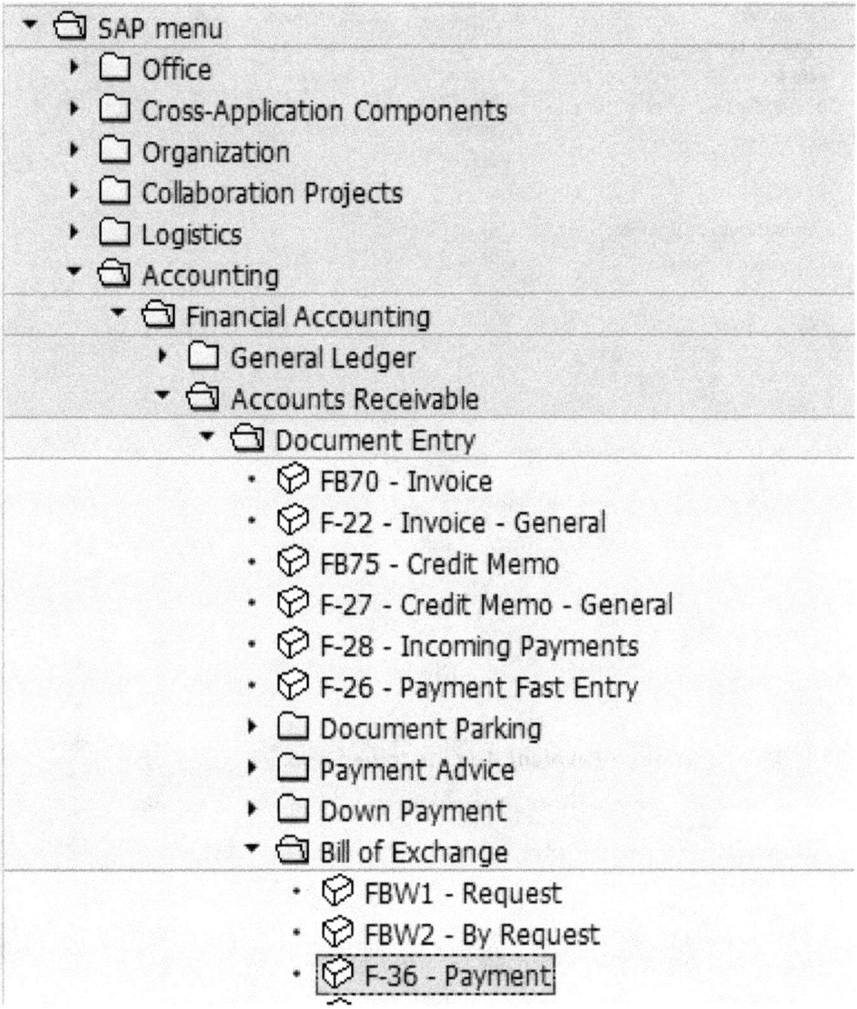

```
▼ 🗁 SAP menu
   ▶ 🗀 Office
   ▶ 🗀 Cross-Application Components
   ▶ 🗀 Organization
   ▶ 🗀 Collaboration Projects
   ▶ 🗀 Logistics
   ▼ 🗁 Accounting
      ▼ 🗁 Financial Accounting
         ▶ 🗀 General Ledger
         ▼ 🗁 Accounts Receivable
            ▼ 🗁 Document Entry
               • 📦 FB70 - Invoice
               • 📦 F-22 - Invoice - General
               • 📦 FB75 - Credit Memo
               • 📦 F-27 - Credit Memo - General
               • 📦 F-28 - Incoming Payments
               • 📦 F-26 - Payment Fast Entry
               ▶ 🗀 Document Parking
               ▶ 🗀 Payment Advice
               ▶ 🗀 Down Payment
               ▼ 🗁 Bill of Exchange
                  • 📦 FBW1 - Request
                  • 📦 FBW2 - By Request
                  • 📦 F-36 - Payment
```

Fig 6

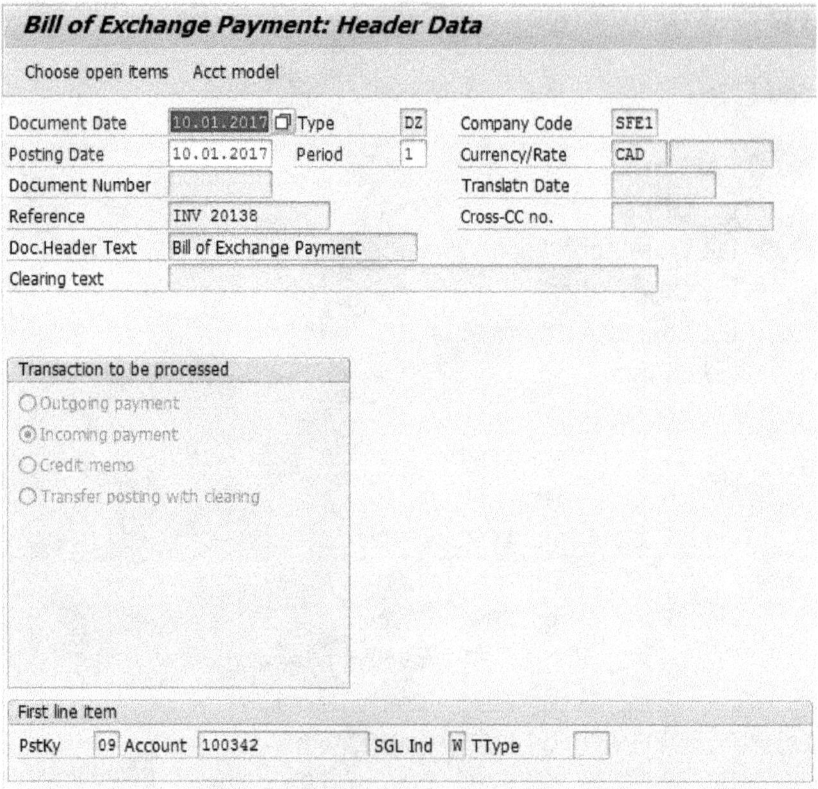

Bill of Exchange Payment: Header Data

Choose open items   Acct model

Document Date	10.01.2017	Type	DZ	Company Code	SFE1	
Posting Date	10.01.2017	Period	1	Currency/Rate	CAD	
Document Number				Translatn Date		
Reference	INV 20138			Cross-CC no.		
Doc.Header Text	Bill of Exchange Payment					
Clearing text						

Transaction to be processed

- ○ Outgoing payment
- ⊙ Incoming payment
- ○ Credit memo
- ○ Transfer posting with clearing

First line item

PstKy 09 Account 100342   SGL Ind W TType ☐

Fig 7

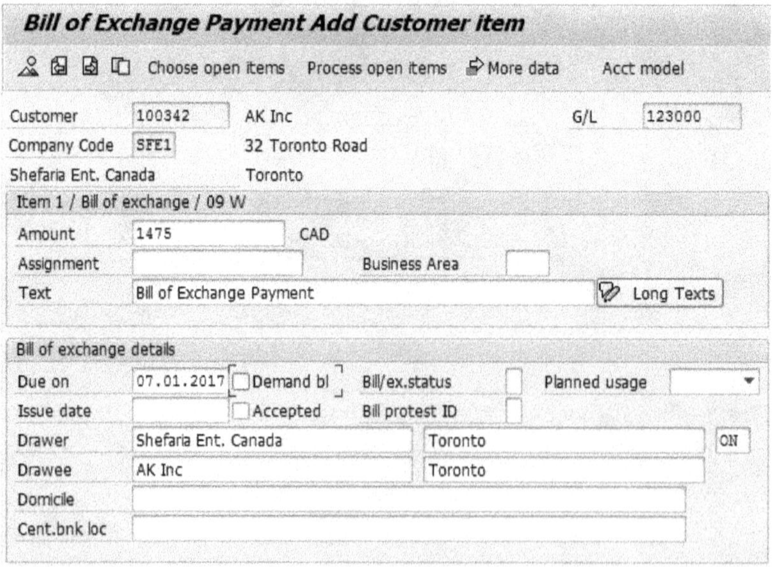

Bill of Exchange Payment Add Customer item

👤 🖫 🖫 🗖 Choose open items   Process open items 🖫 More data   Acct model

Customer	100342	AK Inc	G/L	123000
Company Code	SFE1	32 Toronto Road		
Shefaria Ent. Canada		Toronto		

Item 1 / Bill of exchange / 09 W

Amount	1475	CAD	
Assignment		Business Area	
Text	Bill of Exchange Payment		🖉 Long Texts

Bill of exchange details

Due on	07.01.2017	☐ Demand bl	Bill/ex.status ☐	Planned usage	▼
Issue date		☐ Accepted	Bill protest ID ☐		
Drawer	Shefaria Ent. Canada		Toronto		ON
Drawee	AK Inc		Toronto		
Domicile					
Cent.bnk loc					

Fig 8

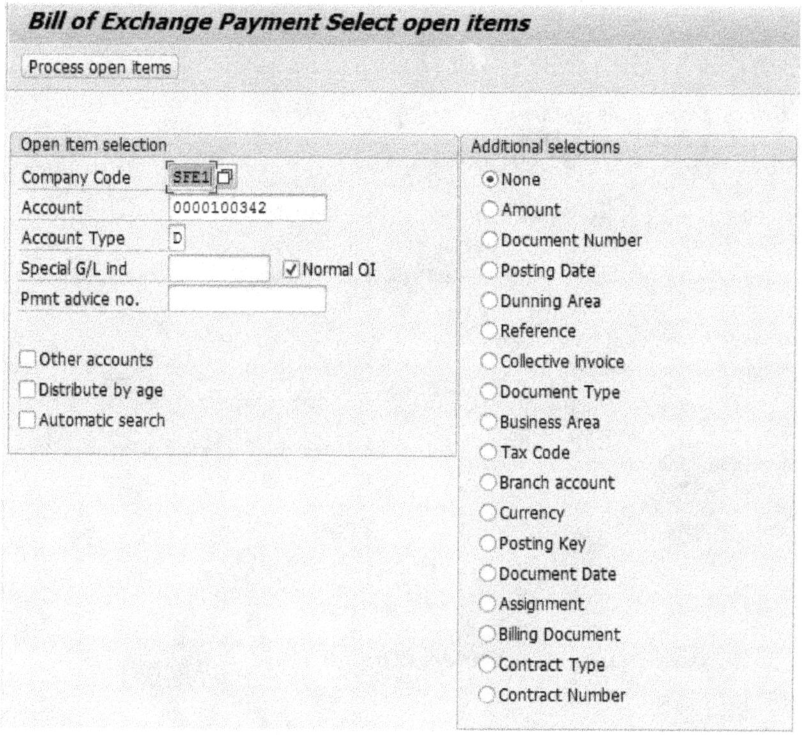

Bill of Exchange Payment Select open items

Process open items

Open item selection

Company Code	SFE1
Account	0000100342
Account Type	D
Special G/L ind	☑ Normal OI
Pmnt advice no.	

☐ Other accounts
☐ Distribute by age
☐ Automatic search

Additional selections

- ⦿ None
- ◯ Amount
- ◯ Document Number
- ◯ Posting Date
- ◯ Dunning Area
- ◯ Reference
- ◯ Collective Invoice
- ◯ Document Type
- ◯ Business Area
- ◯ Tax Code
- ◯ Branch account
- ◯ Currency
- ◯ Posting Key
- ◯ Document Date
- ◯ Assignment
- ◯ Billing Document
- ◯ Contract Type
- ◯ Contract Number

Fig 9

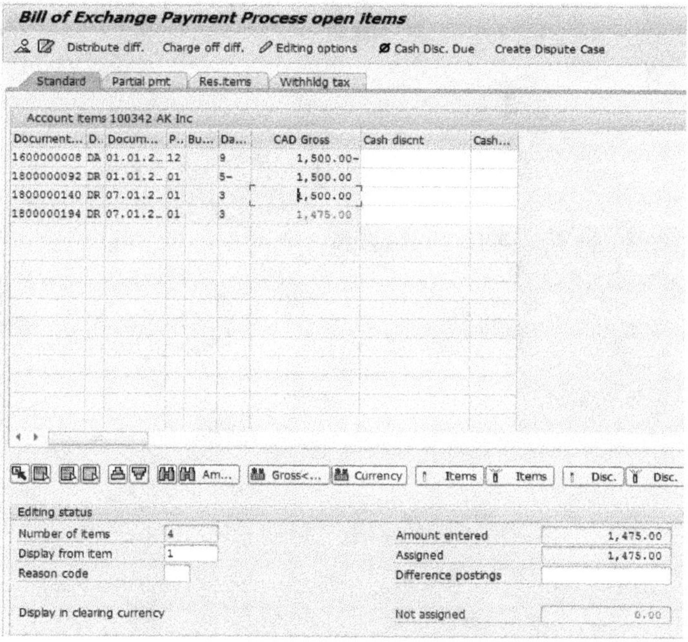

Bill of Exchange Payment Process open items

Distribute diff.   Charge off diff.   ✎ Editing options   Ø Cash Disc. Due   Create Dispute Case

Standard | Partial pmt | Res.items | Withhldg tax

Account items 100342 AK Inc

Document...	D..	Docum...	P..	Bu...	Da...	CAD Gross	Cash discnt	Cash...
1600000008	DA	01.01.2...	12		9	1,500.00-		
1800000092	DR	01.01.2...	01		5-	1,500.00		
1800000140	DR	07.01.2...	01		3	1,500.00		
1800000194	DR	07.01.2...	01		3	1,475.00		

Editing status

Number of items	4		Amount entered	1,475.00
Display from item	1		Assigned	1,475.00
Reason code			Difference postings	
Display in clearing currency			Not assigned	0.00

Fig 10

447

Simulate the Transaction

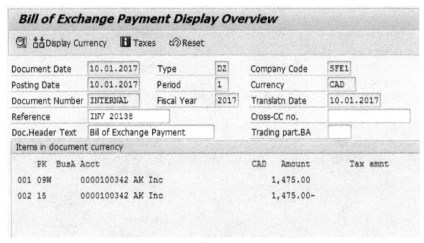

Fig 11

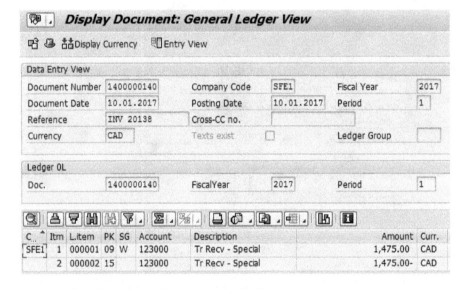

Fig 12

IV. BILL DISCOUNTING (U)

T Code F-33

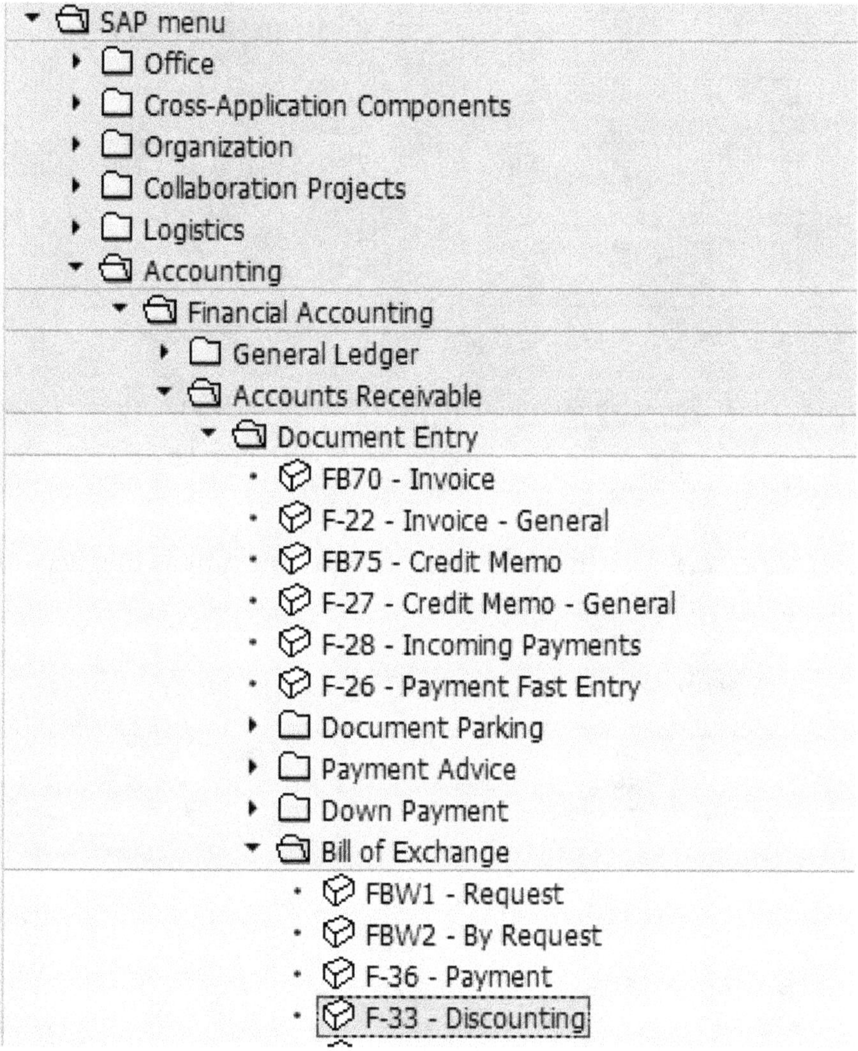

```
▼ 🗀 SAP menu
   ▶ 🗀 Office
   ▶ 🗀 Cross-Application Components
   ▶ 🗀 Organization
   ▶ 🗀 Collaboration Projects
   ▶ 🗀 Logistics
   ▼ 🗀 Accounting
      ▼ 🗀 Financial Accounting
         ▶ 🗀 General Ledger
         ▼ 🗀 Accounts Receivable
            ▼ 🗀 Document Entry
               • ⬡ FB70 - Invoice
               • ⬡ F-22 - Invoice - General
               • ⬡ FB75 - Credit Memo
               • ⬡ F-27 - Credit Memo - General
               • ⬡ F-28 - Incoming Payments
               • ⬡ F-26 - Payment Fast Entry
            ▶ 🗀 Document Parking
            ▶ 🗀 Payment Advice
            ▶ 🗀 Down Payment
            ▼ 🗀 Bill of Exchange
               • ⬡ FBW1 - Request
               • ⬡ FBW2 - By Request
               • ⬡ F-36 - Payment
               • ⬡ F-33 - Discounting
```

Fig 13

Post Bill of Exchange Usage: Header Data

Document Date	10.01.2017	Type	DA	Company Code	SFE1
Posting Date	10.01.2017	Period	3	Currency/Rate	CAD
Document Number				Translatn Date	
Reference	1400000140				
Doc.Header Text	Bill Discounting			Trading part.BA	

Posting details

Usage	D Discounting ▼		Value date	
Bank account	100067		Clearing acct	
Business Area			Profit Center	
Amount	1,200		Amount in LC	
Bank charges			LC bank charges	
Bill/exch.tax			LC bill/ex.tax	
Assignment				
Text	Bill of Exchange Discounting			

Other line items

PstKy	40	Account	400021	SGL Ind

Fig 14

Posting Key 40 : Use the Bank charges G/L Account as that account will take the hit for this amount.

Post Bill of Exchange Usage Correct G/L account item

Select bill of exch.   More data

G/L Account	400021	Bank Charges
Company Code	SFE1	Shefaria Ent. Canada

Item 2 / Debit entry / 40

Amount	275.00		CAD
			☐ Calculate tax
Cost Center	CA1000A	Order	
WBS Element		Profit. Segment	⇨
Network			
		Sales Order	
			⇨ More
		Quantity	
Assignment			
Text	Bill of Exchange Discounting		Long Texts

Fig 15

450

Choose and Enter Bill of Exchange Document No.

Post Bill of Exchange Usage Choose postings

Select bill of exch.

Company Code   SFE1

Relevant bill of exchange details

Doc. Number	Item	Fiscal year
1400000140		2017

Fig 16

Choose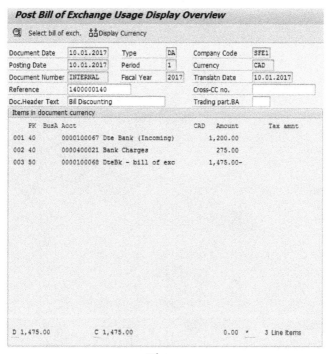

Post Bill of Exchange Usage Display Overview

Select bill of exch.　Display Currency

Document Date	10.01.2017	Type	DA	Company Code	SFE1
Posting Date	10.01.2017	Period	1	Currency	CAD
Document Number	INTERNAL	Fiscal Year	2017	Translatn Date	10.01.2017
Reference	1400000140			Cross-CC no.	
Doc.Header Text	Bill Discounting			Trading part.BA	

Items in document currency

PK	BusA	Acct		CAD	Amount	Tax amnt
001 40		0000100067	Dte Bank (Incoming)		1,200.00	
002 40		0000400021	Bank Charges		275.00	
003 50		0000100068	DteBk - bill of exc		1,475.00-	

D 1,475.00   C 1,475.00   0.00 *   3 Line Items

Fig 17

Choose Simulate and system will display the following message :

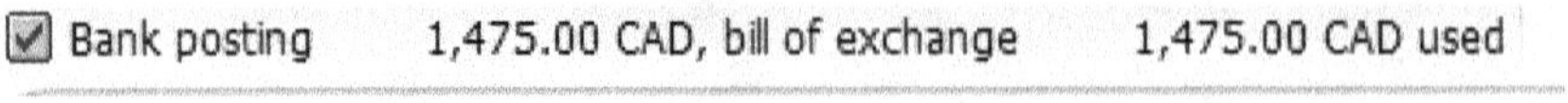

☑ Bank posting   1,475.00 CAD, bill of exchange   1,475.00 CAD used

Fig 18

Choose 💾 to post the document with successful Bill of Exchange Discounting

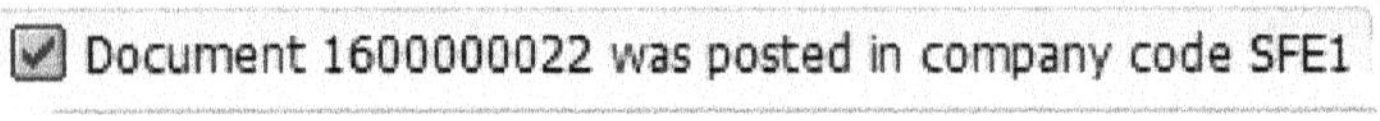

☑ Document 1600000022 was posted in company code SFE1

Fig 19

BANK RECONCILIATION

STATEMENT PROCESSING

Bank reconciliation is the process of matching and comparing figures from accounting records in the system with those presented on a bank statement. Less any items which have no relation to the bank statement, the balance of the accounting ledger should reconcile with the balance of the bank statement.
Bank reconciliation allows companies or individuals to compare their account records to the bank's records of their account balance in order to uncover any possible discrepancies.

Standard SAP provides 2 bank reconciiliation process :

  ➢ Electroninc Bank Reconcilliation

  ➢ Manual Bank Reconcilliation

Electronic Bank statement Process Flow Chart :

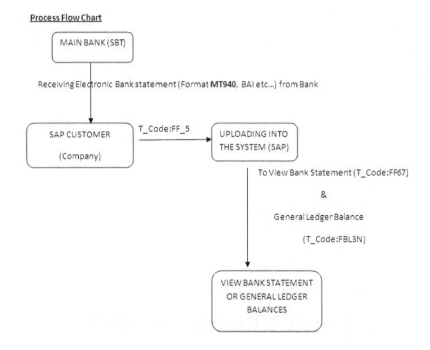

Fig 1

Electronic bank statement overview:

- It is an electronic document sent by the bank, which gives details of the transactions done in the account holder's account with the bank.
- The electronic document can be remitted by the bank in the following formats SWIFT, Multi cash, BAI etc.- these are standard formats with specific sets of data
- This statement is used in SAP to do an automatic reconciliation
- The statement is uploaded in SAP and it clears the various Bank clearing accounts

Next step is to configure the Electronic Bank Statement (EBS).

I. CREATE HOUSE BANK (C)

Transaction Code FI12

In the SAP system, you use bank ID and account ID to specify bank details. These specifications are used, for example, for automatic payment transactions to determine bank details for payment.

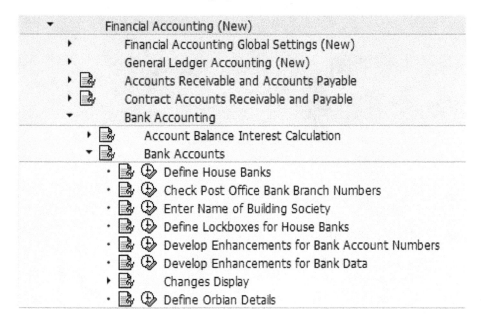

Fig 2

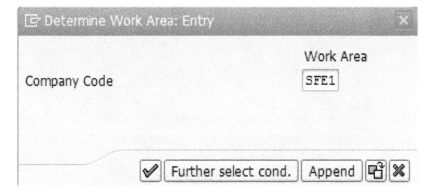

Fig 3

Define your house banks and the corresponding accounts in the system under a bank ID or an account ID.

| Company Code | SFE1 | Shefaria Ent. Canada |
| House Bank | HSBC | HSBC Canada PLC |

House Bank Data

| Bank Country | CA | Canada |
| Bank Key | 1000111111 | |

Create
Change

Communications data

| Telephone 1 | 0102222330001 | Tax Number 1 |
| Contact Person | | |

Address

Address

Bank name	HSBC Canada PLC
Region	
Street	Ontaro
City	Ontario
Bank Branch	Ontario

Control data

SWIFT code	
Bank group	
Post Bank Acct	
Bank number	1000111111

Fig 4

Update Bank Account:

Company Code	SFE1	Shefaria Ent. Canada
House Bank	HSBC	
Account ID	1-101	
Description	HSBC CAD$ Account	

Bank Account Data

Bank Account Number	1000111111	IBAN	Control key	
Alternative acct no.			G/L	100060
Currency	CAD		Discount acct	

House Bank Data

| Bank Country | CA |
| Bank Key | 1000111111 |

Address

Bank Name	HSBC Canada PLC
Region	
Street	Ontaro
City	Ontario
Branch Office	Ontario

Control Data

SWIFT Code	
Bank Group	
Post Bank Acct	
Bank Number	1000111111

Fig 5

456

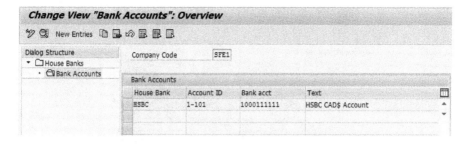

Fig 6

Electronic Bank Statement

In the following activities all the settings necessary for the EBS have been configured in Global Settings for Electronic Bank Statement

```
▼     Financial Accounting (New)
  ▸       Financial Accounting Global Settings (New)
  ▸       General Ledger Accounting (New)
  ▸ 📑     Accounts Receivable and Accounts Payable
  ▸ 📑     Contract Accounts Receivable and Payable
  ▼       Bank Accounting
    ▸ 📑       Account Balance Interest Calculation
    ▸ 📑       Bank Accounts
    ▸ 📑       Bank Chains
    ▼ 📑       Business Transactions
      ▸ 📑         Check Deposit
      ▸ 📑         Bill of Exchange Transactions
      ▼ 📑         Payment Transactions
        ▸ 📑           Payment Request
        ▸ 📑           Payment Handling
        ▸              Online Payments
        ▸ 📑           Manual Bank Statement
        ▼ 📑           Electronic Bank Statement
          · 📑 ⊕         Make Global Settings for Electronic Bank Statement
          · 📑 ⊕         Define Search String for Electronic Bank Statement
          · 📑 ⊕         Simulate Document Number Search Using Strings
          · 📑 ⊕         Define Program and Variant Selection
          · 📑 ⊕         Develop Enhancements for Electronic Bank Statement (General)
          · 📑 ⊕         Develop Enhancements for Elec.Bank Statement (Format Spec.)
          · 📑 ⊕         Error Codes
          · 📑 ⊕         Create Planning Types per Bank Account
          · 📑 ⊕         Create Currency Classes
          · 📑 ⊕         Define Currency Classes
          · 📑 ⊕         Configure Returns Processing
          ▸              Business Add-Ins (BAdIs)
```

Fig 7

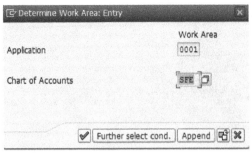
Fig 8

In this activity we make the global settings for the account statement. There are four main steps to be carried out:

- Create account symbol
- Assign accounts to account symbols
- Create keys for posting rules
- Create a transaction type

II. CREATE ACCOUNT SYMBOLS (C)

T Code SPRO

In this activity account symbols has been created to define posting specifications. Before the posting rule is used, account symbols are replaced with the relevant accounts to which posting is to be made. Define an ID for each account symbol & enter a description in the text field. Following Account symbols are created :

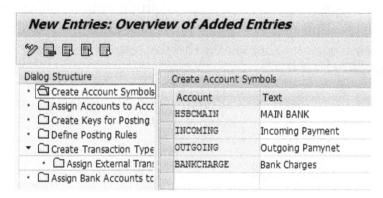

Fig 9

III. ASSIGN ACCOUNTS TO ACCOUNT SYMBOLS (C)

T Code SPRO

In this activity account, determination procedure has been defined for each individual account symbol. Define postings to be triggered by possible transactions in the account statement (such as bank transfer, debit memo). In the posting specifications debit -> credit that has been defined here, we will use the account symbols from step 1, not the G/L account numbers. This prevents similar posting rules being defined several times, as the only difference between them being the accounts to which postings are made.

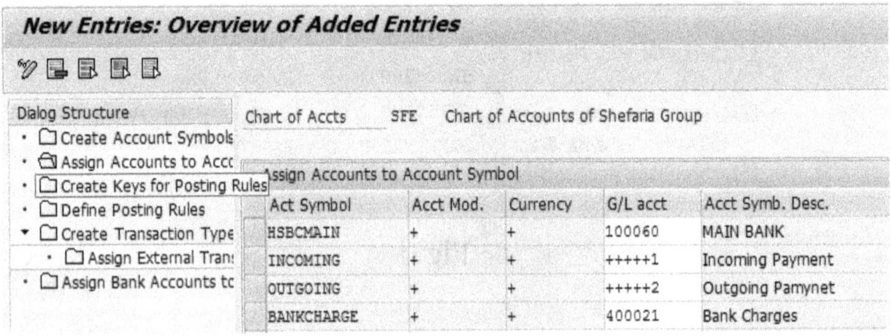

Dialog Structure	Chart of Accts	SFE	Chart of Accounts of Shefaria Group		
· Create Account Symbols					
· Assign Accounts to Acco	Assign Accounts to Account Symbol				
· Create Keys for Posting Rules					
· Define Posting Rules	Act Symbol	Acct Mod.	Currency	G/L acct	Acct Symb. Desc.
▼ Create Transaction Type	HSBCMAIN	+	+	100060	MAIN BANK
· Assign External Trans	INCOMING	+	+	+++++1	Incoming Payment
· Assign Bank Accounts to	OUTGOING	+	+	+++++2	Outgoing Pamynet
	BANKCHARGE	+	+	400021	Bank Charges

New Entries: Overview of Added Entries

Fig 10

The masking is done using ++++++ for the main bank account. For the sub accounts, all the other digits are masked except the last one. For bank charges, the actual G/L account is entered.

IV. CREATE KEYS FOR POSTING RULES (C)

T Code SPRO

In this activity, separate keys are defined for posting rules to be used for banking transactions.

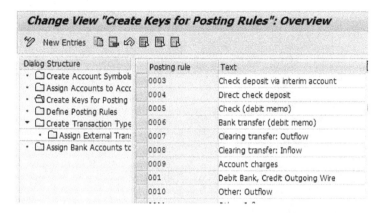

Fig 11

Create New Entries:

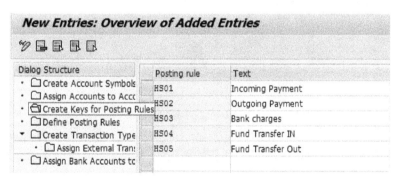

Fig 12

V. DEFINE POSTING RULES (C)

T Code SPRO

For each posting specifications posting rules has been created which will specify how business transaction is to be posted.

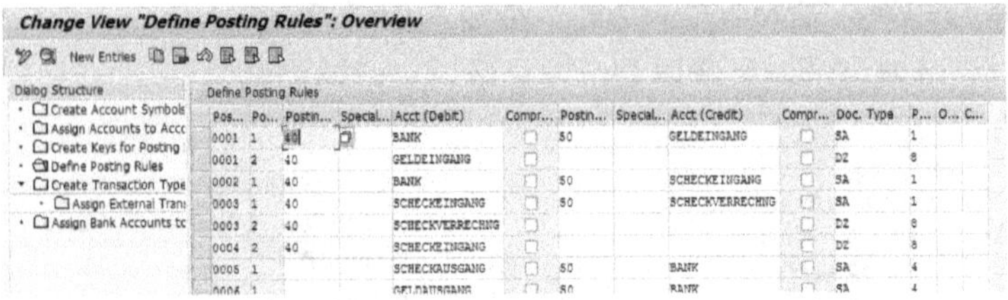

Fig 13

Click **New Entries** to create new posting rules

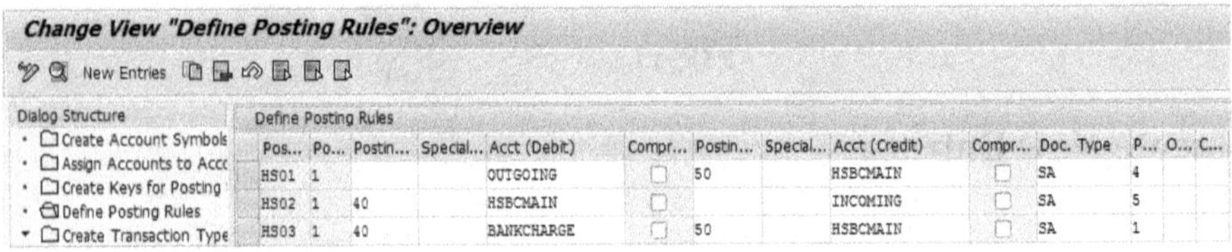

Fig 14

VI. CREATE TRANSACTION TYPES (C)

T Code SPRO

In this activity transaction type: MT940 has been created in order to facilitate Electronic Banking Statement processing.

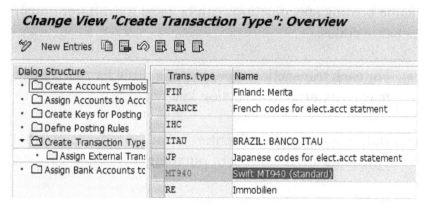

Fig 15

VII. ASSIGN EXTERNAL TRANSACTION CODES TO POSTING RULES (C)

T Code SPRO

In this activity (external) business, transaction codes provided by HSBC are assigned to an (internal) posting rule. This means that the same posting specifications can be used for different business transaction codes.

- For each transaction type, a posting rule has been assigned to each external transaction key

- In the "+/- sign" field, enter "+" or "-" to indicate whether payments are incoming or outgoing

- An interpretation algorithm has been defined for open items relating to outgoing payment in order to clear automatically because of the posting.

Choose Transaction type:

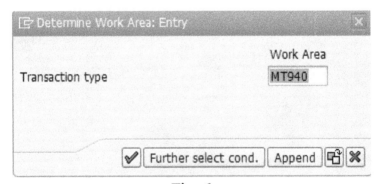

Fig 16

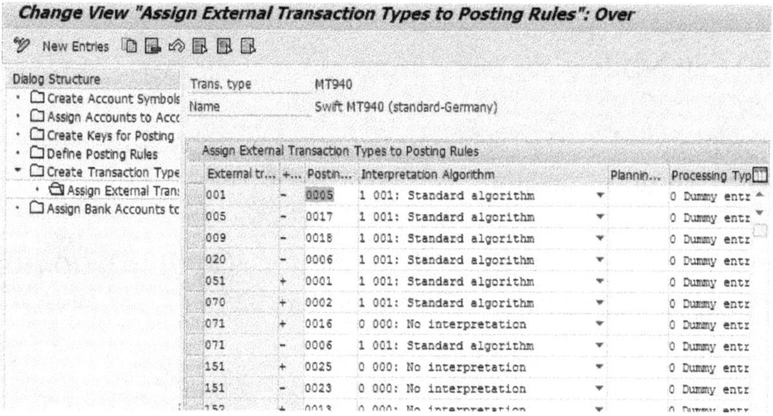

Fig 17

Click New Entries to update the following :

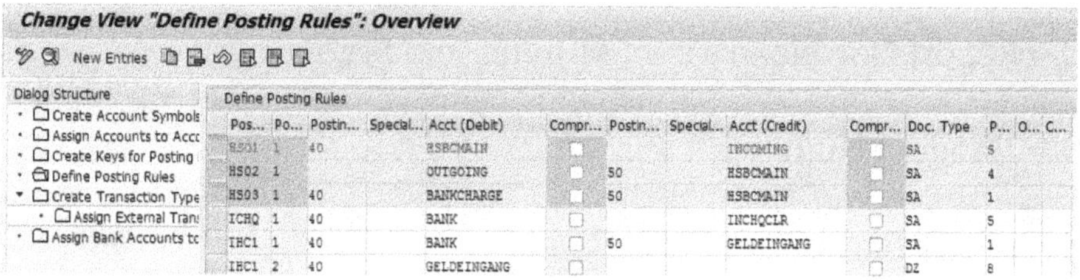

Fig 18

Save the entries.

Details of description (MT940 Format)

: 20: Statement Date

: 25: Account Identification Bank ID/account number

: 28C: Statement and/or sequence number

: 60F: Opening Balance

: 61: Statement line field

: 86: Information to account holder

: 62F Closing Balance

MT940 File Name

The downloaded SWIFT MT940 file will have the similar file name with the following details:

Statement - End of Day (MT940)2004-03-12-06[1].25.45.876474.940

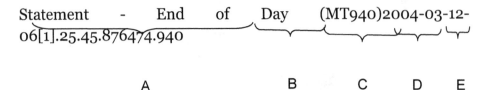

A = Name of the report

B = Report Download Date

C = Report Download Time, Minutes and Second

D = Random Numbers

E = File Extension

SWIFT MT940 Layout Specification

The downloaded report will contain the following fields.

Tag	Field Name Description	Additional Details
:20:	Transaction reference number 16x	YYMMDD, the statement date of the final closing balance
:25:	Account Identification 34x	Internal account number, without '-'
:28C:	Statement Number/ Sequence Number	SWIFT Format option C 5n/3n
:60 (F/M):	Opening Balance (F) Intermediate (M) 25x	1a6n3a15n 1a – 'D/C' debit or credit marker

Tag	Field Name Description	Additional Details
		6n – Statement Date of the opening balance, YYMMDD 3a – Account Currency Code 15n – Amount
:61:	Statement line 48x (52x – R3.2 onwards)	6n4n1a15n4a16a16a34a Subfield 1: Transaction Value Date (YYMMDD) (6n) Subfield 2: Transaction Posting Date (MMDD) (4n) Subfield 3: Debit/Credit Marker (1a) Subfield 4: Not applicable Subfield 5: Amount (15n) Subfield 6: Transaction Type (4a) Subfield 7: Reference for Account Owner (16a) Subfield 8: // [Account Servicing Institutions Reference (16a)] Subfield 9: Supplementary Details (34a)
:86:	Information to Account Holder 6*65x (unstructured) For LVP (Outward)	This field is populated with UNSTRUCTURED information of Transaction Description downloaded from the Bank. 1. full customer batch reference (Line 1 If available)

Tag	Field Name Description	Additional Details
		2. (ED) - identifer to indicate the end of the customer batch reference
		3. AUTOPAY OUT - Constant (Line 1)
		4. Payment setcode (Line 1)
	For HVP (Outward)	5. Payment setcode description (Line 1 if customer reference is NONREF else line 2)
		1. FREE TEXT Beneficiary Name
	For LVP (Return)	2. Narrative
		3. Narrative
		4. Foreign exchange information
		5. Charges information
		1. Standard Narrative
		2. Reject Reason
		3. Payment setcode
		4. Second Party Identifier
:62 (F/M):	Closing Balance (F) Intermediate (M) 25x	1a6n3a15n
		1a – 'D/C' debit or credit marker
		6n – Statement Date of the closing balance, YYMMDD
		3a – Account Currency Code
		15n – Amount

VIII. UPLOADING BANK STATEMENT INTO SAP (U)

Transaction code FF_5

```
▼ ⊟ SAP menu
  ▶ ☐ Office
  ▶ ☐ Cross-Application Components
  ▶ ☐ Organization
  ▶ ☐ Collaboration Projects
  ▶ ☐ Logistics
  ▼ ⊟ Accounting
    ▼ ⊟ Financial Accounting
      ▶ ☐ General Ledger
      ▶ ☐ Accounts Receivable
      ▶ ☐ Accounts Payable
      ▶ ☐ Contract Accounts Receivable and Payable
      ▼ ⊟ Banks
        ▼ ⊟ Incomings
          ▼ ⊟ Bank Statement
            • ⊘ FF67 - Manual Entry
            • ⊘ FEBC - Convert
            • ⊘ S_PL0_09000467 - Convert with DME Engine
            • ⊘ FF_5 - Import
```

Fig 19

Import sample MT940 Statement file from Local
Drive / Application server and   execute

```
:20:170131
:25:1000111111
:28C:00001/001
:60F:C170101CAD100000
:61:1701050104C3200,00NTRF1400000141        //9001XA90M77B
:86:OMC Inc AUTOPAY IN                         C01
CUSTOMER
:61:1701040103D2000,00NTRF1500000070        //LP KLH920990
:86:wood vendor for SFE1
CABLE      CAD4.00
:61:1701240904C100,00NTRFNONREF             //NONREF
:86:MEPS INTEREST  PAYMENT
INVALID ACCOUNT NUMBER 24174527665
C01 SECID001
:62F:C170131CAD101096.00
```

Fig 20

469

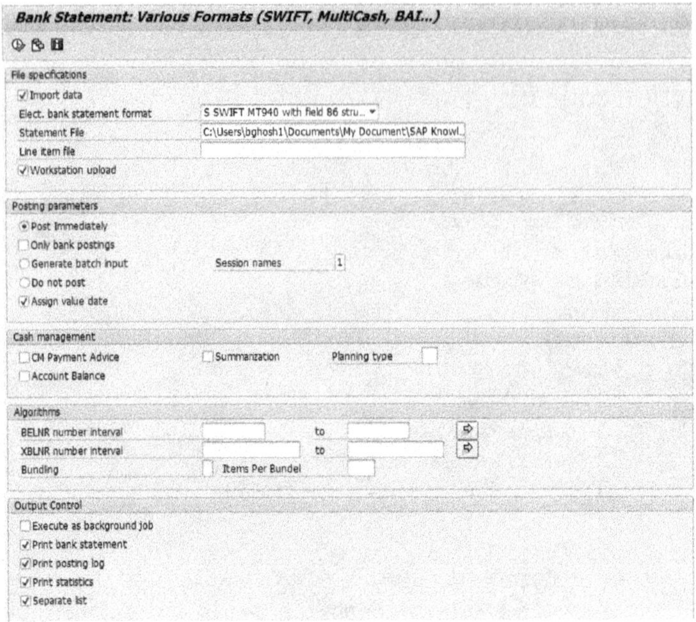

Bank Statement: Various Formats (SWIFT, MultiCash, BAI...)

File specifications
- ☑ Import data
- Elect. bank statement format: `S SWIFT MT940 with field 86 stru... ▾`
- Statement File: `C:\Users\bghosh1\Documents\My Document\SAP Knowl...`
- Line item file:
- ☑ Workstation upload

Posting parameters
- ◉ Post Immediately
- ☐ Only bank postings
- ☐ Generate batch input   Session names `1`
- ☐ Do not post
- ☑ Assign value date

Cash management
- ☐ CM Payment Advice   ☐ Summarization   Planning type
- ☐ Account Balance

Algorithms
- BELNR number interval _____ to _____ ⇨
- XBLNR number interval _____ to _____ ⇨
- Bundling   ☐ Items Per Bundel _____

Output Control
- ☐ Execute as background job
- ☑ Print bank statement
- ☑ Print posting log
- ☑ Print statistics
- ☑ Separate list

Fig 21

Posting Overview: Bank Statement MT940 file has been processed. If some transaction is not posted during MT940 automatic bank reconcilliation it can be later processed via FEBAN – Post Processing

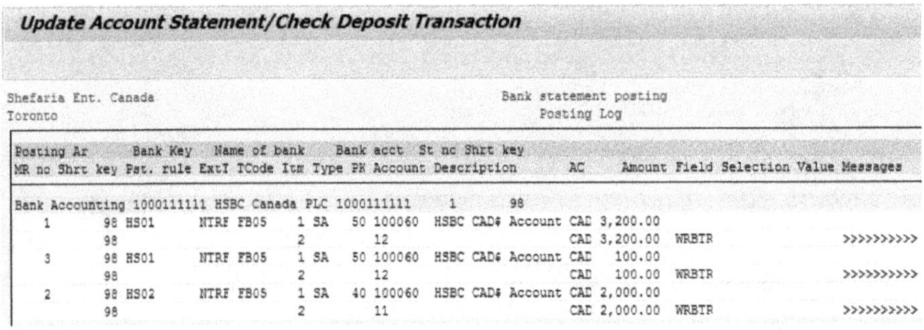

Fig 22

Update in Bank sub-ledger: confirming Payment Cashed in and Out

Update Account Statement/Check Deposit Transaction

Shefaria Ent. Canada   Bank statement posting   Time 12:14:00   Date 14.03.2017
Toronto   Processing Statistics   RFEBBU00/IDES013   Page   2

Posting Ar	Sessn	Group	FB01	FB05	PmtAcc	No Posting	Error	Total	Total Deb.	Total Cred
Bank Accounting			0	0	0	0	3	3	3,300.00	2,000.00
* Bank Accounting			0	0	0	0	3	3	3,300.00	2,000.00
** Bank Accounting			0	0	0	0	3	3	3,300.00	2,000.00
Subledger acctng			0	0	0	3	0	3	3,300.00	2,000.00
* Subledger acctng			0	0	0	3	0	3	3,300.00	2,000.00
** Subledger acctng			0	0	0	3	0	3	3,300.00	2,000.00
***			0	0	0	3	3	6	6,600.00	4,000.00

Fig 23

Bank Statement: Various Formats (SWIFT, MultiCash, BAI...)

Shefaria Ent. Canada   Time 12:17:11   Date 14.03.2017
Toronto   RFEBKA00/IDES013   Page   1
HSBC Canada PLC
Bank no.:   1000111111   Account number: 1000111111   Statement number: 00001   ID: 00000098
House bank: HSBC   Acct ID: 1-101   Statement date: 31.01.2017   Currency   CAD

Opening Balance   100,000.00
Total Debit   2,000.00
Total Cred.   3,300.00
Clos. Bal.   10,109,600.00

MR no	Value date	BkPostDate	Payment Notes	Posting text	Amount	BTC
				Opening Balance	100,000.00	
1	05.01.2017		GMC INC AUTOPAY IN C01 CUSTOMER 9001XKA90M77B Reference 1400000141		3,200.00	NTRF
2	04.01.2017		WOOD VENDOR FOR SFE1 CABLE CAD4.00 LP KLH920990 Reference 1500000070		2,000.00-	NTRF
3	24.01.2017		MEPS INTEREST PAYMENT INVALID ACCOUNT NUMBER 241-CID001 NONREF Reference NONREF		100.00	NTRF
*					101,300.00	

Fig 24

IX. MANUAL BANK RECONCILLIATION (C/U)

1. CREATE AND ASSIGN BUSINESS TRANSACTION (C)

T Code SPRO

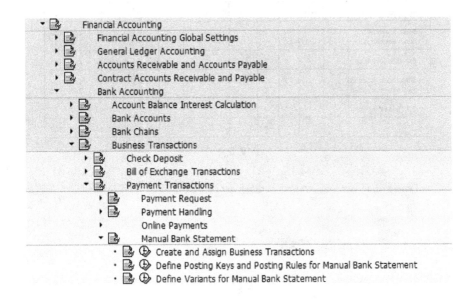

Fig 25

Here new Transaction type is defined and assigned with existing Posting rules

Tran	+-	Post. rule	Acct mod	Int algthm	Text
PMIN	+	HS01			
PMOU	−	HS02			
BNCH	−	HS03			
FDIN	+	HS04			
FDOU	−	HS05			

Fig 26

2. DEFINE VARIANTS FOR MANUAL BANK STATEMENT (C)

T Code SPRO

Here we define the required field during bank statement reconciliation processing.

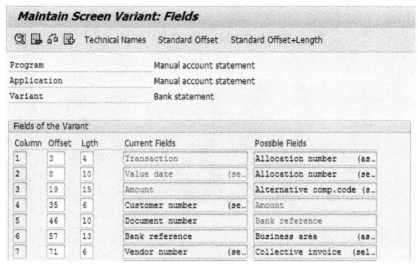

Fig 27

3. PROCESS MANUAL BANK STATEMENT (U)

Process Manual Bank Statement

⛶ Overview   Planning types

Bank Key	1000111111	HSBC Canada PLC
Bank Account	1000111111	HSBC CAD$ Account
Currency	CAD	Canadian Dollar
Statement Number	3	
Statement Date	28.02.2017	

Control

Opening Balance	10,109,600.00
Closing Balance	108,000.00
Posting date	28.02.2017

Selection of Payment Advices

Planning type			
Statement Date			
Planning date from		Planning date to	
Characteristic			

Further Processing

☐ Bank postings only	
Bank posting session	
Subledger session	

Fig 28

Select relevant Transaction an process the statement reconcilliation

Process Manual Bank Statement

Bank acct	1000111111	G/L Account	100060	CoCode	SFE1	Crcy	CAD

Bank statement items

Tran	Value date	Amount	Doc. no.	Cust MC	FC	For.curr.amt
PMIN	04.02.2017	3,200.00	1400000141	100322		
PMOU	05.02.2017	2,000.00-	1500000070			
PMIN	25.02.2017	100.00	1400000110	107000		
PMOU	25.02.2017	10,002,900.00-				

Fig 29

Click 🖫 to save the statement in order to post via further processing.

Update Account Statement/Check Deposit Transaction

Shefaria Ent. Canada   Bank statement posting   Time 18:03:28   Date 14.03.2017
Toronto   Processing Statistics   RFEBBU00/IDES013   Page 1

Posting Ar	Sessn	Group	FB01	FB05	PmtAcc	No Posting	Error	Total	Total Deb.	Total Cred
Bank Accounting	HSBC-1-101		0	4	0	0	0	4	3,300.00	10,004,900.00
* Bank Accounting			0	4	0	0	0	4	3,300.00	10,004,900.00
** Bank Accounting			0	4	0	0	0	4	3,300.00	10,004,900.00
Subledger acctng			0	0	0	4	0	4	3,300.00	10,004,900.00
* Subledger acctng			0	0	0	4	0	4	3,300.00	10,004,900.00
** Subledger acctng			0	0	0	4	0	4	3,300.00	10,004,900.00
***			0	4	0	4	0	8	6,600.00	20,009,800.00

Fig 30

Click button

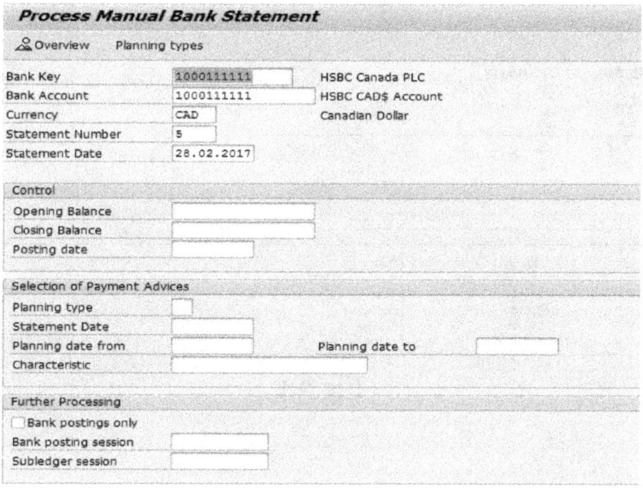

Process Manual Bank Statement
Overview
Planning types
Bank Key
1000111111
HSBC Canada PLC
Bank Account
1000111111
HSBC CAD$ Account
Currency
CAD
Canadian Dollar
Statement Number
5
Statement Date
28.02.2017
Control
Opening Balance
Closing Balance
Posting date
Selection of Payment Advices
Planning type
Statement Date
Planning date from
Planning date to
Characteristic
Further Processing
Bank postings only
Bank posting session
Subledger session

Fig 31

Click Overview button. The Manual Bank Statement Overview screen displays

Manual Bank Statement Overview

Copy New Statement

Bank Account

CCode	Name of bank	Bank Key	Acct		Curr.
1000	Deutsche Bank Gruppe	50070010	10000100	EUR	EUR
1000	Deutsche Bank	62030050	7002335300	EUR	EUR
3000	Citibank	134329042	30050021	USD	USD
SFE1	HSBC Canada PLC	1000111111	1000111111	CAD	CAD

Fig 32

The overview above confirms the status about Statement Posting.

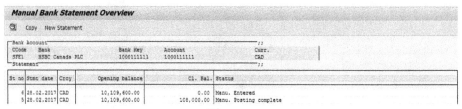

Manual Bank Statement Overview

🔍 Copy New Statement

Bank Account
CCode	Bank	Bank Key	Account	Curr.
SFE1	HSBC Canada PLC	1000111111	1000111111	CAD

Statement

St no	Stmt date	Crcy	Opening balance	Cl. Bal.	Status
6	28.02.2017	CAD	10,109,600.00	0.00	Manu. Entered
5	28.02.2017	CAD	10,109,600.00	108,000.00	Manu. Posting complete

Fig 33

Chose the Statement No. and click 🔍 to get the overview of posted items.

Manual Bank Statement Overview

🔍 Copy New Statement

Bank Account
CCode	Bank	Bank Key	Account	Curr.
SFE1	HSBC Canada PLC	1000111111	1000111111	CAD

Statement
No.	Date	Curr.	Opening Bal.	Cl. Bal.	Status
00005	28.02.2017	CAD	10,109,600.00	108,000.00	Manu. Posting complete

Item

No.	Tran	Value date	Amount	Check number	Status
1	PMIN	04.02.2017	3,200.00		Posted
2	PMOU	05.02.2017	2,000.00-		Posted
3	PMIN	25.02.2017	100.00		Posted
4	PMOU	25.02.2017	10,002,900.00-		Posted

Fig 34

FINANCIAL STATEMENT VERSIONS

(C/U)

This is a very flexible functionality in SAP that enables us to set up the P & L and B/L by configuring the G/L accounts in the statements and then grouping them as needed. We will not go into many details of all here, but will get a good idea of the process involved. In standard SAP, this is a configuration but it is likely that the company will implement this transition because of the high volume of setup and the frequency with which it changes.

This grouping is reflective of how the accounting principles and the laws of the country dictate about this setup – which G/Ls need to be a part of which section or sub-section in the reports.

I. SETUP

T Code SPRO

The path to set this up is:

Fig 1

Fin.Stmt.version	Financial Statement Version Name
ACI1	
ACI2	
AGKR	Commercial balance sheet (Austria)
AJI1	Financial statement vers.for Chinese ind. concern
AUFS	Australian GAAP Financial Statement Versi
BAAR	Commercial balance sheet Canada
BAAU	Balance sheet (Australia)
BABE	Balance sheet Belgium
BACA	Commercial balance sheet Canada
BACN	Financial Statement Version for China
BACZ	Commercial balance sheet - Czech Republic
BADK	Commercial balance sheet (Denmark)
BAES	Commercial balance sheet (Spain)
BAFR	Commercial balance sheet (France)
BAGB	Commercial balance sheet (Great Brian)
BAHU	Commercial balance sheet (Hungary)
BAIT	Commercial balance sheet (Italy)

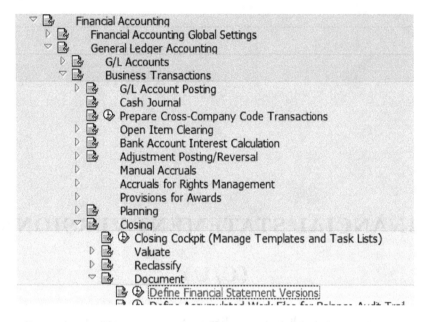

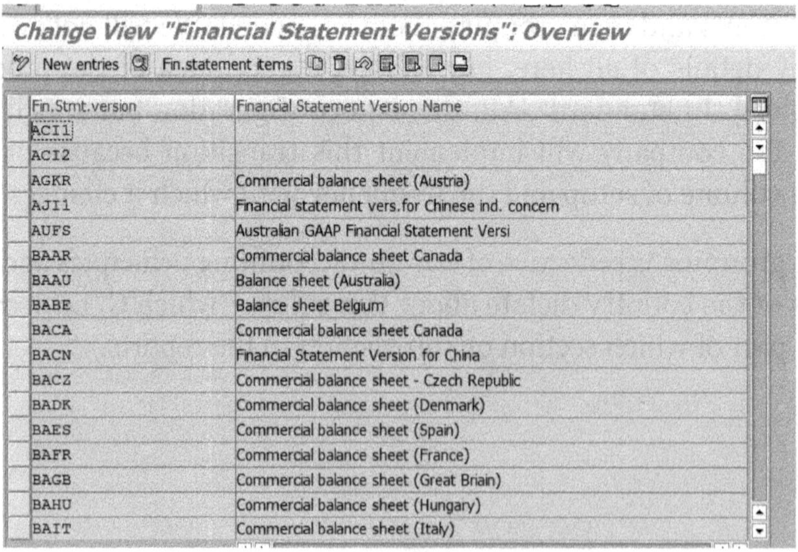

Fig 2

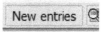

Fig 3

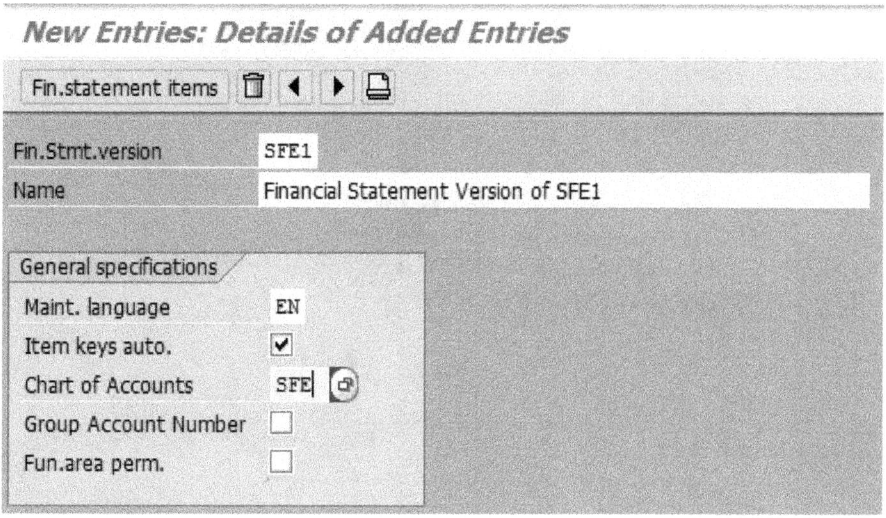

New Entries: Details of Added Entries

Fin.statement items

Fin.Stmt.version	SFE1
Name	Financial Statement Version of SFE1

General specifications

Maint. language	EN
Item keys auto.	☑
Chart of Accounts	SFE
Group Account Number	☐
Fun.area perm.	☐

Fig 4

Save the configuration.

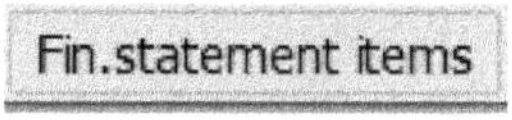

Fin.statement items

To configure the BS and P&L as you would like to, select the Fin Statement version and click on Fin. Statement items:

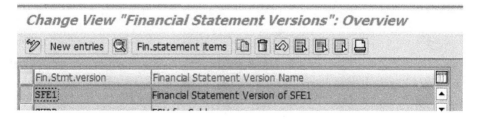

Fig 5

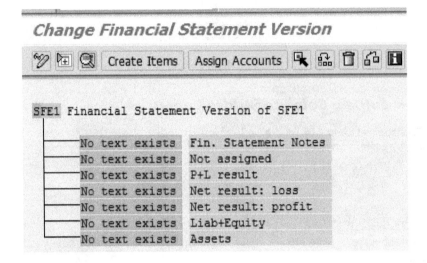

Fig 6

Using the 2 keys:

Fig 7

We can create new headings and sub-headings by positioning the cursor at the required place via the key Create Items. E.g. if we want to create a new heading called Fixed Assets under Assets, we will Click on Assets and then on Create Items:

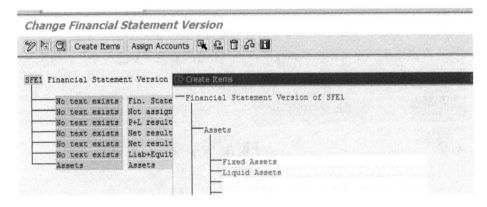

Fig 8

Next, click on Create Items:

Hit Enter and Fixed Assets and Liquid Assets appear as sub-headings of Assets:

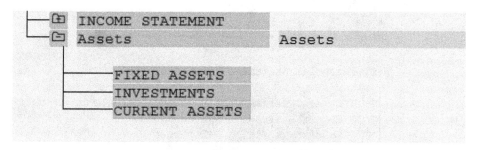

Fig 9

Configuring G/Ls:

Next, we can configure the G/L accounts in each individual sub-heading/bucket. Click on the sub-heading you want to attach the corresponding G/L to, e.g. to Income Statement>Revenue> Revenue from Furniture Division. The click on Assign Accounts:

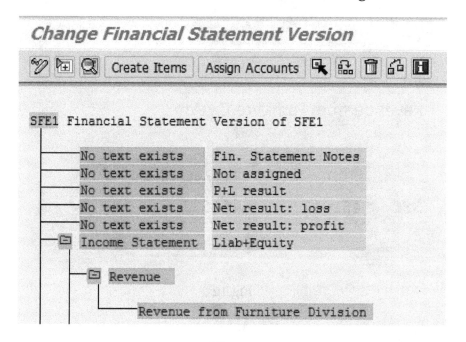

Fig 10

And enter the G/L account e.g. 451011 for this :

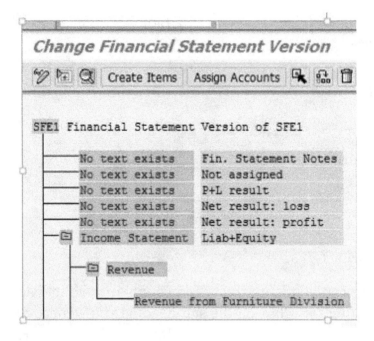

Fig 11

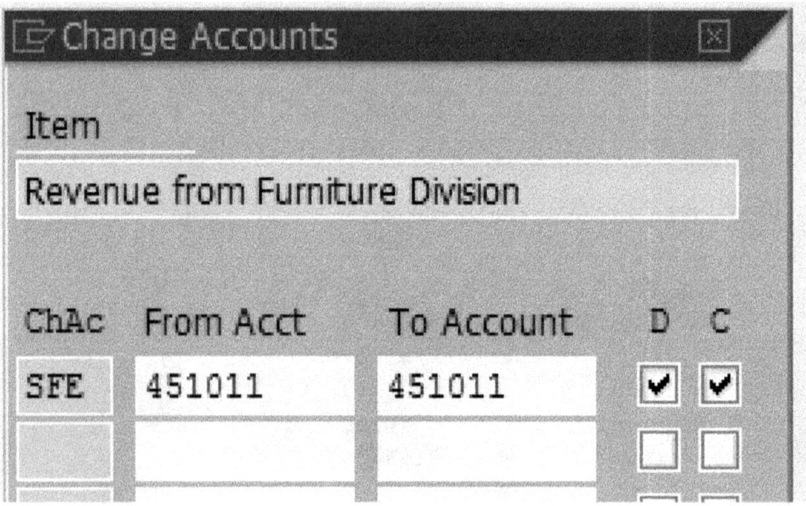

Fig 12

Hit Enter and Save.

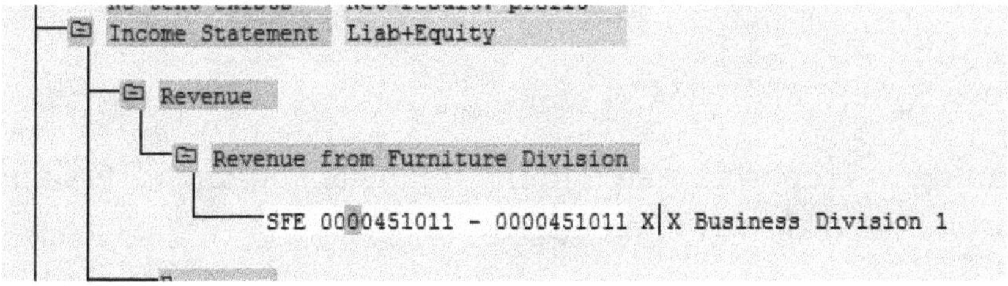

Fig 13

Similarly create all the headings/groups and assign the relevant G/Ls as above. The G/Ls can be repeated over the different areas so long as they follow the norm of P & L and BS numbering sequences. Save.

II.   EXECUTING THE FINANCIAL STATEMENT VERSION (U)

T Code S_ALR_87012284

Running the reports created in the financial statement versions is done via the transaction menu:

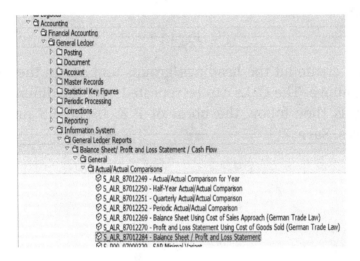

Fig 14

Enter details as needed:

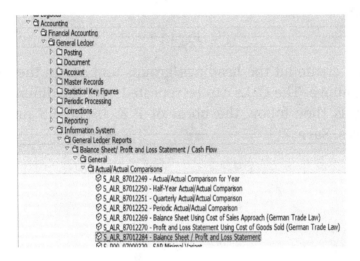

Fig 15

Depending on how much has been configured, the amounts in the G/Ls will be available to view in their respective headings and sub-headings at the bottom of the report – the data in the upper part is not a part of a formal financial statement version but is only G/L balances.

Financial Statements

Financial Statement Version of SFE1

```
OL          Ledger
10          Currency type Company code currency
CAD         Amounts in Canadian Dollar
```

FS Item	Text for B/S P&L Item	Tot.rpt.pr	tot.cmp.pr	Abs. difference	Pct.Diff.
2	460600 Discounts taken from vendors	90.00-	0.00	90.00-	
2	500000 Cost of Goods Sold (without Cost Element)	34,800.00	0.00	34,800.00	
2	530000 Gain/Loss Price Variances	5,522.00-	0.00	5,522.00-	
2	634000 Insurance	22,208.00	0.00	22,208.00	
2	665040 Depreciation Expense - Building	5,007.00	0.00	5,007.00	
2	665041 Depreciation Expense - Furniture & Fixture	909.00	0.00	909.00	
2	665042 Depreciation Expense - Machine & Equipment	1,125.00	0.00	1,125.00	
2	665043 Depreciation Expense - Low Value Assets	1,815.00	0.00	1,815.00	
2	700000 Write Off Fixed Assets	8,520.00	0.00	8,520.00	
2	700001 Clearing Account - Revenue from Account Sale	750.00	0.00	750.00	
2	700002 Gain & Loss Sale of Fixed Assets	950.00-	0.00	950.00-	
2	900100 Under Payment Account	346.00	0.00	346.00	
2	900200 Over Payment Account	341.70-	0.00	341.70-	
2		9,800.00	0.00	9,800.00	
4		9,800.00	0.00	9,800.00	
12	451011 Business Division 1	9,800.00-	0.00	9,800.00-	

Fig 16

COST CENTER ACCOUNTING (U)

Controlling provides us with information for management decision-making. It facilitates coordination, monitoring and optimization of processes and resources in an organization. This involves recording both the consumption of production factors and the services provided by an organization.

In SAP Controlling Cost Center Accounting Concept determines where costs are incurred in the organization. To achieve this aim, costs are assigned to the sub areas of the organization where they have the most influence. By creating and assigning cost elements to cost centers, we not only make cost controlling possible, but also provide data for other application components in Controlling, such as Cost Object Controlling. We can also use a variety of allocation methods for allocating the collected costs of the given cost center/s to other controlling objects.

I. CREATE COST CENTER

T Code   KS01

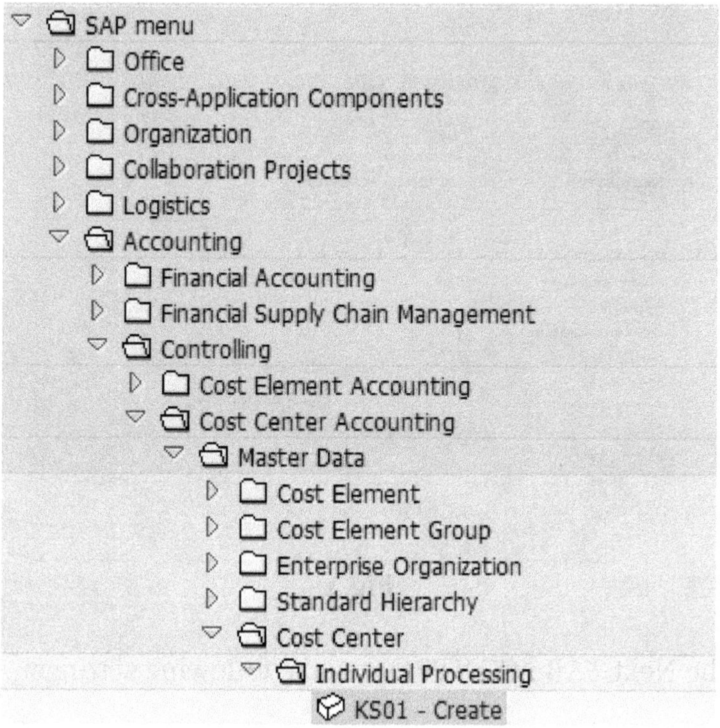

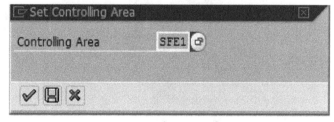

Fig 1

Fig 2

Fig 3

Enter the following details:

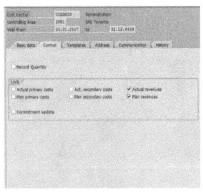

Cost Center	CCADMIN		
Controlling Area	SFE1	SFE Toronto	
Valid From	01.01.2017	to	31.12.9999

Basic data | Control | Templates | Address | Communication | History

Names

| Name | Administration |
| Description | Cost Center - Administration |

Basic data

User Responsible	
Person Responsible	Test
Department	
Cost Center Category	4
Hierarchy area	SFE1_HIER
Business Area	
Functional Area	
Currency	CAD
Profit Center	

Fig 4

Go to the Next TAB : CONTROL make following settings:

Fig 5

Select Save to finish creation of Cost Center: Administration .
System confirms with the

following : Cost center has been created

II.   Using the Cost Center in Transactions

T Code FB60 (example only, can be used anywhere).

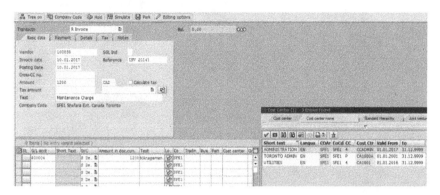

Fig 6

In Cost Center Tab we select applicable Cost Center from the list or enter the one we just created - CCADMIN

	St	G/L acct	Short Text	D/C	Amount in doc.curr.	Text	Lo	Co	Tradin	Busi	Part	Cost center	Or
0 Items (No entry variant selected)													
		400004		S De..		1200 MAnagemen..		SFE1				CCADMIN	
				S De..				SFE1					

Fig 7

Select [Simulate] and [💾] to post the entry to and the booking the cost in cost center: Administration

```
Doc.Type : KR ( Vendor invoice ) Normal document
Doc. Number                Company code    SFE1        Fiscal year    2017
Doc. date       10.01.2017  Posting date    10.01.2017  Period         01
Calculate Tax   ▢
Ref.doc.        INV 20141
Doc.currency    CAD
```

Itm	PK	Account	Account short text	Assignment	Tx	Amount	Cost Ctr
1	31	100838	Wood vendor for SFE1			1,200.00-	
2	40	400004	Office Supplies Exp			1,200.00	CCADMIN

Fig 8

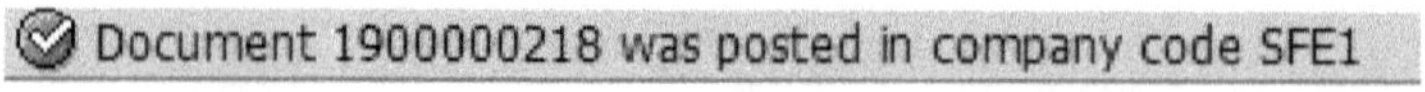

Fig 9

We can now see the cost center we used in the accounting
document at it's appropriate spot:

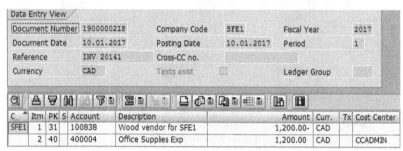

Fig 10

III. REPORTING ON COST CENTERS

T Code KSB1

To look up the postings made to the different cost centers, we use the t-code KSB1 or follow the path:

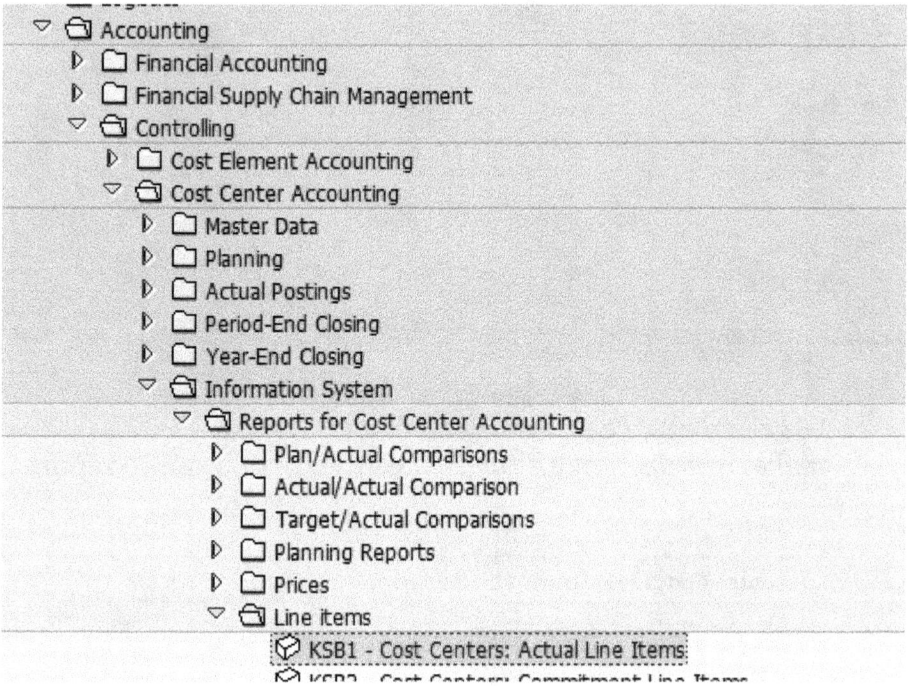

```
▽ 🗀 Accounting
    ▷ 🗀 Financial Accounting
    ▷ 🗀 Financial Supply Chain Management
    ▽ 🗀 Controlling
        ▷ 🗀 Cost Element Accounting
        ▽ 🗀 Cost Center Accounting
            ▷ 🗀 Master Data
            ▷ 🗀 Planning
            ▷ 🗀 Actual Postings
            ▷ 🗀 Period-End Closing
            ▷ 🗀 Year-End Closing
            ▽ 🗀 Information System
                ▽ 🗀 Reports for Cost Center Accounting
                    ▷ 🗀 Plan/Actual Comparisons
                    ▷ 🗀 Actual/Actual Comparison
                    ▷ 🗀 Target/Actual Comparisons
                    ▷ 🗀 Planning Reports
                    ▷ 🗀 Prices
                    ▽ 🗀 Line items
                        �e KSB1 - Cost Centers: Actual Line Items
                        🔒 KCR2   Cost Centers: Commitment Line Items
```

Fig 1

Enter the Controlling Area:

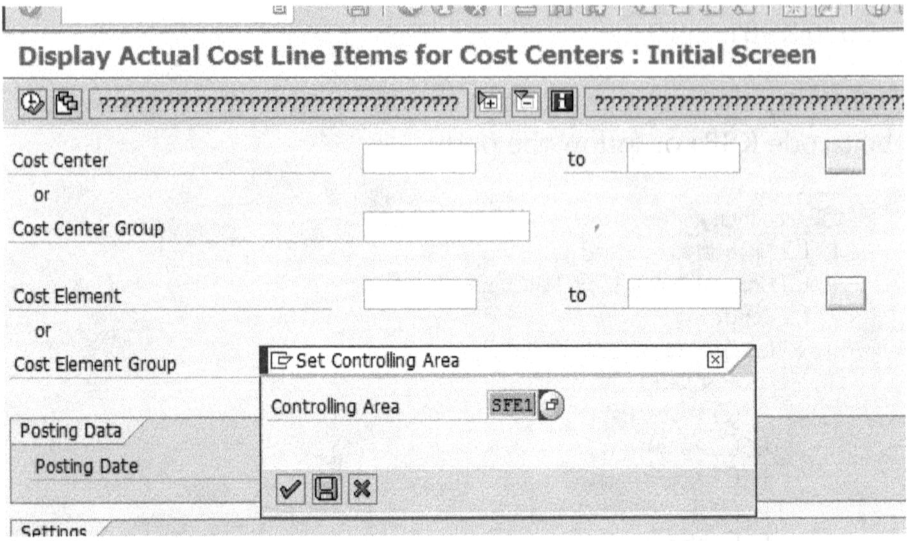

Fig 2

Then make the selection for the cost center/s you want to report on:

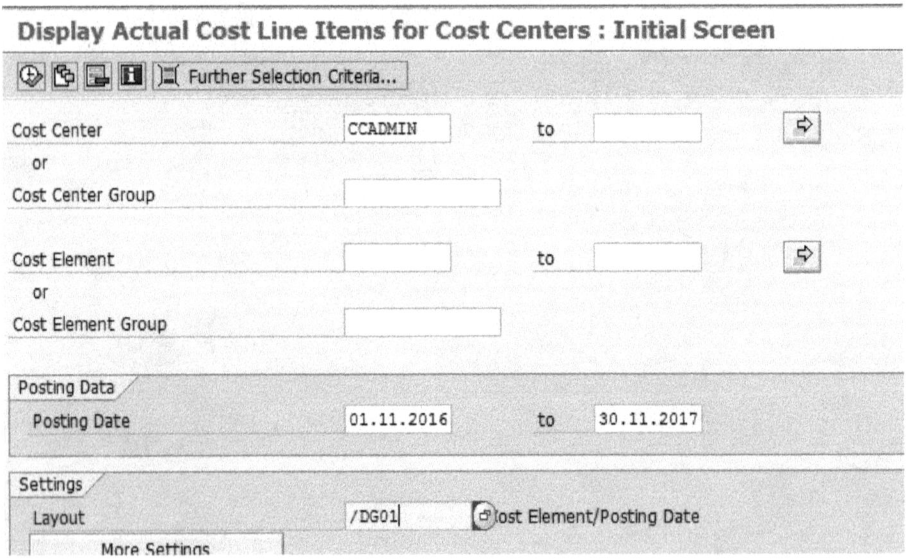

Fig 3

The executable report gives you the postings done to those cost centers:

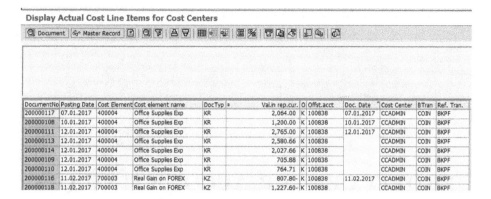

DocumentNo	Posting Date	Cost Element	Cost element name	DocTyp	Val.in rep.cur.	O	Offst.acct	Doc. Date	Cost Center	BTran	Ref. Tran.
200000117	07.01.2017	400004	Office Supplies Exp	KR	2,064.00	K	100838	07.01.2017	CCADMIN	COIN	BKPF
200000108	10.01.2017	400004	Office Supplies Exp	KR	1,200.00	K	100838	10.01.2017	CCADMIN	COIN	BKPF
200000111	12.01.2017	400004	Office Supplies Exp	KR	2,765.00	K	100838	12.01.2017	CCADMIN	COIN	BKPF
200000113	12.01.2017	400004	Office Supplies Exp	KR	2,580.66	K	100838		CCADMIN	COIN	BKPF
200000114	12.01.2017	400004	Office Supplies Exp	KR	2,027.66	K	100838		CCADMIN	COIN	BKPF
200000109	12.01.2017	400004	Office Supplies Exp	KR	705.88	K	100838		CCADMIN	COIN	BKPF
200000110	12.01.2017	400004	Office Supplies Exp	KR	764.71	K	100838		CCADMIN	COIN	BKPF
200000116	11.02.2017	700003	Real Gain on FOREX	KZ	807.80-	K	100838	11.02.2017	CCADMIN	COIN	BKPF
200000118	11.02.2017	700003	Real Gain on FOREX	KZ	1,227.60-	K	100838		CCADMIN	COIN	BKPF

Many other reposts exists for budgeting purposes in which the cost allocations budgeted can be compared with the actuals that took place via the transactions. These reports form a few of the basis of management accounting.

PROFIT CENTER ACCOUNTING (U)

A profit center is a management-oriented organizational unit used for internal controlling purposes. Dividing the company up into profit centers allows us to analyze areas of responsibility and to delegate responsibility to decentralized units, thus treating them as "companies within the company".

Thus, while a cost center is a subunit of a company that is responsible only for its costs, a profit center is a subunit of a company that is responsible for revenues *and* costs.

Example of cost centers are the production departments and the service departments within a factory and administrative departments such as IT and accounting.

Often a division of a company is a profit center because it has control over its revenues, costs, and the resulting profits.

Cost centers and profit centers are usually associated with planning and control in a decentralized company.

I. CREATE PROFIT CENTER

T Code KE51 or the path:

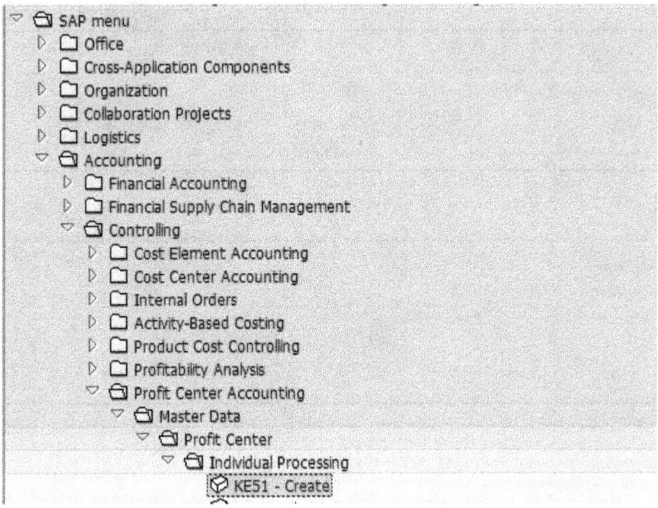

Fig 1

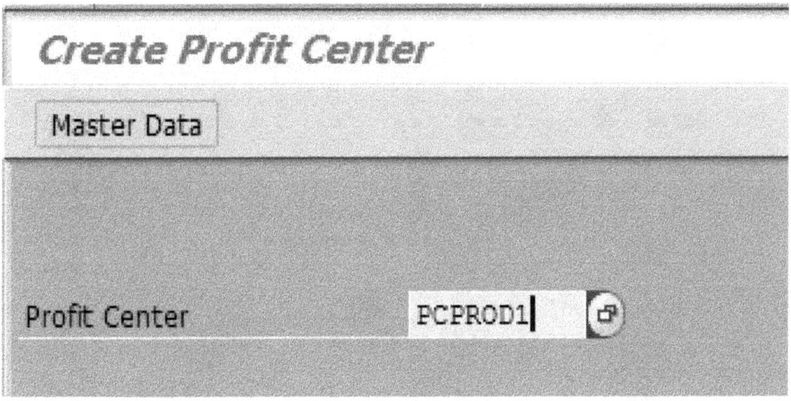

Fig 2

Press Enter and key in the following entries to create Profit Center

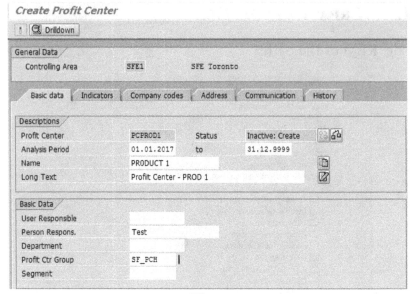

Fig 3

Go to CC tab and confirm the following settings for the active organization for which this profit Center is to be created. This is the way Profit centers are made to be used by different CCs.

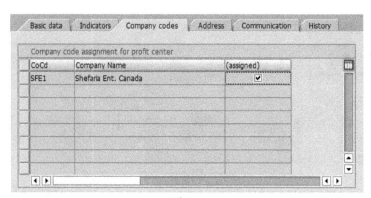

Fig 4

After checking all entries click ⬛ to activate the Proift center. The activation enables the usage of the profit center. The system will confirm with the following message :

✅ Profit center PCPROD1 has been created

II.   USING THE PROFIT CENTER IN TRANSACTIONS

T Code FB70 (example only, can be used anywhere).

Sales & Revenue is subjected to booking in respective Profit center.

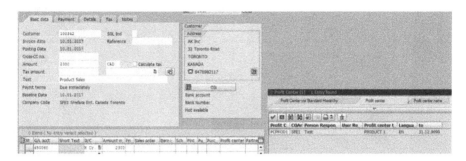

Fig 6

Here we used the Revenue from Sales GL : 450060 and is subjected to profit center booking .

St	G/L acct	Short Text	D/C	Amount in	Fin	Sales order	Item i	Sch	Plnt	Pu	Purc	Profit center	Par
	450060		H Cr...	2300								PCPROD1	

0 Items (No entry variant selected)

Fig 7

Select [Simulate] to process the entry :

```
Doc.Type : DR ( Customer invoice ) Normal document
Doc. Number                 Company code    SFE1    Fiscal year    2017
Doc. date     10.01.2017     Posting date    10.01.2017  Period     01
Calculate Tax  ☐
Ref.doc.      S/O 340000012
Doc.currency  CAD
```

Itm	PK	Account	Account short text	Tx	Amount	Profit Ctr	Text
1	01	100342	AK Inc		2,300.00		Product Sales
2	50	450060	Chair Revenue		2,300.00-	PCPROD1	Revenue Sales

Fig 8

Select 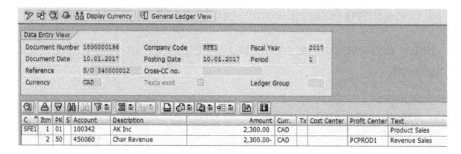 to post the entry to the Profit Center : PRODUCT 1

C.	Itm	PK	S	Account	Description	Amount	Curr.	Tx	Cost Center	Profit Center	Text
SFE1	1	01		100342	AK Inc	2,300.00	CAD				Product Sales
	2	50		450060	Chair Revenue	2,300.00-	CAD			PCPROD1	Revenue Sales

Fig 9

III. REPORTING ON PROFIT CENTERS

T Code KE5Z

Like the cost centers, profit centers can also be reported on for the purpose of analysis and management decision making.

Follow the path:

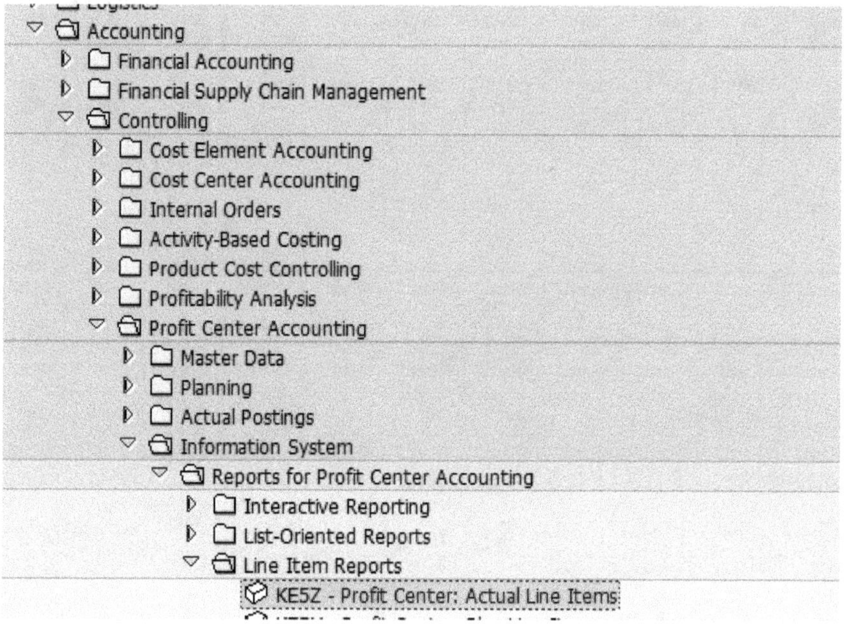

Fig 1

Enter the data as needed on the screen:

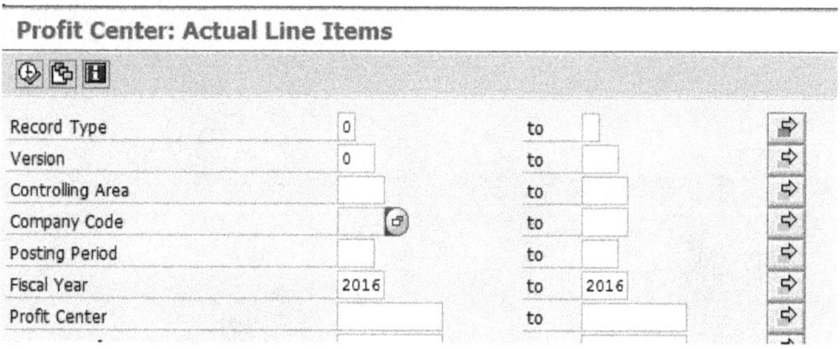

Fig 2

Ledger	8A								
Controlling Area	≈								
Company Code	≈								
Posting Period	≈								
Fiscal Year	2016								
Version	000								

D	Ref.Doc.No.	Itm	Period	Profit Center	Partner PC	Account	Acc.Text	¤	In pctr local curr.	Curr.
W	95099		1	9999	1010	620000	DAA Machine Costs		0.153	EUR
W	95099		1	9999	1010	619000	DAA Production		0.153-	EUR
W	95099		1	1010	9999	620000	DAA Machine Costs		0.153-	EUR
W	95099		1	1010	9999	619000	DAA Production		0.153	EUR
W	95099		1	1010	9999	619000	DAA Production		0.153-	EUR
W	95099		1	9999	1010	619000	DAA Production		0.153	EUR
W	95099		1	1010	9999	619000	DAA Production		0.153-	EUR
W	95099		1	9999	1010	619000	DAA Production		0.153	EUR

Fig 3

CROSS – APPLICATION AND

GENERAL COMPONENTS IN SAP (U)

I.   VARIANTS (U)

Variants are variations of input and output screens. They are not cross application components but 'common' components. Most of the screens in SAP behave similarly for the purpose of creating variants. The purpose of variants is twofold:

- To enable the user to save time by setting up screens with roughly the same data that may be needed every time the transaction is run. In that respect, these input variants can be treated as master data.

- To let different users who may be using the same transaction have their differentiation from each other in terms of inputs and outputs by naming their variants as suitable to them.

    There are 2 primary kinds of variants, best explained with examples.

1. SELECTION/INPUT VARIANTS

Let us call the standard SAP transition to look up account balances, FBL3N:

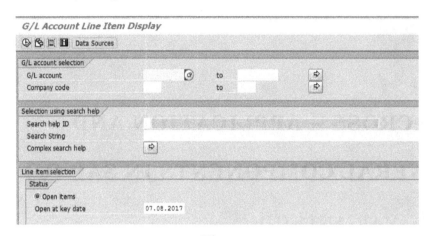

Fig 1

Let us assume that as an accounts person, one responsible for the company code SFE1 and for G/L accounts 100000 to 199999. A simple variant can be set up with these values:

G/L Account Line Item Display

Data Sources

G/L account selection				
G/L account	100000	to	199999	
Company code	SFE1	to		

Selection using search help	
Search help ID	
Search String	
Complex search help	

Line item selection

Status

Open items

Open at key date   07.08.2017

Fig 2

Save the values either by clicking on 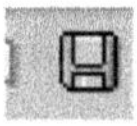 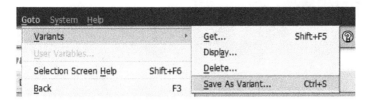 or:

Fig 3

Give it a name:

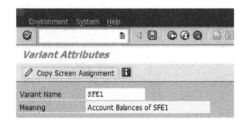

Fig 4

Save it:

Next time when you call the transaction FBL3N simply click on the

button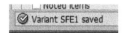

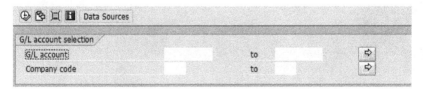

Fig 5

Enter the name of the variant if you know:

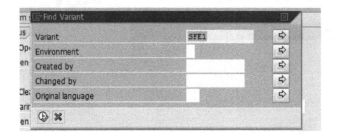

Fig 6

Or simply execute the above window to get a list of all and double click to choose the one you want:

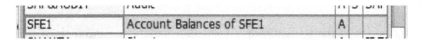

Fig 7

The figures we entered at the time of creating the variant will come on the screen so they don't have to be entered every time.

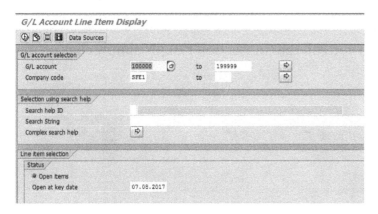

Fig 8

The above was a simple example of a variant. The inputs can be further defined using the feature of multiple values using the icon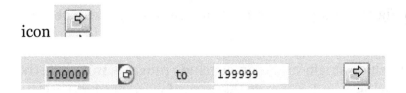

Fig 9

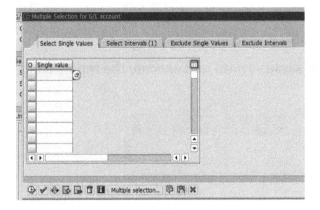

Fig 10

As we notice above, there are 4 tabs:

1. Select single values – here, G/L accounts. You can keep adding the G/Ls you want the balances for, manually or, copy them from a spreadsheet and paste them using the icon ▣. We can also use the button to upload a text file though this is seldom used as the same objective can be achieved by the simpler copy/paste feature.

2. Select Intervals – this is what we have chosen in our current variant:

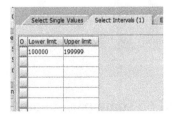

Fig 11

As seen in Fig 11, multiple intervals of different ranges can be chosen.

3 and 4 – Exclude single values and exclude ranges – work exactly the same way as 1 and 2 except these are for excluding the G/L accounts while 1 and 2 were for including them.

2. OUTPUT/DISPLAY VARIANT

Let us stay with our same variant and execute the report using the button Execute:

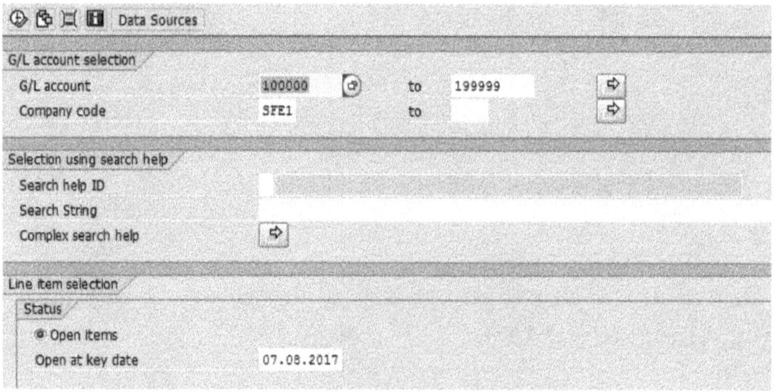

Fig 12

Some kind of a layout emerges based on what the default is:

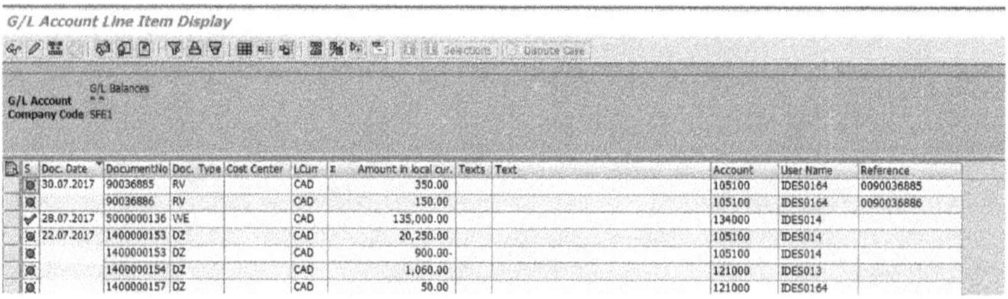

Fig 13

The above is the display of the report based on some parameters. Let us see what they are and how this can be customized to our requirement as it may not be suitable for the data we need.

The first is how to display. As seen above, this is an Excel friendly layout. It can be changed to a more generic layout using:

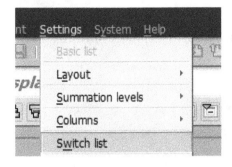

Fig 14

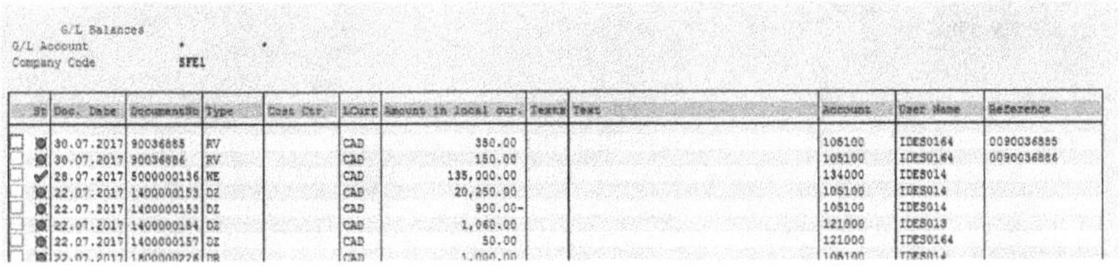

Fig 15

Most people will prefer the Excel type grid so we work with that.

Below are the primary icons (many are Windows based and thus, familiar) that we will work with.

Fig 16

The SAP specific ones, 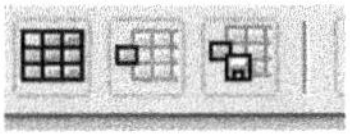 refer to how the layouts can be created and saved. As we notice, the columns currently available to us in this report are:

Fig 17

The source of these columns are SAP tables – in this case, accounting tables (next section, ideally, to be visited only once you have finished the rest of this book).

If we wish to add/delete or re-arrange any of these columns, click on 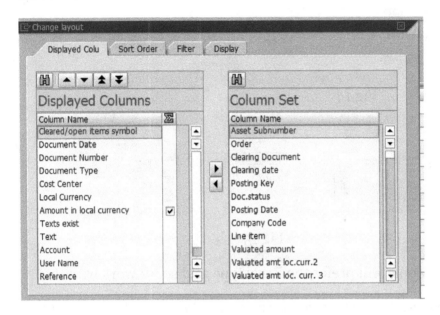 :

Fig 18

As you notice, the section on the left is the list of the columns displayed in the order from top to bottom > left to right in the report. The right section is the list of more fields/columns available though it is not necessary that all of them hold data. If you wish to see something new/additional or want to hide any, just double click on it and it flips from one column to the other as clicked.

The keys _____ are useful to find, or move up or down the list.

Once we are satisfied with what we require in your report and want to save it with the ides of recalling it every time (same way as the

input variant), click on 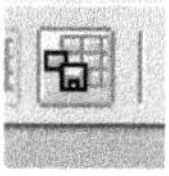 :

Give it a name:

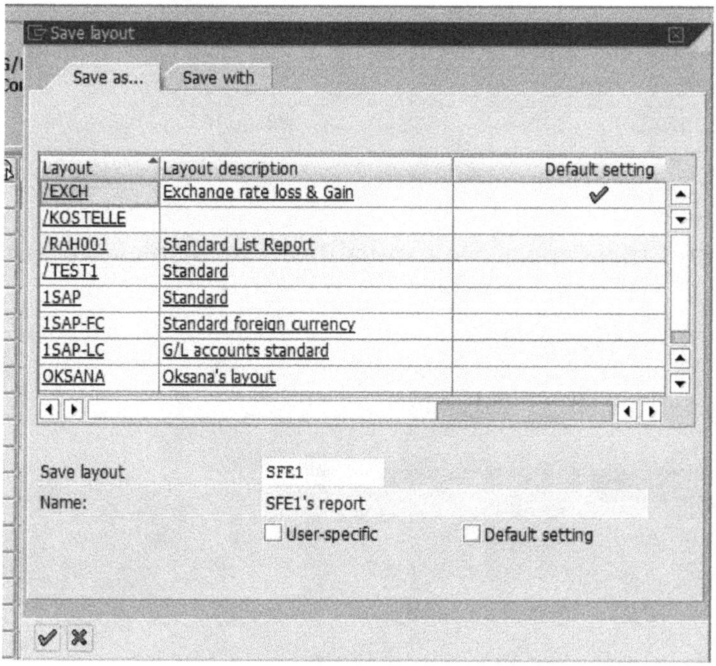

Fig 19

We can only one of the buttons:

☐ User-specific   ☐ Default setting

Fig 20

To save as specific to you OR as a default layout. It is highly recommended not to save as a default layout otherwise everyone will see only that as a default and will have to change it to their requirements which will not be a very kind act towards other users.

So we save this as user specific:

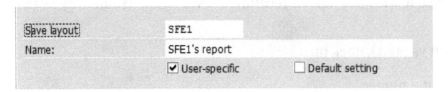

Fig 21

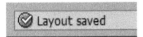

Fig 22

Next time we run this report, we can call for our display variant

using the icon [icon]: (See fig 16)

Click on the hyperlink SFE1 as below:

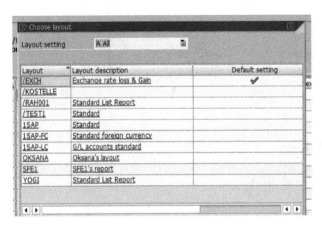

Fig 23

The message displayed at the bottom is:

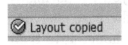

Fig 24

This ensures whatever we had asked for in the layout SFE1 is now on screen displayed for us.

For the most part, this variant functionality in SAP is exactly the same across all screens and all modules thereby making your life infinitely easier.

Not only do variants help us save time, they can also present us with data relating to the documents themselves e.g. by checking any particular line, you can go straight into the document and even change it for whatever is possible to be changed as in Figs 25, 26. Select the line item and then Click on Environment>Options:

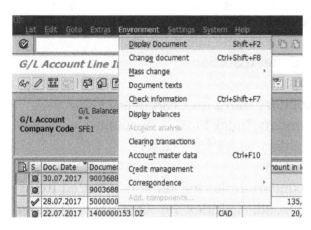

Fig 25

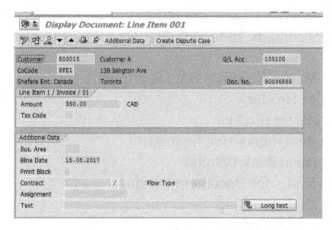

Fig 26

II. TABLES IN SAP (U)

T Code SE16N

Most of the data in SAP resides in tables and structures, primarily in the former. The latter can be read only by technically knowledgeable people but the former is available to all, subject to authorizations. We will peek into how the tables exist in SAP and how they can be read and data extracted from them.

Tens of thousands of tables exist in SAP well apportioned over the different modules. In FI, the few important ones are:

BKPF - Accounting Document Header
BSEG – Accounting Document Line items
LFA1 - Vendor Master (General Section)
T001 - CCs
BSID - Accounting Secondary Index for Customers
BSIS - Accounting: Secondary Index for G/L Accounts
BSIK - Accounting Secondary Index for Vendors
LFB1 - Vendor Master (CC)
BSAK - Accounting: Secondary Index for Vendors (Cleared Items)
BSAD - Accounting: Secondary Index for Customers (Cleared Items)
LFBK - Vendor Master (Bank Details)
KNB1 - Customer Master (CC)
BSAS - Accounting: Secondary Index for G/L Accounts (Cleared Items)
SKAT - G/L Account Master Record (CoA: Description)
AVIK - Payment Advice Header
SKA1 - G/L Account Master (CoA)
KNC1 - Customer master (transaction figures)
KNBK - Customer Master (Bank Details)
VBKPF - Document Header for Document Parking
TTYP - Object Types for Accounting
LFC1 - Vendor master (transaction figures)
T052 - Terms of Payment

512

BSIP - Index for Vendor Validation of Double Documents
LFB5 - Vendor master (dunning data)

The transaction code to look up tables is SE16N:

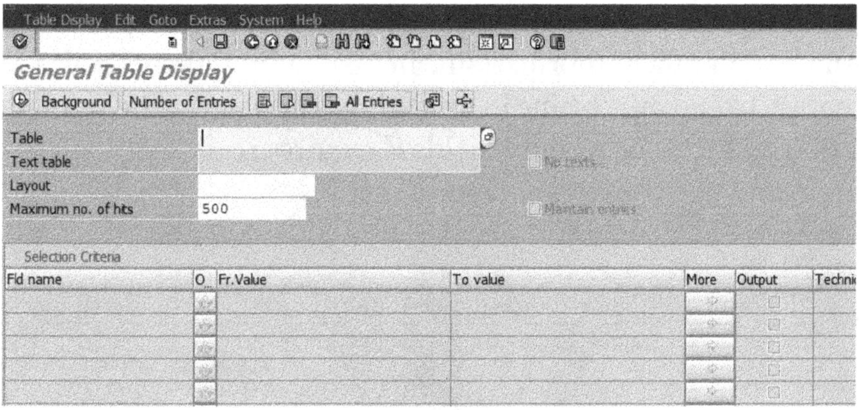

Fig 1

Enter the name of the table you want to lookup and Hit Enter again:

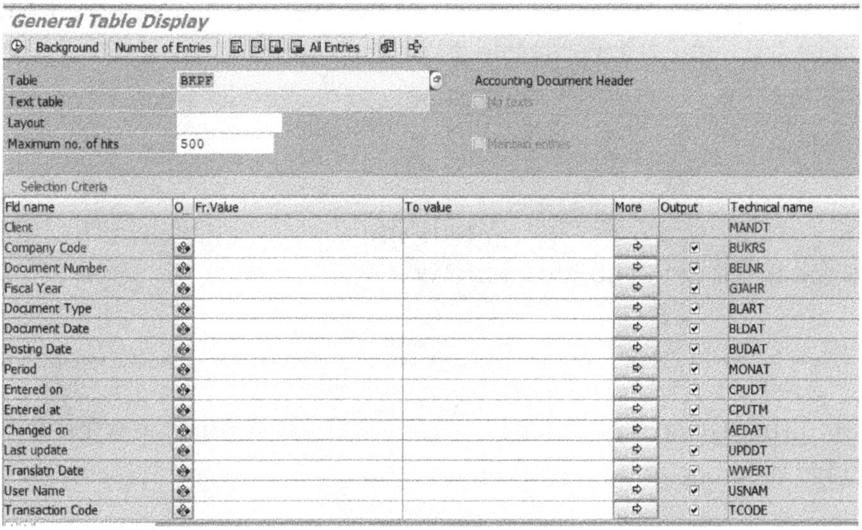

Fig 2

On the left are the names of the fields which are for most part, self-explanatory, on the right are their technical names for those who are more involved in using tables in programming. Enter input data you need to find the results for.

On the right, check the fields that you really want to see in your result as too much information can be clutter and also cause the program to take more time in executing. You can use the scroll bar on the right to look for more fields if required:

Fig 3

Use the keys ![keys] to select or deselect respectively all the fields if needed and then deselect or select the ones you need individually.

The button `Number of Entries` tells you the # of entries in the table for the input data you have entered.

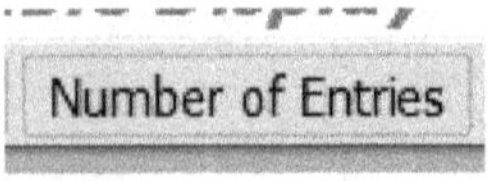

If the result is expected to take a long time, then this can also be run in the background using `Background` by setting up a job for it whose results can be downloaded later.

Unless you are sure the total will be less than 500 (see Fig 2), it is advisable to wipe out this number so you can get the entire list. The default can be changed in the option below though wiping it out is always the best option unless you are looking for only some sample data:

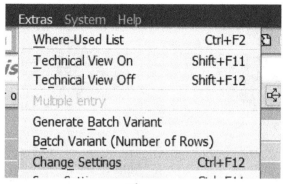

Fig 4

Let's say we want to see only the company code, document number, date of posting and document type, so check only those boxes on the right as 'outputs'. If we want to look for all accounting entries made by any user ID for a certain period, enter these 2 data elements in their respective fields:

General Table Display

| ⊕ Background | Number of Entries | 🗐 🗐 🗐 🗐 All Entries | 🗐 🕀 |

Table	BKPF	⊚	Accounting Document Header
Text table			☐ No texts
Layout			
Maximum no. of hits			☐ Custom entries

Selection Criteria

Fld name	O	Fr.Value	To value	More	Output	Technical
Company Code	⊛	SFE1		⇨	✔	BUKRS
Document Number	⊛			⇨	✔	BELNR
Fiscal Year	⊛			⇨	☐	GJAHR
Document Type	⊛			⇨	✔	BLART
Document Date	⊛			⇨	☐	BLDAT
Posting Date	⊛			⇨	✔	BUDAT
Period	⊛			⇨	☐	MONAT
Entered on	⊛	01.01.2016	30.06.2016	⇨	☐	CPUDT
Entered at	⊛			⇨	☐	CPUTM
Changed on	⊛			⇨	☐	AEDAT
Last update	⊛			⇨	☐	UPDDT
Translatn Date	⊛			⇨	☐	WWERT
User Name	⊛	IDES0164		⇨	☐	USNAM

Fig 5

Execute (F8):

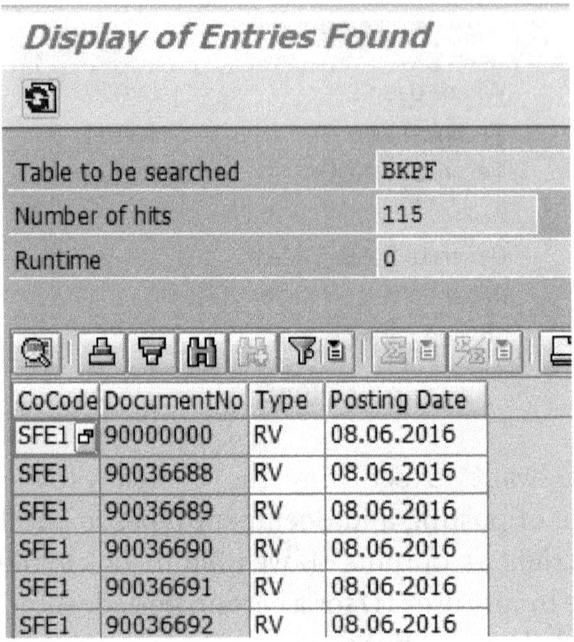

Fig 6

We can either scroll through this list or download it using ![icon]. The rest of the screen icons should be familiar. In this way, all tables can be looked up for the required data.

III. QUERIES IN SAP (U)

T Code SQVI

Queries in SAP link tables to give users results based off their unique requirements. There are 2 kinds of queries; one is a quick view (SQVI) which everyone has access to and the other is more structured queries (SQ01) which require greater skills to develop and execute. Another main difference between the two is that a Quick viewer is available only to the person who creates it while the more structured queries can be made available to everybody using the appropriate user groupings.

In this manual, we will cover the Quick viewer, SQVI as the access to the latter may be very limited in most organizations.

The concept of queries is simple – find one or more fields that are common to 2 or more tables and link the tables by those field/s to 'query' them. Then input your selection in one and get the outputs from that and the other table as desired in one single report instead of doing multiple lookups. However, this link needs to make sense in a few ways:

- The fields being linked must lead up to a unique value else SAP won't find a correct match or will find multiple matches

- There should not be any redundancy of data i.e. the data being linked must have consistency and clarity

- No unnecessary joins should exist between these tables or that can lead to inconsistent results or no results

As an example, we will use 2 tables from the previous section:

LFA1 - Vendor Master (General Section)
LFB1 - Vendor Master (CC)

The intent of our query is to find the vendor data in the CC section along with the vendor's address. From our knowledge of the tables, we know the vendor address exists in LFA1 and the CC data in LFB1. Since the common key that holds them together is the vendor code itself, we will use it in the join to link the two tables together.

To get to the quick viewer use transaction SQVI or the menu path:

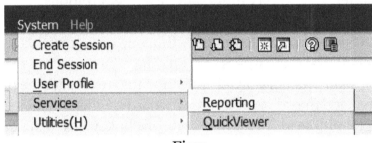

Fig 7

Give it a short name till 15 characters:

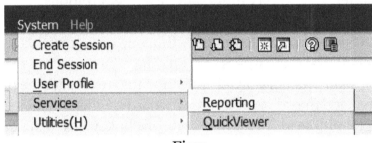

Fig 8

Click on Create

Now we have the ability to give it a longer description/Title:

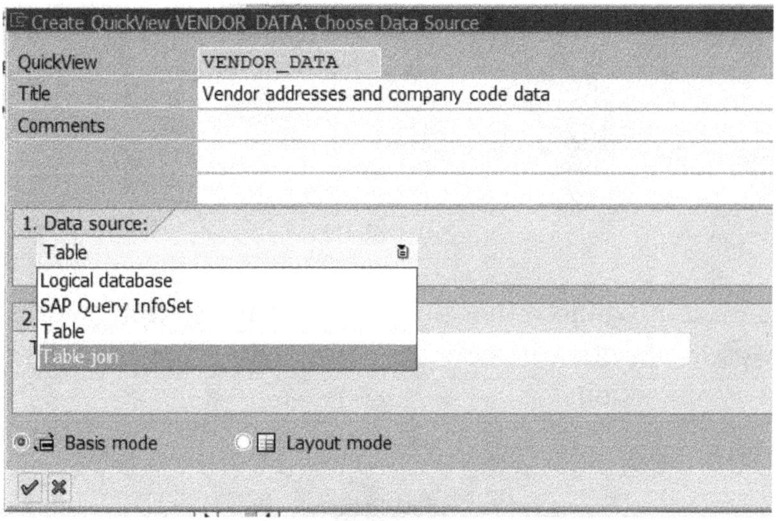

Fig 9

Choose Data source as Table join.

(a) Logical database are complex data structures that have been provided by SAP for some important sub areas like pricing, purchasing, accounting documents etc and are normally used only by IT as they require more complexity to develop

(b) SAP Query Infoset is used in the more structured queries mentioned in the beginning of this section

(c) Table read would be same as SE16N as in the previous section and using it as a query is meaningless and unnecessarily more effort if we have access to SE16N

(d) Table join – this is what we will use and is the most common way of creating a quick viewer

Say OK to come to this screen:

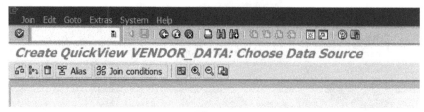

Fig 10

There is a window that appears as a navigation pane which helps to see at a glance when many tables are being used for interconnection:

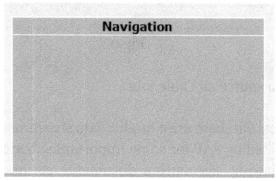

Fig 11

Our first task is to insert the tables we will be using. Use the icon ![icon] to do that:

Enter the name of the first table when the window comes up:

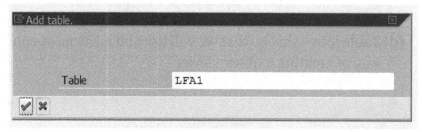

Fig 12

Hit Enter and it should be now available for use along with all it's fields:

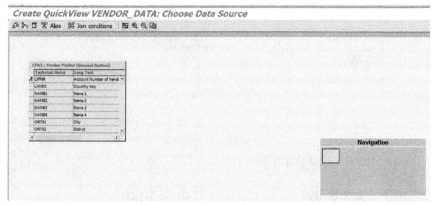

Fig 13

Repeat the insert for the other table LFB1 and SAP will link them together automatically based on the most important field, which is LIFNR (Vendor #):

Fig 14

The link between the 2 tables is now established. It is also possible to change this link to some other if there is any other field that can be more helpful.

Click on Green arrow to step back

Fig 15

Expand on the triangles on the left side of the screen to reveal
all the fields in the 2 tables to choose from

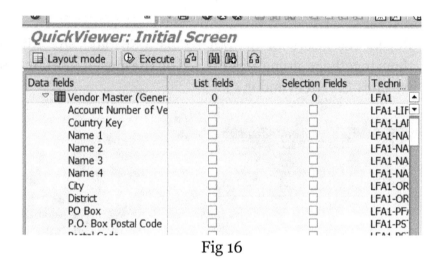

Fig 16

We now have 3 options with respect to the fields of these tables:

1. List fields i.e. show the value in this field in the result – List
   Field. To do that, check it's box.

2. Selection Fields i.e. we use a field to only input what we
   need as a selection criteria. To do that, check it's box.

3. Do both i.e. use it as a selection criterion and also have it's
   data it in the resulting report. To do that, check both boxes.

In our case, we will use the following fields in the general area of the vendor:

Data fields	List fields	Selection Fields	Tec
▽ ⊞ Vendor Master (Gener;	5	1	LFA
Account Number of Ve	☑	☑	LFA
Country Key	☐	☐	LFA
Name 1	☑	☐	LFA
Name 2	☐	☐	LFA
Name 3	☐	☐	LFA
Name 4	☐	☐	LFA
City	☑	☐	LFA
District	☐	☐	LFA
PO Box	☐	☐	LFA
P.O. Box Postal Code	☐	☐	LFA
Postal Code	☑	☐	LFA
Region (State, Province	☑	☐	LFA

Fig 17

And the following in the CC data:

QuickViewer: Initial Screen

⊞ Layout mode | ⊕ Execute | 🔍 | 📇 📇 | ⌂

Data fields	List fields	Selection Fields	Te
▽ ⊞ Vendor Master (Company	5	1	LFB1 ▲
Account Number of Vendo	☑	☐	LFB1 ▼
Company Code	☑	☑	LFB1
Personnel Number	☐	☐	LFB1
Date on which the Record	☑	☐	LFB1
Name of Person who Crea	☐	☐	LFB1
Posting block for company	☐	☐	LFB1
Deletion Flag for Master Re	☐	☐	LFB1
Key for sorting according t	☐	☐	LFB1
Reconciliation Account in G	☑	☐	LFB1
Authorization Group	☐	☐	LFB1
Interest calculation indicato	☐	☐	LFB1
List of the Payment Metho	☐	☐	LFB1
Indicator: Clearing betweer	☐	☐	LFB1
Block key for payment	☐	☐	LFB1
Terms of Payment Key	☑	☐	LFB1
Our account number with t	☐	☐	LFB1

Fig 18

Again, use the scroll bar at the right to see the other fields in the tables.

Save the query. It is common to get a window like this below and in which case, just hit Enter since it is only an info message in Yellow:

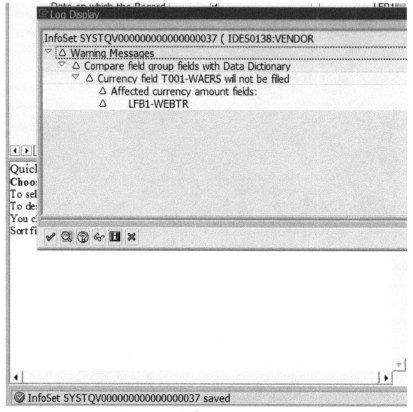

Fig 19

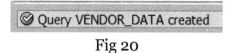

Fig 20

Execute the query F8 or the icon ⊕ Execute

Alternatively, step out and go to SQVI again. This new query will now be available for you to use every time:

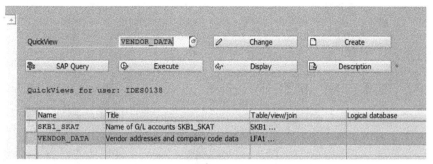

Fig 21

Select and execute:

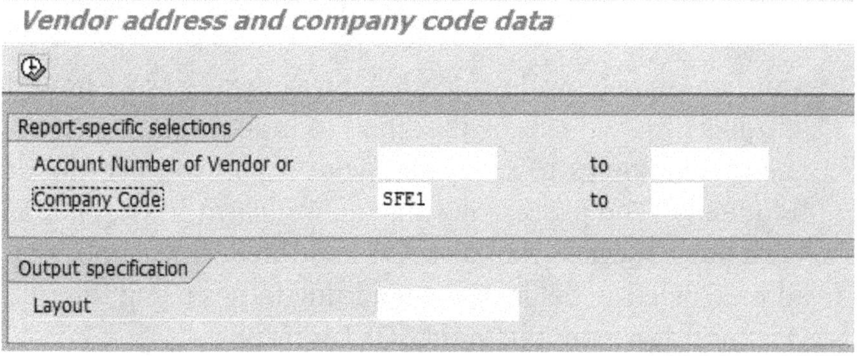

Vendor address and company code data

Report-specific selections			
Account Number of Vendor or		to	
Company Code	SFE1	to	

| Output specification | |
| Layout | |

Fig 22

Recall we had selected only 2 fields as input criteria – Vendor Number from table LFA1 and the CC from table LFB1 and so only those ones show up in the above selection screen.

From here, this selection screen works the same way as in all other transactions in SAP. Since we do not want to look for any vendors in any Co Code other than SFE1, then we enter SFE1 in the Co Code and execute again:

Vendor address and company code data

Vendor	CoCd	Acctg clerk	Name 1	City	PostalCode	Rg	Vendor	Date	Recon.acct	PayT
100863	SFE1	WR	GreenLand Corporation Ltd.	TORONTO	M6N 1B4	ON	100863	06/18/2016	211000	0008
100864	SFE1	WR	Concor Corporation Ltd.		M6N 1B4	ON	100864	06/20/2016	211000	0003
100865	SFE1	WR	Suculant Ltd.		M6N 1B4	ON	100865	06/20/2016	211000	
100844	SFE1	WR	FA Property Canada	Ontario		ON	100844	05/28/2016	211000	0003
100845	SFE1	WR	Ontario Supplier	Ontario		ON	100845	05/28/2016	211000	0003
100846	SFE1		Bolt Supply Company vendor for SFE1				100846	05/28/2016	211000	0003
100847	SFE1		Dubak Electric				100847	05/28/2016	211000	0001
100848	SFE1		Val Electric			ON	100848	05/28/2016	211000	0001
100849	SFE1		Data Enterprise for Devika	Toronto			100849	05/28/2016	211000	0003
100850	SFE1		SP Plus				100850	05/28/2016	211000	0001
100851	SFE1		Jazmin				100851	05/28/2016	211000	0001
100852	SFE1		STONE VENDOR FOR SFE1	TORONTO			100852	05/28/2016	211000	0003
100853	SFE1		xyz company	TORONTO	M6N 1B4	ON	100853	06/02/2016	211000	0003
100854	SFE1		ABC for sfe1	Toronto			100854	06/03/2016	211000	0003
100855	SFE1		Wood for SFE1				100855	06/03/2016	211000	0003
100856	SFE1		QQQ Company Ltd.	TORONTO	M6N 1B4	ON	100856	06/04/2016	211000	0003
100857	SFE1		WEY Campany Ltd.		M8N 7Y6	ON	100857	06/05/2016	211000	0003
100858	SFE1		Burn Company			ON	100858	06/11/2016	211000	0003
100859	SFE1	WR	Free Polution Corporation Ltd.		M6N 1B4	ON	100859	06/14/2016	211000	0008
5000000085	SFE1		Health Corporation Ltd.		M6N 1B4	ON	5000000085	06/15/2016	211000	0008
100860	SFE1	WR	BGW Corporation Ltd		M6N 1B4	ON	100860	06/16/2016	211000	0003
100838	SFE1	WR	Wood vendor for SFE1	Oakville			100838	05/10/2016	211000	0003

Fig 23

This list can be now downloaded the same way as we have done at other times. It can be modified to hide columns you do not need and it helps to save the layout if you will use the query frequently. The process is same as we learnt in the section on Variants. Queries can also be modified the same way by adding/deleting fields or even adding tables using the Change Query button from the main SQVI screen.

ABOUT THE AUTHOR

Yogi Kalra has worked in the SAP field for over 25 years across multitudes of industries and with big 4 Consulting experience. Based in Canada, he has done projects all over Europe and North America. Prior to entering the SAP space, he was in Business handling Sales, Distribution, Depots, Purchasing and Accounting across Chemicals and Computer hardware industries for over 12 years. He is a Certified General Accountant and MBA in Finance from University of Toronto, Canada and has been instrumental in training clients during and after SAP implementations in most of the SAP modules including but not limited to, FI, MM, SD, PP and QM. This book is the second in the series of SAP books in configuration and user training in many of these modules. Prior to this, SAP SCM: A Complete Manual and SAP SD-LE (Configurations & Transactions) is available at most book stores.

www.ingramcontent.com/pod-product-compliance
Lightning Source LLC
Chambersburg PA
CBHW071230050326
40690CB00011B/2061